THE
PRACTICAL

FROM THE GERMAN OF

REV. JAMES NIST
PARISH PRIEST OF BIRKENHOERDT

WITH AN INTRODUCTION BY

REV. JAMES LINDEN, S. J.

EDITED BY

REV. FERREOL GIRARDEY, C. SS. R.

THIRD EDITION

INTRODUCTORY

The Germans during the last two centuries turned their attention in a special manner to the vast field of instruction and education; but in no branch was there more earnest work done than in Catechetics. In numerous cathechetical periodicals and associations, and in a series of catechetical courses men of the greatest talent have devoted all their learning and ability to discuss and test the various methods, and to establish the most fruitful process of teaching Catechism. The movement has not yet met with perfect success; although the views of the weightiest authors now approach unanimity and a number of principles have been adopted as practically reliable, nevertheless it is not an easy matter to reduce them to practice. Of the many who have attempted to do so, only a few have met with satisfactory results. Lacking a thorough understanding of said principles, nearly all have applied them without sufficient care; among these are some who have the reputation of being masters in Catechetics. The Rev. James Nist, parish priest of Birkenhœrdt (Palatinate), easily surpasses all his predecessors, and may be considered by far the best in Catechetics, for he has satisfactorily fulfilled his task. He has, indeed, mastered the true catechetical Method, without allowing it to master him. His catechetical works, therefore, deserve to be recommended as models. Even the older and more experienced Catechists can find much to learn therein, and especially the rare art of becoming little with the little, of accommodating oneself to their mind, heart and will. Wherefore, most willingly complying with the request of the Publisher, I have written this brief Introductory to the English translation of his model

INTRODUCTORY

work. I recommend especially a thorough study of his treatment of the Sixth Commandment, of the Holy Sacrifice of the Mass, and of the Sacrament of Penance (for the first confession).

James Linden, S.J.

March 26th, 1911, St. Boniface's, Emmerich, Palatinate.

PREFACE TO PART I. THE APOSTLES' CREED

Long is the way from a good Catechism to good Catechetics. What the Catechism explains about the doctrines of the faith in clear, short and precise words, Catechetics should impressively develop and bring within the reach of the child's mind and heart. Catechetics should indicate, elucidate and prove the Catholic truth, render it pleasing, lovely, dear and acceptable. It behooves, therefore, the Catechist to possess not only a clear, firm and solid knowledge of the truths of faith, but also the language of children, and a warm, enthusiastic heart for the faith, in order to disclose to their mind the whole depth and beauty of the inexhaustible wealth of comfort and the application of religion to practical life.

Rev. James Nist, parish priest of Birkenhœrdt, has happily made a marked success of his Catechetics on Faith. He teaches not merely, as a genuine priest, correctly and solidly, but he also speaks the language of children in its wonderful transparency and graceful naturalness. We may, perhaps, prefer a different Method; but it will be very difficult to find another book of equal merit. Children will surely not sleep during his instructions, or hardly be tired or distracted, so well does he know how to occupy, win and rivet their attention and good will by the abundance of encouraging comparisons and practical applications.

This is especially the case in the chapters devoted to the life of our Saviour. How eloquently do the lovely pictures of the Child and Boy Jesus, of the august figure of the Teacher and Lawgiver, and the touching aspect of our suffering and dying Saviour, speak to the heart of the child! The Rev. Catechist is well acquainted with all the chords

PREFACE TO PART I

of a child's heart, and he touches them with a masterly hand. These august mysteries of the life of Jesus, the figures of our holy religion and of the Christian life, he discloses in the manifold ways and forms and practices of our divine worship; he possesses the great gift of revealing them all in a surprising manner to the child's mind, and recommending them to his imitation.

I hereby most warmly recommend the work to all pastors of souls, catechists and teachers.

M. MESCHLER, S.J.

Luxemburg, Oct. 25th, 1908.

EDITOR'S NOTICE

Children, in general, do not find the study of the Cate-chism very attractive. It seems to them very dry and abstract and a mere work of the memory. Consequently, the Catechism is often poorly learned and easily forgotten. The best remedy for this is a good, practical Catechist.

The Catechist should 1, possess a correct and clear knowledge of the doctrines of faith; 2, he should be able to speak in the language of children, that is, with great simplicity and clearness; 3, his heart should be filled with an ardent and enthusiastic love for the truths of faith, so as to be able to speak on them from the abundance of his heart; 4, he should have a practical mind, capable of adapt-ing his teaching to the practical religious life of children, for mere theory and speculation are out of place with them; 5, he should dearly *love* children, for without such love, he will scarcely be able to devote his whole energy to their religious training. See how well little children understand their mother. Why? Because the love in her motherly heart speaks directly to their hearts; 6, he needs a large stock of patience; in fact, it should be inexhausti-ble. It is only by dint of numberless and varied repetitions that thorough knowledge is imparted to the young. The Catechist should be especially patient with those who are dull and slow of comprehension. Only a good Catechist will succeed in rendering the least talented of his pupils fairly proficient in the knowledge and understanding of the Catechism.

The teaching of Catechism is an art so difficult and so important as to require that the Catechist should always make a good preparation for it, and follow therein a prac-

EDITOR'S NOTICE

tical and uniform method. However great his experience may be therein, he should consider it a matter of conscience never to omit serious preparation for it.

Of all the methods of Catechetics, that of Rev. James Nist is so thorough and practical, as to be considered the best and the most worthy of serving as a model in every respect. His exposition and explanation of the Catechism is so handled that the children themselves are interested therein, and made step by step to develop, explain and apply in advance the lesson for the following day. The result is that, before studying the lesson in the Catechism, they already know it mostly by heart, and find real interest in studying it. Hence the study of the Catechism becomes for them an easy and agreeable task.

His method, however, presupposes in the children a certain knowledge of Bible History. Where this knowledge is lacking, the Catechist would have to supply it, so as to make the illustrations and applications clear and interesting to the children.

The results of Father Nist's method will not be transitory, but permanent; they are well calculated to produce in the children a clear and precise knowledge of our holy religion, a childlike love for it, and to render its practice like a second nature to them.

The translator has somewhat condensed the work of Father Nist, and adapted certain parts unsuited for the United States, to the wants of our children.

CONTENTS

CONTENTS

CONTENTS

PART I
THE APOSTLES' CREED

1. On Faith.

Dear Children, you have already learned, not only from Bible History, but also from the Catechism, how God created the world. Your teacher teaches you Bible History and the Catechism. Who else teaches them to you? The priest. Where else does the priest teach? In the church when he preaches. There he teaches not only the children, but also the grown people. In every parish there is a priest, who is the pastor of the parish. All priests teach the people. The bishop is above the priests. He also teaches the people. The bishop sends a priest to every parish, to teach the people; and he tells the priest what he must teach. The priests are not allowed to teach differently from the bishop. There are over one thousand bishops in the world. The highest bishop is the bishop of Rome; he is called the Pope. The Pope and the bishops all teach the same. What one of them teaches, all the others teach. (Repeat the above, if necessary.)

Who sends priests to the parishes? The bishop. What must the priest do in a parish? Teach the people about God. What does the bishop also do? How many bishops are there in the world? Who is the highest bishop? The bishop of Rome; he is also called the Pope. The Pope together with the bishops is called the Catholic Church. What other words can we use instead of, the Pope and the bishops teach? The Catholic Church teaches. Before the Pope and the bishops who are now teaching, another Pope and other bishops taught; and others again before them. The

3

apostles were the first bishops in the world. There were twelve apostles. The apostles also taught. Jesus told the apostles what they should teach. The apostles remained with Jesus nearly three years; and during that time Jesus taught them many things. He told them all that we must know about God. Men could never have found out by themselves what we know about God. Jesus had to make it known. To whom did Jesus make it known? He made it known (revealed it) to the apostles.

Who were the first bishops in the world? How many apostles were there? From whom did the apostles learn what they taught? From Jesus. What did Jesus teach the apostles? All that we must know about God. What does reveal mean? It means to make known. The apostles wrote down most of the truths Jesus had revealed to them about God. They are found in the Catechism and in Bible History; but not all. Many beautiful things are related in them. You have already learned about the creation of the world, Adam and Eve, the earthly paradise, and some things about the Child Jesus. I know that these things please you very much. Which story in your Reader pleased you the most? Did you believe what is related in that story about (mention some of the personages)? No. Why not? That is not true; a wise man made it up to please children.

Do you know some one, mentioned in Bible History, who made up a story in order to make men unhappy? Yes; the devil. He wished to induce them to eat of the forbidden fruit. What did God threaten to our first parents, if they would eat of that fruit? That they must die. But what did the devil say (make up)? You shall by no means die. Whom did Eve believe more? The devil. And what did Eve then do? She ate of the forbidden fruit and gave some to Adam. And what did Adam do? He ate it to please Eve. Then Adam and Eve were banished from the earthly paradise. And finally they had to die. Who had foretold this to them? Who, then, had told them the truth? Who had lied to them? The devil always tells lies. He is a liar through and through. But God can never lie. He is always truthful.

Jesus Christ also is God. How do we call all that He says? How do we call all that He revealed to His apostles? All that He revealed to His apostles is true. What must we, therefore, believe? We must believe all that Jesus Christ, who is God, revealed to the apostles. What do we call the Pope together with all the bishops? The Catholic Church. (Repeat.) How can we express in two ways? Who teaches men what God has revealed?

You little children are not yet able to learn and remember all that the Catholic Church teaches. That is a great deal too much for you now. But it is not yet necessary for you to know it all. You should, however, know at least what is the most important. The apostles put together into a prayer the principal truths which we all ought to know. This prayer is short. It contains twelve sentences, or articles. It begins: "I believe in God the Father Almighty." How is this prayer called? The Creed; also the Apostles' Creed. Of how many sentences (articles) is it composed? What is briefly (in few words) contained in these twelve articles? The principal truths which we must believe.

SUMMARY. Which prayer contains in few words the most important truths which we must believe? The principal (most important) truths which we must believe are briefly contained in the Apostles' Creed. Why is it called the Apostles' Creed? Because it comes from the apostles. Recite the Apostles' Creed. What must we believe? We must believe all that God has revealed. Who teaches us all that God has revealed? The Catholic Church teaches us all that God has revealed.

APPLICATION — *Technical.* You will find in your new (larger) Catechism what I have taught you to-day. Open

your Catechism, page   It begins with Q. 1: Why
are we on earth (in this world)? Write this question on
the board. Show it to me in your Catechism. (Examine.) Q. means question; therefore after Q. is asked:
"Why are we on earth?" a line below you see A.; it
means answer. Show it to me. When the children are
asked the Q., they must give the answer A. Next comes
Q. 2. Where? Below is Q. 3. Show it. What does
Q. mean? What do you read in the same line? "What
must we believe?" These are the questions for to-day.
A line further down you see A. What does that mean?
Answer. Who can read the answer? Proceed in like manner with Q. 4, 5, 6, 7. You must read once more Q. 4,
5, 6, 7 at home. What must you read at home? Can you
find it by yourselves? Let us try. Close your Catechism.
When you come home, and your mother asks you: "Which
is your next lesson in Catechism?" open your Catechism,
and show it to her. Which is your next lesson? Show
me. Open your Catechism. Where is your next lesson?
At home say to your mother: "Mother, please question
me." Then your mother will ask you the questions. What
answer will you give her to the question: "What must
we believe?" etc. How do children do, when they study
the Catechism together? One asks the questions, and the
other gives the answers. Let us practise this. Close your
Catechism.

1b. God, the Creator.

There is a prayer which contains in a few words all that
you are to learn in the Catechism and in Bible History.
It begins: "I believe in God the Father almighty." How
is this prayer called? The Creed. It is called also the
Apostles' Creed. The Apostles' Creed has twelve sentences, or articles. You will learn by degrees all that is
contained in the Apostles' Creed. I will explain a part

of it to-day. The Apostles' Creed begins thus: "I believe in God."

OBJECT. I am going to tell you to-day what God has made.

RELATION. In the beginning God created heaven and earth. But the earth was like a desert, without anything on it; it was all dark and covered with water. Then God said: "Let there be light." And then light was immediately there. God called the light day, and the darkness night. That was the first day. Then God said: "Let the firmament be." And the firmament was immediately there. God called the firmament heaven. That was the second day. After this God said: "Let the waters flow into one place, and let dry land appear." And so it happened immediately. God called the dry land earth, and the waters that had gathered together, sea. And God said: "Let the earth bring forth grass, plants and fruit-trees." And so grass, plants and fruit-trees immediately grew out of the earth, and the earth looked green and beautiful. This was the third day. Then God said: "Let there be lights in the heavens." And immediately the lights appeared, for God created the sun, the moon and the stars, that they should give light to the earth. And this was the fourth day. God said further: "Let there be fishes in the water and birds in the air." And God created all kinds of fishes and birds, and blessed them, saying: "Increase and multiply." That was the fifth day.

God spoke again: "Let the earth bring forth all kinds of animals." And immediately all kinds of animals appeared on the earth. And last of all God created man. That was the sixth day. And on the seventh day God rested, and blessed and sanctified that day.

N. B. The children are supposed to know all the foregoing already.

EXPLANATION — *Heaven and earth in six days.* What did God do in the beginning, when there was nothing besides God? In the beginning God created heaven and earth. In what state was the earth then? It was like a desert without anything living or growing on it; it was all dark and covered with water. When is it dark with us? In the night. Just as dark as it is with us those nights when neither the moon nor the stars shine. So dark was it everywhere in the beginning of the world. What does your mother do at night to light up a dark room? She makes a light. How did God make a light in the dark world? He said: "Let there be light," and there was light. In this way the dark night disappeared, and there was daylight. How grand! That was the first day. What did God create on the second day? On the second day God created the firmament. He called the firmament heaven. But the heavens were not yet so beautiful as they are now, for there were no stars, no sun, no moon there. The earth was yet bare, with nothing on it. God wished to make the earth beautiful. What did He create on the third day? On the third day He created the dry land (the earth), and the large body of water called the sea. What did God cause to grow on the earth? He caused grass, plants and fruit-trees to grow on the earth. There were now meadows, plants and trees of every kind. The whole earth became a beautiful garden. There bloomed thereon the sweet-scented violet, the pansy, the rose, the lily and all the beautiful flowers; and there were numberless trees laden with fine fruits, apples, apricots, pears, peaches, plums, cherries.

After making the earth beautiful, God wished to adorn the heavens also. What did God create on the fourth day? The sun, the moon and the stars, that they might shine on the earth. The heavens and the earth were now a beautiful sight. But there was silence everywhere. There was yet no living thing. What did God create on the fifth day? The fishes in the water and the birds in the air. There were more fishes swimming in the water and more birds flying in the air than we can imagine. The birds were happy flying about and singing beautifully. But there was something still wanting on the earth. You know what it was. God created it on the sixth day. On that day God created animals of all kinds on the earth, such as horses, cattle, dogs, cats, elephants, lions, tigers, bears, etc. The woods were full of hares, squirrels, deer and wild beasts. All animals were happy and enjoyed life. And God Himself rejoiced at all that He had made, for it was all very good. But God did not need the earth for His own use. For whom did He make the earth so beautiful? For men. On which day did He create man? On the sixth day. And man was the last thing He made on that day. In how many days did He create the world? He created the world in six days.

The day of rest. After the sixth day God ceased to create new things. What did God do on the seventh day? You must not think that God got even a little tired, for God cannot get tired. But He wished that men should work six days, and should rest on the seventh day. Which day is that? Sunday. God blessed and sanctified the seventh day. Therefore we also should keep the Sunday holy. Where do we go on Sundays? What clothes do you wear there? Sunday clothes. Where do you not need to go on Sundays? Who instituted that day for mankind? You see how God loves us and how He takes our welfare to heart. From whom do you get all the good things you eat? Of which fruits are you especially fond? (Enumerate some.) What pleasure you children find with animals, such as rabbits, dogs, playful kittens; and you like the canary that sings so sweetly in its cage! From whom do all those good things come? From God every good thing comes. From whom do heaven and earth come?

And everything therein. What did God do in the heavens? What has He made to grow on earth? What besides plants? Animals and men. What did God place in the water and in the air? Therefore, God made heaven and earth and everything in them. Heaven and earth and all that they contain are called the world, the universe.

SUMMARY. What things did God make? He made the world (universe), heaven and earth and all that they contain. From whom does everything good come? From God every good thing comes.

APPLICATION. For whom did God create all that is beautiful and good? See, then, how much God loves us.

What do you say to your mother when she gives you something good? Thank you. We must, therefore, thank God for all these good and beautiful things. How can we thank God? By saying: "O my God, I thank Thee." This would please God. But you can please Him more in another way. Who knows? By praying. When should you pray to Him? Where especially should you pray? That is very pleasing to God. Even the flowers, the trees and the birds give Him pleasure. The flowers bloom and smell so sweet. The trees lift their tops heavenward where God dwells. The birds in the woods, in the gardens sing to God such joyful songs. The lark in the field in the early morn ascends towards heaven, singing to God a wonderful song of thanks. That is pleasing to God. Do you also wish to please God? You cannot do it better than by your good behavior and praying devoutly to Him.

2. God is Almighty.

OBJECT. I will tell you how God made all things.

DEVELOPMENT — How? Suppose to-morrow morning your mother would say in the dark from her bed: "Let there be light." What would happen? It would remain dark. Or suppose the carpenter would open his shop and say: "Let there be a new table here right away." What would happen? But how did God create light? God said: "Let there be light." What happened then? And immediately there was light. How did God create the sun, moon, and the stars? He said: "Let there be lights in the heavens," etc. And immediately the great brilliant sun stood in the heavens, the moon was shining in her friendly way, and numberless stars opened their bright eyes in the firmament. (Repeat in like manner the creation of the fishes, birds, plants and animals.) What do we call heaven and earth and all that they contain? How did God create the world (universe)? He said: "Let the world be.' And what happened? And immediately the world was there.

To create. What does your mother need to make light? What does a carpenter need to make a table? What does a contractor need to build a house? Materials, tools, workmen. (Explain briefly.) But how different it is with God! He needs no materials, no tools, no workmen. He made the world out of nothing, without materials, without tools, without workmen, and only by willing it. What did God make out of nothing? God made the world out of nothing. To make things out of nothing is called to create. Instead of: God made the world out of nothing, let us say: God created the world.

Almighty. Name some things which God created on the earth. Grass, flowers, trees. What are the trees made of? Wood. Suppose I would give you plenty of wood and all kinds of tools, and ask you to make a tree that grows, blossoms and produces fruits. What would you say? We cannot do it. Can any man on earth do it? No. Suppose I would give you feathers, flesh and bones and tell you to make a living bird with those things. What would you say? We cannot do it; no man can. Well, then, make a little flower that will grow. That is not possible for us. Well, then, make a blade of grass in the flower-pot. We cannot do it. You see now that you cannot make even a little blade of grass grow. Even if all the men on earth would work together, they could not make a small blade of grass grow. Who made all the grass, all the flowers and all the trees on earth grow? And all the fishes, birds and animals? And how did He make them all? There is not a thing which God cannot do. He can do all that He wills. There is not a thing, however great or difficult, which God cannot make, if He only wills to make it. God is almighty.

The Creator. Because God has created all things, we call Him Creator. What name can we give Him for having created heaven? Creator of heaven. And for having created the earth? Creator of the earth. What, then, do we call God? Creator of heaven and earth.

Creatures. The things which God created are called creatures. What are the flowers, the stars, etc., etc.? They are creatures of God.

The Lord. Suppose you make a boat of paper; whose boat is it? Mine. You are, then, the owner, the master of that boat. Why? Because I made it. Your father makes a table. What is your father with regard to that table? Its owner, its master. Why? Who created the world? God is, then, the Master, the Lord of the world. Who created the earth, the heavens? What is God, on account of that? From whom comes every good? From God. Therefore we say: God, from whom every good comes, is the Creator and Lord of heaven and earth.

SUMMARY. Who is the Creator and Lord of heaven and earth? Why? How did God create the world? God merely said: "Let the world be," and immediately the world was made. Why do we say that God is almighty?

APPLICATION. How powerful, how great is God, who created the world merely by willing it! Would that I could tell you how great and how mighty God is! Suppose all the water in the brooks, in the rivers, in the lakes, in the ocean was ink; and suppose also all the blades of grass, all the leaves of plants and trees were pens; suppose all the worms, caterpillars, butterflies, birds and animals and all men were writers, and the vast firmament was writing paper, and all those writers would write on that paper for thousands of years day and night, in order to explain how great and powerful God is, they could never finish doing so, for He is infinitely great and powerful. And when you see in spring how every plant sprouts and blossoms, you should say: "Almighty God, we praise Thee, and we intend to praise Thee as many times as there are stars in the heavens, flowers in the fields, leaves in the forests, and drops of water in the ocean."

3. God is everywhere. God is a spirit.

OBJECT. I will now tell you where God is.

DEVELOPMENT — *We cannot see God.* When school opened this morning, we said some prayers to God. Where does God dwell? He dwells in heaven. Must we not talk very loud for God to hear us in heaven? But listen: God is not only in heaven; He is also here in this school-room with us. But where? We cannot see Him. (It is not God Himself who hangs on that cross; but only His image.) Can you not see me and all the children here? How do you see? With your eyes; your eyes belong to your body; hence we call them our bodily, or corporal eyes. (Repeat.)

God is a spirit. You see me, my head, my shoulders, my arms, etc.; these are parts of my body. But God has no body, nor anything bodily or corporal, such as, head, eyes, etc. God is a spirit. We cannot see a spirit with our corporal eyes. Why? Because God is a spirit and has not a body. What other things are there, which we cannot see? We cannot see our soul, angels, the air, the wind. We cannot see heat or cold, but we can feel them; and thus we know that they exist. (This admits of further development by questions and answers.)

God is everywhere. Who is here in this room that we cannot see? God. He is also in the church; in your houses; in the streets, in the fields, all over the ocean; in every country; in the air; underground in the mines. If you could fly to the moon, to the sun and the stars, you would find God there also. There is not a place in the whole world where God is not. God is everywhere on earth, in the heavens, in heaven. Is He also in hell? Yes, He is there also; but He does not suffer, but exercises His power by punishing the wicked.

God is immense. You children have been growing larger and larger; you can now reach higher than you did two years ago. But how tall you would have to be, in order to be able to reach with your hand the cross on the church steeple! But God is all over the world; He reaches everywhere; He is infinitely great; He is immense. And yet God has no size, as our body has. We cannot say of Him that He is so tall, so wide. He is everywhere, and in each place He is whole and entire. How can that be? We cannot understand it; but it is so. Our soul makes our body live. Where there is life in our body, our soul is there. But there is life in every part of our body; therefore the soul is in every part of our body; but our soul has no size; it is not so long, and so wide like our body. We cannot divide our soul as our body; and where the soul is, it is all there; not like our body, for each part of our body is in its own place, such as the head, the arms, the feet; where the head is, the arms, the feet are not there; etc. But our soul is whole and entire in our whole body, and in every part of our body. In like manner, God is all over the world, and He is also whole and entire in every little part of the world. God is seen in heaven as He is, face to face.

SUMMARY. Where is God present without being seen? Where is He seen? Is there a place where God is not? God is in heaven, on earth and in all places. He is a spirit and cannot be seen with corporal eyes.

APPLICATION. Suppose you had to go on a dark night through a thick forest, and your father would be with you.

Would you be afraid? Why not? Because your father is strong and able to defend you. But there is One much stronger than your father, who is with you wherever you are, wherever you go. God is always with you, near you, by day and by night, at home, at school, in the street, in the fields. When your mother sends you to a dark place to get something, do you need to be afraid? Is not God there? Is He not with you? Is He not your loving Father and Protector?

4. There is but one God. God knows all things.

OBJECT. I will explain to you that God knows and sees all things.

DEVELOPMENT. There is but one sun. It is very warm to-day. What makes this room so warm? Whence comes the heat in the woods, in the fields, in the streets? It is hot also in .... (mention some neighboring towns, etc.). What makes it hot there also? It is the sun. Is it the same or another sun that makes it hot here and elsewhere? No, it is the same sun everywhere. How many suns produce heat all over the country? One sun only causes all this heat.

Only one God. In like manner, there is only one and the same God everywhere. Is there more than one God for the whole world (universe)? No, there is only one God; He who made all things.

God sees all things. We know that this one God is everywhere. Where are we all now? Therefore we all see what is done in this room. Can your mother at home see what we are doing here? No. Why? Because she is not here. She must be here, in order to be able to see what is going on here. And to see what is going on in your house, you must be there. (Similar questions about other places, countries.) If you were in the woods on a dark night, could you see what would be going on there?

Or if you stood in front of a house, could you see what would be going on in the rooms inside? Why? Because I would not be inside. If you could see at one and the same time all that is going on in all the houses in this place, in every country on earth, in the stars, etc., where would you have to be? Everywhere. Who is everywhere? How much, then, can God see? He can see and sees all things.

Also in the dark nights and places. God can see everywhere, and all things. There is no darkness for God. He has the brightest and most piercing eyes. The darkest night is for Him just as bright as the noonday sun. He can see also all our thoughts. We can see only the outside of things. We can see only what is outward in men. We cannot see into any one's heart. Can you see what N. is thinking in his heart? No. What a person thinks are his thoughts. What is it that we cannot see in men? Their thoughts. But God sees into every man's inmost heart. He sees all our thoughts, all our wishes, all our feelings. God saw in King Herod's mind all his wicked thoughts and intentions, that is, all he intended to do. What did Herod say to the wise men when he sent them to Bethlehem? " Go and find out the new-born King, then come and tell me, and I also will go and adore Him." But in his heart Herod thought (meant) differently. What wicked thoughts had he? Did the wise men know them? Did the scribes, did Joseph and Mary know Herod's secret thoughts? Herod had told no one of these his secret thoughts. Although the wise men did not know them, yet they did not go back to Herod, but returned home by another road. And why? Because God had told them not to go back to Herod. And why did God command that to them? Because Herod intended to kill the Infant Jesus. Who knew Herod's secret thoughts? God knew them. God knows every one's most hidden thoughts, because He reads in every one's mind.

GOD KNOWS ALL THINGS

When you are in the school-room, you see all that is
done there, you hear all that is said there. (The same in
church.) Where is God? Everywhere. Therefore God
sees all that is done everywhere. He sees all you do, when
you are at home, in church, in school, in the street, in the
places where no person sees you, by day and by night. He
sees when you are obedient, when you are good, when you
are doing anything bad. He sees everything that is done
in the whole world. He knows how many stars there are,
how many grains of sand, leaves, drops of water, plants,
insects, animals and men, and all that they do. God knows
every man, everything each one does, each one's most hidden thoughts. In a word, He knows all things.

SUMMARY. How much does God know? How much
does He see? What thoughts does He see? Does God
know all things?

APPLICATION. James and his sister Anna were alone at
home, for their mother had gone out. James tried to coax
Anna to go with him to the pantry to eat preserves. Anna
said: "It is wrong for us to do so. Mother forbade
us." But James said: "There is nobody here; and no
one will see us." But Anna replied: "I will not go; it
is a sin; God sees us." What do you think of James?
Was Anna right? Yes. Remember that, when your
parents are not at home, you are not all alone; for God
is there and sees you. Some children sometimes miss Mass
on a Sunday, or stay away from school, under the pretext
of being sick; but how often is that a lie! The teacher
may be deceived, but God cannot be deceived, for He sees
and knows all things. After death every one of us shall
have to give God an account of every bad word and bad
act, of every bad thought and bad wish. Therefore, bad
boys and bad girls must fear, because God will punish
them. Good children need not be afraid, for God will
reward them in heaven for every good thought, good word

and good deed. God knows they are fond of prayer, that they behave in church, are obedient, tell the truth, etc.

5. God is eternal.

OBJECT. You will hear to-day how long God lives.

DEVELOPMENT — *Everything has a beginning.* When does school begin in the morning? School has, then, a beginning. When does the sun rise? What begins then? The day. The day has a beginning. Many days make a year. How do you call that day on which the new year begins? New Year's day. How old are you? Therefore twenty years ago none of you were born. What have each of you had? A beginning. A hundred years ago your parents were not yet born. They also had a beginning. This town was not yet here a thousand years ago. It also had a beginning. A million years ago there were not yet any sun, moon or stars. They all had a beginning. All that we see around us had a beginning.

God has no beginning. Who made all things? God was already before there were any earth, sun, moon and stars. He saw how all of them had a beginning. Heaven and earth, plants, fishes, birds, animals, all began. God was already long before all of them. God always was, for He had no beginning. (Repeat with appropriate questions.) What has everything in the world, which God has not? A beginning.

The world has an end. The things in the world do not always remain. The flowers, now in bloom, will wither and die, and disappear; they will have an end. The same will happen to all plants, animals; to all our clothing, to all our houses. Our bodies will die, rot and disappear. No matter how young, healthy and strong you are, you shall have an end; death will come, and take you out of this world. The sun, moon and stars will fall from heaven, and fire will destroy this earth and all it contains.   Therefore the whole earth will one day have an end.

God alone has no end.   Only One will be always.   Who is it?   God.   Even if every creature would disappear and end, God will still be.   God has no end.   What is it that God has not?   An end.   What else has He not?   A beginning. God, therefore, had no beginning and shall have no end. God is always.   God is eternal, that is, without beginning and without end.

God remains forever.   God was before all time; before there was any day, any year.   He was before all things and all time.   At the end of the world "time shall be no more."   No more days, no more years; it will then be always; eternity; and God remains forever.   (Repeat with appropriate questions.)

SUMMARY.   Had God a beginning?   Will He have an end?   No; God is always; He is eternal; He is without beginning and without end.   He is before all time; He remains forever.

APPLICATION.   How long the eternal God lives, we cannot even imagine.   Have you not already seen a little canary bird in a cage drinking out of his little glass?   The glass contains only a little water.   The bird drinks only a little at a time, but often; but he cannot empty the little glass in a day.   How much water is there in the ocean? Suppose every thousand years a little bird would come and drink one little drop of water out of the ocean.   Oh, how long would it take that little bird to drink all the water in the ocean, and entirely empty the ocean!   And yet after he would have drunk the whole ocean dry, not one minute of eternity would have passed away; eternity would not have become one minute shorter!   And God lives always, without end.   How old is God?   Old men have grey hair and grey beards; and God is so painted; why?   Old people at last die.   Can God die?

I will now relate an anecdote of a woman who dreamt that God had died. There was a workman and his wife; they were very, very poor, and became poorer every day. At last they had nothing to eat. The man said: "Oh, if I could die!" His wife said: "Do not speak so; God has always helped us; He will help us again." But the man would not believe her, and became very gloomy. She also got sad, and would not eat any more. This continued for two days. He asked her: "What is the matter with you? Why are you so sad?" She replied: "Oh, I had an awful dream. I dreamt I saw God lying in His coffin. His long hair was white like silver, and the angels stood around in a circle, and were weeping. Oh, how unfortunate we are, since God cannot help us any more, for He is dead." The man then burst out laughing, and said to her: "How stupid you are! do you not know that God cannot die? That God is eternal, that He always was and always will be?" She then said: "Oh, you know that too! And why do you imagine that God will not help us any more? He is almighty, goodness itself, and has promised to help those who trust in Him." This cured her husband of his melancholy. Dear children, no matter what misfortunes may come to you, do not despond; even if your parents were to die. Trust in the good God, and He will always care for you.

6. The Blessed Trinity.

N. B. As an object lesson bring along three equal pieces of a wax candle.

OBJECT. I will speak to you to-day of God, of the Father, of the Son and of the Holy Ghost.

DEVELOPMENT — *The Father, a divine Person.* What sign do we make when we begin our prayers? The sign of the cross. Make it, John. What do you say when you put your right hand to your forehead? " In the name of the

Father." The Father you mention is God the Father, who is in heaven. Every child has a father at home. The father at home is a person; the mother is a person; each child is also a person. Mention other persons. The priest, the teacher. Your father is a man; therefore he is a human person; and you and your mother are also human persons. The Father in heaven is also a person; but He is not a man. What is He? God. Therefore He is a divine Person. (Repeat with appropriate questions.)

The Son, a divine Person. In making the sign of the cross, what do you say when you put your right hand to your breast? "And of the Son." "John," your father says to you, "you are my son." To Mary he says also: "Mary, you are my daughter." What does your father say to you, Fred? To you, Rose? God the Father in heaven also has a Son. He is called Jesus Christ. He died for us on a cross. Look at the crucifix; it is His image. It is He whom we mean, when we say: "And of the Son." The Son of God is also a person. He is God also like His Father. What kind of person is God the Son? A divine Person. (Repeat.)

The Holy Ghost, a divine Person. What do we say when we put our right hand, first to the left, and then to the right shoulder? "And of the Holy Ghost. Amen." The Holy Ghost is also a person. He is God, like the Father and the Son. What kind of person is the Holy Ghost? A divine Person. (Repeat with appropriate questions.)

The three divine Persons. Count the divine Persons. How many are there? Three divine Persons: the Father, the Son and the Holy Ghost. The Father is the first Person; the Son is the second Person, and the Holy Ghost is the third Person. How is the first Person in God called? The second? The third? How many Persons in God? Three. Name them.

Each Person is true God. I have here three small candles. What are all three made of? Of wax. Compare them with one another. They are all of the same size; the first is not larger than the second, nor the second larger than the third; all three are equal to one another. Is any one of them thicker or longer than any of the other two? In like manner the three divine Persons are equal to one another in all things. God the Father is infinitely great. How great is God the Son? How great is God the Holy Ghost? How great are the three divine Persons? All three are infinitely great. Infinite means without end, without limits. (Repeat a similar explanation to show that none of them is older than the others; all are equally eternal, without beginning, without end, without limits. Also to show that they are all three equally almighty. Then briefly repeat all the above by asking appropriate questions.) Because the Father is infinitely great, eternal, almighty, He is true God. Because the Son is infinitely great, etc., He is true God. Likewise the Holy Ghost.

The three divine Persons are only one God. If you were to count as follows: The Father is God (lift up one finger); the Son is God (lift up another finger); the Holy Ghost is God (lift up a third finger); how many Gods would that be? But to count up in this manner would be entirely wrong, for there is only one God. The three divine Persons are only one God. You cannot understand how that is; neither can I, nor can any one else, for it is a great and deep mystery.

Illustrate with the three candles. I light these candles. How many candles do I hold? Three. How many lights (flames)? Three. But now I put them together. I have three candles, but only one flame, one light. So it is with the three divine Persons. As the three candles put together have only one and the same flame (light), so the three divine Persons are but one and the same God.

The Blessed Trinity. The three divine Persons together are called the Blessed Trinity. Trinity means three Persons in one God. How do we call the three divine Persons together? The three divine Persons together are called the Blessed Trinity.

Each of the three divine Persons is good to us. God the Father created us; you and you, every one of you; otherwise none of you would be in the world. Fred, what good did God the Father do for you? God the Father created me. It was the will of God the Father that all men should go to heaven. But our first parents, Adam and Eve, sinned, and God closed heaven against them and their descendants, against all men. Then God the Son came down from heaven on the earth and became man. He died for all men, for each man, for every one of you, on the cross, and opened heaven again to men, so that we can now go to heaven. Wherefore we say: God the Son redeemed all men, each one of us. What good, what benefit did God the Son bestow on you? He redeemed me. The Holy Ghost also has done much good to us. When you were a little baby the priest baptized you. Then the Holy Ghost came into your soul and made it holy and wonderfully beautiful. He whose soul is holy, is fit to go to heaven. What good did the Holy Ghost do to you? He sanctified my soul, that is, He made it holy. (Repeat.)

SUMMARY. Is each Person of the Blessed Trinity true God? Are the three Persons but one and the same God? What is the Blessed Trinity?

APPLICATION. 1. I will now tell you something about the three divine Persons of the Blessed Trinity. When Jesus was thirty years old, He went to the river Jordan, where many people came to St. John to be baptized. They went into the river, and St. John poured water over their heads. Jesus also came to him to be baptized. When Jesus came out of the river, He knelt down and prayed. The heavens opened, and the Holy Ghost in the form of a beautiful white dove, came down and remained over

His head, and a voice from heaven was heard saying: "This is My beloved Son, in whom I am well pleased."

Who came to St. John to be baptized? Jesus. Jesus is the Son of God. What did Jesus do after He was baptized? When He was praying a voice was heard from heaven. What did it say? Who can call Jesus His Son? The Father of Jesus. Who is the Father of Jesus? God the Father in heaven. Who was over the head of Jesus? The Holy Ghost in the form of a dove. Here you have the three divine Persons of the Blessed Trinity. What did the Father do? What did the Son do? What did the Holy Ghost do?

2. We sometimes see a picture of the Blessed Trinity. Here is one. Show me God the Son. How do you know that it represents Him? How can you distinguish the Holy Ghost? How does the Father look? Like a venerable old man. Why? How do you call the three divine Persons? The Blessed Trinity.

3. Each of the divine Persons did much good to us. What did the Father do? What did the Son do? What did the Holy Ghost do? We can never thank, honor or praise them enough. Say the Glory be to the Father, etc. Say another prayer in their honor. The sign of the cross. What do you do, when you say that? By this sign we honor the Blessed Trinity.

7. God cares for the world. God is good.

TRANSITION. You have learned that God created the world. What did God create in the heavens? What did He create on earth?

OBJECT. You will now hear what God still does for the world.

DEVELOPMENT. 1. *God causes the world to continue to exist.* The grass, plants, trees, birds, animals and men that God created in the beginning, are no longer. And yet there is grass, there are trees, vegetables, fruits and flowers. And God causes them to grow. But what must men do, in order to have vegetables, fruits, etc.? They must sow their seeds. And trees? They must sow or transplant them. Each plant has its own seed. It is God, who enables them to have seed. How wonderful! A man sows in the ground a grain of wheat, of corn, a peach-stone, an apple-seed, a piece of a potato, and the grain grows and produces hundreds of other grains; the piece of a potato grows and produces sometimes many dozens of whole potatoes. And of these other grains, when planted, each produces hundreds of others. (Illustration may be prolonged and diversified according to the products of each region.)

Plants grow from seeds. But where do the little birds come from? And the fowls? From eggs laid and hatched by the older ones. Horses, cows, cats gets little ones, and these grow up, and also get little ones, and so on. God cares for all.

The sun, moon and stars are in the heavens as God created them. They continue to do what God has created them for. The sun still gives us light and warmth, the moon lights up the night, and the stars shine and twinkle at night. Tell me how God cares for the world; for plants; for birds; for animals; for the sun, etc.

God cares for young animals. Where are the little birds at first? In the nest made by the older ones, where they were hatched. To grow larger and strong, to be able to fly, they must eat. But how can they get food? The older ones bring them worms, etc., and feed them as a mother feeds her baby with a spoon of mush, and keep them warm at night by covering them with their wings. If the older birds did not do this, the little ones would perish. Who taught the older ones to procure food for the little ones, to feed them and keep them warm? God. God cares for the older ones, by enabling them to find worms, insects, grains of wheat, corn, etc. He cares for them in winter, lest they should freeze; He makes them fly South for hundreds of miles to a warmer climate, and come back in time for warmer weather. The birds that stay, get a thicker coat of feathers to keep them warm. The cattle have also a thicker coat of hair in winter.

God cares for the plants. How beautiful are the flowers! The snow-white lilies, the forget-me-nots with their blue mantle; also the fruit-trees in spring with their beautiful blossoms, the orange trees with their sweet-scented blossoms! No King is so beautifully clothed as they! In winter the ground is covered with snow to protect certain plants, and to prevent the ground from freezing too deep, otherwise nothing could grow in spring, for it would take too long to thaw the ground. Winter is to the earth and to plants what sleep is to us.

RECAPITULATION. For which things does God care? Animals, plants. God cares for His creatures, for the beings He created.

APPLICATION. God cares for even the smallest creature, and has provided for it means of subsistence. (How the egg of a butterfly becomes a worm, a caterpillar, and lastly a butterfly.) He who cares for all things, cares also for me.

2. *God cares as a father for us His children.* Who cares for you at home? Father and mother. They reflect and work all day, so that nothing may be wanting to you. For whom especially do they work? For their children. And why do they do so? Because they love their children. Father and mother love you more than all else in the world. But far better than your father and mother care for you, does God care for all His creatures. Therefore call God also your Father. He is the Father of the whole world. Where does He dwell? In heaven. Therefore we call Him our Father in heaven, our heavenly Father. More than your father and mother at home does God love you.

He cares for us with a special love. You know already how He cares for birds, for animals. They sow not, they reap not, nor do they lay up into barns, and yet they have their daily food. They have no other wants, and they are so joyful. And does not God esteem you far more than a little bird? You are children of God. Look at the flowers; they work not in summer, do not spin in winter, nor do they sew, and yet they are more magnificently clothed than the richest monarch. If God so cares for flowers, how much greater care will He bestow on you! Are you not worth more than a little flower? You all are God's beloved children. Let us see how He cares for you.

God gave you parents, that is, a father and a mother, saying to them: "Here is this dear child; care for it; give it all it needs." And to enable them to do this well, God gave them a deep love for you. You are to grow larger and stronger. What do you need for this? Who gives you food? Your parents give you   (enumerate some of the foods, such as, bread made from wheat flour, meat, milk, eggs from animals, fruits from trees.) Who made the wheat and the fruit-trees grow? Who made the cows, the cattle, the chickens? Therefore we pray daily to God: "Our Father who art in heaven, give us this day our daily bread" (food).

You are all well and comfortably clothed. Of which things are your clothes made? Hemp, cotton, wool, leather; plants, sheep and cattle. Who made these? Who then cares for your clothing? At night you sleep in a warm, soft bed of moss, etc. Who made these things grow? God cares, then, for you during the night. How many sick persons cannot sleep at night, on account of their great pains? And you get up in the morning refreshed and with a good appetite. Who has cared for you?

God loves some children with a special love; He calls them to Himself in heaven, when they are yet infants.

How happy they are! How good it is for them to go straight to heaven! We should not grieve over them. You now see how God loves all men as His children and cares for them. God made for men, His children, everything in the world; the sun, moon, stars, flowers, plants, fruits, birds, fishes, all animals. From heaven God looks down on all men; He hears their prayers; He helps them in their wants. Your parents cannot always help you; but your heavenly Father can always help you. If your father at home dies, you still have a Father in heaven, the best, the most loving and powerful of fathers. For whom, then, does God care with a special love? For us, His children.

Divine Providence. Sometimes God allows misfortunes to happen to men. Even this is a mark of His love for them. A very holy man wished to go by sea to a certain place. He was just about to enter the ship, when he fell down and broke his leg. He had to remain on land until his leg would be healed. His servant was very mad because they had to remain where they were. But the holy man told him not to get mad, saying: "All that God does is good. Who can now tell why He allowed my leg to get broken?" They were told later, that the ship on which they intended to embark, was wrecked, and that all on board had been drowned. The saint and his servant would also have been drowned, if he had not broken his leg. So you see that what at first appeared to be a misfortune, was a real blessing. Why? Therefore all that God does, is good. Nothing can happen without God knowing it. He knows how many hairs we have on our head, and not one of them falls off without His knowing it.

Often God sends misfortunes to the wicked who will not obey Him. He sends sickness, fearful storms, hailstorms, frost, cyclones, floods, etc., which destroy houses, plants, fruits, etc., and the people get poor and suffer want. He does this, that they may reflect on how wicked they have been, pray to Him, repent of their sins, be converted and lead a good life. If they remain good, where will they go after death? How many there are, who, if they had not met with misfortune, would have remained bad, and would never go to heaven, but would be condemned to the everlasting fire of hell.

SUMMARY. What does God always do for the world? He cares for all His creatures. For whom does God care with special love? God cares especially for us, His children. God's care for the world and all creatures is called Divine Providence.

APPLICATION. 1. You now see how good God is towards us. What does a good child say to him who makes him a nice present? You have perhaps already seen your mother give some money, or some food, to a poor person. What did the poor person then say? And if he did not say it, does not your mother remark: "That person does not even say 'Thank you.'" Little Bertha, coming home one day from school, found there a basket of fine apples, which her godmother had sent her. She exclaimed: "Oh, how good is my godmother to me. Mother, may I not go at once to thank her for her loving kindness?" "Yes," replied her mother, "it is right for you to go to thank her."

Dear children, you receive every day from God a thousand times more than Bertha received from her godmother. God daily gives you your life, food, drink, etc. What do you owe to God for all this? How do you thank Him for it? Do you pray before and after your meals? What do you say before meals? What do you say after meals? Do you sit down to eat, and get up after eating, without thinking of God who gives you your food, without a word of prayer, of thanks? Do you ever think of thanking God for all His other benefits? How often must you be reminded of your morning prayers, of your night prayers? Are those children who neglect their morning or their night prayers, thankful to God? Children who do not pray and thank God, are like animals that lie down, get up, eat and drink without a thought of God.

2. When a misfortune happens to you, you should not get angry, for God who allowed it to happen to you, knows that it is good for you. Remember that nothing happens without God's permission and for our good. Tooth-ache, sickness, and death in the family, even of your mother. God permits all this for our good, because He loves us.

7b. God rules the World.

OBJECT. I will tell you to-day of other things that God does in the world.

DEVELOPMENT — *God preserves all things.* God created the world. What does He do to keep it from perishing? God preserves the world; He preserves men, animals, plants, etc. He so arranges things, that there are always on earth men, animals, plants, etc. How does it happen that there are always plants? Plants produce seeds, and seeds planted produce new plants. Animals grown up have young ones; and the young after growing up, also have young ones. Birds and fowls lay eggs, and young birds and fowls are hatched from the eggs. (Repeat here from 1 of preceding 7 God's care for animals, plants, etc.)

God orders all things. Who cares for everything at your house? Who in the school? In school you should behave well, and study diligently. Are you allowed to come when you like? To go out when you like? To sit where you like? To do as you like? Who would not suffer or permit it? Why? Because everything would be in confusion; and no one could learn anything. How long must you remain in school? Where must you sit? Who takes care that everything is properly done in school? The teacher. The teacher keeps order in the school. In school there must be order, or the children will not be able to learn anything.

There must be order in the world. The sun may not rise or set when or where it likes. Where must it rise? Where must it set? So has God ordered it. The stars may not go where they like. God has appointed a place for each star. He said to one: "Here is your place"; to another: "There is yours." They rise at the appointed time, not a minute too soon, not a minute too late. So it is in the heavens. On earth some animals (birds) live in the air, others on the land, and the rest in the water. Some of the birds build their nests in trees, others on houses, others in hedges, and some on the ground. Some animals eat grass and herbs, others eat insects, others feed on nuts, on fruits, and others on flesh. Some trees bear apples, others, peaches, others, oranges, others, nuts. Man lives on cereals, eggs, meat, fish, vegetables, fruits. There is order all over the world. Who orders all things in the world? God orders everything in the world.

God directs all things. God does not merely give each thing its place. The driver does not merely hitch his horse to the wagon, and let it go or run where it likes. Whom must the horse obey? The driver. The horse must go where the driver wills. Therefore the driver holds the reins in his hands. What does he do when he wishes the horse to turn to the right? He pulls the rein on the right side. And to make the horse turn to the left? The driver directs his horse with the reins. As the driver directs his horse, so God directs all things in the world. It is God, and no one else, who in the fall directs the birds to fly hundreds of miles over rivers, mountains and forests to seek a warmer climate for the winter, and to come back in the spring. In like manner, God directs the sun in its course. He directs the clouds to rain where rain is needed, and the rivers in their course to the sea. He directs each thing where it has to go, and what it has to do. He directs all things as He pleases.

God directs all things for good. He directs (or governs)

men also. Some He allows to live long, others only a few years. Some He allows to get rich, and others to remain poor; some to be healthy and strong, others to be weak and sickly. God does all that He wills, as it pleases Him, and as it is good for each one and for all. To some He sends good fortune, and misfortune to others. (Repeat the anecdote of the saint who was prevented to sail in a vessel by falling and breaking his leg.) This shows how well God directed everything for the welfare of that holy man. God often sends sickness, or some misfortune, to wicked or worldly persons, in order to convert them; for instance, St. Ignatius who was wounded, and could find nothing else to while away time than to read the lives of the Saints.

SUMMARY. The other day I explained to you what God does to preserve the world; and you have just heard how He directs and governs the world. God, therefore, preserves and governs the world. How does God preserve the world? He causes the world to continue, as it pleases Him, and as long as He pleases. How does He govern the world? He cares for all things, orders and directs all things, just as He wills.

APPLICATION. The same as in the foregoing number.

8. The Creation and Fall of the Angels.

OBJECT. To-day I will speak to you on the angels.

RELATION. Before creating heaven and earth God created the angels. Seated on His brilliant throne, God said: "Let the angels be." Immediately there were there many, very many angels. They were brighter than the sun. And then God said further: "The angels shall dwell with Me in heaven, stand before My throne and praise and adore Me. They shall protect men and bring them to heaven." At that very moment the angels stood before the throne of God. They began to praise and adore God. The angels loved God very much, and cheerfully obeyed Him. They were perfectly happy.

But many of the angels grew proud. They wished to be equal to God, and would no longer obey Him. There arose a battle between the good and the bad angels. The leader of the good angels was Michael. The bad angels were conquered by the good angels and driven out of heaven. And as lightning comes down quickly from the heavens to the earth, so the bad angels fell down like lightning into the abyss of hell. They suddenly became fearfully ugly and horrible to look at. They are now called devils or demons. But the good angels remained in heaven. God rewarded them with eternal happiness (bliss).

EXPLANATION — *Invisible spirits.* When you go out of the house, you can see the heavens above and the earth below. How are the heavens and the earth called? The world (universe). We can see the world, for it is visible, and is called the visible world.

But above the visible heavens is another heaven. This heaven we cannot see. There God is seated on His bright throne. What did God say when, seated on His throne, and before He created heaven and earth? " Let there be angels." To count the angels is as difficult as to count the stars in the heavens on a clear night. Can you count the stars in the heavens? No. Why? There are so many, that we cannot see or distinguish all of them. It is even much more difficult to count the angels. They are countless. How many angels did God create? The angels have no head; but they can think; they have no eyes, but they can see; they have no ears, but they can hear; they have no tongue, but they can speak; they have no hands, but they can work. In a word, the angels have no body. God Himself has no body. How do we call God, because He has no body? God is a spirit. The angels have no body. What, then, are the angels? The angels are spirits.

God is a far better and more perfect spirit than the

angels. Compared with God, the angels are like a tiny spark of fire compared with the sun. Because God is a spirit, we cannot see Him; He is invisible. The angels also are spirits. What, then, are the angels? The angels are invisible. The angels are invisible spirits. How many invisible spirits did God create? God created very many invisible spirits. When did God create these invisible spirits? Before He created heaven and earth. Therefore God created two kinds of things. Which kind did God create first? Which kind did He create afterwards? Did God create something else besides the visible world? God created also many invisible spirits, the angels.

All good. When God created the angels, did He say where they were to dwell? What should they do in heaven? Praise and adore God. And the angels did so. Some placed themselves around the throne of God; others knelt in front of it, joined their hands and bowed their heads. And all began to sing very beautifully, in order to praise and adore God. The angels sang many hymns in praise of God. One time one angel would sing alone; then two would sing together; then all the angels would sing together. Sometimes they would sing so softly and sweetly, and then so loud, that the whole heaven would tremble. All the angels loved God very much. They obeyed God in everything. It made them happy to obey and please God. He who loves God, prays willingly, obeys well and is good. What were all the angels when God created them? Good.

And all happy. The angels were all so beautiful. How beautifully the stars twinkle on a clear night! But near the bright sun a little star is almost as nothing. But an angel shines more brightly than the sun. So beautiful are the angels. There are nine kinds of angels; each kind seems more beautiful than the others. But God is hundreds of millions of times more beautiful still. The angels resemble God. The angels were exceedingly happy with God in heaven. Nothing was wanting to them; they had all they wished. Their life was a continual joy and pleasure. He who has continual joy and pleasure, is truly happy. What, then, were all the angels, when God created them? The angels were all happy; all good and happy.

Learned and powerful. The angels are very learned and smart. Do you know how many blades of grass grow on the earth, how many flowers are blooming, and the name of each kind? But an angel knows all this. An angel knows more than all the men on earth. They are also strong and powerful. An angel can lift with ease the largest building, carry the highest mountain, and break the thickest chain more easily than you can break a small thread. An angel by a single breath can open the largest and heaviest gate that is locked.

God's messengers. Many times did God send angels on earth to men. To whom did God once send an angel? To Mary; to Joseph. Where did an angel stand in the earthly paradise? To whom did very many angels appear one night? To the shepherds. What was the angel to do for God, when God sent him to Mary? When he was sent to St. Joseph? What did the angel announce to the shepherds? All these angels had to bring a message from God, and to speak in the name of God. The angels are God's messengers. Men also send messengers to bring news to other men, or to transact business with them in their name. The letter-carrier is a messenger; also the carrier of telegrams. What the messenger is to say or do, is called a message. The angels bring messages to men from God. What message did the angel bring to Mary? To Joseph? To the shepherds?

Pictures or portraits of the angels. The shepherds, Mary and Joseph could see the angels. These angels had put on the form of a human body, just as we put on a coat, etc. They looked like men; only they were much more beautiful. When an angel is painted, he is painted like a man, a child. Look at the picture of the Annunciation. Where is the angel? How do you know it is an angel? He looks like a beautiful large boy, with wings on his shoulders. But angels have no wings. Birds fly fast with their wings. Wings denote speed. The angels go very fast from place to place. The wings spread out denote that the angels are always ready to go where God sends them.

The sin of the angels. For some time all the angels were good and happy. They saw how beautiful, learned, smart and powerful they were. What do children, who are beautiful and smart, often become? Proud. What did many angels become, when they saw how beautiful and smart they were? Many angels became proud. They wished to ascend to God and place themselves on thrones like His, alongside of Him. To whom did they wish to be equal? They wished to be equal to God. Therefore they would not obey God any more. He who disobeys God, commits a sin. What did those angels commit by not obeying God? A sin. They sinned. They were no longer good angels, and God was not pleased with them.

The punishment. God would no longer look at them. He spoke: " Put them out of heaven." What happened then between the good and the bad angels? What is the name of the leader of the good angels? Michael. He said to the leader of the bad angels: " What! you wish to be like God? Who is like God? " And now there was a great battle between the good and the bad angels. But it did not last long, for God helped the good angels and made them much stronger than the bad ones. And what then happened to the bad angels? The bad angels were cast into hell. In hell there is a great and terrible fire. In this fire the bad angels must burn. They weep and howl for pain and curse horribly. And that will last forever!

Did all the angels remain good and happy? No. Why not? Many angels sinned. How did they sin? How did

God punish them for their sin? They were cast (precipitated) into hell. As long as they obeyed, those angels were good spirits. What kind of spirits are they now? Bad or evil spirits, or devils, or demons. Who has seen a picture of the devil? Where? The devil is thousands of times more ugly than he can be painted. It was only one sin that made him so ugly and hideous.

The reward. Where did the good angels remain? In heaven. Because they obeyed God, they were, from that time, enabled to see God in all His beauty and magnificence. Just as you can now see my face, so the good angels now stand before the throne of God, and see Him face to face in all His splendor and glory. They never get weary admiring Him, so beautiful He is! The very sight of God in His infinite beauty makes the angels perfectly happy. And in their joy and happiness, they constantly sing: "Holy, holy, holy Lord of hosts! Glory be to the Father, and to the Son, and to the Holy Ghost." How long will their happiness last? Always; for all eternity!

SUMMARY. Did God create anything besides this visible world? How were the angels when He created them? Did all the angels remain good and happy? How do we call the angels that sinned?

APPLICATION. The punishment of the angels shows us how severely God punishes sin. Like lightning the wicked angels were put out of the beautiful heaven, and cast into the everlasting fire of hell. How frightful it must have been for them suddenly to lose all their beauty and splendor! How painful it must have been for them to see themselves suddenly changed into ugly and hideous devils! And what for? For one mortal sin. And there are children who commit mortal sin, and do not care about it! They miss Mass on a Sunday, and then say: "It matters not, if I miss Mass!" So they speak. But will it not matter a great deal when they shall have to burn for it in hell? Some eat meat on Friday, and say: "There is nothing wrong in that." Is there nothing wrong in committing a mortal sin, which deserves the everlasting fire of hell? Who would like to be punished like the bad angels? Hence, dear children, never commit a mortal sin, not even for the whole world! Remember how terribly God punishes a mortal sin in the next life. The example of the bad angels should be a powerful warning for us. A single mortal sin turned angels into devils! Beware, then, of committing a mortal sin.

9. God is holy and just.

OBJECT. I will explain to you to-day that God rewards what is good, and punishes what is bad.

DEVELOPMENT. 1. *God loves the good.* What were the angels when God created them? The angels were good and happy. They obeyed God in all things. God loved them for this. But God did not always love all the angels. Which angels did God always love and still loves? God loves also all good men. There is a child, who is poor and not very smart; but he is very good. God loves that child. There is a sick man lying in bed; he is poor, but pious and good. God loves him. There is a cripple; there is also a man who has only one eye; there is another man who has only one leg; but all three are good and pious. How does God look upon them? With love. What kind of persons does God love? God loves all who are good.

God detests the wicked. After the angels had sinned, God did not love them any more. He could no longer bear them. When you pass in summer near a dead animal, such as a dog, a cat, which is already corrupting, you turn your face away. Why? Because you cannot bear looking at, staying near it, or its offensive odor; you detest it. God has a greater horror of the bad angels, than you can have of rotten dead animals. But God detests and abhors far more than that a man, a child who has committed a mortal sin. For instance, there is in a large city a very rich man, living in a fine house, dressed in the height of fashion; he is loved and admired and envied by many people. But he has committed a mortal sin by breaking one of God's commandments. But God justly detests him. There is in a certain school a child who is very, very smart, so well dressed, for his parents are rich; all his schoolmates envy him. But he is bad. How does God feel towards him? God detests him. What kind of persons does God detest? Which angels does God detest? Which angels does He love? And which persons does He love? God loves the good and detests the wicked.

God loves all that is good. How does God see that some one is good? God loves those who go regularly to church, who are fond of praying, charitable towards the poor, who suffer for the love of God. Even the smallest good act is pleasing to God. For instance, you please God, whenever you devoutly make the sign of the cross, obey punctually, study diligently, behave well in church, in school, at home; when you are kind to your companions. God is then greatly pleased with you, for He loves all that is good.

God detests all that is bad or evil. How does God see that some one is bad? God detests cursing, stealing, telling lies, disobedience, quarreling, fighting, jealousy, immodesty, impurity, misbehaving in church, missing Mass on Sundays, eating meat on Fridays. God does not love, but detests those children who commit these sins. God loves all that is good and detests all that is bad or evil.

Because God loves all that is good, and detests all that is bad, we say that He is holy. Why do we say that God is holy? The angels also are holy. The angels are as pure and white as the snow that has fallen. But God is more than a hundred millions of times more pure and holy than they. God is most holy, infinitely holy. What do the angels sing constantly before the throne of God?

2. *God rewards the good.* God showed the good angels how much He loves those who are good. How did He reward them for obeying Him? He placed them in heaven, where they will be happy with Him forever. God rewards men also for doing good. When you say your morning prayers devoutly, you receive a reward from God. Also when you study well in school, when you are obedient to your parents, etc.

God rewards also the smallest good act. You need not do great things to receive a reward from God. For instance, to give a sick person a drink of water, is nothing great, but God will reward it, if it is done for His sake. In like manner, to give a little alms to a poor person, to make devoutly the sign of the cross. God rewards even the smallest good act. He often rewards these acts on earth, but not always, by enabling men to prosper, by imparting peace and joy to their hearts. But it is only after their death that the good receive the greatest reward, for God then takes them up to heaven.

God punishes the wicked. God punished the bad angels for their disobedience. How did God punish them? In like manner, God punishes men also when they do evil; for instance, thieves, murderers, those who wilfully miss Mass on Sundays. He punishes the children also who do not mind their parents.

God punishes the smallest evil. He punishes a bad word, and even a wilful bad thought. What does God punish? All that is evil. God often punishes in this world. A father punishes his child with a rod. God punishes some persons by permitting them to get sick, to meet with some accident or some misfortune, or a child's parents to get sick, or his father to get out of work. But it is after death that He punishes men most severely for their sins. Where do the wicked go after their death?

CONNECTION — *God is just.* What would you say, if

God would take the wicked to heaven, and cast the good into hell? You would say that God does not act right. Or if God would take all men to heaven, both the good and the wicked? You would say that it would not be right for God to treat the good and the wicked alike. Or if God would give only a slight reward to those who have been very good, and a great reward to those who have done only a little good? What kind of reward will God give to those who have done much good? To those who have done only a little good? The more good a person has done, the greater the reward which God will give him. And also, the greater the evil a person has done, the greater will be the punishment he will receive from God. God rewards all that is good, and punishes all that is evil. Therefore we say: "God is just." What is God? Just; infinitely just.

SUMMARY. Why do we call God just? Why do we call Him holy?

APPLICATION. God does not pay attention if a person is beautiful, rich, smart, or has a great name. He loves a poor and a dull child who is good, more than a rich and smart child who is wicked, or even not so good as the other child. God is infinitely holy. If you wish to be with God in heaven, you must become holy, for only those who are holy are admitted into heaven. Let us see how far you are from being holy. Are you fond of praying? Do you obey as promptly as the angels? Do you never tell a lie? Do you always behave well in church? You see now that you are still far from being holy, from being saints. Take pains henceforth to become daily more and more pious, obedient and holy, that you may be admitted into heaven to sing with the angels: "Holy, holy, holy the Lord God of hosts."

10. The Guardian Angels.

OBJECT. I will tell you to-day how the good and the bad angels act towards us.

DEVELOPMENT — *The bad angels hate us.* The bad angels hate God, and constantly curse and blaspheme Him. If they only could, they would dethrone Him and cast Him into hell. But that is impossible. The bad angels hate us also, because we are the image and likeness of God; and because they were cast out of heaven, they do not wish us to go to heaven, but would like to drag us with them into hell. Therefore they are always doing all they can to induce us to commit sin. When you tell lies, pilfer, steal, disobey, you can think that the devil prompted you to do it.

OBJECT. The good angels are willing to help us to go to heaven.

RELATION. When you were born, God chose for each of you a good angel. He said: " In   a child is born; I give him to thee as thine own. Take care that no harm happens to his body, but especially that he do nothing bad. Now go to that child, and stay near him day and night, as long as he lives; and when he dies, bring him to Me in heaven to be happy forever." The angel obeyed, and ever since is always near you and has never left you.

EXPLANATION — *The guardian angel is always near us.* Who is always near you? Our guardian angel. Who sent that angel to you? When? What has your guardian angel to do? Take care of me. In cities there are men appointed (policemen) to watch that no one steals, that no property be damaged, that no one does harm to his neighbor. What are they called? What must they do? Guard the life and property of the inhabitants. What do our angels care for? Therefore they are called guardian angels. How do you call that angel who is always near you? He accompanies you to school, to church, wherever you go or remain. He is with you when you are awake, and when you are asleep; when you are praying, studying, playing, eating; by day and by night. He never leaves you.

The guardian angel protects our body. In a certain city there was an old wall falling to pieces. A good woman was walking along with her five-year-old boy holding her hand. When they came near that wall, the boy stopped, and made his mother stop. She said to him: "Come on." But he would not move. All at once an awful crash was heard, and down came the old wall in a cloud of dust. A few more steps, and both mother and child would have been killed and buried under the ruins. When they reached home, the mother asked: "Why did you stop suddenly and would not go on?" He said: "Did you not see?" "See what?" she asked astonished. "That beautiful youth dressed in long bright clothes; he stood right before me, and I could not pass." Where did the boy stop short? What did his mother say to him? Did he obey? In what direction was he looking? What did he see? Who was it? What did the angel do to keep the boy back? Why? What then happened? Did any harm happen to the boy and his mother? How was harm and death prevented? Now, dear children, had it not been for your guardian angel, how often you would have been hurt when you fell down, when you were playing in the streets and nearly run over by some vehicle? Who protected you? What did he then protect?

The guardian angel protects us in our soul. There was once a very pious girl thirteen years old. Her name was Agnes. A wicked man tried to make her commit sin. But she would not. He then tried to force her against her will. But Agnes said: "You cannot force me to do evil, for my guardian angel helps me." The wicked man tried to take hold of Agnes, but the angel struck him dead. What was the pious girl's name? What did the wicked man wish her to do? Who helped Agnes against him?

Hence we say: "The angel protected Agnes." Perhaps you would have committed sin many a time; perhaps the devil would have induced you to sin as he did Eve; or perhaps a bad child or a wicked person would have led you into sin; but your guardian angel did not permit it, and protected you. Or you might often have seen or heard evil things, but your guardian angel closed or turned away your eyes, that you might not see it, or kept you from understanding what you heard. And thus you escaped committing sin. Those sins would not have injured your body, but your soul would no longer be pure and holy, and perhaps they would have caused you to be cast into hell. Who kept you from committing those sins? Your guardian angel protected you. What did he protect in you? Your soul. What else does he protect in you? Your body. Our guardian angel protects us in soul and body.

Our guardian angel prays for us. Our guardian angel prays daily for us, that we may remain good and pious. When we pray, he prays along with us. And when we pray to God for something, he prays with us and for us. Many sinners would already be in hell, if their guardian angels had not interceded with God for them. The guardian angels of many bad children have prayed to God to put off their punishment, and give them another chance to become good. What does our guardian angel do for us before God's throne?

Our guardian angel admonishes and warns us. Where should our guardian angel bring us in the end? To heaven. For this reason he tries to keep us from sin. Have you not sometimes gone to the pantry to take cakes, sweet meats, etc., without permission? Did you not then seem to hear some one telling you: "Do not take that; that is wrong; God sees you"? It was your guardian angel speaking to you. He warns you against taking things without permission, against stealing, against cursing, against disobedience, against going with bad companions. He warns you against all that is evil. When you rise in the morning, your guardian angel reminds you to say your morning prayers; and at night, to say your night prayers. He also admonishes you to go to church, to study, to obey, to behave well; in a word to all that is good. What does he warn you against? When your parents and teachers admonish or warn you, they speak aloud to you; but your guardian angel does it silently, for he speaks only to your heart. Pay attention, and you will often hear his voice interiorly in your heart. What he then tells you is called an inspiration.

CONNECTION — *The good and the bad angels.* The devil also gives inspirations. The devil and your guardian angel would each wish to have you for himself. Where does the devil try to bring you to? Where does your guardian angel wish to bring you to? What does the devil inspire you with? To what does your guardian angel admonish you? What does he do for your soul and your body? What does he do for you before God's throne? What does his conduct towards us prove? That he loves us. All the other good angels love us, and act towards us like our guardian angel.

SUMMARY. What do the good angels do for us?

APPLICATION — *Follow the inspirations.* What should you do when your parents tell you to do something? Obey. You should obey cheerfully and promptly. Your guardian angel admonishes and warns you oftener than your parents. He knows all you think about and all you intend to do. What should you do when he inspires you to go to church, to obey, to study, to keep away from bad children?

Pray devoutly. One night there was a large house on fire. Two children were sleeping upstairs. They awoke only when the house was already all on fire. They could not get down the stairs, for they were on fire. The elder girl cried out: " Holy guardian angel, help me," and then jumped out of the window; she fell on the hard frozen ground, but did not hurt herself. Then she said to her sister: " Do as I did." The little girl then said: " Holy guardian angel, help me," and she also jumped, and fell upon the hard frozen ground, but did not get hurt. How did the two girls get out safely from the burning house? How easily they could each have broken a leg, or even their necks! But they were not hurt at all. What did they say before jumping? Who protected them? When you are in any danger whatever, invoke your guardian angel. Invoke him also when the devil tempts you to disobey, to steal, etc., and when he fills your mind with bad thoughts. But pray to him devoutly, for only then will he help and protect you. Be sure always to follow his inspirations and heed his warnings.

11. The Creation of the first Man.

PREPARATION. Last time I spoke to you about the angels; to-day you will hear something about men. There are now many men on earth. God created all of them. But did God create so many in the beginning? No, God first created only one man.

OBJECT. I will tell you how God created the first man.

RELATION. When God was about to create the first man, He said: " Let us make man according to our own image. He shall rule over all animals and over the whole earth." Then God made a human (man's) body out of clay, and breathed into it a living soul. It was in this manner that God created the first man. God called him Adam, that is, a man of clay.

CONSIDERATION — *Creation of the body.* What did God say when He was about to create man? What did God then make first? A body. Of what did he make that body? Out of clay. That body had the appearance of a grown-up man, with head, eyes, etc., etc. It appeared like a man's body; but it was cold and stiff, without life, and was very much like a dead body. What can a dead body do with its hands and feet, eyes and ears, etc.? Nothing.

Breathing in of the soul. God blew in the face of that body. Fred, blow into your hands. Can you see your breath? It is not visible. But you feel it. How is it? Warm. When God breathed on the deathlike cold body, His warming breath went through the nostrils and mouth into every part of that body. The heart now began to beat, the whole body grew warm, the cheeks rosy. What God breathed into that body was invisible, just like your breath. The invisible thing which God blew into that body was the soul. How was the body after God had breathed into it? Alive. The first man was now finished. He did not remain lying on the ground, but got up, and began to see, to walk and use every part of his body. (Repeat all the foregoing in questions and answers.) The first thing God created in man was his body; and then his soul. We are all men like Adam. We are composed of body and soul. The soul is, in some manner, the breath of God.

We cannot live without a soul. Although we cannot see the soul, we can know whether the soul is in the body. How was it remarked in Adam? He got up and walked; he was alive. How could it be known that there was yet no soul in his body? His body was yet cold, stiff and like dead. So it is with every man. No man can live without a soul.

The body is mortal. Every man's soul shall once leave his body; and his body will then be dead. Therefore we say: "The body is mortal." A dead body, or corpse, is first laid in a coffin, and then brought to the graveyard. Where will it then be placed? In the grave, and then will be covered up with earth. When after many (some) years a grave is opened, there is found in it only earth and dust. What became of the body? It turned gradually into earth and dust. It was made of earth. Why did God call the first man Adam? What became of Adam's body after his death? It turned into earth and dust. We are made of dust, and we shall return into dust.

The soul is immortal. What becomes of a man's soul after his death? It also returns whence it came. Whence did it come? From God's breath. The soul returns to God, from whom it came. If the soul is perfectly pure, God immediately places her in heaven. If she is defiled by grievous sins, God at once casts her into hell. If she is stained with only small faults, God places her in purgatory until she is entirely purified. After thousands and millions of years the soul still lives. The soul cannot die. So has our Saviour said. Does not the soul die with the body? No, the soul never dies. Therefore we say: " The soul is immortal." What is it that we cannot do without our soul? Wherefrom did God take the soul? Repeat what you have learnt about the soul.

The soul has understanding. You learn in school also reading, writing, arithmetic. Animals learn and remember many things; for instance, the horse and the ox learn to draw wagons, to plow, to turn to the right and to the left. They recognize your house, their stable, and stop there of themselves. When a shepherd brings his flock home in the evening, the sheep run of themselves to their stable. How many things can some dogs learn! Parrots learn to say some things, and babble them the whole day, and give wrong and foolish answers to questions; they have no sense, no understanding. If a little child would give such queer answers, everybody would laugh at him. What should a child do, before answering a question? He should think (reflect), that he may find out what he should answer. If I ask you: " What did you write the day before yesterday? " what should you do before answering? Think. Why does not the parrot also think before answering? Because he cannot think. Animals cannot think. Why? Because they have no understanding.

Where have you got your understanding? In my head. But animals also have heads. Do not forget that the understanding is in the soul, belongs to the soul. What does man's soul possess? Understanding. The soul is a spirit and is immortal. Animals have no immortal souls, that are spirits, as men have. Therefore they have no understanding. Parrots learn from men how to prattle certain words; but other animals do not learn to speak words. A child can learn how to speak well. Why? Because he has understanding. What a happiness to be able to speak! If you could not speak, you would not be able to tell your wants to your parents and what happens to you. Some children, however, cannot keep still, they talk all the time, even in church. Animals can make known their hunger etc., in different ways (such as dogs, chickens). What is it that they cannot do? Why? They have no understanding.

The soul has free-will. You have something else which animals have not. Mary pays a visit to some friends who are careless Catholics. They invite her to dine with them. It is Friday. They have meat. They urge her to have some. But she remembers it is Friday, the day on which meat is forbidden. She is very hungry, and the meat looks and smells so nice. Now Mary, if she only wills, can refuse to eat and willingly suffer great hunger rather than commit a sin. And, in fact, she preferred to remain hungry, rather than even taste the meat. Now an animal that is hungry and has food before him, has not the power to keep from eating, unless through fear of a stick, etc. What is the difference in this matter between men and an animal? Man has free-will; an animal has not. A good man says: "I will pray, I will go to Mass, I will work, I will keep away from bad company." Man can, therefore, do what he wills; he is free; he has a free will. Animals have no free-will, because they have no spiritual soul. Why has man a free will? Because he has a soul.

We cannot think without a soul. Man alone has an immortal soul. Animals have not. (Repeat in questions and answers the differences between man and animals.) Children forget what they have learned; they forget the letters of the alphabet. What must they then do? They must think over, reflect. Men can reflect; animals cannot. Why? Because they have no souls. Man has a soul.

If we had no soul, we could not speak. God knows what we think of; even our inmost, hidden, secret thoughts. Men cannot. How can you make known to men what you are thinking about? By speaking. You can, therefore, make known to others your wants, your opinions, and relate what you have done, seen and heard; you can tell them how you rejoice with them in their good fortune, how you sympathize with them in their misfortunes; you can tell your parents how you love them, give instructions, show what you know, consult, ask questions, admonish, encourage, etc. Can animals do that? Why not?

SUMMARY. Tell me the gifts or qualities our soul possesses. The soul is a spirit, immortal, possesses understanding, free-will, the power of communicating our thoughts and feelings, and of learning. How did God create Adam?

APPLICATION. You have heard that God gave Adam a beautiful body and an immortal soul. Adam knew that he had received all from God. What was the first thing Adam did after he saw that God had created him so beautiful? He knelt down and thanked God for it. God gave you also a body and a soul and life. How good He is! Therefore thank God for it from your heart, saying: " O God, Thou hast given me so beautiful a body, eyes to see, ears to hear, a tongue to speak. How good art Thou! I thank Thee from my inmost heart." Some children use their tongues principally to tell lies, curse, scold, speak harshly and cross. Have you also done that? Oh, how ungrateful have you been to God! Do not again use

your tongue in such a sinful manner. God has given you
an immortal soul to enable you to think; should you, then,
think on evil things? Your souls should often think on
God. God gave you a free will; you are able to do as
you will, either good or evil. But you cannot do either
without serious consequences. There is a reward for every
good thing you do, and a punishment for every evil thing
you do. For which will you use your free-will? God gave
it to you to do good.

12. Man is God's most noble Creature on earth.

OBJECT. To-day I will explain what man is worth on account of his soul.

DEVELOPMENT — *The soul is like unto God.* What is
man's soul? It is a spirit. A spirit is not thick and coarse
like a body, but like the breath, very fine and invisible.
Who else is a spirit? God. Why is the soul an image
of God, or like God? Because it is a spirit. God is a far
greater and more perfect spirit than the soul. God is immortal. What is the soul also? In what is the soul similar to God? In being immortal. God knows all things.
You also already know many things. Every day you learn
more things. In what is your soul like God? In being
able to know things. But you cannot know all things, as
God does. If you did, you would not only be like God,
but would be His equal. (Institute similar comparisons
between man's power and God's omnipotence, man's in-
tellect and God's, man's free-will and God's, etc.)

Image and likeness. Man is like (similar to) God in
many things. A boy looks like his father, in eyes, mouth,
nose, hair, gait, and talent. Your father, for instance,
looks into a mirror. What does he see? His likeness;
the picture of his face, eyes, etc., all like himself. The
child is also his father's likeness, his living likeness, but
smaller than his father.

The soul also a likeness of God. God wished to have
on earth a small living likeness of Himself. Which creature did God say He would make like Himself? What did
God say when He was about to create man? Man's body
cannot be a likeness of God. Why not? What is fit in
man to be a likeness of God? His soul. There must be
many things in man's soul which make it similar to God.
We have already learned them. (Man's soul a spirit, immortal, having knowledge, power, understanding, free-
will.) His soul is similar to God, God's likeness. God
created man after His image and likeness.

Man is God's most noble creature on earth. Let us suppose two children stand here side by side: a millionaire's
son and a poor laborer's son. The millionaire's son has
finer clothes, his features look more delicate, he can talk
nicely; he is more vain and proud. His outward appearance is nicer, more noble than that of the laborer's son.
But in their souls there is no essential difference. What
is the poor boy in his soul? The rich boy? Both are
God's likeness in their souls.

Now suppose all the animals in the world were assembled
together. How many would there be? How many large
and beautiful ones! Suppose also that alongside of all
the animals there would be all the beautiful, many colored
flowers and all the gold, silver and precious stones in the
world in a heap like a mountain. Now put in the midst
of all these creatures the poor child with patched clothes.
He could hardly be seen, for he is so small. No one
would care to look at him. And yet that poor boy has
something which all those animals, flowers, gold and precious stones have not. What is it? An immortal soul.
And his immortal soul is a million times better, more
beautiful, more precious than all the animals, flowers, gold
and precious stones in the world! After what was his
soul created? After the image and likeness of God. He
is therefore more noble, more excellent than all else in

the visible creation. Tell me in which things man's soul is more excellent than animals.

Man's body is more noble than animals. Animals, such as the horse, the dog, walk bent down, looking towards the ground, to show that they are made only for the earth. Man walks erect, holding his head towards heaven, to show that he is made for heaven. He has two hands, and how many things he can do with them! Animals have no hands; they cannot do what man can do. No animal has such a fine, handsome face as man. And in his face his two eyes shine like two stars, and enable him to look up heavenward. Where is man destined to go? No animal can go there. What must we do to reach heaven? We must pray, we must obey. When should you pray? To whom do you speak when you pray? You must love God. Think how wonderful it is to be able to speak to God, to love God! God is so great, so powerful; He carries the whole world on His finger. And with this great God you may speak in prayer; you need not fear Him; for, when you pray, God bends down to you like a good father and graciously listens to you. A child that prays is like the angels in heaven. No one on earth, except man, can pray. Now tell me in how many things man's body is more noble, more excellent than animals. There are creatures more noble and excellent than man. Who are they? The angels. There is One who is infinitely more noble and above the angels. Who is it? God.

CONNECTION. What is God? What are the angels? What is our soul? Who is the greatest spirit? How great is God? What do we mean when we say God is eternal? Will the angels ever die? Is our soul immortal? Our soul and the angels had a beginning. God had no beginning. How much does God know? How much do men and the angels know? How much can God do? How much can men do? How much can the angels do? Are the angels above men? God placed men a little below the angels.

SUMMARY. Whom did man resemble after his creation? What is man with regard to God? His likeness. Are the angels more like God than men? Why? All other creatures on earth are not the images of God. Why? Is man more noble and more excellent than they?

APPLICATION. 1. Man is the lord of the other creatures on earth, because he is more noble and excellent than they. God made him their lord. What did God say, when He was about to create man? He said: " Let us make man to rule over the earth." Man is the lord of all animals, and also of the earth itself. Man therefore uses some animals to help him or work for him, to be useful to him in other ways, such as the domestic animals; and he cultivates the earth, and uses its materials to build houses, railroads, etc. God rules over men, and they must obey Him, and not waste earthly things, for they are gifts of God to supply their wants.

2. Our soul is a wonderfully beautiful image (likeness) of God, but not an inanimate image on paper, etc., but a living image. If you have a very beautiful picture, you take great care not to soil or tear it. Therefore do not defile, soil or destroy your soul. How can your soul be soiled or destroyed? By sin, such as, telling lies, stealing, cursing, missing Mass on Sunday, disobedience, impure thoughts, words or deeds. If another child would soil or damage a very nice picture of yours, what would you say? " Oh, my fine picture!" You would even cry over it. And would not that child deserve to be punished? Therefore, remember that your soul is a beautiful image of God, most beautiful in itself, and say: " I will never soil or defile it by sinning."

3. You are created in the image of God. You have learned to know God; you must continue to learn still more about Him, and you will see always more and more how good God is, how much He loves you, and you will be able to love Him every day more and more. A child

that loves God is fond of praying to Him, and will try
to resemble the angels in heaven before God's throne. A
child that does not pray is like a mere animal. He is even
worse than an animal. Why does not a beast pray? A
beast cannot pray. Why does a child not pray? Because
he does not wish to pray; he is too lazy to do so. Therefore when you rise in the morning, say your morning
prayers; and before you retire at night, say your night
prayers, and do not act like cattle and other animals. But
always pray devoutly.

13. The Creation of Eve. Paradise.

1. PREPARATION. What was the name of the man who
was alone on earth in the beginning? Adam. Adam was
well off. He had all that he wanted. But it would have
been more pleasant for him, if he had had company. Suppose you were, like him, alone in such a beautiful garden,
and neither your father and mother, nor your brothers
and sisters were with you. You would feel lonesome, and
not perfectly happy. That was the case with Adam at first.
He had no one to speak to, for the animals did not understand him. That was not very pleasant for Adam.

OBJECT. I will now tell you how God created a wife
for Adam.

RELATION. God said: " It is not good for Adam to
be alone. Let us make him a helpmate like himself."
God sent a deep sleep on Adam. Whilst he slept, God
took one of his ribs, and made a woman of it. When
Adam awoke, God brought her to him. Adam was glad
and called her Eve; this word means " Mother of all the
living."

EXPLANATION — *The Creation of Eve.* Who was the
first man on earth? Why was it not good for him to
remain alone? God then wished to create a being like
Adam, having like him a body and an immortal soul.

What could it be? Only a human being. God, therefore, created a woman as a helpmate and companion of Adam. What did God say, when He was about to create woman? "It is not good," etc. Relate how God created woman. What did He make her body of? A rib is a bone in our side. Animals also have ribs. You can see the marks of the ribs on the skin of a lean horse.

Adam did not feel God taking one of his ribs, for he was sound asleep. What did God make Adam's body of? And that of Eve? God also breathed an immortal soul into Eve's body. What did God do, when Adam awoke? You may be sure Adam was glad when he saw Eve. He named her Eve. How many persons were then on earth? Two, Adam and Eve.

Our first parents. Adam and Eve got children, and their children also had children in the course of time. And there are now hundreds of millions of men on earth. All of them come from Adam and Eve. A large tree has many branches and twigs; all men on earth are like a large tree. Adam and Eve are like the trunk of the tree, and all the other men are its branches and twigs. As the branches and twigs of a tree come from its trunk, so do all men come (or descend) from Adam and Eve. From whom do you descend? Adam is the ancestor or forefather (first father) of all men, and Eve is the mother of the living, the foremother of all men.

SUMMARY. Relate how Eve was created. How were the first man and the first woman called? Of what did God make Eve's body? What do we call Adam and Eve? Our first parents.

2. OBJECT. I will relate to you how Adam and Eve lived.

RELATION. God had planted a wonderfully beautiful garden for our first parents. It was called the earthly paradise. It was full of all kinds of trees bearing delicious fruits. In the center there was a great spring, from which flowed four streams of running water irrigating the garden. God placed our first parents in paradise to take care of it. God said to them: "You may eat of the fruits of all the trees in the garden; but you must not eat of the fruits of the tree in the middle of the garden; if you eat of them, you shall die." Adam and Eve lived very happy in paradise. They were holy and just, and had no knowledge of evil. God therefore loved them much.

EXPLANATION — *Happy in paradise.* What had God planted for our first parents? What was that garden called? In this garden God placed our first parents. They were to dwell there. Rich people have fine houses; the rooms are splendidly adorned with rich carpets, large mirrors, splendid paintings, silken draperies, etc. But no rich man, no monarch has ever had so beautiful a dwelling as our first parents had in paradise. What was there in paradise? Beautiful trees, a great spring, fine rivers. (Enumerate some of the fruit trees, with delicious fruits hanging on them.) There were in paradise many fine cool spots, where Adam and Eve could sit down and have a pleasant talk. What could they do, when they felt hungry? They could choose what they wished among so many delicious fruits. They could have the finest eggs, milk and meat from the animals, and the most refreshing clear water from the spring. The animals were all tame; they would come and eat out of the hands of our first parents. (It is well to enumerate some of the animals.) The birds would joyfully flutter about the trees, singing so sweetly, and would come down to perch on their hands or shoulders. They would watch sometimes the various kinds of fish swimming in every direction in the rivers. There were there also all kinds of domestic animals and fowls. Adam, after his creation, had reviewed all the animals, given each kind its name. So you see that Adam and Eve had much pleasure in paradise. God often came to Adam and Eve in the evening. They awaited His coming with joy. Sud-

denly the trees would move their branches and bend their
tops in reverence. Then the hearts of Adam and Eve beat
with joy; soon God appeared. He was so kind and friendly
with them, as a father with his children. Oh, how fast
the time in paradise passed for them! They wished God
would never leave them. Tell me how many different joys
Adam and Eve had in paradise. They lived happy
there.

Nothing to suffer, never to die. Adam was not to remain idle in paradise. Why had God placed him in it?
To care for it. What kind of work is required in a garden? Adam had to perform it. But work was like play
to our first parents. When men work long and hard, what
do they become? Tired. But Adam and Eve did not get
tired in paradise. The work was not hard, and the weather
was always mild and the sun was shining. How do people
working in the sun in summer feel? Very hot. And in
winter? Very cold. But our first parents never felt hot
or cold in paradise; the weather was so mild and pleasant.
They never were sick or suffered pain; they were never
to die. What was to happen at the end of their life on
earth? To go to heaven in body and soul.

EXPLANATION — *Holy.* God intended at the end of the
life of Adam and Eve on earth to take them in both body
and soul to heaven. Who were already in heaven with
God? The good angels. They are holy. They are as
pure and white as the recently fallen snow, and they shine
as the sun. Who is millions of times more holy than the
angels? God is infinitely holy. Only those who are holy
can go to Him in heaven. What had our first parents to
be, in order to go to heaven? Holy. Therefore God had
placed something wonderful from His heart into the hearts
of Adam and Eve. That was sanctifying grace. It was
like a bright garment for their souls, and made their souls
holy. He who has this garment of grace in his soul, is a
child of God. What were Adam and Eve with this gar-

ment in their souls? God was well pleased with them and loved them very much.

Just. Adam and Eve also loved God and tried to please Him. They were fond of praying to Him. They cheerfully did all that God required of them. They never did anything that was not right; they never thought of doing anything wrong. All they did was right and just. Therefore they were just. Because they had on the garment of grace, they were holy and just. So they were after their creation.

SUMMARY. What were Adam and Eve in the beginning? Holy and just. Were they also happy? They had nothing to suffer, and were never to die.

APPLICATION. How glad I would be, if I could say that all of you children here always do what is right before God. But there are some that do not like to pray, to be obedient. They miss Mass even on Sundays. They need to be often admonished. And yet these children wish to go to heaven. When they were baptized, they also received the garment of sanctifying grace. When they tell lies, disobey, quarrel, misbehave, they defile their garment of grace, and become unfit for heaven. If you are fond of praying, of going to Mass, and love God and do all He commands you, the garment of grace remains clean in your soul, and becomes daily more beautiful; and you feel happy on earth. And when you will die, God will take you to Himself in the beautiful heaven. In heaven it is far more pleasant than it was in paradise for Adam and Eve. In heaven there is no sickness, no trouble, no suffering, but only pleasure and happiness without end.

14. The Commandment of God in Paradise. Why are we on earth?

OBJECT. I will tell you to-day why God created man.

DEVELOPMENT — *To serve God.* How did our first

parents live in paradise? Where were they destined to go? But God wished first to see whether they would obey Him. Therefore He forbade them to eat of the fruit of one of the trees. What did God say to them? " You may eat of the fruits of all the trees in paradise, except of the fruit of the tree in the center. If you eat of the fruit of this tree, you shall die." This was what God forbade them. God has given us also and all men some commandments, such as, to pray, to honor our father and mother, not to tell lies, not to steal. What must you do, when your father bids you to do something? You must obey him. You must obey your superiors also, such as the Church, the priest, your teacher, the government. (Servants, etc., must obey their masters, their employers.) We are all servants of God; all, the Pope, bishops, priests, monarchs, must obey God. We are all on earth to serve God, to do what He commands us.

Heaven is the reward. Servants and workmen get their wages, according to their work and the length of time they work. Adam and Eve were to get their wages (reward) in heaven, if they served God faithfully. What would happen to them, if they did not serve God, did not obey Him? They should die. We also are destined to go to heaven, which is to be given to us as an exceedingly great reward or pay for serving God faithfully during our life. That is why God has placed us on earth; to serve Him and gain heaven.

SUMMARY. Why are we on earth? Where shall we go, if we serve God? We are on earth to serve God and go to heaven by doing so.

APPLICATION. The angels and saints are in heaven. There they continually serve God. They cheerfully do all that He wills. The will of God is always done in heaven. It should be done always on earth also. Who should do the will of God on earth? Who does the will of God on earth? All those who keep His commandments (enumer-

ate). But God has to help us to do always His will on
earth. Therefore we pray in the Our Father: "Thy will
be done on earth as it is in heaven." If all men on earth
would do God's will as the angels do it in heaven, this
earth would be almost as good and as happy as heaven
itself, and we would all go to heaven, the kingdom of God.
For this also we pray to God: "Thy kingdom come."

15. The Fall of our First Parents.

PREPARATION. Have you ever seen boys trying to catch
fish with a hook? How is a hook made? But if the boys
would throw the hook just as it is into the water, no fish
would bite. What do they put on the hook to draw the
fish? Bait. And now the stupid fish, seeing only the bait,
and not the hook hidden by the bait, takes hold of the bait
and bites the hook, and thinking how good the worm tastes,
tries to swallow the bait and hook, and moves its tail and
pulls the hook and is caught! Just as boys catch fish with
a hook and bait, so did the devil try to lead our first
parents to disobey God and make them unhappy.

OBJECT. I will now tell you how the devil acted to induce our first parents to disobey God's commandment.

RELATION. The devil was very envious of the happiness
of our first parents. He resolved to lead them into the
sin of disobeying God. Therefore he hid himself in a
serpent. The serpent was on the forbidden tree. One day
Eve went near the forbidden tree and saw the serpent on it.
The serpent said to Eve: "Why hath God commanded
you, that you should not eat of every tree of paradise?"
Eve replied: "Of the fruit of the trees that are in paradise we do eat; but of the fruit of the tree which is in
the midst of paradise, God hath commanded us that we
should not eat; and that we should not touch it, lest perhaps we die." But the serpent said to Eve: "No, you
shall not die. For God knows that, when you shall eat of

it, your eyes shall be opened; and you shall be as gods, knowing good and evil." And Eve " saw that the tree was good to eat, and fair to the eyes, and delightful to behold; and she took of its fruit, and did eat, and gave to her husband who did eat."

EXPLANATION — *Envy of the devil.* Where did Adam and Eve dwell in the beginning? Were they happy there? Who is it that could not bear to see them happy? He who cannot bear to see others happy, is envious. The devil envied (was envious of) the happiness of our first parents. Why was he so envious? The devil was at first so happy. What had he been? Where had he dwelt? In heaven. Why was he cast into hell? The devil was anxious that men also should be cast into hell. Therefore he thought: " If I could only induce men not to keep God's commandments. I will try." What did the devil intend to do? To tempt our first parents to disobey God.

The temptation. In what animal did the devil hide himself? Where was the serpent? Who came near that tree? What did Eve see on the tree? The devil showed himself very friendly, and asked her: " Why hath God commanded you," etc. Eve was astonished at hearing the serpent speak. What did she answer? Whose commandment did Eve know quite well? And she knew the punishment also, for she said: " Lest we perhaps die." But what had God said? " You shall die, if," etc. She thought that what God had said, might not be true, for she said " perhaps." The serpent laughed, saying: " By no means; you shall not die, and your eyes," etc. He meant that Adam would see that they were equal to God.

The devil was anxious that men also should wish to be like or equal to God, so that God should at once cast them also into hell. The devil knew that men could not become like God, and yet he said they would. He was the first liar; he is the father of lies. Whom should Eve have believed, the serpent or God? And Eve should have gone away, and not stood to listen to the serpent's lies. But the words of the serpent pleased Eve. She would have liked so much to become equal to God. Therefore she stayed longer near the tree, and looked at its fruits. What did she think of them? That they looked nice and tasted good. There were many, very many other fruits in paradise. Why did these please her more? Because she believed that, if she ate of them, she would become like God.

The fall. Then Eve went nearer the tree, and looked more closely at the fruit. Then there happened to her what happens to the fish looking at the bait on the hook. The fruit pleased her so much, that she longed to taste it. At last she took and ate some, and gave some to Adam. And what did Adam do? How great was the joy of the devil, when he saw that!

EXPLANATION — *The first sin.* What had God forbidden our first parents? Did they obey God? They did not obey Him. They transgressed (broke) His commandment. He who transgresses a commandment of God, commits a sin. What did our first parents commit by disobeying God? They committed a sin; they sinned. Was God's commandment very hard to keep? No, for there were very many other trees with delicious fruits, besides the forbidden tree. There was no need of their eating the forbidden fruit. The sin of our first parents was great, grievous before God.

Pride. Why did Adam and Eve eat of the forbidden fruit? Because they wished to be equal to God. But no one can be equal to God. How do you call those persons who wish to be more (greater) than they are? Proud. What were Adam and Eve? Proud. Who before Adam and Eve wished to be like (equal to) God? Those angels were proud. What did they commit thereby? A great sin. Pride is a sin.

Lying. The devil knew very well that Adam and Eve

could not be like God. Yet he said: "You shall be as gods." What do you call his saying that? A lie. The devil was the first liar. Whom does a child who tells lies, imitate? By his lies the devil succeeded in causing our first parents to commit sin.

SUMMARY. What commandment had God given to our first parents? What did they do? Transgressed God's commandment, and sinned.

APPLICATION. The devil seeks to lead you also into sin; for instance, when you are alone at home, he suggests to you to go to the pantry to take and eat of the sweetmeats that are there, telling you how nice and good they are, and that your mother will not see you, or know that you have taken or tasted them. When there is some change lying loose in the house, he suggests to you to take some to buy candy, etc. How often does he not suggest to you to tell lies, in order to escape punishment; to strike others, to call them abusive names; and often he sends a bad companion to lead you into mischief, into sin!

If Eve had gone away, she would not have sinned. You also must go out of the way of temptation, out of bad company, or else you will fall into sin. Pray to God not to let great temptations come to you; say: "Lead us not into temptation." And when temptation comes, ask God to help you to overcome it. "Jesus and Mary, help me to keep from sin."

16. The Confession and Punishment of our First Parents.

OBJECT. I will relate to you how God punished our first parents for their sin.

RELATION. After Adam and Eve had sinned, their eyes were opened, and they saw that they were naked. Full of shame, they made for themselves aprons with fig-leaves. When they heard the voice of God, they hid themselves among the trees of paradise. And God called Adam: "Where art thou? And Adam said: I heard Thy voice in paradise, and I was afraid, because I was naked, and I hid myself. And God said to him: And who hath told thee that thou wast naked, but that thou hast eaten of the tree, whereof I commanded thee that thou shouldst not eat? And Adam said: The woman that Thou gavest me to be my companion, gave me of the tree, and I did eat. And God said to the woman: Why hast thou done this? And she answered: The serpent deceived me, and I did eat. And God said to the serpent, because thou hast done this thing, thou art cursed among all cattle and beasts of the earth. I will put enmities between thee and the woman, and thy seed and her seed; she shall crush thy head. To the woman also He said: I will multiply thy sorrows from thy children; thou shalt be under thy husband's power, and he shall have dominion over thee. And to Adam he said: Because thou hast hearkened to the voice of thy wife, and hast eaten of the tree, whereof I commanded thee, that thou shouldst not eat, cursed is the earth in thy work; with labor and toil thou shalt eat thereof all the days of thy life. In the sweat of thy face thou shalt eat bread, till thou return to the earth, out of which thou wast taken; for dust thou art, and into dust shalt thou return." Then God clothed Adam and Eve with garments of skin, and cast them out of paradise.

EXPLANATION — *The trial.* What did the devil tell Eve to induce her to eat of the forbidden fruit? He said that they would not die, but that their eyes would be opened, and they would be like God, if they would eat of it. One thing which the devil told them, was true; that their eyes would be opened. But they saw something very different from what the devil had made them believe. What did they see? That they were naked. They got ashamed and covered themselves with aprons made of fig-leaves. Do you remember what was the garment of the souls of Adam and Eve when God created them? The garment of grace. It made their souls exceedingly bright and resplendent; this brightness penetrated their bodies and made them bright also, and this brightness served as a garment for their bodies; hence they needed no material clothes as we do. But when Adam and Eve sinned, they lost sanctifying grace, the bright garment of their souls, and all the brightness of their bodies disappeared.

What injury did the sin of our first parents cause to their souls? It robbed them of the garment of grace, and defiled them with a mortal sin; so that their souls looked ugly and repulsive (disgusting). Therefore Adam and Eve were no longer children of God. And now their consciences reproached them with having disobeyed God, and they got afraid. Their hearts beat violently. And they heard the voice of God. This time they did not feel glad that God was coming to them. They ran away. What did they do to keep God from seeing them? They hid themselves. But God had seen them. Why? Because He is everywhere, and no one can hide himself from Him.

Then God called out: "Adam, where art thou?" Then Adam and Eve had to come out of their hiding-places. Adam did not tell the exact truth why he had hidden himself. What did he say? But God knew Adam's sin. He knew why Adam was afraid. What did He say to Adam? Adam should then have said: "Lord, forgive me." But what did he say? He tried to excuse himself by putting all the blame on Eve (and remotely on God Himself who had given her to him as his companion). What did God then say to Eve? How ought Eve to have spoken then to God, and begged His forgiveness? But what did she say instead? She blamed the serpent for deceiving her. But should she not have believed God rather than the serpent? What should she have done, when the serpent began to speak to her? Was she not guilty? And was Adam bound to take and eat the forbidden fruit given him by

Eve? No. He also was guilty. Both were guilty. Who was most guilty? The serpent. All three were punished. How was each of them punished?

The punishment. What did God say to the serpent? (Will be explained further on.) Who was punished after the serpent? Eve. What did God say to her? You know how babies often cry all night, and their poor mothers cannot sleep, for they must be all the time with their crying babies. How much do poor mothers suffer and complain! God foretold that. Why was Eve so punished? Whom did she seduce (lead into sin)? Hence God said to her: " Thou shalt be under the power of thy husband." Finally, Adam got his punishment. What did God say to him? " Cursed be the earth," etc. On account of this curse the earth no longer so easily produces eatables, no such fine fruits as there were in paradise. What should it produce henceforth of itself? Thorns and thistles (weeds). If Adam and Eve wished to eat, Adam would have to work so hard, that the sweat would pour from his brow down his face. How did God say that? As Adam would sweat in summer, so he would freeze in winter; and he would be liable to get sick, to suffer pains of all kinds, in every part of his body, during his whole life. God told him also that he must die. From what did God make Adam's body? What would his body become in the grave? Dust. God said: " Thou art dust," etc.

God's mercy. When Adam and Eve heard these punishments, they began to weep bitterly. Even then God showed them how much He loved them. As they were naked He made them clothes out of the skins of animals. Where were Adam and Eve no longer allowed to remain? What did God do to them? How many times did they not look back towards paradise, to see if God would not call them back! But they were nevermore allowed to return to it. They had lost paradise forever. God placed an angel with a flaming sword before its gate to keep our

APOSTLES' CREED

first parents from entering it again. When Adam and Eve left paradise, the animals, hitherto so tame, began to make horrible noises, ran away and became wild. (Explain a picture of Adam and Eve's expulsion from paradise.)

CONNECTION. We shall now again consider how our first parents were punished for their sin.

In their souls. What garment had Adam and Eve in their souls before their sin? What was the effect of their sin on this garment of grace? That was the first punishment of their sin. What was their soul before their sin? Beautiful, bright, pure and holy. And after their sin? It was all defiled, ugly and disgusting. That was the second punishment. Whose children were Adam and Eve before their sin? And after their sin? That was their third punishment. Where were Adam and Eve to go later on, if they had remained faithful? Where were they no longer able to go after their sin? That was their fourth punishment.

In their bodies. Where did Adam and Eve dwell before their sin? What did God do to them after their sin? Cast them out of paradise. That was the fifth punishment. What kind of work did they have before their sin? And after their sin? This was the sixth punishment. After their sin their bodies were liable to undergo all kinds of sickness and suffering and death, and to return to dust. That was the seventh punishment.

SUMMARY. Our first parents, in punishment of their sin, were cast out of paradise, became liable to many sufferings, and were to die.

APPLICATION. You have often heard of some child punished by its good father; and each time the thought came to you: "That child must have done something bad." God was a good father to Adam and Eve; and yet He punished them severely. Why did God do that? All those misfortunes would not have come over our first parents, if they had not sinned. This shows you how wicked sin is in the sight of God. Suppose an ugly reptile, a snake, would creep up your clothes. It would make you afraid and scream aloud, and you would at once shake it off and jump away from it. Now sin is more horrid and dangerous than a poisonous snake. You should prefer to suffer hunger rather than to steal, to be laughed at rather than to go with bad companions, to take punishment rather than to escape it by telling a lie.

The holy Queen Blanche often said to her little son: "Louis, I love you more than anything on earth, but I would rather see you dead than to hear that you have committed a sin." Little Louis took these words so much to heart during his whole life, that he never committed a mortal sin, and became a great saint. Dear children, I love you also very much; but if I would know that any of you would later on fall into a mortal sin, I would pray to God rather to let you die now. For if you die without grievous sin, you shall forever dwell in heaven; but if you commit a mortal sin and die in it, you shall be cast forever into hell. Every good child tries hard to avoid even the smallest sin.

17. Original Sin.

PREPARATION. I told you the other day how Adam and Eve became unhappy by their sin.

OBJECT. You will hear to-day how all men have been made unhappy by the sin of our first parents.

DEVELOPMENT — *To inherit.* After they were cast out of paradise, Adam and Eve had children. When the parents are rich, their children also are rich. When the parents are poor, the children also are poor. Now, think a little, and tell me, when the parents die, who gets all that belonged to the parents; their houses, furniture, fields, money? The children. Therefore we say: "Children inherit the property of their parents." If their parents are poor, or if they are rich, the children inherit accordingly. Before their sin Adam and Eve were rich in paradise; they were not only rich, but good and happy. Their children were to be like them, rich and happy, because they would have inherited riches and happiness from them. All men are children of Adam and Eve. Why? Therefore all men were destined to inherit the riches and happiness of Adam and Eve.

Original sin. But Adam and Eve did not obey God. What did they do? Therefore thé children of Adam and Eve were born with sin in their souls, and also all the children born since then have inherited the sin of Adam and Eve. That is a great misfortune for all of us. The sin which all men have inherited from our first parents is called original sin.

Inclination to evil. Because all men inherited the sin of Adam and Eve, they have in themselves an inclination to evil. Therefore all children have an inclination to steal fruits, sweetmeats, to tell lies, to quarrel, to strike others. Who was the first to let the inclination to evil come into her heart? Eve. All men have inherited that inclination from Adam and Eve.

The punishments. What did Adam and Eve lose in their souls through their sin? When we were born we did not have the garment of grace in our souls. The sin of our first parents is the cause of this. Whose children did Adam and Eve cease to be after their sin? God's. When we were born, we were not children of God. Why? And where could Adam and Eve no longer go after their sin? To heaven. Heaven was closed against them and against all men by their sin. In what other way did God punish Adam and Eve? They had much to suffer, and at last to die. How did they have to suffer? Hard work, sickness, troubles. We also must suffer like them, and at last die. Why?

SUMMARY. What have all men inherited from Adam

and Eve? First, original sin, and secondly, the punishment of original sin.

APPLICATION. You have not yet suffered much. Perhaps a little headache or toothache, a few punishments. But you have perhaps seen others suffer great pains, and heard their cries and complaints. There are a great many sick persons on earth; how much do they suffer! Some die of hunger, others freeze or burn to death, or are drowned, or killed in accidents. How people grieve over the death of their relatives and friends, in the house, in the graveyard. One hundred thousand persons die daily on earth. What are all these pains, deaths and grief? The punishment and consequence of sin.

Moreover, you have an inclination to evil, to be disobedient, to steal, to tell lies, etc. When you feel inclined or tempted to do wrong, do you not act like Adam and Eve? Do you keep away from bad companions and all danger of sin? Do you pray when you are strongly tempted?

18. Promise of the Redeemer.

OBJECT. I will relate to you how God showed Himself kind and merciful to men after the sin of our first parents.

DEVELOPMENT — *All men were lost.* Whom did Adam and Eve obey, when they sinned? The devil. Therefore they belonged after that to the devil. They deserved hell by their sin. Sin was like a rope, with which the devil tied them and tried to drag them into hell. Who inherited the sin of Adam? All men. Therefore when children are born, they are not the children of God. And where does original sin prevent men from going? But the devil was not satisfied with preventing men from going to heaven; he wished to bring all men to hell with him. Therefore he made the plan to lead all men to commit all kinds of sins, and to use their sins as ropes to drag them all into hell. No man could ever free himself, by his own efforts, from these ropes. No, not all men together could break the ropes of sin; even if they tried as hard as they could. Nor could any angel, no, not even could all the angels together break the rope of sin and free men from sin. And yet no man could ever go to heaven, if he did not get free from that rope. God alone could free men from it, and redeem all of them. (Ask questions on the foregoing.)

God shows mercy. God did not redeem the bad angels from their sin. Where did He cast them? God could have treated Adam and Eve in the same manner and cast them into hell. But Adam and Eve were not so enlightened as the angels; also Eve did not of herself alone disobey God. Who had deceived her and induced her to disobey God? The devil. Therefore God had pity on men. And the Son of God in heaven spoke to His Father: "I will help man to be free from sin." For the Son of God had pity on men in their misfortune, and wished to show them mercy. But the heavenly Father asked Him: "How wilt Thou help men?" The Son replied: "I will choose a holy Mother, and become man. I will then combat the devil, and My Mother shall crush his head, and then men shall be free from sin." This pleased God the Father.

Promise of the Redeemer. God had said this to the serpent in paradise. How did He say it? "She (the woman) shall crush thy head." This He said after He had cursed the serpent. Because the serpent was cursed by God, men hate it, pursue it and kill it. What do children do when they see one? What is the meaning of all that God said to the serpent? "Thou thinkest that, because thou hast seduced Eve, and Adam through her, that thou wilt bring all men into hell. But there shall come a holy woman with a holy Child, and she shall crush thy head, and her Child shall free men from sin." Who was to come? What was the Child to do? And what should the woman do to the serpent? When the head of a snake is crushed, the snake can no longer bite or do harm. Therefore when the promised woman would crush the devil's head (power), the devil would no longer be able to harm men, to drag them by the rope of sin into hell. Therefore the devil got no good from his joy at seducing Eve.

The Redeemer is the Son of God. Who said to God the Father, that He would free (deliver) men from sin? The Son of God. How was He to do this? By becoming man. He would take a body and soul like ours, and would be born as a little baby. And what would His Mother do in consequence? Who is that Child, who, as God promised, would free men from sin? And who is the woman that would crush the head of the serpent?

Mary, the Mother of the Redeemer. Explain the picture of God punishing Adam and Eve, and the serpent. You see on the right a lovely little picture of a woman with a child in her arms. What is her foot treading on? The head of the serpent. This represents what God said to the serpent in paradise. Who is this woman? And who is the Child she is holding in her arms? Of what woman and of what Child was God speaking?

Who in heaven had already said that Mary with her Child would crush the serpent's head? But God did not call her Mary. How did He call her? Whose mother is Mary? Mary is the Mother of the Son of God. Therefore she is the Mother of God. Who is the Child Jesus she is holding in her arms? The Child Jesus is the Son of God. Mary and the Son of God were to crush the serpent's head. And from what did the Son of God wish to free us? And what is He, therefore, called? The Redeemer. To whom did God promise a Redeemer? When? Immediately after the fall (sin) of our first parents God promised them a Redeemer, who would free them from sin. He did this out of pity for men. What would have become of mankind, if God had not had pity on them?

The expectation of the Redeemer. Adam and Eve were very sorry for their sin. They did not afterwards get angry for having to suffer so much on account of it. They thought: "We will willingly suffer everything, for we have deserved it." They said to God: "Lord, forgive us; we will never sin again. Send us the Redeemer soon." Therefore God took away their sin from their souls, and restored His friendship to them; that is, He forgave them. They related to their children that God had promised a Redeemer; and their children related it to their own children, and thus all men knew it and expected the Redeemer.

The corruption of the world. But men did not remain good; not even all the children of Adam and Eve. One of them, called Cain, was wicked; he killed his brother Abel. Later on men became still worse; they made statues of wood and stone, and said: "These are our gods." And they adored the sun, moon and stars. In a certain city they had a large statue of iron, which was hollow inside. They would make in it a great fire, and when the statue was red-hot, parents would place their little children in the red-hot arms of the statue, and the children would roll from the arms into the big mouth of the statue, and were burnt up inside. These men knew nothing of God and the Redeemer.

The great Advent. But there were still many men on earth who knew that the Redeemer was to come. Every day they would go to church, and pray thus to God: "O Lord, send us the Redeemer." But the Redeemer did not come yet. At last these good men thought they could wait no longer until the Redeemer would come. They would get up during the night, kneel down and pray God to send the Redeemer. Sometimes they wished that the Redeemer would grow out of the ground at night as a beautiful flower, or would at early morning come down from heaven as the dew falls from heaven on the earth, or that the clouds would pour Him down like rain. But it was only after several thousand years that the Redeemer came. The long waiting of men for the Redeemer is called Advent.

19. The Announcement of the Redeemer's Birth.

PREPARATION. How did God show mercy to men? Immediately after the sin of our first parents God promised them a Redeemer, who would free them from sin. Whose son was the Redeemer to be? To redeem us, the Redeemer had to become man. What did He wish to seek for Himself on earth? A mother. There were many rich and beautiful women on earth. They were all anxious to be His Mother. Whom do you think He chose as His Mother? A queen, or an empress? Listen: He chose a poor virgin. You know her name? Mary lived at Nazareth, a poor little country village. It is far from here in Asia. To get there, it is necessary to travel many days on a railroad and in a vessel on the sea. Mary was poor, but very pious. She often prayed the heavenly Father to send the promised Redeemer; but she never imagined that she was to be His Mother. She thought she was of too little account for that great honor.

OBJECT. But, as I will now relate to you, God sent her a message to inform her that she would be the mother of the promised Redeemer.

RELATION. The angel Gabriel was sent by God to a poor, pious virgin named Mary. She was espoused (married) to a holy man called Joseph. Mary was praying in her little room, when the angel Gabriel came in and said to her: " Hail, full of grace, the Lord is with thee; blessed art thou among women." When Mary heard these words, she got frightened; but the angel said to her: " Be not afraid, Mary, because thou hast found grace with God. Thou shalt conceive a son, and shalt call His name Jesus. He will be great and the Son of the Almighty." Mary asked: "How will this happen?" The angel replied: "The Holy Ghost will come over thee, and by His power thou shalt become the Mother of God." Mary then said: "Behold the handmaid of the Lord; be it done to me according to thy word."

St. Joseph also lived at Nazareth. He was a poor carpenter. To Joseph also an angel appeared and said: "Take Mary to thee; the Holy Ghost came over her, and she will have a Son, whom thou shalt call Jesus, and He will save His people from their sins."

EXPLANATION — *The Virgin Mary.* Where did Mary live? What was Mary? A poor, pious virgin. To whom was she espoused? Therefore St. Joseph is called the spouse of Mary. Mary had but little money and no fine dresses. And yet God loved her more than all the other women in the world. Why? She was already very pious and so holy that there has never been any one in the world so holy as she. You have seen pictures of Mary with a lily in her hand. Of what color is the lily? Pure white, without the slightest spot or stain. Inside the leaves are golden threads, from which golden dust falls on the leaves.

But Mary's soul was much more beautiful than the most beautiful lily. She had never committed a sin. What sin stains the soul of every man that comes into the world? Now listen: Mary's soul was never stained with original sin. Mary alone among all the descendants of Adam and Eve, did not inherit original sin. She never had the least stain of any sin in her soul. Her soul was as pure white, and as shining like gold as the finest lily, and even far more beautiful. Her soul was rich in grace. No virgin was ever so rich in grace as Mary, for the heavenly Father willed that the soul of the Mother of the Redeemer should be the most beautiful, pious and holy of all women and virgins. Therefore we call her the Most Holy Virgin Mary.

The greeting of the angel. Mary was very fond of prayer and prayed often. On a certain day when she was at prayer, her room suddenly became wonderfully bright. Who was standing in front of Mary? An angel dressed in purest white, and his face was as bright and as beautiful as the sun. The angel made a low bow to her, and greeted her. What did he say?

How did he begin his greeting? He said: "Hail, full of grace." Just as if he said: "A beautiful greeting to thee from the Lord." When your father, or your mother, sends you to greet your uncle, or a friend, in their name, they show that they love the one to whom they send their greeting. From whom did the angel bring the greeting to Mary? What did God intend to show to Mary? That he loved and honored her; that she was more pleasing to Him than any one else. Why did God love Mary so much? Because she was so good and so holy; she was without sin. How beautifully pure was her soul! Her soul possessed more grace than all men and angels together. She was "full of grace."

Because Mary was full of grace, she became the Mother of the Son of God. She was allowed to carry the Lord God in her arms. The Lord was always near her and with her. Mary is the most happy of women, because she is the Mother of God. Therefore no woman is so greatly praised and honored as Mary. The angel truly said: "Blessed art thou among women." Repeat now the whole of the angel's greeting (salutation).

The message of the angel. When Mary so suddenly saw the angel and heard his wonderful greeting, she was frightened. The angel saw it, and said to her: "Fear not, Mary, etc., thou shalt," etc. And the angel at once told her what would be her Son's name, saying that He "shall be called Jesus." What else did the angel tell her about Him? "He shall be called the Son of the Most High." Who is Most High in heaven and on earth? God. Whose Son will the Son of Mary be called? The Son of God. How great is God? Infinitely great. Therefore

the angel implied that Mary's Son would be great. But
Mary could not imagine how this could be. She asked
the angel about it. The angel said that she would conceive
Him by the Holy Ghost.

Mary's consent. The angel's answer satisfied Mary.
.What did she then say? " Behold the handmaid of the
Lord; be it done to me according to thy word." So many
rich and noble women had longed to be the mother of the
Redeemer. But God preferred Mary. Mary is therefore
better and more noble than all those great ladies. But she
is not proud of it; for what does she call herself? Only
a servant (handmaid) of God. You know what a servant
is; whom must a servant obey? The mistress of the house.
Mary calls herself the servant of God, to show that she
would always be ready to do what God would bid her.
Then the angel returned. Where? To God's throne, to
bring to God Mary's answer. What was her answer?

St. Joseph. Who was St. Joseph? The spouse (husband) of Mary. Where did he live? What was his trade?
He was poor like Mary. You have already seen a picture
of St. Joseph. What does he hold in his hand? How do
the leaves of the lily look? St. Joseph's soul was as pure
and white as the lily. What does the lily in his hand teach
us? St. Joseph did not know that Mary had been chosen
to be the Mother of God; and Mary did not tell him a
word about it. But an angel came to him and told him to
call the Redeemer's name Jesus. What was St. Joseph
expected to do? To support and protect Mary and Jesus,
her Son.

EXPLANATION — *Redeemer, Saviour, Christ.* What did
the angel say to St. Joseph about the name he should give
to Mary's Son? Why should He be called Jesus? " Because
He shall save His people from their sins." What means
Jesus? Saviour. Jesus has yet another name. What is
it? Christ. How is the Redeemer called? Jesus Christ.

The only-begotten Son of God. Whose Son is the Re-

deemer? God's; God is His Father. A father on earth
has often more than one son. But Jesus is the only Son
of God the Father.

Our Lord. Who is God? The Lord of heaven and
earth. Jesus is also our Lord. Why? Because He is
God. To whom did men belong after the fall (sin) of
our first parents? To the devil. Who freed us from sin?
Jesus. Therefore we belong to Him, and He is our Lord
and Master.

SUMMARY. Jesus Christ is the only-begotten Son of
God. Why do we belong to Jesus Christ? Therefore we
call Him our Lord, as the Apostles' Creed teaches. Who
is His Mother? Mary. She is the happiest of women.
What do we call her? The Most Blessed Virgin Mary.

The Angelus. Who came to Mary when she was praying? Whose messengers are the angels? What message
from God did the angel Gabriel bring to Mary? Mary
could not understand the message; she asked the angel to
explain it. What did the angel reply? "The Holy Ghost
shall come upon thee." And thus make her the Mother
of the Son of God. Was Mary satisfied with the angel's
answer? What did she say?

The Angelical Greeting, or Salutation. When you say the
Hail Mary, you should think: "O Mary, I greet thee
from my heart." Who first greeted Mary? It is for this
reason that the Hail Mary is called the Angelical Salutation. How greatly you would rejoice, if an angel would
come to you and say: "God sends you greeting." What
a joy Mary must have felt when the angel greeted her in
the name of God, and delivered and explained to her his
message! She must often have thought of it afterwards.
Where is Mary now? God has made her Queen of heaven,
Queen of all the angels and saints. Mary is very much
pleased when we greet her as the angel did.

The words of Elizabeth. Then after "blessed art thou
among women," we add: "and blessed is the fruit of thy

womb." These words were first spoken to Mary by her
cousin St. Elizabeth. When Mary knew that she was to
be the Mother of God, she went quickly to St. Elizabeth.
When Mary entered Elizabeth's house and greeted her,
Elizabeth knew at once that Mary would be the Mother
of God, for the Holy Ghost inspired it to her. And now
Elizabeth greeted Mary as the angel had done, saying:
" Blessed art thou among women, and blessed is the fruit
of thy womb." And as Jesus is Mary's Son, we add
" Jesus."

The prayer of petition. We thus continue the Angelical
Salutation : " Holy Mary, Mother of God, pray for us, sin-
ners, now and at the hour of our death. Amen." We beg
Mary to pray for us. John's mother is sick. John would
like her to get well. And so he says to Mary: " O dear
Mother of God, pray God to make my mother well again."
And Mary prays to God for John's mother, and she
will get well. Why? Because God does all that Mary asks
of Him, for He cannot refuse anything to the Mother of
His Son. Therefore, when we need anything, let us say:
" Holy Mary, Mother of God, pray for us for   ." We
need Mary's prayers, for we are all poor sinners. With
what sin in our soul were we born? And we have also
committed sins of our own, and perhaps grievous sins, for
which God can justly cast us into hell. Therefore, let us
beg Mary to pray for us *now,* that is, every day, that God
may forgive us.

But the most dangerous time for us is the hour of our
death. Men dread death. They fear hell on account of
their sins. And the devil is watching when men are dying,
for he does not wish them to be sorry for their sins; he
tries to make them commit more sins. No one can better
help those who are dying than Mary. The devil is greatly
afraid of her. If she prays for us, the devil cannot harm
us. What do we wish Mary to do for us? When do we
ask her to pray for us? Why especially at the hour of our

death? You should all reflect on this when you recite the Hail Mary. By doing so, you will give Mary great pleasure.

20. Birth of the Redeemer.

OBJECT. I will tell you to-day how the Redeemer was born.

PREPARATION. You know already who is our Redeemer, who is His Mother, and who is her spouse. Where did Mary and Joseph live? Bethlehem is also in Palestine. It was called the city of David, because that great king was born there. Mary and Joseph descended from King David; hence we say that they were of the family of David. When the Redeemer was born Herod was king of Judea. He lived in its capital, called Jerusalem. Herod had to obey a much greater monarch than himself. This was the Emperor Augustus, who lived in Rome and governed a great part of the world. Augustus wished to know how many people lived in his empire. What must I do to find out how many children are here? Count them. Now Augustus had to get the people in his empire counted, in order to find out their number. The same is done every ten years in the United States. This is called taking the census. (Appropriate questions.)

RELATION. Therefore Augustus ordered the census to be taken in his immense empire. Every one had to go to his city to give in his name, and all about his family. St. Joseph and Mary went to Bethlehem, the city of David, because they were of the family of David. But when they came there, the hotels, boarding-houses, and private houses were all full because of the crowds that had come there; they could find no place to lodge in. They had to go into a poor, abandoned stable just outside of the city. In this miserable place Jesus Christ, the Son of God, was born; and Mary wrapped Him in swaddling-clothes, and laid Him on straw in the manger.

EXPLANATION — *The command.* Under what emperor was Judea? What did Augustus wish to know? What means did he use to find it out? Where had Joseph and Mary to go on that account? Taking the census in the United States is done differently. Who knows how it is done?

The journey. Where did Joseph and Mary go to get their names inscribed in the census book? Why had they to go there? There were no railroads in those days. Rich people could travel in wagons. But how had Joseph and Mary to travel? On foot for three days. They were very tired, and would have been glad to get lodgings in some house.

Their arrival. When they came to Bethlehem, it was late in the evening. They had no friends or relatives in Bethlehem to whom they could go. They sought the public inn or lodging place for strangers. There was no more place for them. They sought a lodging elsewhere, but no one would give it to them, no one wanted them, for they were too poor. Suppose you would come to a strange town on a cold night, and you could find no place to lodge, to spend the night! How would you feel? Imagine, then, how Mary and Joseph felt. They did not get angry, or complain. They looked around, and at last found that wretched abandoned stable just outside the walls. They went in and were glad to get that poor place. It was night. The lights of Bethlehem were put out one by one, until there was darkness all over the city, and the people were all asleep. Mary was still praying, and Joseph tried to fix and clean up the miserable place.

The birth of the Redeemer. All at once, at midnight, a great bright light lit up wonderfully the poor stable, and Mary saw on her dress a beautifully bright Baby looking at her and smiling. Then it began to cry and hold out its little hands to Mary. She saw it and prostrated herself before it, adored it, and lovingly and tenderly kissed it

over and over again, and held it in her arms. She could
not get tired looking at its beautiful bright little face. St.
Joseph looked at it with reverence and joy, knelt down
and adored it, and tenderly kissed it. Then Mary wrapped
up the Infant Saviour (Redeemer) in swaddling-clothes;
and where did she put Him? In a fine cradle? No; she
had none; the only place she could find for Him was the
manger out of which cattle eat; in it there was a little
straw, and there she laid the sweet divine Infant. Oh, how
poor was the Saviour born, on a cold night; He had no
bed to lie on; no fire to warm Him; nothing to make Him
comfortable.

FURTHER EXPLANATION — *The Infant Jesus is the only-
begotten Son of God.* That Infant in the crib, or manger,
is wrapped in swaddling-clothes, like all the other children
in Judea; He is as weak and helpless as other children at
their birth. From the angel Gabriel we know that He is
much more than other children. Whose Son was He to
be called? The Son of the Most High. Therefore He is
the Son of God; the only Son of God the Father.

God became man. Therefore the Son of God became
a little infant. He did not cease to be God. As God He
could not be seen. Why? But He could be seen as an
infant in the manger. His face, His eyes, His mouth, His
hands and feet, His whole body could be seen. There was
one thing in Him that could not be seen. It was His soul,
for He had a body and soul like ours, which He took when
He became man. He remained God. Therefore He is
both God and man.

The Redeemer, or Saviour. Where was it that God the
Son told God the Father that He was willing to become
man? In heaven. Why did He wish to become man?
To save us. What name was Mary told to give Him?
Jesus. What does Jesus mean? Saviour. The Saviour
is the only-begotten Son of God, who became man to save
us.

The Word was made flesh. We can also say: "The Word was made flesh to save us." Why? Because the Son of God is called also the Word; and to be made flesh means also to become man. In what prayer do we say: "And the Word was made flesh"? In the Angelus. Where was Jesus, the Son of God, born? And for thirty-three years He dwelt among us. It is nearly two thousand years since the Son of God came on earth.

APPLICATION. Why did the Son of God come upon earth? What would have become of men, if the Son of God had not come upon earth? They would all be lost. Therefore we cannot be grateful enough to Him. We should thank Him for it by reciting the Angelus three times a day, when the church bell rings in the morning, at noon and in the evening.

The Angelus. The Angelus begins as follows: "The Angel of the Lord declared unto Mary; And she conceived of the Holy Ghost." When saying this, think of the angel entering Mary's room when she was praying, and announcing to her that she was chosen to be the mother of the Redeemer; and say the Hail Mary. Then say: "Behold the handmaid of the Lord; Be it done unto me according to thy word." This was Mary's answer to the angel's message; she consented to become the mother of the Redeemer, in obedience to God's will. Then say another Hail Mary. After this say: "And the Word was made flesh; And dwelt among us." As soon as Mary gave her consent, God the Son took a body and soul like ours and dwelt among us for thirty-three years. When you say these words, strike your breast, if you are kneeling; but if you are standing, make a genuflexion. Then add a third Hail Mary. After this recite the following: "Pray for us, O holy Mother of God; that we may be made worthy of the promises of Christ. Let us pray. Pour forth, we beseech Thee, O Lord, Thy grace into our hearts, that we, to whom the Incarnation of Christ,

Thy Son, was made known by the message of an angel, may by His passion and cross be brought to the glory of His resurrection, through the same Christ our Lord. Amen."

When the Angelus bell rings in the morning, children are usually asleep. They should then recite the Angelus after rising. If you are at home, when the Angelus bell rings at noon and in the evening, say it when the bell rings. If you are outside, you ought to stop your play, your conversation, and say the Angelus quietly, the boys with their hats off. Always say it devoutly.

21. The Shepherds adore the Infant Saviour.

PREPARATION. The first persons who knew of the Saviour's birth were Mary and Joseph.

OBJECT. But, as I am going to relate to you, God had it announced on the same night to some pious shepherds.

RELATION. In the neighborhood of the stable there were some pious shepherds in the fields keeping night-watch over their flocks. Suddenly there was around them a very bright light, and they feared very much; an angel stood before them, saying: "Fear not; I announce to you tidings of great joy. To-day in the city of David is born to you a Saviour, who is Christ the Lord. And this shall be a sign to you; you will find an infant wrapped in swaddling-clothes, and laid in a manger." And suddenly there was with the angel a multitude of the heavenly army, praising God and saying: "Glory to God in the highest, and on earth peace to men of good will." Then the angels returned to heaven. The shepherds then said to one another: "Let us go over to Bethlehem, and see what has been told us." They hastened to the stable, and found Mary and Joseph, and the Infant lying in the manger. And after this they returned to their flocks, thanking and praising God.   Eight days later the Infant was circumcised and named Jesus, as the angel had foretold.

EXPLANATION — *The apparition of the angel.*   On the night that Jesus was born the stable was empty.   The sheep were in the fields guarded by the shepherds.   The shepherds had lighted a fire, and were seated around it. They had been speaking about the Saviour who was expected to come soon.   Then they fell asleep, and only one shepherd remained on the watch, walking up and down. The night was calm and clear and the stars were shining so nicely.   All at once the watching shepherd saw a bright light in the heavens coming down nearer and nearer, and making everything as bright as the noon-day.   Greatly astonished, he awoke the other shepherds; they sprang up; the light around them was so bright that they could no longer see the stars or the fire.   They were dazzled and got afraid.   In the midst of the bright light they beheld an angel clothed in shining white garments; his face looked heavenly.   They were so much afraid that they fell down to the ground.   But the angel had come to bring them good news.

The message of the angel.   What did he say to them? Why should they rejoice?   How did the angel call the Saviour?   Did he tell them where He was born?   In which city?   Did he tell them how they would find Him?

The hymn of the angels.   The shepherds listened joyfully and devoutly to what the angel said to them.   Then they saw a multitude of other bright angels in the air around them, so that there was like a street of light up to heaven.   And all the angels sang.   What did they sing? How sweet and beautiful was their singing!   It was a heavenly melody in the quiet night extending from earth to heaven.   Since then men also sing the beautiful hymn of the angels.   The priest intones (begins) it at the high Mass, and the choir continues it.   It is called the Gloria. But men cannot sing it so beautifully as the angels.

The shepherds seek the Infant Saviour. Suddenly the angels all disappeared. Whither did they return? The shepherds stood a long time looking up to heaven after the angels. But they at last remembered what the angel had told them about the Infant Saviour, and said to one another: "Let us go over to Bethlehem, and see what the Lord hath told us." You may be sure the shepherds hastened as fast as they could in order to go to Jesus. They came to the stable, knocked at the door, and St. Joseph came to open it and asked them what they wished. They related what the angel had told them, and what they had seen and heard.

The shepherds find the Infant Saviour. Full of joy St. Joseph let them in. There they found everything as the angel had told them. Whom did they see there? Greatly wondering, they stood around the Infant Saviour lying on straw in a manger. His Mother had not even a little room or a little bed for Him. For Jesus, the Lord of heaven and earth, Mary, the best and holiest of mothers, had found only a stable, the dwelling of cattle. The cold wind was blowing through the cracks in the walls. Jesus had to endure cold at His very birth. But the shepherds knew from the angel that the poor Infant in the manger was the long expected Redeemer.

The return of the shepherds. Where did the shepherds go after seeing and adoring the Infant Jesus? On their way back to their flocks they thanked and praised God, sang pious hymns, and spoke of the Infant Saviour just born.

The Circumcision. What happened when Jesus was a week old? He was circumcised. His skin was cut, and He bled a little. On that day He received the name of Jesus. Who foretold that He would receive that name? The angel. When?

EXPLANATION — *Jesus.* Why did the angel say that He should be named Jesus? What does Jesus mean? From what was He to save or redeem us? Sin had made our souls slaves of the devil, and Jesus was to redeem them from sin. The angel, when speaking to the shepherds, had called Him Saviour. Why was Bethlehem called the city of David? His father was a shepherd, and David also had been a shepherd in his youth.

Christ. David was very good, pious and pleasing to God. Therefore God intended that he should become king of the Jews. The prophet Samuel, a man of God, was ordered by God to anoint David's head with oil in His name. David was an *anointed* of God; by this anointing he was made king of God's chosen people. Jesus is also a king, the King of heaven and earth. He is also called "the Anointed," or Christ, for Christ means the Anointed.

Our Lord. Who called the Redeemer Christ? What other name did the angel give Him? The Lord. Jesus Christ is our Lord. Why? Because He is God. Who had become our master on account of sin? The devil. But the devil did not always remain our master. Why? Who is now our Master, or Lord? Jesus Christ is, then, twice our Master, our Lord. How is that?

Humiliation. God is infinitely rich and powerful. To Him belongs all that is in heaven and on earth. The Son of God could, if He had wished, when He became man for us, have been born in a splendid palace, and laid on a bed of the finest silk in a golden cradle. But in what kind of building was He born? What kind of bed had He? He wished to be born in great poverty and suffering. For our sake He wished to suffer already from His very birth.

SUMMARY. Let us recite all the names given to the Infant Jesus in the manger (crib). How did the angel, that was sent to Mary and Joseph, call Him? Jesus. How do you call Him? The Infant Jesus. Whose Son did the angel say that Jesus was? The Son of the Most High. Whose Son is He then? The Son of God. We, there-

fore, call Him also the Divine Infant. How is He called, because the Father has only one Son? The only-begotten Son of God. How did the angel call Him, when speaking to the shepherds? The Saviour, Christ, the Lord. Who were the first to come and adore the Divine Infant? Where did they come from? From the neighborhood. And how did they find out that the Saviour was born? An angel came from heaven to tell them.

APPLICATION — *Poverty*. Some of you have parents that are poor; therefore you have no fine clothes, and suffer from cold in winter. But none of you are so poor as the Infant Jesus. You have a soft bed to sleep in, and you do not live in a stable. When you see other children with better clothes and many more good things than you have, do not envy them, do not be displeased, but say: " For the love of me Jesus, the Son of God, became poor, and for the love of Him I will willingly bear my poverty." Blessed Herman Joseph was very poor. Many a time he had to go to school very hungry and without any breakfast. He would then each time kneel down and pray before a statue of the Blessed Virgin, holding the Infant Jesus in her arms, saying: " Dear little Infant Jesus, this morning I got only a very small piece of bread to eat, and I am still so hungry. But I will be contented. Thou art the Son of God, and Thou hast suffered want." Then Herman Joseph would go cheerfully to school. Dear children, like Herman Joseph, be content, for the love of the Infant Jesus, with the little you have.

Christmas. We all rejoice very much because our Saviour was born. He was born during the night. That night has been blessed and sanctified. What is it called? Christmas night. In memory of that night we celebrate every year on the twenty-fifth of December the great feast of Christmas. In Catholic countries, and where the bishops allow it, Mass is then celebrated at midnight, because the Infant Jesus, our Saviour, was born at midnight. On

Christmas night Almighty God presented to us what He loved above everything else, His only-begotten Son. In remembrance of this most precious of gifts, children receive Christmas gifts. (Santa Claus is not Catholic; it is a Protestant invention and institution, a corruption of the Catholic practice of honoring and rejoicing over the birth of Jesus Christ.) Christmas is essentially a Catholic feast, on which we remember, and thank God for the gift of His divine Son as our Saviour.

Advent. Children rejoice long beforehand on account of Christmas; they can hardly wait for it. The Church has set apart four weeks to prepare for Christmas in remembrance of the four thousand years, during which men were anxiously waiting for the coming of the promised Redeemer. These four weeks are called Advent. During this time the Church repeats the prayers and sighs of the holy persons yearning for the coming of the Redeemer. (*Rorate coeli.*)

Veneration of the name of Jesus. Who is the Just One, whom the clouds should rain down from heaven? The Redeemer, Jesus Christ. The name Jesus was given Him by God Himself. It is a most holy name. When it is pronounced, all the angels bend the knee. When we say the Hail Mary, we bow our head at the name of Jesus. In some Catholic countries those who meet a priest, say: " Praised be Jesus Christ." And the priest answers: " Forever." That is a much better and more appropriate greeting than " Good morning," " Good evening."

The picture. Explain the picture. Where is the Infant Jesus? In what is He wrapped up? On what does he lie? Where are the shepherds? Where is Mary? Where is St. Joseph? How do you know it is a stable? The ox and the ass. Where is the manger? But it is night. Where does the light come from? From above, or from the Infant Jesus? Where are the angels? What do they remind you of?

22. On Holy Mass.

(Adapted from Canon Meyerberg's Catechetical Instruction.)

Dear Children, what did the angel say on Christmas night to the shepherds? " I announce to you tidings of great joy. This night the Saviour was born in the city of David." I will announce to you a similar event you have yourselves witnessed. It is Sunday. In this town (city) everything is quiet. (The catechist should give some local details.) The carpenter, the blacksmith, the farmers are not engaged in their every-day work. Everything is so quiet, so solemn. The large church bell suddenly rings in the quiet morning, beautifully, earnestly and long. The people are going out of their houses. They are better dressed than on other days. From every side people are coming to church. The children also are coming. The bell continues to ring. It seems as if it was speaking. It tells something to all the people, to the children. And the bell causes all to come from far and near. What does the bell say? The bell says almost the same thing as the angel of Christmas said: " I announce to you a great joy this day; come to church; the Saviour is born." What does the bell say? (Answered by the children.) The bell tells you also: " My child, I announce to you a great joy; to-day during Holy Mass the Saviour will be born." You know, dear children, that the shepherds were very happy. The angel had said to them: " You shall see the Saviour." And we all wish to be as happy as they. Just think of how holy and great a thing is about to take place! Our dear Lord Himself, our Saviour, will be born during Mass in this church. He will come to us.

What did the shepherds do? They hastened to Bethlehem. They did not stop on the way and stand looking all around. And they found Mary and Joseph and the Infant Saviour lying in the manger. There is a school-

boy, a schoolgirl, who are going to church; the bell tells
them: " I announce to you a great joy; to-day the Saviour
is born." But they stop and look around, and perhaps
are doing some mischief. The bell continues to ring; but
they do not hear the bell any more. Other children come
along and join them. They walk a few steps towards the
church, and something else attracts their attention, and they
stop to look. But the bell continues to ring, saying:
" Come, I announce to you a great joy." At last the bell
stops ringing; it has spoken loud and long enough. The
children enter the church late, much too late. Are these
children like the shepherds? Are their guardian angels
pleased with them? (Here admonitions may be given appropriate to the circumstances of the people and the place.)

Divine service will soon begin in the church. There the
little bells will also begin to ring. On Christmas night an
angel said: " I announce to you tidings of great joy."
Suddenly a multitude of angels joined him and all praised
God, singing " Glory to God on high," etc. In like manner, the little bells will repeat what the large bell has said.
What will they say to us?

Entering the church. You now come to the church.
But I must first relate something to you. There was once
a holy man called Bernard. He was fond of going to
church. When he would come to the church door, he
would first turn around and look back. And then only
would he go in. One day his pupils asked him: " Father
Bernard, why do you always turn around and look back,
when you come to the church door? " He said: " I will
tell you. I stand still in front of the church and look
back. Then I say in my heart: You worldly thoughts,
you street thoughts, you must now stay outside. I will
think on God only."

Dear children, you must do likewise. Of course, you
need not turn around in front of the door. That would

cause great confusion among those who are going in. But I will tell you how you must act. What do you find on entering the church? Who knows? What do grown people take there? Yes, holy water; water blessed by the priest. His blessing has made it holy. On entering the church you devoutly take holy water, not with your whole hand, but only with the tip of your fingers. (Do not play in or with the holy water.) And then what do you do? Make the sign of the cross. When you place your right hand on your forehead you should remember that it means: " My child, leave all your street thoughts, your thoughts of school, of play, outside. Think of God; you are now in His house, and He is there in the tabernacle waiting for you. Remember where you are; think on God, and adore Him really present." Then look closely at the priest who says Mass, and if you have a prayer-book, recite the prayers in it for hearing Mass. Do not look around. If you catch yourself thinking of things outside, check yourself, try to drive away such thoughts, and begin to pray again and pay devout attention to the priest saying Mass. By acting in this way, you will please God and draw His blessing upon yourself.

In church, especially during Mass, you must not speak, but keep silence. You should speak to God only, that is, pray to Him. In ancient times there was a holy man, a prophet of God. He spoke in the name of God, and foretold things that were going to happen, for God had made them known to him. He spoke to the Jews about behaving in church. What he said was very beautiful. Listen attentively: " The Lord is in His temple; let the whole earth keep silence before Him." Remember, then, that God is in the church, and every one should keep silence in it, and not talk. The whole earth, all men should keep silent in His presence. What, then, should we think of those boys and girls, who talk, whisper to one another in church, and never think of God. Are they more than the whole earth? God is in His own house, and those who come into it, must not talk with their companions, but must speak only to God, that is, pray to Him.

When you bless yourself, you next place your right hand on your breast, in which your heart is placed. And this means as if God said to you: " My child, give Me thy heart. Give Me all that thou hast. Give Me thy inmost heart, the best thing that thou hast. Give Me thy whole soul, all thy strength. Give me, especially in church, thy heart with thy pious prayers. Give Me a pure, obedient, pious, upright heart, a heart that tries always to be good." And when you touch your shoulders with your right hand, it means this: " My child, be ready to carry thy little cross for Jesus as He carried His for thee. Take upon thy shoulders the burden of keeping the commandments of God and of His Church. For only by doing this, thou canst gain heaven."

And when, on entering the church, you make the sign of the cross with holy water, say devoutly: " In the name," etc. And go into the church in the name of God the Father, who created you, and all the stars, plants, flowers, birds, fishes and animals. To Him all things belong. He is everywhere, but especially in the church, which is His temple. Let the whole earth keep still before Him. You enter the church also in the name of God the Son, in the name of Jesus, our Saviour. In the church, you will, like the shepherds, find Jesus. The bell truly says: " I announce to you a great joy. To-day in this church, during Holy Mass, the Saviour will be born." You enter the church also in the name of God the Holy Ghost. He will Himself descend into your heart. The Holy Ghost breathes (distributes His gifts) when and where He pleases. You do not know where He comes from, nor where He goes. But He comes down to the children who are devout in church, for He loves children very much, and He quietly comes down into their souls like a soft wind in spring. He helps you to pray from your inmost heart, and to say: "Our Father who art in heaven."

23. The Presentation of Jesus in the Temple of Jerusalem.

PREPARATION. In Catholic countries it is customary for a mother to bring her month-old baby to church. There she kneels before the altar to thank God for giving her that child; she promises God that she will raise him so piously, that he may be able, at the end of his life, to go to heaven. In ancient times it was the custom among the Jews that mothers should bring to church their first-born boys, forty days after they were born. There was only one church in all Judea; it was in Jerusalem. It was very large, and was called the Temple. Here the mother would hand her baby to the priest; and the priest, holding it in his arms, would offer it to God. This was called the presentation of the child to God. In offering her child to God through the priest, the mother meant to say: "I wish to offer my child to God; it should belong to God." What did the Jewish mothers offer to God in the temple? How did they do it?

OBJECT. I will now tell you how Mary and Joseph presented the Infant Jesus to God.

RELATION. When Jesus was forty days old, Mary and Joseph brought Him to Jerusalem, in order to present Him to God. At the same time they made the offering of the poor — two young doves. At that time there lived in Jerusalem a God-fearing old man, named Simeon. He longed and prayed ardently for the coming of the Redeemer. Inspired by the Holy Ghost, he came to the temple just as Mary and Joseph were bringing Jesus in. Simeon took the Infant Jesus in his arms, praised God saying: "Lord, I can now die in peace, for my eyes have seen the Saviour."

In Jerusalem there was a pious widow eighty-four years old, called Anna. She served God day and night in fasting and prayer. She also came to the temple at the same time, praised God for having been able to see the Saviour, and spoke of the Infant Saviour to all who were waiting for the redemption.

EXPLANATION — *The journey.* After Jesus was born Mary and Joseph remained for a time in Bethlehem. Where did they bring Jesus when He was forty days old? On the way Mary sat on a donkey, carefully holding the Infant Jesus in her arms. She had covered Him with her large veil. Joseph walked, leading the donkey by the bridle. Spring had already begun, and the early flowers were already in bloom. In two hours they reached Jerusalem, that beautiful city. Just as a young bird peeps from its nest through the leaves of the tree, so the Infant Jesus was peeping with His lovely eyes through Mary's veil on the city and temple. How the little heart of the Saviour was beating! Our Saviour had long dwelt there as God. Now He came as man for the first time into the temple. With great joy He looked at everything, for He knew that the temple was the house of His Father. Jesus is the Son of God; He was therefore the Lord and God of the temple. Why did Joseph and Mary bring the Infant Jesus to the temple? How did they present Him in the temple? They handed the Divine Infant to the priest, and the priest held Him towards heaven to offer Him to God, as if he would say: "Dear Lord, this Child shall belong to Thee." The priest then gave Him back to Mary and Joseph.

Mary's Offering. Jewish mothers had to do also something else. The rich ones had to offer a lamb to God in the temple; but the poor mothers had to offer only two doves. Which offering did Mary make? Why? Because she was poor.

Simeon and Anna. Who can tell me which two persons came into the temple just when Mary and Joseph were bringing the Infant Jesus? Were they young? No; for Simeon is called an old man. He was pious and feared offending God by committing sin. At that time all pious persons were expecting the Redeemer. Simeon was expecting the Redeemer; but because he was very old, he feared he would not live long enough to see the Redeemer. So he prayed to God every day to send the Redeemer, so that he might see Him before his death. The Holy Ghost rewarded his intense desire by promising him that he should not die before seeing the Redeemer. That was a great joy for him. He used to go daily to the temple to pray and wait for the Redeemer to come. On the day when Mary and Joseph came to the temple with the Infant Jesus, the Holy Ghost made known to him: "To-day the Redeemer will surely come to the temple. Go there and you will see Him." Did Simeon go that day to the temple to see the Redeemer? Yes, he went that day very early to the temple, that he might not miss seeing Him, just like children, who go very early to see a parade, so that they may not miss seeing it. Simeon was led by the Holy Ghost to the temple. When Mary and Joseph came with the Infant Jesus, Simeon was already there waiting. As soon as he saw them, he recognized the Infant Jesus as the Redeemer. He at once came to them, knelt down, bowed deeply before the Divine Infant. Probably the Infant Jesus bent down towards him, to show to Mary that He wished to go to him. Simeon held out his arms to Jesus, and Mary put Jesus in Simeon's arms. Oh, with how great reverence and love the holy old man pressed the Infant Jesus to his heart! Then holding Him out in front of him, to take a good look at Him, he gazed at the Infant Jesus with unspeakable love. He saw in the Infant's eyes a light that grew brighter and brighter, and at last enlightened the whole world. Oh, how happy Simeon felt! He felt as if he would now willingly die, since he had seen the Redeemer. What did he say?

Who praised God after Simeon for the coming of the Redeemer? Anna. What was she? A very old widow. She was much bent in walking, and had to lean on a stick. She was very lean, because, for the love of God, she used to fast, that is, she ate very little. Moreover, she prayed much day and night. The Holy Ghost made known to Anna that the Infant Mary held in her arms was the Redeemer. How did Anna manifest her joy? She praised God, and in doing so, her thin, pale face looked flushed (red) and beautiful, and her eyes brightened with joy. The people who were then in the temple listened to her words. She said: " The Redeemer, whom· we have so long expected, has now come. He is here in the temple; look at Him; there He is; that Child in His Mother's arms." Our Infant Saviour was much pleased with those two holy persons, and gave them His blessing. And Mary and Joseph wondered how Simeon and Anna had found out that the Infant Jesus was the Redeemer. Although He was only an infant, the shepherds, Simeon and Anna had praised Him as the Redeemer.

FURTHER EXPLANATION — *The intention in the offering.* Why did Mary and Joseph bring the Divine Infant to the temple? How was the ceremony of His presentation performed? What did the priest mean to say? Whilst the priest was holding Him towards heaven, the Infant Jesus offered Himself for us to God the Father, saying in His Heart: " Dear Father in heaven, Thou hast willed that I should become man to redeem all men. I am willing to suffer and die for them, as Thou willest that I should do." Mary also offered the Divine Infant to God at the same time, for she said in silence: " Dear Father in heaven, I will not keep this Child for myself. I offer Him again to Thee. Thou willest that He should suffer and die for men; I am satisfied with Thy holy will. May it always be done! "

SUMMARY. How old was the Infant Jesus, when Mary

and Joseph brought Him to the temple? And why did they bring Him there? Because Simeon saw a great light in the eyes of the Infant Jesus, when He was presented (offered) in the temple, we celebrate a feast every year, in which wax candles are blessed and carried around in procession. That feast is called Candlemas-day. It is celebrated on the second of February, forty days after Christmas.

APPLICATION — *The Offertory of the Mass.* As Mary and Joseph went with the Infant Jesus to the temple, so you go to church on Sundays and Holydays to assist at Holy Mass. When the priest says Mass, he has before him on the altar, a gilt silver chalice, and on it a gilt silver little plate, and on the plate is a thin round white bread, called the host. Over all this is a nice silk cover. When the priest takes off that cover, the altar boy rings a little bell. The priest next takes in his hands the little silver plate with the host on it, and raises it towards God in heaven, just as the priest in the temple raised the Infant Jesus heavenward. The altar boy then brings wine and water to the priest, who pours some of each into the chalice, and then raises the chalice heavenward. What did the priest in the temple mean to say, when he raised the Infant Jesus towards God? The priest in the church says the same to God when he raises heavenward the host and the chalice, saying (in substance) "O God, I offer these to Thee; deign to accept them; they belong to Thee." (Appropriate questions on the foregoing.) What is the Offertory in the Mass? What does the priest do at the Offertory? During the Offertory you should imitate the Infant Jesus. What did He say to His heavenly Father, when the priest was offering Him to God? So ought you also to do during the Offertory, saying to God from your heart: "Dear Lord, I wish to be all Thine; I give Thee my body and my soul, my whole self." When should you say this in your heart? How do you know when the Offertory begins? You must, therefore, pay attention to the priest during Mass.

24. The Wise Men from the East adore the Redeemer.

PREPARATION. Mary and Joseph, the pious shepherds and Simeon and Anna rejoiced greatly because the Redeemer was born. They had long expected Him. How did they know that a Redeemer was to come? To whom had God promised Him? To whom did Adam and Eve relate this? To prevent men from forgetting during four thousand years the promise of a Redeemer, God repeated from time to time this promise to the Jews. This He did through holy men, called prophets. God made many things known to the prophets about the coming of the Redeemer. One of them told the Jews that the Redeemer would be born when a wonderful star would be seen in the heavens. Another said that the Redeemer would be born at Bethlehem. (Appropriate questions on the foregoing.)

What the prophets foretold about the Redeemer was written in the Holy Scriptures, or the Bible. The Bible contains holy things revealed or inspired by God. The Jews were fond of reading the Holy Scriptures. Some of them became so learned, that they knew almost all the Holy Bible by heart. They were called scribes. But the Jews were not the only people that knew that the Redeemer would come. Even the pagan nations knew it; they had heard it from the Jews, etc.

OBJECT. When the Redeemer was born, three kings came from pagan countries to adore the Infant Jesus. I will now tell you all about it.

RELATION. When Jesus was born at Bethlehem, wise men came from the East to Jerusalem. They asked:

"Where is He that is born king of the Jews? For we have seen His Star in the East, and are come to adore Him." When King Herod heard this, he was frightened. He called all the scribes together, and asked them where Christ was to be born. They answered: "At Bethlehem in the tribe of Juda." Then Herod sent the wise men to Bethlehem, and said to them: "Go there, and seek the Child carefully, and when you have found Him, come and let me know where He is, and I also will go to adore Him."

The wise men set out immediately for Bethlehem. And the wonderful Star went ahead of them to show them the way. When they got near the stable, the Star stopped directly over it. When the wise men saw the Star, they were overjoyed. They went into the stable, and found the Child with Mary, His Mother. They prostrated themselves and adored the Infant Jesus. They also offered Him gold, incense and myrrh. During the night God commanded them not to go back to Herod. They returned to their country by another route.

EXPLANATION — *The wise men come to Jerusalem.* Show me where the sun rises. The countries in that direction are called the East. The East was far from Jerusalem. Who came from the East when Jesus was born? How many were they? They were smart and learned. They were as rich as kings, and were very pious. Later on they even became saints. Hence they are called "the three holy kings." They rode on camels, and had many servants with them.

Where did they first seek the Redeemer? In Jerusalem. How did they inquire for Him? They thought that He was the son of a king. Why did they seek Him in Jerusalem? Because King Herod dwelt there. How did they know that the Redeemer was born? They had seen a new and wonderful Star suddenly shining in the heavens. The Star came towards them, and grew always larger and brighter. They had never before seen such a star. It was truly wonderful. Now they knew that that wonderful Star was the Star foretold by the prophet. What was to happen when that Star would appear? Therefore, when they came to Jerusalem, they said: "We have seen His Star." How did Herod feel, when he heard this? He was frightened, and thought in his heart: "Who is this newly born king? Shall I be no longer king?" What was it that Herod could not tell the wise men? Whom did he ask about it? Why could the scribes know it? What answer did they give?

Herod sends the wise men to Bethlehem. Where did Herod tell the wise men to go? What did he tell them to do? What did he mean by this? He meant that the wise men should seek Him and inquire about Him, until they should find Him. To whom were they to make known where the Redeemer was? And why should they tell it to him? Herod only said so, but he meant something very different. He meant to go and kill the Infant Jesus.

The wise men on their way find the Infant Jesus. The wise men left Herod. Where did they go? But they did not know which of the infants in Bethlehem was the Redeemer. Who showed them the way to the Infant Jesus? The Star. From the time they had left their country they had not seen the Star any more. But as soon as they got out of Jerusalem, the Star suddenly appeared before them. But it did not do this of its own accord. Who commanded the Star to go before them? Now they knew for sure that they were on the right road. How did they feel, when they saw the Star? Where did the Star stop? The Star shed bright rays of light on the entrance of the stable, as with a lighted finger pointing to it.

The wise men find the Infant Jesus. Before entering the stable the wise men put on their finest clothes. Then they went slowly with their servants in procession into the stable. Whom did they find in it? Mary was sitting down

with the Infant Jesus in her lap. She bowed kindly to the
three wise men and showed them the Infant Jesus. They
looked at Him with reverence and joy. How did they call
the Infant Jesus when they inquired about Him in Jerusalem? What, then, was the Infant Jesus? He was truly
a king, but not a king like Herod, nor an emperor like
Augustus. He is a much greater and better king. Where
is His throne? In the kingdom of Heaven. He is the
King of heaven and earth. And even much more. Whose
Son is He?

The wise men worship the Divine Infant. How did
the wise men wish to worship the Divine Infant? Mary,
for that reason, held Him standing on her lap turned towards them. The wise men (holy kings) knelt before
Him with hands joined, and adored Him. The Divine
Infant looked at them with His bright little eyes in a kind
and friendly way, and raised His little hands upwards, as
if to give them His blessing. Probably Mary allowed them
to kiss His hands and to hold Him a little while in their
arms. After the wise men their servants likewise knelt
and adored the Infant Jesus.

The gifts of the three wise men. Each of the wise men
had brought a gift for the Infant Saviour. They were glorious gifts, the best of the things the country of each of them
produced. What did the first one offer? Gold. You all
know what gold is. What things are made of gold? What
did the second wise man offer to the Infant Jesus? Incense. You have already seen incense in church. What
is it used for? It is laid on burning coals in the censer,
and then rises heavenward as a sweet fragrant smoke.
What did the third wise man offer? Myrrh. We have
no myrrh in our country. It is a fine resin. Why did
the wise men bring most precious gifts to the Infant Jesus?
They thought that, since the Infant Jesus was God, they
should give Him the best of what they had. They stayed
a whole day with Jesus. They related about the wonderful

Star and their journey. When taking leave of Mary they wept, for it pained them to go. They asked Mary and Joseph to remember them. They also invited them to come and see them, saying: "All that we have shall be yours." Then they again adored Jesus and departed.

The wise men return to their country. They remained over night in Bethlehem, and soon fell asleep. They had a dream. Who appeared to them in their dream? What did God say to them? "King Herod intends to kill the Infant Jesus." To which city did they not return? How did they return to their country? What was it that Herod did not find out? How did Herod fail to murder the Infant Jesus? Who protected Him?

EXPLANATION — *Meaning of the gifts.* Who were the first to hear of the birth of the Infant Jesus? How did they find it out? Where did the wise men come from? How did they learn of the birth of the Redeemer? Why did they go to Him? What did the first wise man offer Him? Gold. Why? Because Jesus Christ is King, and kings wear crowns of gold. What did the second wise man offer Him? Incense. Where is incense used? How is it used? Towards whom does incense rise? Heavenward to God. Jesus is God, and to honor Him as God the smoke of burning incense is made to rise heavenward. What did the third wise man offer? Myrrh. Myrrh is bitter. Our Saviour suffered bitter pains to redeem us. The bitter taste of myrrh should remind us of the bitter passion of Jesus Christ. Why did the wise men offer to the Infant Jesus gold, incense and myrrh?

APPLICATION — *The Infant Jesus comes to us at the Consecration of the Mass.* Where did the three wise men (kings) come from? The distance from the East to Bethlehem is very great. They had to travel many days to reach Bethlehem. They did not fear hardships and fatigue; nothing seemed too difficult to them, if they could only come to Jesus. You boys and girls need not go so

far to find Jesus.   Where do we find Him?   In the church.
Every day Jesus comes on earth at the Consecration of the
Mass.   He is hidden in the Sacred Host; therefore we can-
not see Him.

Adoration at the Consecration.   The priest raises heavenward the Infant Jesus in the Sacred Host, and the altar
boy rings the little bell; and there is a deep silence all
over the church.   You should then adore the Infant Jesus,
as the three wise men adored Him.   How did they adore
Him?   Therefore, kneel down, bow your head, then look
at the Sacred Host, whilst you say in your heart: "Jesus,
my Lord and my God; I adore Thee, I love Thee."   When
the priest raises the chalice containing the blood of Jesus
Christ, the altar boy again rings the bell.   Then bow your
head, and then look up at the chalice and strike your breast,
saying: "O Jesus, have mercy on me, for whom Thou
didst shed all Thy blood."

The offering.   But it is not enough to adore the Infant
Jesus; you should, like the wise men, make Him an offering.   The Infant Jesus does not ask of you gold, incense
and myrrh; but He wishes you to give Him something
more precious.   During Mass you should offer yourselves
to the Infant Jesus.   How do you call that part of the
Mass, in which you should do this?   What should you then
say?   "O Jesus, I offer Thee my body and my soul, my
whole self to Thee."   The Infant Jesus wishes especially
for your heart.   Therefore, give Him your heart.   Therefore when the priest raises the little silver plate with the
host on it, you should in thought place your heart on that
little plate, and say: "Sweet Infant Jesus, I now offer
Thee my little heart."   But not every heart pleases the Infant Jesus.   What kind of heart pleases Him?   From what
must such a heart be free?

The Communion.   The Infant Jesus comes into a pure
heart.   He comes during every Mass into the heart of the
priest.   But before He enters it, the priest strikes His

breast three times, saying each time: "Lord, I am not worthy," etc.. This part of the Mass is called the Communion. It follows some time after the Consecration. Each time the priest then strikes his breast, the altar boy rings the bell. You also should then strike your breast three times, saying each time, like the priest: "Lord, I am not worthy," etc. After the third time say: "O Jesus, sweet Jesus, come to me. See, my heart longs for thee." Or you may say: "Dear little Infant Jesus, come to me and make me good and pious." And Jesus will joyfully come and dwell in your heart.

The presence of Jesus in the Blessed Sacrament. The wise men could not remain long with the Infant Jesus. They had to return home. You remember how sorry they felt when they took leave, for they would never again have the chance to come to Him. But you can go every day to the Infant Jesus; for He not only comes on the altar at the Consecration of Holy Mass, but He remains all day in the church. The church is His house; He stays there in the tabernacle. The tabernacle is like His manger. We cannot, indeed, see the Infant Jesus as the shepherds and the wise men saw Him. But He is always there. The wonderful Star is also there. It is not so large and so bright as the wise men saw it. It is the perpetual light, the lamp that is always kept lighted before the tabernacle. Have you not remarked how it flares and trembles? It is like a fiery little tongue speaking to you: "Child, Jesus dwells here." Jesus is glad if you often visit Him; He expects your visits; He dearly loves those who visit Him.

How to go into the church. The wise men went slowly and orderly, as in a procession, into the stable where Jesus was. So you also should go slowly and orderly into the church, taking holy water and blessing yourself with it when going in, and making a genuflexion towards the tabernacle before you go into the pew. The genuflexion should be your greeting to Jesus in the tabernacle. After entering and kneeling down in the pew, what prayers should you say? "In the name of the Father," etc. In leaving the church, you should make the sign of the cross before going out of the pew, and genuflect two by two towards the tabernacle, turn towards the door, looking neither to the right nor to the left to gaze at the people, and at the entrance bless yourself with holy water before you are out of the church. (Practise this with the children.)

25. Flight of the Holy Family to Egypt.

PREPARATION. Who came first to adore the Infant Jesus? Who told them that the Redeemer was born? Who were the two pious persons that worshiped the Infant Jesus in the temple of Jerusalem? Who came a great way from the East to adore the Infant Jesus? How did they find out that He was born? All these persons rejoiced, because they were allowed to see the Redeemer. Herod also had heard of His birth. But this news gave him no joy. What did he mean to do to the Infant Saviour? Why? Because he thought Jesus would later on take away his kingdom and become king in his place. But Herod had no reason to fear the Infant Jesus, for Jesus did not intend to take away from any one what he had. He came to redeem men and make them happy. Herod wished to find out from the wise men where the Infant Jesus was; but he had not told them what he meant to do to Him. He had not told it to any one. But God saw all those evil thoughts in Herod's heart. How did God take care to prevent Herod from finding out where the Infant Jesus was? What did he command the wise men to do? The wise men did not go back to Herod. But the danger was not yet over. What had Herod learned from the scribes about the Infant Saviour? He also knew about how old Jesus was. Thus he had still a good chance to find Him out.

OBJECT. Now listen, and you will learn how the Infant Jesus was saved.

RELATION. During the night an angel of God appeared to Joseph and said to him: "Arise, take the Child and His Mother, and flee to Egypt, and stay there till I tell thee; for Herod is seeking the Child, that he may kill Him." Joseph got up at once, and during that very night he took the Child and His Mother and started for Egypt. Herod had waited for some time for the return of the wise men. Seeing that they did not come back to him, he got very angry. He sent soldiers to kill all the baby boys under two years of age in and around Bethlehem. The soldiers obeyed, and killed all they could find. There arose great lamentations, and the mothers of those little ones would not be consoled. Not long after Herod died a most awful death. Later on the angel of God appeared to Joseph in Egypt, and said to him: "Arise, and take the Child and His Mother, and return to the land of Israel." Joseph immediately obeyed, and left Egypt, went to Galilee and dwelt at Nazareth.

EXPLANATION — *The angel's order.* How did St. Joseph find out that Herod wished to kill the Divine Infant? An angel appeared to him during the night. What did the angel say to him? "Arise," etc. What was Joseph to do with the Child and His Mother? Flee, that is, go away as fast as he could. Where should he go? To Egypt, a country very far off, where Herod had no power.

The flight. Joseph did not wait till morning. How did he fulfil the order of the angel? Oh, how hard it was for Joseph and Mary to start so hurriedly in the night, to go so far to a strange country, where they were perfect strangers. Mary wept, because the Infant Jesus, so young, had to flee. But Mary and Joseph were not mad about this; they thought: "God wills it." Mary awoke the Infant Jesus, wrapped Him carefully and took Him in her arms. Then she sat on the donkey, and Joseph led the donkey by the bridle. In this way they left Bethlehem in the middle of the night. The moon was shining. They went through the streets and alongside of the houses, in which all were sound asleep. Mary and Joseph traveled many days. There were hardly any roads, and they often suffered from hunger and thirst. They often got very tired, especially Mary, because she had to hold the Infant Jesus continually in her arms. In the evening they sat down under some tree; they ate a little. The Infant Jesus slept in their midst, and Mary and Joseph usually slept on the ground in the open air. Sometimes they stopped over night in some small village. At last they reached Egypt. There they lived in a very small house. St. Joseph worked as a carpenter, and earned hardly enough for their wants. Mary employed herself in spinning, making woolen cloth and sewing.

The stay in Egypt. In Egypt nearly all the inhabitants were pagans. They adored cats, alligators and other animals. This greatly pained Mary and Joseph. Mary would sit in the evening outside their little house, and St. Joseph would cull some wild flowers to amuse little Jesus. It was there that Jesus learned how to speak, that He put on His first dress and took His first steps. Often when sitting at Mary's feet, He would play with other children. When Joseph came home in the evening, Jesus would go to meet him. Joseph usually brought Him some fruit. Jesus would bring and show it to His Mother. Already little Jesus began to help Mary and Joseph a little.

The massacre of the Innocents at Bethlehem. What happened in Judea when Mary, Joseph and the Infant Jesus were on their way to Egypt? The wise men on their way home had not passed through Jerusalem. Herod in vain waited for them. He suddenly found out that they had already long before started on their way home. He got fearfully angry. He said: " Yes, I will yet catch that child. I will order all the baby boys under two years of age in and around Bethlehem to be killed, and I shall be sure of having the Infant Jesus among them." Therefore Herod sent soldiers to Bethlehem with strict orders to kill at once all the baby boys under two years of age. Where were the soldiers ordered to go? What should they do?

The soldiers obeyed Herod's cruel order. They entered all the houses in Bethlehem, and all the houses in all the places near Bethlehem, and where they found a little boy two years old and less, they pulled him out of his mother's arms or out of his little bed, and stabbed him to death with their swords. The poor mothers did all they could to save their baby boys, and wept and sobbed aloud. In every house were heard loud cries and lamentations. The mothers would say: "Oh, my dear little boy! How cruelly they have killed you!" The friends and relatives of the mothers came and tried to console them; but the mothers would not be consoled, and continued to cry and lament for many days.

Herod's death. Who was the cause of all this grief and sorrow? Herod. But God punished Herod for his cruel deed. God sent him a terrible disease. Fearful sores broke out all over his body, and these sores were all full of worms eating up his flesh; and the sores spread a most horrible stench, so that no one could stand it. And he died in the most intense pains.

The return to Nazareth. How did Joseph find this out in Egypt? An angel appeared to him and said: "Arise," etc. Israel here means the land of the Jews. How did Joseph obey the order of the angel? The land of Israel was large; there were many towns and villages in it. In what town were Mary and Joseph living before they went to Bethlehem? In Nazareth. It was to Nazareth that Joseph and Mary with the Child Jesus went after returning from Egypt. Nazareth is a town of Galilee; and Galilee was a part of the land of the Jews. (Questions on the foregoing.)

FURTHER EXPLANATION — *Joseph, the foster-father of Jesus.* Joseph and Mary worked and cared for the Child Jesus, just as your father and mother do for you. Whose Son was the Child Jesus from all eternity? The Son of God. Who was His Father? God the Father in heaven. St. Joseph was not His real father, but he cared for the Child Jesus, as a good father cares for his son. He worked in order to provide Jesus with food and with all His needs. How did he save Jesus from being killed by Herod? On the way to and from Egypt St. Joseph had to take care that no harm should happen to Jesus, and that He should have a place to rest at night. Therefore he is called the foster-father of Jesus. St. Joseph represented God the Father on earth towards Jesus.

The Holy Family. Who is the Mother of Jesus? Father, mother and children make and are called a family. What were Jesus, Mary and Joseph together? A family. All three are holy, and are, therefore, called the Holy Family.

The Holy Innocents. Why did the Son of God come upon earth? To redeem us. He wished to redeem us by suffering, and finally by dying for us. He wished first to grow up as man and teach men. Therefore the heavenly Father protected Him against Herod. How was the Infant Jesus saved from death? Who were killed by order of Herod? Many baby boys. These little boys had to die to save the Infant Jesus. They were entirely innocent. Therefore they are called the Holy Innocents. They have a beautiful place in heaven. They are near the throne of God, and pray for the children on earth. They pray especially for those who invoke them. We invoke them when we say: " Holy Innocents, pray for us." The Church celebrates every year a feast, on which we especially honor and invoke the Holy Innocents. How is it called? Feast of the Holy Innocents.

CONNECTION. The Holy Innocents are in heaven with

God. Who else are also in heaven? The saints and angels. What do they do? Praise, sing, pray and serve.
Since the Infant Jesus came on earth angels often come
down from heaven on earth. To whom did an angel first
appear on account of the Infant Jesus? To the Blessed
Virgin Mary. What did he announce to Mary? Who can
tell me to whom else did the angel appear on account of
the Infant Jesus? Three times to St. Joseph; to the shepherds first one angel, then many. On no one else's account
have so many angels and so often come, than on account
of the Infant Jesus. Why? Because He is the Son of
God.

SUMMARY. Did the Holy Family always remain in the
Jewish country? No. Where had they to flee? To
Egypt. Why? Where did the Holy Family live after re-
turning from Egypt? In Nazareth.

APPLICATION — *St. Joseph our protector.* St. Joseph was
the foster-father and protector of Jesus Christ. He
watched over Him and protected Him. St. Joseph protects us also. He is greatly pleased, when we invoke His
protection; and he always helps us, if we pray earnestly
to Him. Therefore he is also our protector. We ought,
then, to pray daily to him. It was St. Joseph's guardian
angel who told him to flee with the Infant Jesus. God
has given to each of us also a guardian angel to remain
day and night near us, and to protect our body and soul.
What should we do to have him protect us against all
evil? Pray to him. How can you do so?

26. The twelve-year-old Child Jesus in the Temple of Jerusalem.

PREPARATION. Where did the Holy Family live after
their return from Egypt? How did Jesus behave in Nazareth towards His parents? The Child Jesus grew in age
and size just like other children. When He was twelve

years old He went again to Jerusalem. When had He been there before? At His presentation in the temple. The temple was the most beautiful and grand building in Judea. It was built on a hill; and many wide steps led to it. The doors were covered with gold; golden flowers adorned the walls, and even the floor was gilt. Before the holy place in it there was a large silk curtain beautifully embroidered. It was in that temple that the Jews made their offerings to God, prayed to God, and sang holy hymns. We have a church in almost every town. But among the Jews there was only one temple. Where was it? In other places there was only a small house of prayer. Where had the Jews to go when they visited the temple?

OBJECT. When the Child Jesus was twelve years old, He went to Jerusalem with His parents, and remained there three days after they had departed. I will now relate this to you.

RELATION. When Jesus was twelve years old He went with His parents to Jerusalem for the feast of Easter. After the days of the feast were over, Joseph and Mary returned. But the Boy Jesus remained in Jerusalem without His parents knowing it. They traveled a whole day, and then sought Jesus among their relatives and friends; but they did not find Him; therefore they went back to Jerusalem. And it was only on the third day that they found Jesus in the temple. He was sitting among the doctors and men learned in the law of God, listening to them, answering them and asking them questions. All those who heard Him, wondered at His knowledge and answers. His Mother said to Him: "Son, why hast Thou done so to us? Behold Thy father and I have sought Thee sorrowing. And Jesus said to them: How is it that you sought Me: did you not know, that I must be about My Father's business?" And Jesus went with them to Nazareth, and was subject to them, and remained with them till He was thirty years old. And Jesus advanced in wisdom and age, and grace with God and men.

EXPLANATION — *The journey to Jerusalem.* Pious children are fond of going to church. On which day must we go to church? That is not very difficult for us. Why? The church is not very far off. But it was not so easy for the Jews. How many churches were there in their country? How was that church called? Where was the temple? Most of the Jews lived very far from Jerusalem. They had to walk not only for hours, but for whole days, to get there. Therefore the Jews were obliged to go to the temple at most only on the three great feasts in the year. Easter was the chief of those feasts. Mary and Joseph used to travel every year for Easter to Jerusalem. People went there from all the towns and villages, so that there was a procession on every road. In a procession the people walk in order. Who go first? Who go next? Who follow? So it was among the Jews going to and returning from Jerusalem. The little children had to stay at home.

How old was Jesus when He first went for Easter to Jerusalem with His parents? The people of Nazareth traveled together. It was a long procession. The boys went first. With them was the little Saviour Jesus. On the way there was praying and singing. Jesus prayed and sang along such psalms as: "I rejoiced in what was said to me: We shall go into the house of the Lord." And: "How lovely are Thy tabernacles, O Lord of hosts; my soul longeth for the courts of the Lord." It was in spring; the flowers they saw on the way were in full bloom. The journey lasted three days; much of the way was over steep hills. Jesus surely felt tired; but He went along willingly. He rejoiced at the thought: "I shall see the temple and pray in it."

The parents lose Jesus. There were many sights in Jerusalem. It was full of large and beautiful buildings and fine stores. It was filled with people from every country. Many had come on camels. There was much to delight, astonish and amuse boys. But our little Saviour paid no attention to all this. Where did He go? What took place in the temple? In the temple there was also a school in which learned men explained Holy Scripture. They sat on a platform. The feast of Easter lasted eight days. Jesus was nearly the whole time in the temple. What did Mary and Joseph do when the feast was over? They started for home with the other people from Nazareth. They returned home in the same order as they had come. What was this order? The children were not with their parents. In this way Mary and Joseph traveled a whole day. But where was the Boy Jesus? Joseph and Mary believed He had been with the other boys in front. When did they miss Him? What did they then do? Among whom did they seek Him? But, as they did not find Him, they got very anxious about Him. What did they then do? On the whole way back to Jerusalem they inquired about Jesus. How long did they seek Him? Where did they find Him?

Jesus listens to the teachers in the temple. Our divine Saviour had remained in the temple. After praying a long time, He went to the school in the temple. He took a seat among the listeners, and paid great attention to what the teachers said. He was also asked questions. He easily answered every question they asked Him. He knew everything much better than even the teachers themselves. His answers were so clear and correct, that every one looked at Him with astonishment. They could have listened to Him for hours without getting tired. They said: " There never has been so smart and prudent a twelve-year-old boy like Him." In the evening Jesus went out of the temple and sought a place to sleep in. The next morning He went early to the temple, and after praying long and devoutly, He visited the school. The people there were

waiting for Him and made Him sit in front. He again
listened very attentively, and gave the very best answers.
At last the most learned and smart men came to question
and examine Him.

Jesus also teaches. Now the little Saviour began also
to ask questions and examine the teachers. He asked them:
"Will the Saviour come?" They answered: "Yes."
Then He asked: "Of what tribe is the Saviour to be?"
They replied: "Of the tribe of Juda." He then asked:
"Of what family?" They said: "Of the family of
David." Then He asked: "In what city was He to be
born?" They answered: "In Bethlehem, the city of
David." You see that they gave correct answers. After
this He asked them: "When is the Redeemer to come?"
They replied: "When a wonderful Star shall appear in
the heavens." Then He asked them: "Has the Redeemer
come already?" They said: "No." But little Jesus
said: "He has come already; for has not that wonderful
Star already appeared?" They answered: "No, it is not
true." And they grew envious and got very angry and
vexed. But Jesus continued: "Have you not heard how
the three wise men from the East came to Jerusalem, and
asked about the newly born King of the Jews? This King
is the promised Redeemer. Have you not heard how
those wise men related that they had seen the Redeemer's
Star? Did not Herod call the scribes together, and ask
them where the Redeemer was to be born? Did not Herod
send the wise men to Bethlehem? And have you already
forgotten that, on account of it, Herod later on ordered
the children in and around Bethlehem to be massacred?"
The teachers and the scribes could not say: "No; that
is not true." But they became furious. They got up
from their seats, and the head teacher came down also,
and all cried out: "How can you, a mere little boy, undertake to teach us, old men? Do you, perhaps, claim to be
the Redeemer?" And they tried to surround Jesus; but

He fell back (retreated), and they came nearer and nearer to Him.

Jesus on the Chair of Moses. But Jesus retreated always more and more till He got to the platform; He then ascended it, and took the head teacher's chair. Now He was the teacher. And there stood around Him the very much astonished teachers and scribes and many others listening to Him teaching them.

Mary and Joseph find Jesus. Just then Mary and Joseph came in and saw with astonishment the little Jesus in the head teacher's seat teaching. As soon as Jesus saw His parents, He rose and came down from the platform, and went to them very respectfully. Mary began to weep for grief and joy, held out her hands towards Him, in order to embrace Him. And how did she speak to Him? Very sweetly and lovingly. She did not scold Jesus. But Jesus raised His little right hand towards heaven. And what did He answer her? He meant to say: " You did not need to be anxious about Me. You know where I must be." When saying this, His face became bright, and His eyes were shining like two stars. All present kept still, and looked at Him with respect and astonishment. Then our Saviour went to His mother, gave her one of His hands and the other to St. Joseph, and went away with them walking through the crowd.

Jesus in Nazareth. Where did Jesus then go with His parents? And how did He behave towards them? " He was subject to them," that is, obedient to them. At Nazareth Jesus grew up to be a young man, and then to be a full grown man. Hence we say: " He grew in age." Jesus was the Son of God; therefore He was very wise; He was full of wisdom. When He was still an infant, people could not remark that He was full of wisdom. What is it a little child cannot do? He cannot speak. But as Jesus became older, He gradually let people see that He was wise. Where did He especially show His wisdom? In the temple. Therefore we say: "Jesus increased in wisdom." People became also more and more fond of Him. Why? And even His heavenly Father looked upon Him with greater pleasure. Hence we say: "Jesus increased in grace before God and men." In what did Jesus Christ increase at Nazareth? How long did He remain there with His parents? He was then already a full grown man; and continued to obey His parents.

EXPLANATION. Why did Jesus Christ continue to obey even after He had become a man? He wished to show that all children, even when they are grown up, should obey their parents. But He was still more obedient to His heavenly Father than to His parents on earth. The heavenly Father had made known to some persons that the Redeemer had come. To whom? To Mary, Joseph, the shepherds, Simeon, Anna, the wise men. Whom did He send to tell it to Mary? To Joseph? To the shepherds? How did the wise men, Simeon and Anna find it out? Now twelve years had passed since His birth. Jesus was then about to show to men that He was the Redeemer and the Son of God. Therefore He remained in Jerusalem, when His parents departed for Nazareth. And therefore also He asked the scribes, whether the Redeemer had already come; whether they had not heard of the Star, of the wise men that were seeking the newly born King of the Jews, and of Herod's slaughter of the children on account of the newly born King. The scribes knew that Jesus was right. Therefore they got very angry at Jesus. And what did they then ask Him? "Dost Thou perhaps claim to be the Redeemer?" What did He answer His Mother, when she asked Him: "Son, why didst Thou remain here?" Jesus is in the house of God, and is there doing the will of His Father. He therefore calls the house of God the house of His Father. Who, then, is His Father? If His Father is God, who is Jesus? He is, as He said: "I am the Son of God."

SUMMARY. What did Jesus do when He was twelve years old? How long did He remain in the temple after His parents were gone?

APPLICATION. How glad did Jesus feel when He was permitted to go into the temple of Jerusalem! How devout He was there! He then thought only of His Father in heaven. He paid no attention to the people coming in and going out. Do you behave like Jesus in the house of God? At home you may eat, drink, talk, laugh, play, look around to see who is passing by. But not so in church; there you must not talk, whisper, laugh or look around. The church is a holy house. Who is in the church? God. And in the tabernacle He dwells, who, when a boy, behaved so well in the temple. He looks at you, and sees all you do. If you look devoutly towards Him, or pray and sing well, you give Him pleasure. He will love you, and when you pray to Him for some favor, He will give it to you. But He sees from His tabernacle those children who misbehave, talk, laugh and disturb others. That greatly displeases Him. Are you one of those children? How do you after this intend to behave in church? Will you not try to be like Jesus?

Also in school, in studying and paying attention, you should be like the Boy Jesus. He did not need instruction. He was the Son of God. And yet how attentive He was in the temple! You do not yet know much about God; you must first learn more. But how much pains are needed to teach you! And yet some of you do not pay attention, do not properly study the catechism. And I am sometimes obliged to admonish and even punish you. How ashamed should such children feel before the Child Jesus! Endeavor after this to be more diligent and attentive in school and in church. How happy would I be if there were no more careless and inattentive children among you! How pleasing would you all then be to our dear Saviour! Do your best now, all of you, to give Him great pleasure. You will please God, if you willingly pray, study and obey.

27. The Life of Jesus at Nazareth.

OBJECT. To-day I will tell you how the Holy Family lived at Nazareth.

RELATION. Where did the Holy Family go after their return from Egypt? They owned a small house there. Near by was the workshop of St. Joseph. In that house the Child Jesus grew up. Let us imagine we are now all in that little house to see what the Child Jesus does. It is now morning before sunrise. The little Saviour is still sleeping and resting in His little room. How nicely He rests! Like an angel He lies in bed with one hand under His head, and the other over His breast. Now He awakes; He looks up heavenward to His Father in heaven, and most lovingly says: " My dear God, to Thee I offer up My awakening." He arises immediately and dresses quickly, but quietly, so as not to disturb any one. Then He kneels down and says His morning prayer. He prays long and devoutly; He could pray better than any one else. He was fond of reciting the Our Father.

After His morning prayer, Jesus went to the kitchen, prepared and arranged all that His Mother would need during the day. He probably also swept that little room, for everything in that house was clean and neat. Then He greeted His dear Mother and St. Joseph with great respect. This He did daily with an ever fresh love. Then He asked them what they wished Him to do. He would bring water from the well to His Mother, prepare the wood for the kitchen; He would go on errands to the stores to get what was needed. Then He would go with St. Joseph to the workshop. He wished to learn the carpenter trade from St. Joseph. And St. Joseph would show Him how to work, and sometimes would hold in his large hand the small hand of Jesus to direct it in the work. Jesus at work was industrious and quiet; and He worked without stopping. And when the weather was hot and drops of perspiration poured down His forehead, He did not stop, but continued to work till His tender hand became gradually hard. At work our Saviour never lost any time standing around and talking, and He would immediately do everything St. Joseph commanded Him. At noon our Saviour accompanied St. Joseph back to the house. The Blessed Virgin had, in the meanwhile, prepared the dinner. St. Joseph said grace, and Jesus prayed with him. Our Saviour took the last place at table, and waited till St. Joseph served Him. He was satisfied with what was given Him. All that His Mother had prepared was to His taste. During meals the Holy Family spoke to one another in a friendly and devout manner. Dinner over, they prayed again. And after awhile St. Joseph and the Saviour went to work again. Sometimes Mary would come with her work into the shop, and would look at Jesus full of joy. In the evening our Saviour put everything in its proper place and cleaned the workshop, and then accompanied St. Joseph to the house. After supper they would sit for some time on the bench in front of the house. Perhaps Jesus then read aloud some passage of Holy Scripture and explained it. Then they all said night prayers together, and afterwards retired to rest.

On Sunday (the Sabbath) the Holy Family did not work. Jesus put on His best suit of clothes and went with His parents to the little church (the synagogue) of Nazareth. There He joined the congregation in reciting aloud or singing the beautiful psalms. He listened devoutly to the sermon. He could have preached much better, but He did not put Himself forward. On Sundays the Holy Family sometimes went out for a short walk, or to visit relatives, neighbors or acquaintances. Jesus loved especially to visit the sick, and to speak kindly to them and exhort them to suffer patiently. Thus was our Saviour's life at Nazareth holy and beautiful. God and men were pleased with Him.

EXPLANATION — *Pious.* About whom were our Saviour's first thoughts on awaking in the morning? What did He say the very moment He awoke? But He was not satisfied with this short prayer. What did He do after dressing? What can you say about His morning prayer? At what other times did He pray? Could any one pray better, more devoutly or more willingly than He? Jesus knew how pleasing prayer is to His heavenly Father. He loved above all to please the Father. Do you also wish to please our heavenly Father? Do as our Saviour did. Of whom should you think first when you awake? What should you say to him? Do you say your morning prayer after you are dressed? What prayers do you say during the day? You should do your best to pray devoutly like our dear Saviour.

Docile. What did our Saviour do after His morning prayer? How beautifully He acted! He could have thought: "I am the Son of God, the Lord of heaven and earth; I need not do anything for others. I am much greater than My Mother, than My foster-father." But such were not our Saviour's thoughts. He knew that Mary and Joseph represented His heavenly Father towards Him, and that it was His heavenly Father's will that He should obey them as He would obey the heavenly Father Himself. Our little Saviour loved obedience above everything else. It was a pleasure for Him to obey. He was always thinking: "How can I obey My parents, for I wish to please My Father in heaven."

Industrious. Where did our little Saviour go with St. Joseph after breakfast? You have already seen a picture of St. Joseph in his workshop. He is sawing a beam. St. Joseph pulls one end of the big saw, and who pulls the other end? Or you see our Saviour chopping wood. Jesus worked constantly. Even when only a little child,

He tried to help His parents, and was always ready and pleased to do so. The larger He grew, the harder He worked. How did He work especially in hot weather? *Subject.* What did He do when St. Joseph commanded Him something? He did it immediately. Whether His parents ordered Him to perform something easy or difficult, something important or insignificant, pleasant or disagreeable, or whether He had to work alone or near Joseph and Mary, it was all the same to Jesus. Nothing was too much for Him. As soon as something was commanded Him, He thought: "This is the will of My Father in heaven;" and then He did it cheerfully. His parents knew that they could not please Him better than when they commanded Him to do something. Otherwise they would not have dared to command Him anything. And why? And the heavenly Father was pleased more by His Son's silent obedience, than by anything else on earth. God the Father could say all the time of Jesus: "This is My well-beloved Son; I am well pleased with Him." How did Jesus conduct Himself towards His parents in Nazareth? Did He obey only in important things? In what things was He obedient? What did He ask His parents every morning? How He could help them. When He knew that they would like Him to do something, He did it of Himself, and did not wait to be told to do it. He was the Son of God, and yet He subjected Himself to His earthly parents. He knew better than St. Joseph how to work, and yet He let St. Joseph teach Him how to work. He could have taken the first place in the house; but which place did He take? He could have required His parents to come first to greet Him in the morning, but what did He do? He made Himself lower than His parents, and was subject to them in all things. He, the Lord of heaven and earth, made Himself subject to His creatures, and came to serve them, and not to be served by them. Oh, how different it is in the world!

APPLICATION. Why did the Son of God wish to be subject to His creatures? Do you remember how Adam and Eve in paradise did not obey God? Just on account of their disobedience, our Saviour wished to be obedient. He wished to teach men to be obedient, and how beautiful obedience is in the sight of God. Therefore you should not seek to do always only what you please. You should, before all, do what your parents command you. The children who do all that their parents and teachers require, do enough, for they do what God wills of them, and all they do is good and holy before God. Not every child can be rich, smart or beautiful. That is not necessary to please God or to go to heaven. But every child can obey. Are you always obedient like our Saviour? Do you at once do what your parents command you? Do you obey also when they order you to do something you do not like? Whether you like it or not, you should at once obey. Remember how the Son of God was obedient in all things.

28. Jesus teaches, works miracles and chooses His Apostles.

OBJECT. To-day I will relate to you how Jesus taught the people and cured the sick.

RELATION. Where did Jesus live after His return from Egypt? How long did He remain at Nazareth with His parents? He left Nazareth when He was thirty years old, and went from place to place through the whole Jewish country. Wherever He came, He went first to the little house of prayer. When the people had come there, He would begin to teach and to preach. This He did especially on the Sabbath. He would tell them that He was the Son of God, the promised Redeemer. He taught them all that is necessary to bring men to heaven. He spoke wonderfully well, but so simply that every one could easily understand Him. The people, therefore, all liked to hear Him. When they learned that He had come to a place, the people from all around came in hundreds and thousands to hear Him, so that the little church there was by far too small to contain them. Then He would go outside, and preach in the open air. Sometimes even the towns were too small for the crowds that came; then He would go to preach in large fields, in places, where no one lived; and sometimes even on a mountain. There the immense crowds would partly stand around Him, and partly sit on the ground. Whilst He preached, there was no noise, no disturbance, no want of attention, no looking around. All looked at Jesus the whole time, and paid great attention to every word He said. Jesus would begin to speak to them of the Kingdom of heaven so beautifully. His voice and His words penetrated into the inmost depth of their hearts. And when He had finished speaking, the people would say: "We have never heard such good preaching. That is Jesus, the teacher, Jesus the divine Teacher."

After the sermon many sick persons were brought to be cured. When a blind man was brought, Jesus would merely say: "Be thou seeing," and the blind could see after that. When a lame man was brought to Him, Jesus would say: "Arise and walk;" and the lame man was able to walk. Thus with a word or two, He would heal persons of every kind of disease, and even raise dead persons to life. At the funeral of a young man, He merely said: "Young man, I say to thee: Arise." And the dead young man came to life again. To a dead girl Jesus said: "Little girl, I say to thee: Arise." And the dead girl arose full of life. The people wondered much about these miracles, and praised Jesus, saying: "He has done all things well." He gave sight to the blind, hearing to the deaf, speech to the dumb, made the lame walk, and raised the dead to life.   Many believed in Him and followed Him everywhere.   These persons were called the disciples of Jesus.

Once our Saviour had prayed all night on a mountain. In the morning He came down where many persons were waiting for Him, for He was to preach again.   His disciples were there also.   Jesus said that from among His many disciples He was going to choose twelve; these twelve should always be with Him and become His messengers, or apostles.   The sun had just risen and had lit up the whole country around with his golden rays.   The Saviour stood solemnly before the people, and they all looked at Him with wonder.   And now Jesus called out the names of those whom He had chosen for His apostles: Peter, James, John, Andrew, Thomas, James, Philip, Bartholomew, Matthew, Simon, Thaddeus and Judas.   Each of these twelve full of joy and love came forward when Jesus called out his name.   They all knelt before Jesus. Jesus blessing them laid His hand on the head of each, and ordained them as His apostles.   Then He made them sit alongside of Him.   And from that time the twelve apostles were always with Him and accompanied Him everywhere.   They were later on to preach to the whole world what they had heard Him preach.

EXPLANATION — *Jesus teaches.*   How old was Jesus before He left His parents?   Where did He go?   All over the land of the Jews.   What did Jesus do wherever He went?   Where have we preaching in this place?   In church.   Where did Jesus sometimes preach?   Where else did He also preach?   Why did Jesus go out of the church to preach outside or in the fields?   Why did the people like to hear our Saviour preach?   What did He preach about Himself?   What else did He preach about?   Who went and who were allowed to hear Him preach?   Because He preached to all who came to hear Him, we say: " Jesus preached in public."   When did He begin to preach?

Jesus performs miracles. Why were sick persons brought to Him after His preaching? Who is now called to see the sick? What does the doctor do for the sick? What must the sick person then do to get well? Often the medicine does no good, or takes a long time to cure. But what happened to the sick who were brought to Jesus? To the blind, the deaf-mutes, the lame? How did Jesus cure them? He cured them at once, without medicine, and only by saying to the blind: "Be thou seeing;" to the lame: "Arise and walk." What would happen, if doctors would try to cure the sick, etc., in that way? The blind would remain blind, etc. It would be a miracle if doctors would cure the sick as Jesus did. The cures Jesus wrought were miracles. But Jesus performed still greater miracles than these, for He raised to life a dead young man, a dead girl twelve years of age, merely by telling them to arise. God alone can raise a dead person alive again. Why could Jesus do it? Because He was God. Mention some of the miracles Jesus performed? When did Jesus begin to perform miracles? When He was thirty years old. Because of these miracles the people believed in Jesus Christ; they believed that He could do all He wished, and that He spoke the truth, when He preached to them. What did Jesus teach about Himself? That He was the Son of God and the promised Saviour. What do you call those who believed in Jesus? His disciples. He had many disciples on account of His miracles. But the high priest and the scribes were greatly displeased at this. They envied Him and would not believe in Him; they were too proud.

Choice of the twelve apostles. How many of His disciples did Jesus make apostles? Where were they to be always? Near Jesus to hear Him preach, to witness His virtues and His miracles. What were they to do later on? Teach. Teach what? What Jesus had taught, that is, His doctrine. Where were they to teach His doctrine?

All over the world. How did Jesus call these twelve disciples on account of this? Apostles (messengers). Mention some of the apostles.

SUMMARY. What did Jesus do when He was thirty years old? Whom did He choose to preach His doctrine all over the world?

APPLICATION. The teaching of Jesus came from heaven. It is called the Gospel. The apostles preached the Gospel all over the world. It is now also preached all over the world. Much of it is written in the Holy Bible. The priest reads a portion of it on Sundays from the pulpit. You ought to pay close attention to it. You will often hear the priest read: " At that time Jesus said to His disciples," that is, to the people. Before the priest begins to read, the people stand up and make the sign of the cross. You must do likewise. What should you do, when the priest is about to read the Gospel? When the priest reads the name of Jesus in the Gospel, you should bow your head a little. Why? And why does the priest kiss the book after reading the Gospel? Because the words of the Gospel are holy. You can always tell when the priest reads the Gospel during Mass, for the Mass-book (Missal) is carried by the altar boy to the left side of the altar, and all the people stand up when the priest reads or sings the Gospel. In beginning the Gospel the priest makes with his right thumb the sign of the cross on the Missal, then on his forehead, lips and breast. You should do the same. When the priest has read the Gospel, he kisses the Missal in the place where the Gospel is.

How happy you are to hear the beautiful and holy teaching of Jesus Christ! Listen to it in the sermon and the Catechism class with great attention; and then do what Jesus and the priest teach you. That is the sure way to heaven.

29. Jesus raises Lazarus from the dead.

OBJECT. I will tell you to-day how Jesus made a dead man, called Lazarus, alive again.

RELATION. 1. Lazarus lived at Bethania near Jerusalem with his sisters Martha and Mary. Lazarus took suddenly sick. His sisters sent a message to Jesus, saying: "Lord, he whom Thou lovest, is sick." But Jesus stayed two days more where He was. On the third day, He said to His apostles: "Lazarus is dead; I will now go to awake him." When Jesus came to Bethania, Lazarus was already four days in the grave. Martha went to meet Jesus, and said to Him: "Lord, if Thou hadst been here, Lazarus would not have died." Jesus said to her: "Your brother will rise again." "Yes," said Martha, "I know that he will rise again at the general resurrection at the last day." But Jesus said to her: "I am the resurrection and the life. He who believes in Me shall live, even if he be dead. And every one who believes in Me, shall not die forever. Dost thou believe this?" Martha answered: "Yes, Lord, I believe that Thou art Christ, the Son of the living God, that came into this world."

2. Then Martha went to call her sister Mary, and said to her: "The Master is there and calls thee." Mary at once hastened to where Jesus was. She knelt at His feet, saying: "Lord, if Thou hadst been here, my brother would not have died." Mary wept; and the Jews who had followed her, wept also. Then Jesus grieved and said: "Where have you laid him?" They said: "Come and see." And Jesus wept. The Jews said: "See how He loved him." The grave was a large hole (or chamber) cut into a rock; the opening was covered with a large, heavy stone. When they came to the grave, Jesus said: "Remove the stone." But Martha said: "Lord, the stench is great, for he is buried already four days." But Jesus said to her: "Did I not tell thee, that, if thou

didst believe, thou wouldst see the glory of God?" So
they removed the large stone. Jesus then raised His eyes
towards heaven, and prayed to His heavenly Father. Then
with a loud voice He said: "Lazarus, come forth." And
Lazarus came out at once, but with difficulty, for his hands
and feet were tied up with bandages. Therefore Jesus
said: "Untie the bandages, so that he may walk."

3. Many of the Jews present at this extraordinary miracle, believed in Jesus. Others went to the Jewish priests
and told them what Jesus had done. And the chief priests
said: "What shall we do? This man works many miracles." They resolved to put Jesus to death, in order to
get Him out of the way. But Jesus went far away into a
retired place.

EXPLANATION — *The sickness of Lazarus.* How was
the dead man called, whom Jesus made alive again? How
were his sisters called? Where did they all live? Where
was Bethania situated? Lazarus, Martha and Mary believed in Jesus, and were much attached to Him. Therefore Jesus also loved them. He often came to their house.
What suddenly happened to Lazarus? His sisters sent for
a doctor. But Lazarus grew worse, and his sisters feared
he would die. Who could have surely cured Lazarus?
His sisters knew it; but Jesus was far away.

The Saviour does not come immediately. How did
Jesus know that Lazarus was sick? What message did
they send to Jesus? They could also have asked Him to
come and cure Lazarus. But they did not do so; they
knew how much Jesus loved their brother. They thought
that Jesus would come of His own accord, if He believed
it necessary. But our Saviour did not come immediately.
How long did He still remain where He was? In the
meantime Lazarus got worse, and the sisters said to each
other: "Oh, if our Saviour were here, Lazarus would
not die."

Lazarus dies. But Lazarus died. And our Saviour had

not arrived. The sisters wept very much. Lazarus was buried, and Jesus had not yet come. But even now the sisters hoped that our Saviour would yet come and help them. Jesus knew well that Lazarus was dead. How did He know it? What did He say to His apostles on the third day? Where was Lazarus when Jesus arrived? How long had he been buried?

Jesus and Martha. What did Martha do, when she heard that Jesus had arrived? Martha knelt at His feet and wept very much. What did she say to our Saviour? She meant to say: " O Lord, Thou didst love my brother so much, that, if Thou hadst been here, Thou wouldst have cured him." What did Jesus answer? Jesus meant: " I will make your brother alive again. He shall rise alive from the grave." What did Martha reply? Martha did not rightly understand what Jesus had said. She thought only of the resurrection of all men at the end of the world, when Lazarus would rise also. Therefore Jesus said to Martha: " I am the resurrection and the life," etc. What was Martha's reply?

Jesus and Mary Magdalen. Whom did Martha call? What did she say to her? What did Martha call Jesus? The apostles often called Him Master. Master means Lord. What did Mary then do? Who followed her? What did Mary do, when she came to Jesus? And what did she say? How could people know that she grieved very much over her brother's death? And Mary wept again; and all the friends and relatives of the two sisters wept also when they saw them weep. All wept for grief and looked imploringly to Jesus, for they knew that He alone could help them. What did Jesus then feel in His heart? He had compassion on the two sisters. How did He show it? He also wept. It was very touching to see Jesus weep. What did the Jews say, when they saw Him weeping?

On the way to the grave. What did Jesus ask the sisters

about Lazarus? What did they answer? Where did they all go? The Jews did not dig their graves deep in the ground; but they cut out holes in the rock; and after wrapping up the corpse in a sheet, and tying bandages around it, they laid it in the grave in the rock and covered the opening with a great stone. What do you know about the grave of Lazarus?

The resurrection of Lazarus. What did Jesus command, when they reached the grave? When a person is dead, after two or three days his body begins to corrupt (get rotten) and to send forth a great stench; and nobody cares to look at it any more, or to stay near it. But Lazarus was already four days buried. What did his sisters say about this to Jesus, when He ordered the stone that closed the grave to be removed? What did Jesus reply? Did they remove the stone? All were standing around the grave, wondering very much about what was going to happen. What did Jesus do first? What did Jesus then say with a loud voice into the grave? What took place after He had said that? How they all got greatly frightened when Lazarus came out of the grave! How did he look? Some people screamed, others fell on their knees before Jesus and adored Him. What order did Jesus give about Lazarus? The apostles untied the bandages around his hands and feet. Lazarus then knelt before Jesus, adored and thanked Him. Jesus blessed him, took him by the hand and led him to his sisters. They were overjoyed and embraced him. And they also knelt before Jesus, adored and thanked Him. Many of the Jews present believed in Jesus Christ. Others got angry and still more envious of Jesus Christ. To whom did they relate what Jesus had done? What did the chief priests say? What did they intend to do? Where did Jesus go after this?

INTERPRETATION — *The Saviour is almighty and knows all things.* Have you ever heard that a dead man in this town ever became alive again? Such an event would be a great miracle. You have already heard that people deathly sick got well again. What did the sisters of Lazarus wish Jesus to do to their brother who was deathly sick? What message did they send to Jesus? Our Saviour knew beforehand that Lazarus was dangerously ill. He knew also that Lazarus would die. Why did He know all this? I have already seen the picture of a certain man; when you stand in front of it, he is looking at you; when you stand on the right, he is also looking at you; and he still looks at you when you stand on the left. No matter which way you turn, he is looking at you. So does our Saviour look at us wherever we are. No mother watches so carefully at the bedside of her sick child, as our Saviour watches over us. He watched over Lazarus also. Nevertheless He did not go directly to Lazarus. He would let him die, for He wished to do more for him than to cure him. He wished to raise him from the dead. He can still help us, when no one else can. For what is He? Almighty. How did He show it with the dead Lazarus? What do you call making a dead person alive again? Jesus had previously raised to life a dead girl and a dead young man. Those were great miracles. But the corpse of Lazarus was already corrupting, and the stench was insupportable. How long had he already been buried? And yet with a word Jesus made him alive again. How great was this miracle! What did Jesus intend to show by it? And many on account of it believed in Him.

APPLICATION. Lazarus is a proof that our Saviour does not always help immediately. After receiving the news of the illness of Lazarus, He remained where He was two days longer. The sisters of Lazarus thought He would come immediately to cure him. Jesus did not come, and Lazarus died. The sisters still believed that Jesus would yet help. And Jesus did help. He did much more for them than they expected. What did He do for them?

Our divine Saviour has now as good a heart as He had then. He helps us also as willingly, as He helped Lazarus and his sisters. And He is always very near us. Where does He dwell? In the tabernacle in the church. What must we do to obtain His help? Ask Him; pray to Him. But He does not always help immediately. Sometimes He makes us wait long for His help. You should not then think: "My prayers are not good." But you must continue to pray and hope for help, and He will surely help you. And then the same will happen to you as happened to the sisters of Lazarus. He may give you much more than you ask for and expect.

30. Jesus sweats blood in the Garden of Olives.

PREPARATION. What were the feelings of the chief priests towards Jesus Christ, because many people believed in Him? The greater the number of those who believed in Him, the more also the envy of the chief priests increased. When Jesus had raised Lazarus to life, the chief priests became still more angry with Him. They began to fear that, in the end, everybody would follow Him and believe in Him, and no one would any longer care for them. What did they intend to do to Him? But they were afraid to arrest Him publicly, in the daytime, lest the people would say: "We will not let you do Him any harm." Therefore they intended to arrest Him in the night. But they did not know where He stayed at night. Who were always with Jesus? Who knew where Jesus was at night? How many apostles were there? You will say: "Surely none of the apostles would tell the chief priests where Jesus was at night." And yet one of them did tell. His name was Judas. Formerly Judas was good and pious. But of late he no longer cared to pray. He became covetous, that is, he wished to make plenty of money. And in order to get money, he became a thief.

Then the devil whispered to him: "If you go to the chief priests, and tell them where they can easily arrest Jesus, you will earn plenty of money." At first, Judas did not listen to the devil; but he began to think of the amount of money he could make by telling the chief priests where they could easily arrest Jesus. At last he went to the chief priests and said: "What will you give me, if I tell you where Jesus stays at night?" They promised him thirty pieces of silver. Judas was satisfied with that sum. But Jesus knew very well what the chief priests intended to do to Him, and that Judas was going to betray Him. But He did not leave Jerusalem. For why had He come on earth? How did He wish to redeem us? To die for us. When did He first promise to do so? And God the Father accepted His offer. Now the time had come, when Jesus was really to die for us. But before dying, He wished to suffer very much for us.

OBJECT. I will now relate to you how Jesus began His bitter passion for us.

RELATION. On the night before His death Jesus went with His apostles to the Mount of Olives. There was a garden there called Gethsemani. Jesus entered the garden. At the entrance He said to His apostles: "Sit down here, whilst I go there to pray." Now He took Peter, James and John with Him into the garden. He began to be sad and to tremble. He told the three apostles: "My soul is sad even unto death; stay here, and watch and pray with Me." Jesus went a little distance away from them, and fell with His face on the ground and prayed saying: "Father, if it is possible, take this chalice from Me. But not My will, but Thine be done." In this manner Jesus prayed three different times. Then an angel from heaven came to strengthen Him, that He might not die then of sadness and sorrow. But He fell on the ground in an agony (as if He was dying), and a deathly sweat came upon Him like drops of blood, trickling to the ground.

Jesus prayed then only the longer and the more earnestly. After this He arose from His prayer, and said to His apostles: "Arise, and let us go; see, My betrayer is approaching."

EXPLANATION — *Jesus enters the Garden of Gethsemani.* What is the name of the garden Jesus went to before His death? Who were with Jesus? How many apostles were with Him? Judas was not among them. Where was he probably at that time? Where was the Garden of Gethsemani? The garden was near Jerusalem. Red flowers and rosemary grew in it, and also plenty of olive trees. Oil is made from olives. It was a quiet, pleasant place. Jesus often went there at night to pray. The apostles also knew the place very well. Jesus entered it with them; but He wished to be alone. What did He intend to do? To pray. What did He say to the apostles at the entrance of the garden? Did they do so? Which three apostles did He take with Him further into the garden? Now Jesus began to feel very, very sad. What did He say to His three apostles? What did He tell them to do? "Watch ye and pray." He did not wish that they should leave Him alone, or fall asleep. But our Saviour did not remain near them, but went a short distance from them. What did He then do?

Jesus prays the first time. Around Jesus is the darkness of the night. What do you do at night? Perhaps you have already had a terrible dream, that you saw some wild beast about to spring upon you and tear and eat you up. You were very much afraid and perhaps screamed in your dream. Just as you saw in your dream frightful things, so our Lord saw something really dreadful before Him. He saw how His enemies were coming to arrest Him; how they would beat Him till He would bleed so that His blood would flow and cover the ground; how they would make Him carry a heavy cross and then nail Him to it. These frightful sights surrounded our Saviour and rushed upon Him, as the wild beast in the dream was rushing upon the child. At last all these terrible things seemed to Jesus to be in a chalice, which the heavenly Father gave Him, to drink everything in it. Where have you seen a chalice? Who drinks out of it? Now suppose a chalice was full of poison, and that you were compelled to drink out of it! Would you not get much afraid and do your best to keep from drinking out of it? Why? Because drinking out of it would cause death. But the frightful things in the chalice our Saviour saw, were worse than poison. How did Jesus feel about them? He trembled, and felt as if He could not drink all that was in the chalice. What did He do in His fear and anguish? He fell with His face to the ground; that is, He knelt down and bowed so low that His face almost touched the ground. He stretched out His hands, as if He was seeking help, and He prayed. How did He pray? What did He ask of His heavenly Father? He meant to say: " Father, if it is possible do not make Me suffer all that. But if Thou willest that I should suffer it all, I will obey Thee. Not My will, but Thine be done."

Then Jesus rose and went to His three apostles. He could hardly walk, for He was so weak and faint. His whole body trembled, and His face was deathly pale, when He came to His apostles. What had Jesus told them, before He went to pray? " Watch and pray." But the apostles slept, because they felt tired. Jesus awoke them. The apostles were frightened when they saw Jesus so pale and trembling. But Jesus said to them: " You are asleep! Could you not watch one hour with Me? Watch and pray."

Jesus prays the second time. Our Saviour returned to His place to pray, and again fell on His face. Now He saw more frightful things. He saw all the sins Adam and all men had already committed, and also all the sins men would commit until the end of the world. Oh, how many

sins our Saviour saw then! For instance: your disobedience to your parents and teachers; your neglect of
prayer, your misbehavior in church; your lying, etc., etc.
Jesus then saw all, all. It was to Him, as if a thousand
rivers of filth flowed to Him, and that He should drink all
that out of the chalice! He felt such a terrible repug-
nance to do this, that He was filled with sadness. Therefore He prayed a second time, as He did the first time.
After His prayer Jesus rose and went again to His apostles and found them asleep. He awakened them. But
when the apostles saw by the moonlight Jesus so pale
and trembling, they thought He would fall down. They
therefore held Him up under the arms to keep Him from
falling. They were so frightened that they did not know
what to say. But our Lord said to them: " Do not fall
asleep again. Oh, watch and pray with Me." Jesus then
returned to His place.

Jesus prays the third time. He again prostrated Himself
to the ground, and now saw the most frightful things. He
saw so many millions of men who do not believe in Him.
They will not obey Him, and do not even will to be redeemed by Him. They prefer to follow the devil, to be
seduced by him and to be cast into hell. And even for
them Jesus must die! Jesus sees them all passing in long
rows before Him and the devil in their midst. The sight
greatly grieved our Saviour. He loved them so much and
would so willingly die to save them all. But they do not
want to be saved by Him! That pained Jesus most of all,
and made His chalice more bitter than all else. Jesus
prayed now the third time as before to His heavenly Father.

The agony of Jesus. Now His anguish became terrible,
so much so that He felt as if He would drop dead. What
do we call the anguish He felt then? His agony. In His
agony He fell to the ground as a person dying.

Jesus sweats blood. A man, when about to die, falls

into a cold sweat; His forehead is all covered with it. The anguish of Jesus was so great, that His whole body was covered with sweat; but it was not drops of water that oozed out of his pores, but drops of blood! It was a heavy sweat of blood that covered His body and trickled down His face, filled His eyes and fell to the ground. In His extreme anguish He did not stop praying. In that prayer He wept and called aloud to His Heavenly Father for help.

The Father does not take away the chalice. Whom did His heavenly Father send to Him? The angel held a little chalice, and offered it to Jesus, as if he would say: " The Father will not take the chalice away from Thee. Thou must suffer and die for men." And Jesus accepted the chalice, because He was going to do the will of His Heavenly Father.

Jesus is comforted. But the angel brought to Jesus consolation from His heavenly Father. He showed Him all the men who would go to heaven through His passion and death. Our Saviour sees Adam and Eve, Simeon and Anna, the three wise men, the Holy Innocents, and an immense number of persons who would enter heaven with Him. The apostles, His disciples, the martyrs, the virgins, the Popes, bishops, priests, religious, pious men and women, Jesus sees them all passing before Him wearing crowns, clothed in costly garments. It was a wonderful and touching sight. They were around His Sacred Heart as a wonderful flower wreath, thanking their Saviour for having suffered and died for them, that they might enter heaven. Oh, how that sight consoled our Saviour! It renewed His courage. He felt so strong, that He would have suffered every torment and died even to save only one soul! And now He sees the numberless souls His sufferings and death will save and bring to heaven. He remained yet a little while in prayer, and then went to His apostles; He was still pale, but He no longer trembled. He was full of courage. The apostles were still sleeping. What did Jesus say to them? Who was the traitor?

EXPLANATION — *Jesus suffers through obedience.* How were our first parents punished for their sin? What misfortune did Adam bring upon all men? How is the sin called, which we inherit from Adam? What would happen to men, if God had not shown them mercy? How did our Redeemer intend to free us from sin? To whom did, He say that in heaven? And God the Father accepted His offer.

When our Saviour on the Mount of Olives saw the sufferings He was about to endure, He was seized with a great dread. What did He pray for to His Heavenly Father? What was there in that chalice? Our sins and His sufferings. How often did Jesus address that prayer to His heavenly Father? But what did He add each time to His prayer? But His Father did not take away the chalice. What did the Saviour do then? He who does what the Father wills, is obedient. How did our Saviour show Himself obedient to His Father? For whom was Jesus going to suffer and die? For all men; for each one of us also. He willed to take upon Himself the punishment we deserved for our sins. If we had not sinned, our Saviour would have had no need to suffer and die. For whom did He suffer on the Mount of Olives? What did He suffer there for us? How great was His agony? He sweat blood. Think of this when you recite the first sorrowful mystery of the rosary.

APPLICATION. In His great anguish Jesus began to pray. To whom did He pray? Now, children, sometimes you have some little thing to suffer; for instance: when you dread something; when you, your father or mother are sick, or some misfortune has happened in the family. What should you then do? If God does not immediately grant you what you pray for, you must not stop praying.

Our Saviour did not stop praying. How many times did He pray? So you also should pray again.

Our Saviour did not tell the heavenly Father: "Father, Thou must take away that chalice and My bitter passion, for I do not want to suffer." But how did He pray? Therefore you must not pray: "Dear Lord, Thou must help me." How ought you to pray? "Not my will, O Lord, but Thy will be done." What should you think? "If God does not wish to take away this suffering from me, I will bear it cheerfully." Then if God does not take it away, your prayer is not in vain. Our Saviour's prayer was not in vain, for the heavenly Father sent Him an angel to console and strengthen Him. In like manner, God will console and strengthen you, so that you may be able to bear that suffering.

31. The Arrest of Jesus.

OBJECT. I will relate to you how Jesus was arrested.

RELATION. Whilst Jesus was telling His apostles: " See the traitor is coming," Judas came with many soldiers and servants. They were armed with swords and clubs. Judas had said to them: " He whom I shall kiss is the one you must arrest." Then he went to Jesus and said: " Hail, Master!" And he kissed Jesus. But Jesus said to him: "Friend, for what art thou come? Dost thou betray the Son of man with a kiss?" Then Jesus went to meet the crowd, and asked: "Whom do you seek?" They replied: "Jesus of Nazareth." And Jesus said: "I am He." And they fell backward to the ground. Jesus again asked them: "Whom do you seek?" They answered: "Jesus of Nazareth." Jesus then said: "I have told you that I am He. If you seek Me, let these go their way " (let these alone). And they laid hands on Jesus. Then Peter drew a sword and hit Malchus, a servant of the highpriest, and cut off his right ear. Jesus said to Peter: " Put back thy

sword into its scabbard." And Jesus touched the ear of
Malchus and healed it. Now Jesus was seized and bound.
But the apostles left Him and ran away. Only Peter and
John followed Jesus from afar.

EXPLANATION — *The band.* What had Jesus said to the
apostles, when He came to them after His third prayer?
Who was the traitor? But Judas did not come alone.
Who accompanied him? The soldiers and the servants of
the highpriest. Priests and scribes went along in the rear.
That was a large crowd. What had the soldiers and serv-
ants brought along? And what else? Ropes and chains.
Why?

The traitor. Many of the soldiers and servants did not
know Jesus. They might have mistaken one of the apostles
for Jesus. What means did Judas use to point Jesus out
to them? He said: " He whom I shall kiss, is Jesus. Arrest Him; and take care that He does not escape." But
when Judas saw Jesus, he got afraid, and began to tremble. But He nevertheless went up to Jesus. How did he
greet Jesus? And what did he do?

Jesus and the traitor. To kiss someone is a mark of
love. What did Judas wish Jesus to believe when he kissed
Jesus? But Jesus knew well that Judas was betraying
Him with his kiss, and yet He allowed Judas to kiss Him.
He also kissed Judas. Oh, how many saints would have
been overjoyed, if Jesus had deigned to kiss them! But
Jesus did not. But He permitted Judas to kiss Him, and
He also kissed Judas. What did Jesus say to Judas, when
Judas had kissed Him? Jesus looked sadly at Judas. He
meant to say to him: " Judas, with a kiss people are wont
to show their love; but thou kissest Me, in order to enable
My enemies to recognize Me." Our Saviour said this in
a friendly manner to Judas. Do you know why Jesus was
so friendly to Judas? Jesus wished to remind Judas of
what a horrible sin he was committing, and how deeply it
pained Him. Judas ought then to have knelt down before

Jesus and said to Him: "O dear Saviour, forgive my great sin. I am sorry for having so shamefully betrayed Thee." But Judas did not do that. Had he done it, Jesus would have forgiven him.

Jesus and the armed band. Now the soldiers and servants knew Jesus. Jesus advanced to meet them. What did He ask them? What did they answer? What did Jesus then say? And what happened to them when Jesus had said this? It happened like a sudden clap of thunder; they fell down all at once as if they had been struck dead. Who caused them to fall down so suddenly? Jesus wished to show His enemies: "If I wished, you could do Me no harm, for I could by a single word suddenly strike you all dead; and then I could go away where I wished, and none of you could touch Me even with a finger."

Jesus is arrested. Slowly the soldiers and servants got up one after the other, and stood up in ranks. What did Jesus ask them the second time? What answer did they give Him? And what did Jesus then say? Whom did He forbid them to harm? What did the armed band then do? The soldiers went up to Jesus, surrounded Him, and laid hands on Him.

Peter defends Jesus. Which apostle tried to help Jesus? What kind of weapon did he use? He drew his sword out of his scabbard (case). Whose ear did he cut off? What was Malchus? But Jesus did not want Peter to fight for Him. He could have helped Himself, if He had wished. What did He say to Peter? Jesus was sorry to see Malchus bleeding so much. What did He do therefore? He healed Malchus. What could the Jews have concluded from this? That Jesus was God. What should they have done then?

Jesus is led away. What did they do instead with Jesus? Jesus quietly gave His hands to be bound. And they bound His hands tight together, and dragged Him away. On the way the soldiers kept pulling and pushing Him and striking Him. They treated Him so roughly that He fell down several times before reaching Jerusalem. The priests and scribes rejoiced like devils over all this. They thought: " Now we have got Him. He shall never escape us. He shall die." But Jesus bore all this in silence.

The apostles flee. When the apostles saw that Jesus willingly allowed Himself to be bound, they did not know what was going to happen to them, and they got frightened. What did they do through fear? But not all. Who did not flee? What did they do?

FURTHER EXPLANATION — *Jesus suffers freely.* Jesus knew beforehand that Judas was going to betray Him to His enemies. He knew also where His enemies would bring Him after His arrest. Where? What could Jesus have done to prevent His enemies from arresting Him in the Garden of Olives? And Jesus went there. Why? When Jesus had prayed the third time in the Garden of Olives, He knew that Judas was coming with His enemies. What did He say about it to His apostles? What could Jesus have done even then to escape from His enemies? But He did not go away. On the contrary, He advanced to meet Judas and His enemies. What does this prove? What could Jesus have done when all His enemies had fallen down? And why did He not wish Peter to defend Him? And if our Saviour had prayed for it, His heavenly Father would have sent Him a hundred thousand angels to protect Him. Indeed, Jesus needed only to say the word, or to breathe, and He could have made Himself free. No one could compel Him. But He did none of these things. Why? Because He wished to suffer and die for us. Therefore He suffered of His own free will.

SUMMARY. How did our Saviour suffer? He suffered of His own free will.

APPLICATION. How beautiful would it be, if you would sometimes willingly suffer a little for our dear Saviour's sake! Suppose on a certain week-day you had no school, and you hear the bell ringing for early Mass. You are still in bed; and it feels so good to remain in it. And you think: "To-day I will stay in bed, and not go to Mass, for it is no sin not to hear Mass on a week-day." But now comes another thought: "For the love of our dear Saviour, I will get up and go to Mass." And you do so. You thus do something difficult for you, and resemble our Saviour. And your heart tells you: "You have done well." And you feel happy over it.

I will now relate how a certain boy suffered something willingly. A man wished to take a walk in the forest with his three sons on a Sunday afternoon after Vespers. But their sister was sick, and she would have to remain alone the whole afternoon in bed. Their mother had long been dead. Now a voice from his heart said to the eldest boy: "Will you not stay home with your sick sister, so that she may not feel lonesome?" That boy had already the whole week before been rejoicing at the prospect of that fine walk, and he felt so anxious to go along. But at last he thought: "For the love of our divine Saviour I will stay at home with my sick sister." How beautiful was his conduct! Did it not cause him more pleasure than if he had gone out walking? In this way you can please our divine Saviour every day by doing something good which you are not bound to do; and you would find every day more and more pleasure in doing so. This is a very good way to thank Jesus for having willed to suffer so much for you. Try it all of you.

32. Jesus is scourged.

PREPARATION. What must a child do, when his father commands him something? Obey. The child must obey his father. He who does not obey his father, commits a fault. What does the child deserve for that fault? Punishment. Suppose a child steals a dollar, he commits a fault and deserves punishment for it. Which fault is the greater, to disobey or to steal a dollar? To steal a dollar. What then should be the punishment for stealing a dollar? Greater than for disobedience. Hence the child who steals should be punished with the rod. Stealing is an evil deed, or rather a misdeed, a crime. What, then, is the child who steals? A thief, a criminal. He who steals only a trifle, is a petty criminal, an evil-doer. A criminal is a thief that steals much, or a person that robs, kills, etc. What kind of punishment does such a criminal deserve? A great punishment. Who punishes criminals? The police arrest him and bring him to the judge of the Criminal Court, and he is tried by the judge and jury. The witnesses tell what they saw or know of his crime. After this the jury brings in a verdict of "guilty" or "not guilty," and, if he is not guilty, the judge sets him free; but if he is guilty, the judge condemns him, according to his crime, either to death or to the penitentiary, and hard labor for a number of years or for life. The greatest crimes, such as murder, are punishable with death (hanging or electrocution). (Who appoints or elects the judge?)

In the time of our Saviour the judges were appointed by the Roman emperor. The Roman emperor did not live in Judea; but appointed a governor for Judea, who had the power to govern and to judge the greater criminals and condemn them to death. Among the Jews highway robbers and murderers were condemned to be crucified, that is, to be nailed to a cross and to die on it. The chief priests wished Jesus to be crucified; therefore they brought Him to the Roman governor, Pontius Pilate, that he should condemn Jesus to be crucified, as if He was one of the greatest criminals.

OBJECT. I will relate to you what the Roman governor did to Jesus.

RELATION. In the morning Jesus was brought to Pontius Pilate, that he might condemn Jesus to death. But Pilate easily saw that the chief priests had brought Jesus through envy to be condemned. He sought to set Jesus free. But the priests and scribes excited the people, and they all cried out as loud as they could: " Crucify Him, crucify Him!" Pilate replied: " What evil has He done? I will have Him scourged, and then I will set Him free." Then he commanded Jesus to be scourged.

EXPLANATION — *Jesus is brought to Pilate.* The Jews had arrested Jesus during the night. On what day? Then, on Friday morning the Jews brought Jesus to the Roman governor. What was his name? Why did they bring Jesus to the Roman governor? Why did they wish Jesus to be put to death? If Jesus were put to death, He would be looked upon as a great criminal.

Pilate finds Jesus not guilty of any crime. The chief priests, therefore, accused Jesus of many wicked deeds; but they lied, and could not prove what they said. You know that Jesus had done many good things to men. Mention some of them. Pilate examined everything that the chief priests said against Jesus. What did Pilate find out about the chief priests? And what was it that he did not find out about Jesus? Guilt. It is not allowed to put an innocent man to death. What should a judge do to an innocent man? What should Pilate have done to Jesus? Pilate wished to set Jesus free.

The chief priests excite the people. But the chief priests did not want him to do that. Therefore they told the people: " Jesus must not be set free. Do not allow it. He must be crucified!" They made the people wild, just like bad boys excite a dog. And what did the people (rabble) cry out? What did Pilate ask them? What did Pilate declare Jesus to be? Innocent. What then ought Pilate to have done at once?

Pilate condemns Jesus to be scourged. But Pilate was afraid. He thought: " If I do not punish Jesus, the people will become still more wild. I must give him a punishment to quiet them." What punishment did he order to be inflicted on Jesus? The scourging. With what does a father punish his bad child? Pilate ordered Jesus to be beaten with heavy rods and big whips, whips far worse than those of teamsters, for each of them had several thongs, and at the end of the thongs there were pieces of sharp iron or balls of lead. These whips were called scourges.

The scourging. Jesus was scourged outside the court building, and not before Pilate. The soldiers tied Jesus to a stone column after pulling off His clothing. Jesus had to stand half naked. Oh, how he felt ashamed! And now two soldiers began to scourge Him with those terrible whips. They hit Him with all their might. Every blow makes a red and blue mark on His skin; but soon the skin is cut through and the blood of Jesus flows; and still they continue to strike Him as hard as they can. When the first two soldiers get tired striking Jesus, two other soldiers take their places, and then not only is the skin of Jesus all torn, but His flesh also, and His blood runs in streams down to the ground. Soon the flesh of Jesus is so torn, that in some places His very bones can be seen. And thus Jesus is so cruelly scourged until all the soldiers are so tired that they must stop! The whole body of Jesus is a dreadful wound; He is all bloody and bleeding from head to foot, and the ground is covered with a pool of His blood! Oh, how Jesus suffered! Every blow convulsed Him with pain; and His body was so delicate, so sensitive to the slightest pain. He wept aloud for pain; His crying could be heard between the blows He received; and the Jews stood around Him rejoicing, laughing at and making fun of Him, and shamefully insulting Him! When He was untied from the column, He was so weak and so faint, that He fell down half dead on the ground! But He was made to get up and to put on His clothes Himself. There was no one to help Him, who had helped so many!

FURTHER EXPLANATION — *Jesus suffers innocently.*
If Jesus had been a criminal, He would have deserved
that no one should help Him. But what evil had He done?
What did Pilate say about His innocence? Jesus was perfectly faultless. Jesus therefore suffered innocently.

Jesus suffers patiently. Suppose some other man, who
was innocent, had been scourged as cruelly as our Saviour,
would he not cry out aloud, complain, scold, and show the
greatest impatience? But how differently did Jesus act?
What did He do, when He was scourged? He wept, and
thought in His heart: "My Heavenly Father wills that I
should suffer this." Therefore Jesus quietly held out His
bare back to the blows and allowed the soldiers to scourge
Him so cruelly! When we suffer quietly and do not complain, but think: "Our dear Lord has sent me this pain,
and I will suffer it willingly," we suffer patiently. What
is it that Jesus did not do whilst He was scourged? Show
impatience. What did He think in His heart? How did
He suffer?

For our sins. Jesus took upon Himself the punishment
due to our sins, as if He really deserved it. But there was
no guilt in Him. All men were guilty. Each sin is a
debt to God's justice. Who committed the first sin on
earth and contracted the first debt to God's justice? Every
sin contracts a debt to God's justice. Just think now how
many and how great debts all men have since the first sin
contracted to God's justice! And each of you has already
contracted many such debts. And our Saviour took all
these debts upon Himself, and allowed Himself to be
scourged for them! And He received on His innocent and
tender body the fearful blows which all men deserved!

Especially for impurity. In the scourging Jesus not only
suffered cruel blows, but He was especially greatly pained
and put to shame in appearing half naked before a great
number of people. And there are children who are not
ashamed to stand around in the house half naked morning

and evening, or who unnecessarily uncover themselves
during the day even before others! Woe to those immodest children! It was especially on account of their
sins that Jesus was so cruelly beaten on His bare body before so many people.

SUMMARY. For whom did Jesus allow Himself to be so
cruelly scourged? For all men. But for whose sins especially was he scourged? For the sins of the immodest
and the impure. How did He suffer the scourging? Innocently and patiently. From what words do you see that
He was innocent? How do you know that He suffered
patiently?

APPLICATION. 1. Suppose when you go home, you
would find your father or your mother lying on the floor
all bleeding and covered with wounds, and hear them
groaning with pain! Would you not grieve very much,
especially if you knew that they were suffering this on your
account? Now see our divine Saviour lying down near the
pillar, all covered with fearful bleeding wounds and moan-
ing for pain, and that on account of your sins! Does not
this sight, this thought grieve you? You should, therefore, resolve to be pure and modest, never to look or touch
with pleasure anything impure.

2. Was it not cruel for the soldiers to scourge our innocent Saviour so unmercifully? But our Saviour bore
it patiently. Perhaps you may have yet to suffer something without being guilty (deserving it). How much you
would please our Saviour, if you would bear it patiently.
For your sake Jesus suffered so patiently. Strive, therefore, also to suffer patiently for His sake. 3. Let us, when
we recite the second decade of the sorrowful mysteries of
the rosary, reflect on the fearful pains Jesus endured in
His scourging.

33. Jesus is crowned with thorns.

OBJECT. I will relate to you how Jesus, after being scourged, was reviled and mocked by the soldiers.

RELATION. After scourging Jesus the soldiers put on Jesus an old tattered purple cloak. They also plaited a crown of thorns, and put it on His head, and placed a reed in His right hand. Then in mockery they bent their knee before Jesus, saying: "Hail, king of the Jews." Some spit upon Him; one after another slapped Him, took the reed out of His hand, and hit Him on the head with it.

EXPLANATION — *Jesus as a mock king.* After the scourging Jesus was led into Pilate's yard; the soldiers guarded Him. Our Saviour stood there trembling with pain. How good it would have been for Him, if He could have had a little rest! But His sufferings were far from being over. The soldiers had heard that He claimed to be a king. Now they thought they could have a little fun with Him. A king, in those days, usually wore a rich purple cloak; and Jesus would need one, if He were to be presented as a king. The soldiers soon found an old, worn out, ragged red cloak. They then roughly pulled off by force all His clothing, which was now sticking close to His terrible wounds, and cause His wounds to bleed afresh, to His great suffering. Suppose you had badly cut your finger, and your mother bandaged it with a piece of linen, and the linen were now sticking closely to the wound of your finger; how greatly would it hurt you to pull off roughly that piece of linen from your finger! And would not the wound of your finger begin to bleed again? But our divine Saviour had not merely one wound, but His whole back was covered with large, deep wounds, and His clothing was sticking fast to His wounds, and the soldiers most roughly pulled off His clothes to hurt Him the more! How greatly He must have suffered! His wounds must

have burned like fire! What did the soldiers place after
this on His shoulders! Now Jesus was wearing a king's
cloak!

A king, in those days, sat on a golden throne. What
does Jesus need more to be a king? Therefore the soldiers lead Him to a large stone. That was to be His
throne. They made Him sit on it. But the king on his
throne wore a golden crown on his head. Therefore the
soldiers said: "This king must have a crown." They
then made Him a crown, not of gold, but one of thorns.
They took branches full of thorns, and plaited them into
a crown, and then set that crown. on His head. They
pressed it down on His head as hard as they could, so as
to make the thorns sink deep into His head. Those thorns
were very sharp and as hard as nails. How it hurts when
a little thorn has entered our finger or our foot! But the
long, sharp and hard thorns of our Saviour's crown sank
deep into His head. How terrible were the pains they
caused Him!

A king on his throne held a costly rod, called sceptre,
in his hand. What kind of sceptre did the soldiers place
in our Saviour's hand? It was a reed. Relate how the
soldiers adorned Jesus as a mock king.

The mockery. A king on his golden throne was rev-
erenced by the people. Those who approached him, used
to kneel on one knee very respectfully. What did the
soldiers do to Jesus Christ? They bent their knee before
Him and pulled out their tongue at Him. They did not
intend to honor Jesus, but to mock and revile Him by
their kneeling. A king is greeted by the words: "Long
live our king!" But the soldiers greeted Him in mockery:
"Hail, king of the Jews!" Costly presents are offered
to a king. What presents did the soldiers give to Jesus?
They slapped Him, they spat in His face! In kneeling before a king, the people kiss his sceptre. How did they

mock Jesus with the reed as His sceptre? Finally to complete the mockery, they threw Jesus down on the ground from the stone. Look at the picture representing Jesus crowned with thorns. He is seated on a stone; His head is bent down; His beautiful forehead is covered with the crown of thorns; His hair is entangled in the thorns; blood is flowing from every part of His head, and running in streamlets down His face, dyeing His shoulders red, and gluing His hair together. Around are the soldiers mocking Him. How this causes pain and shame to our Saviour!

FURTHER EXPLANATION — *How painful and undeserved the mockery.* Let us suppose that some children had done wicked things in a house. Only one of the children there had nothing to do with it. All the others blame him for it; and he is severely punished by his father. The innocent child weeps bitterly. When the father is gone, the wicked children stand around the innocent child, and mock him. Now tell me what hurts the innocent child more, the punishment, or the mockery of the other children?

Our Saviour also is innocent. For whom did He suffer such terrible punishment? He suffered for all men, out of love for them. Men should therefore have had compassion on Him in His suffering. But instead of pitying Him, what did the soldiers do? How greatly must it have pained Jesus! Every word and act of mockery must have been like the thrust of a big thorn into His heart. Which hurt Him the most, the thorns piercing His head, or the mockery piercing His heart?

Jesus suffers mockery for us. How could Jesus have acted towards the soldiers? Had He wished, He could have defended Himself, reproached the soldiers for their shameful conduct, and by a single word or breath He could have made them fall dead to the ground. But what did our Saviour do against all this mockery? He was perfectly silent, meek and gentle. And why? Because He wished to suffer for mankind. He allowed Himself to be reviled, because men so often unjustly revile their neighbor. Mockery is like the stroke of a whip in one's face, so greatly does it hurt. Mockery is like the thorns with which we would pierce and pain our neighbor. Oh, how it pained Jesus to be so outrageously mocked! Oh, how it made Him feel ashamed! What a fearful penance He did for the sins of mockery we commit against our neighbor!

Our Saviour, being the King of heaven and earth, could have worn a gold crown glittering with diamonds. But He wished to wear a crown of thorns, because men have their heads so full of proud and other evil thoughts, and wish to be and to have more than others. By wearing such a painful crown Jesus wished to do penance for our evil thoughts.

APPLICATION. You have probably at home a picture of Jesus crowned with thorns. Who does not feel compassion for Jesus when he looks at it? Did not Jesus deserve to be better treated? How sad He looks in that picture! When you are inclined to feel proud, just look at that picture, and think that Jesus suffered it all for the many sins of pride men commit. And when you are tempted to make fun of, to ridicule other children, old people, then remember that picture of Jesus crowned with thorns. Does He not wear that crown of thorns to atone for the sins of mockery men commit? When you are unjustly laughed at or mocked, remember again the picture of Jesus crowned with thorns. He did not get angry or mock back. Do then as He did.

The crown of thorns worn by our Lord is a thousand times dearer to us than if it were of gold. Our Saviour wore the crown of thorns, because He loved us. Now as a reward for it, He wears in heaven a crown of bright stars. Instead of the soldiers bending their knee before Him in mockery, there now bend the knee in love and adoration before Him the Pope, the bishops, millions of the best people on earth, and in heaven countless angels and saints kneel before Him, adore Him and sing His praises forever!

34. Jesus is condemned by Pilate to die on the Cross.

PREPARATION. Jesus had already terribly suffered in the scourging and crowning with thorns. But His enemies were not satisfied. They insisted that Pilate should condemn Him to be crucified. But Pilate wished to set Him free. Why?

OBJECT. I will now tell you how it happened that Pilate at last condemned Jesus to be crucified.

RELATION. Pilate attempted once more to free Jesus. He had Him brought before the people. Jesus came forth wearing the crown of thorns and the purple cloak. Pilate said to them: "Behold the man!" The chief priests and their servants cried out: "Crucify Him, crucify Him!" Pilate said: "I find no crime in Him." The Jews answered: "We have a law, and according to this law, He must die, because He made Himself (claims to be) the Son of God." Pilate tried for the last time to set Jesus free. But the Jews became furious and cried out: "If thou set Him free, thou art no friend of Cæsar" (the emperor). Pilate then called for water and washed his hands before the people, and said: "I am innocent of the blood of this just man. See you to it." Then all the people cried out: "His blood be upon us and upon our children." And Pilate gave Jesus up to be crucified.

EXPLANATION — *Jesus is presented to the people.* After crowning Jesus with thorns and mocking Him, the soldiers again brought our Saviour to Pilate. Pilate had pity on the innocent Jesus so cruelly beaten and torn. He thought: "I will now show Jesus in His terrible condition to the people; perhaps they will have pity on Him and let me set Him free." What did he then do with Jesus? Jesus stood before the people all wounded and bloody and crowned with thorns. He wore that torn purple cloak, and His hands were tightly bound together. All the people could see Him. Pilate pointed to Him with his hand. What did he say to the people? He meant by these words: "Oh, look at that poor terribly scourged man! He can scarcely be recognized. He hardly looks like a man, for He is so disfigured. Have you, then, not a spark of compassion for Him! Oh, let Him go free now; He has been punished enough." All eyes were now turned to our Saviour. He was a fearful sight, wearing a crown of thorns and a ragged cloak, with His face covered with blood and spittle, His body torn by the scourging, and a reed for a sceptre in His bleeding and trembling hands. He was bent down, and His eyes looked so sad at that ungrateful people. The people felt shocked at seeing Jesus in so pitiable a state. Around Him all was as silent as death. And Pilate thought: "Now the Jews will not say anything against my setting Him free."

But who felt no pity for Jesus? They were more cruel than wild beasts. What did the chief priests and their servants cry out? They looked as if they were possessed by the devil. Jesus had always done nothing but good to the Jews, and yet they cried out over and over again: "Crucify Him, crucify Him!" Pilate was unwilling to condemn Jesus to be crucified. He ought also to have set Him free. Why? Because he declared that Jesus was innocent, that Jesus had done no evil. What did the Jews answer, when Pilate said: "I find no cause (crime) in Him"? "He must die, because He made (claims to be) Himself the Son of God." But is not Jesus really the Son of God? Was it, then, wrong for Him to say: "I am the Son of God"? Did He deserve death for this?

Pilate did not wish to condemn Jesus to death. He tried for the last time to free Jesus. What did the Jews then cry out? They meant: "If you set Him free, we will get you into trouble with the emperor by bringing charges against you." Pilate wished to remain a friend of the emperor, in order not to lose his office. He, therefore, got afraid: "I will rather yield to the demand of the Jews than get into trouble with the emperor, therefore I will condemn Jesus to be crucified."

Pilate washes his hands. The blood of those who are crucified flows out from their hands and feet; and those who nail them to the cross get their hands all bloody. As Pilate was condemning Jesus to be crucified, it was as if he himself actually nailed the hands and feet of Jesus to the cross and stained his hands with our Saviour's blood. But Pilate did not wish to be responsible for shedding the blood of Jesus on the cross; he wished the Jews to be alone responsible for the death of Jesus. Therefore he ordered a servant to bring him some water. What for? What did he do? And what did he say? Whom did he call "that just man"? Why does he call Jesus "that just man"? What did Pilate mean by these words and by washing his hands? "I will take no responsibility for the blood of Jesus that will flow on the cross. You chief priests and Jews alone are responsible. Beware, for you may soon be severely punished for it." Pilate in placing all responsibility for the death of Jesus on the Jews, thought that they would get afraid and suffer Jesus to be set free.

But Pilate hoped in vain. What did the people cry out with all their might? They meant: "His blood must be shed, whatever may be the consequences. We will take the responsibility. We are not afraid of punishment falling upon us; it will not be much; and even if our children are punished on our account, they will be able to stand it." They cared no more for the death of Jesus, than for the death of an insect, which any one may crush with his foot.

Our Saviour standing there had seen and heard all. How it must have pained His loving heart to see that people so cruel and so ungrateful! How many had He benefited among those fiercely clamoring for His death! He had blessed their children, cured their sick. He could have reproached them for their conduct. But He kept silent and prayed for those ungrateful persons.

The sentence of death. Pilate then sat down in his judicial seat. Armed Roman soldiers stood on each side of him. Jesus was brought before him. Pilate said to Jesus: "You are condemned to be crucified." Then he said to the soldiers: "Bring the cross." To what was Jesus condemned? What were the Jews allowed to do to Jesus? To whom did Pilate turn Jesus over?

EXPLANATION — *Pilate's fault.* Pilate seemed to think that he was not responsible for the death of Jesus. What should Pilate have done with Jesus after declaring Him innocent and just? Set Him free. What should he never have done to Jesus? Condemn Him. It is never allowed to condemn an innocent man to death. Was not Pilate very guilty in condemning Jesus to death? The water with which he washed his hands, could not wash away this great crime from his soul. Because Pilate was guilty of making Jesus suffer so much we say in the Apostle's Creed: "Suffered under Pontius Pilate."

Jesus suffers freely. Jesus could have said to Pilate: "Only the greatest criminals are condemned to be crucified. You know that I am innocent; why, then, do you condemn Me to be crucified?" But what did our Saviour say? Nothing. Why did not Jesus defend Himself? Because He willed to suffer and die. No one could have compelled Him against His will. Therefore He suffered death willingly, freely.

For us. Who had deserved death and the torments of hell? Who, of His own free will, took our sins upon Himself? Who, then, had to suffer the punishment they deserved? Our Saviour. Many a child among you, for instance, has sinned by lying and disobedience. What has he deserved for those sins? Which of you would be willing to take upon you the punishment deserved by another child? How are thieves punished? Imprisoned. Which of you would be willing to be imprisoned instead of a thief? Not one. What punishment does a murderer deserve? Which of you would offer to be executed (put to death) instead of a murderer? Now see how Jesus freely did what none of you, what no one on earth would be willing to do. For us He allowed Himself to be arrested, scourged, crowned with thorns, mocked and condemned to be crucified.

Out of love. What does this prove? That Jesus loves us. Out of love for us our divine Saviour came upon earth and became man. Out of love for us He willed to be born in a stable, to be laid in a manger. Out of love for us He suffered an agony and sweat blood in the Garden of Olives. Out of love for us He allowed Himself to be cruelly scourged, crowned with thorns and condemned, as a great criminal, to be crucified.

Out of infinite love. And this He did for all men. For all men He willed to suffer and to die, and this even for His enemies, for the chief priests and scribes, for the soldiers and the wicked Jews. [Yes, even for the traitor Judas, Jesus wished to suffer and die. When Judas saw that Jesus was condemned to death, he took a rope and hanged himself on a tree. Judas had no reason for doing this. If he had said to Jesus: " I am sorry for betraying Thee," Jesus would have forgiven him and enabled him to go to heaven.] So great was our Saviour's love for men. No one has ever had such great love. There can be no greater than our Saviour's for sinful men. His love for us has no bounds; it is an infinite love.

SUMMARY. Therefore we say: " Jesus, out of His infinite love for us, suffered a cruel death." Was Jesus obliged to suffer death? No. Jesus suffered death for us of His own free will.

APPLICATION. Dear children, because Jesus, out of His

infinite love for us suffered so many and such painful torments, we ought, out of love for Him willingly suffer a little. This was so beautifully done by little Maria Josepha. She got very sick and had great pains in the chest and in the side. A pious lady once visited her, and said: "Oh, poor child, how much you suffer!" But Maria Josepha replied: "My dear Jesus suffered a great deal more for me; His whole back was covered with wounds; His whole head was pierced with thorns; and I feel only a little pain in the side. Because Jesus suffered such great pains for me, I will also, for His sake, bear my pains willingly."

Dear children, imitate that pious child. If you have headache or toothache, or some other pain, think: "O my beloved Jesus, Thou hast suffered much greater pains for me. Therefore, I will bear my pains also for Thy sake." Those who do this show themselves grateful to Jesus and please Him very much.

35. Jesus carries His heavy Cross.

PREPARATION. Among the Jews the criminals condemned to death were executed in a public place. The place of execution for Jesus was outside of Jerusalem and quite near to it. It was a hill, or a small mountain. It had two names: Golgotha and Mount Calvary. It had the form of a man's head; hence it was called the mountain of skulls. Those who were condemned to be crucified, had to carry, each his own cross.

OBJECT. I will now relate to you how Jesus carried His cross to Mount Calvary.

RELATION. The executioners laid hold of Jesus, took off His purple cloak, put on Him His own clothes, and led Him out to be crucified. And Jesus went out of the city carrying His cross to the place called Calvary, or Golgotha, that is a place of skulls. With Jesus two murderers were led out. A certain man, called Simon, coming from the fields, was passing by. The soldiers stopped him and obliged him to carry the cross behind Jesus. A great crowd accompanied Jesus. Among them were women crying and lamenting over Jesus.

EXPLANATION — *The cross laid on Jesus.* The soldiers who had scourged and mocked Jesus, were ordered to accompany Him to the place of execution. We call them executioners, for they were to crucify Jesus. As soon as Pilate had condemned Jesus, they lay hold of Jesus. He should no longer wear the purple cloak. What, then, did the executioners do? And what did they put on our Saviour? But they left the crown of thorns on His head. Then they brought the large, heavy cross, and threw it down at His feet, and ordered Him to take it up and carry it. The cross was twice as high as a man. A carpenter had made it with two heavy boards. When our Saviour saw the large cross, He was, at first, frightened. He thought of the fearful sufferings He would endure on it, and also of the great shame it was for Him to die on the cross. But He knew also that His heavenly Father sent Him that cross, and that He was going to redeem men by dying on that cross. Our Saviour had also thought on that cross all His life; and now it was ready for Him. He knelt down, put His arms around the cross and kissed it. And then He took it up courageously in His arms, and laid it Himself on His shoulders with childlike respect. The soldiers now led Him out on the way to be crucified.

The march to Calvary. Jesus was not led alone to the place of execution. Who were led out with Jesus? It was a long and sad march. In front went a Roman captain on horseback. Then came Jesus with the cross on His shoulder, between four soldiers leading Him by a rope. Then came the two murderers, each between four soldiers. After them came the executioners who were to nail Jesus and the two murderers to their crosses. Then came the chief priests and the scribes and the rabble. They rejoiced like devils that Jesus was to die on the cross. And who else went with Jesus?

The way to Calvary was very painful for our Saviour. He had become very faint from the sweat of blood in the Garden of Olives, from the scourging and crowning with thorns, and from having had nothing to eat or drink for sixteen or more hours. Before taking the cross He could scarcely walk. And now He must carry that heavy cross on His bruised and wounded shoulder. He staggered along under its great weight. He walked very much bent down. His face was all swollen and bloody. His eyes looked so sad and so imploring under the painful crown of thorns. And His lips moved in prayer. Everywhere in the streets, at the doors and windows of houses people stood looking at Jesus, mocking and insulting Him. Where was He going? To Calvary, the place of execution. The procession stopped at every corner. A soldier blew the trumpet, and everything became quiet and still. Then the soldier cried out in a loud voice: " Know you that Jesus of Nazareth has been condemned to be crucified, because He said that He is the king of the Jews." Then the procession continued on its way.

Jesus falls. The way was very rough. After going a short distance, Jesus, all faint and worn out, fell down, with the cross upon Him. Jesus stretched out His hand for help. When a poor horse falls down under his load and cannot get up, everybody runs, out of pity, to help him to get up. But for Jesus neither the soldiers nor the executioners had any pity. No one helped him. The soldiers began to curse, to pull Him by the rope and to strike Him, till He got up and went on.

Simon of Cyrene. When our Saviour had fallen a second time, He could not get up. The soldiers feared He would die before reaching Calvary. This did not please them, for they wished to see Him die on the cross. Therefore they wished to get someone to help Jesus to carry His cross. But no one was willing to do so. Whom did they then meet? Simon. He was not from Jerusalem, but from a distant city, called Cyrene. What was he therefore called? Simon of Cyrene, or the Cyrenean. He had been at work and was returning home with his two boys. He did not come to help Jesus. He refused. What did the soldiers do, so that he should help Jesus? Simon looked upon it as a great shame to carry the cross for Jesus. He would rather have done anything else. It made him afraid merely to look at Jesus, for Jesus looked so horrible. His clothes were covered with mud and blood stains. Therefore Simon did not wish to help Jesus to carry His cross. He refused to do so. But Jesus, lying on the ground and weeping, stretched out his hand to Simon, looking imploringly at him. Then Simon's heart softened. He took the cross and helped Jesus to carry it. Then the more he looked at the bleeding and patient Saviour, the more willing he was to help Him; and at last he carried it willingly and cheerfully. How fortunate was Simon to help Jesus to carry His cross! He was sanctified by doing so, and now he is praised in the whole world.

The weeping women. Not all who accompanied Jesus were His enemies on His way to death. Among the great number of the wicked there were also some good persons who had compassion on Jesus. Who were they? How did those women show their compassion? They wept aloud and shed many tears over Jesus. That was good on their part.

Veronica. Another woman was standing along the way when Jesus passed. She saw how drops of sweat ran down the bloody face of Jesus. This greatly moved her to compassion. She pushed her way through the soldiers, knelt down before Jesus, handed to Him a white cloth, which she used as a veil, that Jesus might wipe away the sweat and blood from His face. That was a good act on the part of Veronica. Jesus kindly took the veil, wiped His face with it, and gave it back to Veronica. And there was impressed on that veil the picture of our Saviour's face. Thus did Jesus reward her loving compassion.

The Mother of Jesus. The Mother of Jesus was waiting at a certain place to see Jesus carrying His cross pass by. She wished to see her beloved Son, and remain near Him till His death and die with Him. And now she sees Jesus coming with the cross on His shoulder, tired and worn out, staggering and bleeding. Oh, how great a sorrow was in her heart, when she beheld her divine Son in so wretched a state! It seemed to her that she felt seven swords piercing her heart. She would gladly have gone to her Son to speak a few words with Him. But the soldiers would not let her pass. Then she held out her arms towards Jesus, and Jesus remarked that His Mother was there. And Jesus and Mary looked at each other with unspeakable compassion, sadness and love. Mary, weeping, followed her Son.

EXPLANATION AND APPLICATION — *The sins of all mankind made the cross of Jesus so heavy.* How heavily does the cross press on Jesus! Three times He fell down under its weight. And do you know what made His cross so heavy? The sins of all men. They are so many, that no one could count them. If they were made into a tower, they would reach from earth to heaven. The big mountain of the sins of mankind pressed on the cross of Jesus. No wonder He fell three times under His cross!

Thanks. Our Saviour carried His cross loaded with all the sins of men, in order to redeem all men. We can never thank Jesus enough for this. We thank Him every time we recite the fourth decade of the sorrowful mysteries of the rosary. Let us think on this, and recite it with devotion.

The Way of the Cross. The way Jesus passed along

carrying His cross on His shoulder, starts from the house of Pilate and ends at Mount Calvary. It is over a mile long. Later on the Mother of Jesus and the apostles made the way of the cross, stopping a little at those places on the way where something remarkable had happened to Jesus; for instance, where Jesus fell the first time under the cross. There they would stop and reflect how greatly He suffered there, and how the sins of men had prepared those sufferings for Him. Then they would compassionate with Jesus, saying in their heart: "We would rather die than commit a sin." After that they would go to the next station. Where Jesus met His Mother, they stopped again, and so on, till they finished the way of the cross at the sepulchre, where Jesus was buried. Altogether they stopped and reflected fourteen times. Those fourteen places are called Stations. (Ask appropriate questions on the foregoing.)

Later on at each station a picture was placed, on which was painted what happened there to Jesus. Soon people went there from every country in the world to make the Way of the Cross, where Jesus had made it. The people would look at the pictures and think on them, pray devoutly before them, and thank Jesus for all He had suffered for them. And now the Fourteen Stations are in nearly every church in the world. And you sometimes see people going from one picture to another, look at each, and then kneel down and pray. This is called making the Way of the Cross. This greatly pleases our Saviour.

You children also can make the Way of the Cross. Do it in this way. First kneel before the altar and say: "Dear Saviour, Thou didst make the bitter way of the cross for the sins of the whole world; and also for my sins. I am sorry for my sins. O Jesus, forgive me. I will now for the love of Thee make the Way of the Cross." Then go to the First Station. Look at the picture, and think a little while on what it shows that Jesus suffered;

then recite devoutly one Our Father. Then go to the next Station and do the same there; do this until you have finished the fourteenth (last) Station. Now tell me how you can easily make the Way of the Cross. Which of you will make it? You will then find out how happy you will feel in your heart, whenever you make the Way of the Cross with devotion. A child that likes to make the Way of the Cross will surely go to heaven.

36. Jesus is crucified.

OBJECT. I will relate to you how Jesus was crucified.

RELATION. Jesus reached Mount Calvary about noon. The soldiers gave Him wine mixed with gall. Jesus tasted it, but would not drink it. Then they crucified Him. With Jesus they crucified two criminals, the one on His right hand, and the other on His left, and Jesus in the middle. After this the soldiers took the clothes of Jesus, and divided them into parts, one for each soldier. The woven tunic, which had no seam, they would not divide; they cast lots for it. Then they sat down and watched Jesus. Our Saviour hung on the cross for three hours. The chief priests and many Jews mocked and reviled Jesus, saying: " If Thou art the Son of God, come down from the cross. He helped others, but He cannot help Himself! " But Jesus prayed: " Father, forgive them, for they know not what they are doing."

At noon the sun was eclipsed and a great darkness came over the earth, which lasted three hours. Then Jesus said: " It is consummated." Not long after Jesus cried out with a loud voice: " Father, into Thy hands I commend My spirit; " and then He bent down His head and gave up His spirit. And now the earth trembled, the rocks split, graves opened and the bodies of many of the holy dead arose. The captain and the soldiers watching our Lord got frightened and said: " Truly this man was just; He was the Son of God." And all the people struck their breasts and returned in silence to Jerusalem.

EXPLANATION — *The wine with myrrh.* On what day was Jesus condemned to be crucified, and was led to the place of execution? At what hour did He reach Calvary? Our Saviour was exceedingly tired, deathly pale and covered with perspiration. What did the soldiers give to Jesus to drink? With what was the wine mixed? Who knows how gall tastes? The bitter wine was intended to prevent Jesus from feeling His pains so much. Some good women had sent Him the wine. But what did our Lord not wish? He did not wish to be insensible to pain, but to suffer all the fearful pains of the crucifixion. But He also wished to please the good women who had sent Him the wine. Therefore He tasted it.

Our Saviour's clothes taken off. Then the soldiers took off His clothes very roughly. But His clothes stuck to His wounded body. What then happened to His wounds? They were opened again. Did that hurt Jesus very much? It hurt Him like a fresh scourging, for His blood again flowed all over His body and made it all red.

Jesus nailed to the cross. Now the soldiers gather around Jesus, and the most terrible thing is going to be done. The executioners stretched out their hands to lay hold of Jesus. You may imagine how the heart of Jesus must have beaten out of dread. But He allowed the executioners to lay Him down on the cross. What a hard bed it was, especially for the sore back of Jesus! And yet how touching it was to see Him lying on it! Now one of the executioners kneels on the breast of Jesus; another on His right arm; a third takes hold of His right hand and lays it on the arm of the cross, and with a hammer drives a big sharp nail through the Saviour's right hand into the cross. A trembling passes through every part of our Lord's body. The blood squirts out from His hand, and His fingers, through pain, close up around the nail. The same happens with the nailing of the left hand to the other arm of the cross. Hot tears pour out from the eyes of Jesus, and He weeps aloud. Now is the turn of the feet. Pain had cramped up His feet. The executioners roughly stretched His legs and nailed His feet to the cross; the bones cracked while the nails cut their way between them! How terrible that pain! At last our Saviour is nailed to the cross; His body is fearfully stretched on it. His face is deathly pale, and covered with blood. His whole body is red with blood, and blood streams from His hands and feet.

The raising of the cross. The cross is now raised by means of ropes, poles and ladders. The cross staggers for some moments, rises a little, staggers again, rises a little more; after some more staggering it is up and with a frightful jerk its foot falls into the hole prepared for it, and the sufferings of Jesus in His hands and feet are increased. The hole is then filled with ground, and the cross is up and stands fast in its place.

Jesus hangs on the cross. The cross of salvation is now erected for the first time on earth. On it hangs the Son of God between heaven and earth. His head is covered with the crown of thorns. Jesus cannot move. The blood from the crown of thorns continues to flow and trickles down into His eyes and mouth. And from His hands and feet streamlets of blood run over His arms and down the cross to the ground.

Who were crucified with Jesus? In what order were the crosses placed? Jesus was placed in the middle, as if He were the worst of criminals.

When the cross was raised, the chief priests and scribes yelled for joy! They rejoiced like devils, and all hell rejoiced with them. They thought: "We have got Jesus at last! He shall no more escape us. Now He must die."

Compassion of friends under the cross. There were also friends of Jesus standing under the cross: St. John and

Mary, the sister of Lazarus, and other pious women. Weeping they raised their hands towards Jesus, and looked at Him full of grief and love. Also the Mother of Jesus stood under the cross, that bed on which her Son and her God was dying! Oh, how much she suffered near that terrible death-bed of Jesus! Mary and Jesus looked at each other's eyes, and spoke together in silence with their looks. What a love! What a sorrow! Because Mary underwent so great a sorrow at her Son's death, she is called the Mother of Sorrows.

Division of the clothes of Jesus. How many soldiers led Jesus to execution and helped to crucify Him? These four soldiers took possession of the clothes of Jesus; His shoes, a girdle, an upper garment, an inner one, and a cloak. What did the soldiers do with the clothes, so that each one should get as much as any of the others? They divided them so that he who got the shoes, got also a piece of the upper garment; and he who got the girdle, got also a piece of the cloak. The four parts were equal in value. The under garment was left. This garment the Blessed Virgin had woven herself as a single piece without seam. The soldiers would not cut it into pieces, for it was too good to be cut up. Only one of them was to get it. They threw dice to see who would get the largest number, for the largest number would win the inner garment. This was the way in which they cast lots for it. Did the soldiers then go away? How long did they remain on Mount Calvary? Until Jesus died. At what hour of the day did He die?

Jesus reviled and mocked. In the meantime what were the chief priests and the other Jews doing to Jesus? They made fun of Jesus and insulted Him. They would not give Him a moment of rest or let Him die quietly. We must never make fun of an unfortunate person. That gives him fearful pain. Much less should we make fun of a person dying. How did the chief priests and Jews revile and insult the dying Jesus? They said: "Ah, Thou Son of God, show now what Thou canst do: come down from the cross." You know that Jesus could easily have come down from the cross, if He had wished. Why? But why did He not come down? What else did they say to revile Jesus? But Jesus prayed for those who insulted Him. What did He say?

The eclipse of the sun. What wonderful thing happened in the heavens while Jesus was hanging on the cross? At what hour? It became as dark as the darkest night over the whole earth. The birds stopped singing, the animals, greatly frightened, ran about and hid themselves. The men also were in great fear, looked at the heavens to see what was the cause of the darkness. How long did the darkness last?

Jesus dies. As long as He hung on the cross, Jesus was praying silently to His heavenly Father for all men. At last He had suffered enough. He raised His head crowned with thorns, and said: "It is consummated" (finished). What was consummated? His suffering. He had finished all that His Father had commanded Him. He had atoned for the sins of mankind. Men were redeemed. And now for the last time on the cross He opens His lips. What did He say with a loud voice? "I commend," that is, I give up. To whom did He give up His soul? How beautiful! Jesus knows no one to whom He would rather give up His soul than to His heavenly Father. What did our Saviour then do with His head? He bowed His head. He wished to give a signal to death, as if He said: "Now, death, you can come; I will now die." Then Jesus drew one breath more, and then breathed out His soul, that is, gave up His soul. Jesus was dead.

The wonders at the death of Jesus. At the moment Jesus died, great wonders took place. What were these wonders? What did the earth do? It trembled. People thought the houses would fall down, and ran out into the streets and the fields. What happened to many large rocks? They split like wood cut with an axe. Mount Calvary was split in two. What happened to some graves? Who came out of the graves?

The impression made by these wonders. The soldiers were still on guard around the cross. Their captain was also with them. He was very near the cross of Jesus, and looked all the time at the face of our Saviour. How did the captain and the soldiers feel when the earth trembled and the rocks split? Who caused these wonders to take place at the death of Jesus? What should the Jews have concluded from these wonders? Who made the right conclusion? What did they say? What did they believe about our Saviour? How did the people act? On what did they probably reflect when they went home in silence?

FURTHER EXPLANATION — *Tree of the cross; tree of paradise.* The Redeemer hangs dead high up on the cross. The cross is like a tree with two dry (withered) branches. Our bleeding Saviour is the red fruit on the tree of the cross. The tree of the cross reminds us of another tree, on which fruit was hanging. Who knows which tree I mean? The tree of paradise. What command had God given to our first parents concerning that tree? What would happen, if they would eat of its fruit?

All men lost. How did they obey that command? What did they commit by their disobedience? What did their sin do to their soul? Where could they no longer go? God closed heaven to men. What punishment were they to undergo after their death? Where would their soul go? Who inherited their sin and punishment? Most of men have also committed actual sins, personal mortal sins. Where should such men go after their death? To hell, the endless punishment due to their sins.

Our Saviour took upon Himself the sins of all men. But the Son of God undertook to wash away in His own blood the pains of hell and the sins of all men. Therefore

He took upon Himself our sins, the sins of all men. He was so overloaded with these sins, that His heavenly Father saw nothing but sins when He looked at Him. And our Saviour loaded with all these sins allowed Himself to be hanged on the tree of the cross between two criminals, as if He were the worst of criminals. He took upon Himself all the sins of all men. And let us see how He atones for them.

Our Saviour atones for our sins. What did our Saviour receive by being nailed to the cross through His hands and feet? How did He before this receive many wounds? His wounds pained Him very much, especially those in His hands and feet. The big nails burned Him like red hot irons. He felt as if there came from every one of His wounds flames of fire. He felt as if He was lying in the fire of hell, for His pains were like those of hell itself. And how many hours did He suffer all this? Three hours. Whilst He is hanging on the cross, what flows from His wounds? And the blood of Jesus, thus flowing down the tree of the cross, washes the sins from the souls of men. What happened to Jesus when all His blood had flowed out of His wounds? He died.

We are redeemed. At that moment heaven was opened again. What punishments did our Saviour atone for by His pains? What did He wash away from our souls with His blood? Now we have been freed from the slavery of sin and the pains of hell. And what is now open to men? Men are redeemed. Oh, how lovely is Jesus on the cross! Already in the manger He was lovely! But He is more lovely to us with His wounds on the cross. He loved us and washed us from our sins with His blood.

SUMMARY. No one could have obliged Jesus to suffer death for us. But what induced Him to suffer for us? The infinite love He has for us induced Him freely to suffer and die for us, in order to redeem and save us. Where was Jesus crucified? On Mount Calvary, near

Jerusalem. How long did He hang on the cross? What did Jesus do at last with His head? Bowed it down. And what then took place? He died. After hanging three hours on the cross, Jesus at last bowed His head and died. Let us repeat what Jesus suffered for us. What did He suffer in the Garden of Olives? Agony and a bloody sweat. What then happened to Him? He was arrested, scourged, crowned with thorns, and finally nailed to the cross.

APPLICATION — *Holy Week.* On which two days did Jesus suffer all this for us? On which day did He die for us? Good Friday is the day on which our Saviour died. When the father dies, the children are sad. The day of his death is for them a day of sadness and mourning. So is the Friday, on which our Saviour died, a day of mourning for all men. That Friday is called Good Friday; it is called Good, because on that day Jesus redeemed us from sin and hell. On Maundy Thursday the bells stop ringing and the organ becomes silent.

Abstinence. The last two (three) days of Holy Week are days of abstinence from flesh meat. Why? Because Jesus suffered for us. And because Jesus died on a Friday, we are not allowed to eat meat on Fridays during the whole year, except on the feasts of obligation that fall on a Friday (Pope Pius X.).

Veneration of the cross. On Good Friday a picture of our Lord on the cross, called a crucifix, is exposed for the veneration of the faithful. The people go to that crucifix, kneel down before it, pray to and thank our Saviour for dying on the cross for us, and then they kiss our Saviour's wounds on the crucifix. You children should do this as well as the grown people. Therefore, like them, kneel before the crucifix, pray to Jesus crucified and thank Him for dying for you, and devoutly kiss our Saviour's wounds. The crucifixion is the fifth sorrowful mystery of the rosary. In the house of every Catholic there should be a crucifix. There is one in every church, on every altar. Whenever you see a crucifix, think how Jesus died on the cross for us. Pious people love to pray to Jesus before a crucifix, and this is very pleasing to Jesus. Thank Jesus for dying for you on the cross, and say to Him: " My dear Jesus, I thank Thee for dying on the cross for me. May Thy blood not be shed in vain for me."

The passion of Jesus should not be in vain. Our Saviour died, indeed, for each one of us. And yet it might happen that some of you will be condemned to hell. Why are some persons condemned to hell? It is not the fault of Jesus; it is their fault; on account of their sins, of which they do not and will not repent, Jesus died in vain for them. In vain He suffered for them, in vain He shed His blood for them, in vain He died on the cross for them. It would be the greatest possible misfortune to be of the number of those persons! Our Saviour can help a child never to commit a mortal sin; He can help a child who has committed a mortal sin to be really sorry for it, and He will pardon the child who is really sorry for his mortal sins. Such a child will go to heaven. For such a one the sufferings and blood of Jesus are not in vain. Often pray to Jesus: " I thank Thee, O Lord, for having died for me. Let not Thy sufferings and Thy blood be lost for me."

Everything for the love of Jesus. You can thank Jesus also in this way: " My dearest Jesus, Thou hast done all for the love of me; I wish to do also all for the love of Thee." When you work, when you study, when you find it hard to obey, when you suffer pain or are sick, say: " O Jesus, all for the love of Thee." If you do this, your whole life belongs to Jesus, you live for Jesus.

At the Elevation. When Jesus is raised up by the priest at the Elevation of the Mass, it is as if He was dying on the cross for us. Then you should love Him so much, that you would be ready to die for Him. You ought then to say to Him: "O Jesus, for Thee I live, for Thee I die. I am all Thine in life and in death."

37. The dead Body of Jesus is pierced and buried.

OBJECT. I will tell you to-day what was done with the body of Jesus after His death.

RELATION. Towards evening one of the soldiers opened the side of Jesus with a spear (lance). Blood and water immediately flowed out of it. Then two members of the Great Council of the Jews took the body of Jesus down from the cross, wrapped it up in fine linen and laid it in a new grave cut out of a rock. They then covered the entrance with a large heavy stone. The next day the chief priests sealed the stone, and placed a guard of soldiers over the grave.

EXPLANATION. How long did Jesus hang on the cross before dying? What happened to the sun when Jesus was hanging on the cross? After the death of Jesus the sky became gradually clear, and the evening sun cast gloomy rays through the clouds on the Redeemer's dead body hanging on the cross. Where are dead bodies placed? In graves. But not immediately; they are usually kept a day or two before being buried. A dead body is called a corpse. The dead body of Jesus was buried the same evening. A Roman soldier wished to see if Jesus was really dead. What did he do to find it out? With what did he pierce the side of Jesus? A spear, or lance, is a weapon with a long handle or pole, having a sharp piece of steel at the end. With this spear the soldier struck the side of Jesus so hard, that the sharp piece of steel went through His breast deep into His very heart. When he drew out his spear there was a large and deep wound in the side of Jesus, out of which Jesus shed the last drops of His blood. Jesus was then really dead. How many large wounds were there now in the body of Jesus? They are called the Five Sacred Wounds of Jesus. Which was the largest? The wound in His side. It was so large that a man could put his hand inside of it. It was wide open, and through it the heart of Jesus could be seen. Why did the soldier open or pierce the side of Jesus? The wound in the side of Jesus is like an open door through which we can reach the Heart of Jesus. When the Blessed Virgin saw the soldier piercing the heart of Jesus with his spear, she cried out greatly frightened.

Jesus is taken down from the cross. Now Mary would have wished to take down the body of her divine Son from the cross and bury it. But she was not able to do it. Who came to help her? Two influential members of the Great Council. One was Joseph, of the town of Arimathea, and the other Nicodemus of Jerusalem. They bought fine white sheets of linen and plenty of aromatic (sweet smelling) spices, and went to Mount Calvary. Mary was very glad when she saw them coming to her assistance. They first knelt devoutly before the cross to adore their dead Saviour. Then they placed ladders against the cross, and went up on them. One of them pulled out the nails from the hands and feet of Jesus. He kissed the nails and handed them down below. The other received in the linen sheet the body of Jesus, holding it tight. Then both carried it down from the cross with great reverence. They spoke only what was necessary, and in a whisper, as if they were in church.

The Saviour's dead body in His Mother's lap. Mary sat down on a mat, and both men slowly and carefully laid the body of Jesus in her lap. The Infant of Bethlehem lies again in His Mother's lap. Mary, holding Him by the neck, kisses Him, and lays her face long on His face; then she draws His head to her breast, just as if He was asleep. But, alas! He is dead. His lovely face is pale, swollen and bloody. Mary can hardly recognize it. His eyes are closed in death. His arms are rigid and stiff. His head is pierced with thorns. His right shoulder is badly bruised from carrying the cross. The hands and feet bear the cruel marks of the nails. And in His side there is a wide, deep wound reaching into His very heart. Mary saw and considered all. She felt as if she had had her heart suddenly pierced by seven sharp swords, and as if she would have to die of grief. Who has seen a picture of Mary holding her dead Jesus in her lap?

Mary cared for the body of Jesus. Mary first removed tenderly the crown of thorns from the head of Jesus. Then she washed His head and face. She washed also the bloody wounds in His shoulder and in His back, and His pierced hands and feet. Lastly she combed His hair and poured on it some sweet-scented ointment.

The embalming. Jesus was now to be buried. Joseph and Nicodemus wrapped His body in the winding sheet, placing all around the body inside the sheet plenty of sweet aromatic herbs and spices. This they did, in order to prevent the body from corrupting and emitting stench.

The burial. They then carried the body of Jesus to the grave. The graves of the Jews were different from ours, as I have already explained to you, when I related to you the resurrection of Lazarus. What did I say about his grave? People could go into it as in a little room. Sometimes several corpses were placed in one grave. Our Saviour's grave was like that of Lazarus, cut out of a rock. No corpse had yet been laid in that grave. What was it, therefore, called? A new grave. The grave was in a garden near Mount Calvary, belonging to Joseph of Arimathea. He had got the grave made for himself, for he wished to be buried in it after his death. Into this grave the body of Jesus was carried by Joseph and Nicodemus. The Blessed Virgin, St. John and the holy women followed the body of our Lord. In the grave our Saviour's body was gently and reverentially laid in a coffin of stone. His body, though full of wounds, no longer bled. The sweet-scented herbs and spices spread an agreeable odor. Outside the grave there grew palm-trees, shrubs and flowers; and the garden was already full of blooming spring flowers.

Taking leave of the dead Saviour. The holy Mother of Jesus entered the grave to take a last look on the body of our Saviour now lying there surrounded by so many beautiful flowers and blossoms. She bent down weeping over the body of Jesus and gave it a last kiss. Then the men and holy women also entered the grave to adore our Saviour and kiss His wounds.

The closing of the grave. The entrance of the grave was now closed with a stone so large that it could not be carried. How did they bring it and place it against the opening? Then they went away sorrowful and silent. Their eyes were red from much weeping. After reaching home they thought all the time about the Saviour's body in the grave.

The guard over the grave. The chief priests were still very much afraid. They feared that the apostles would come in the night and carry away the Saviour's body, and then tell everybody that Jesus had risen from the dead. Therefore, early on Saturday morning they went to the grave with sixteen soldiers. The soldiers were strictly ordered to keep a close watch over the grave. What were the soldiers, therefore, called? Guards. The chief priests said to the guards: " Stay here day and night, and take good care that no one comes here and steals the body of Jesus."

The sealing of the large stone. But this was not enough for the chief priests. They placed a sign on the grave, so that no one could move the stone closing the grave without its being found out. Who knows what that sign was? What did they do to the stone? Who has already seen a sealed letter? The seal is placed just where the letter is closed. And if the letter is opened, what happens to the seal? The seal is broken. You can tell by the seal if the letter was opened. Our Saviour's grave could not be sealed exactly like a letter. The priests placed some tape or large strings around the large stone and fastened the ends on each side of the grave. Now how could they find out, if somebody had opened the grave? Why did the chief priests seal the grave of Jesus?

SUMMARY. What was done to our Saviour's side after His death? After His death His side was pierced with a spear. And after that what happened to His dead body? The dead body of Jesus was taken down from the cross and laid in the grave.

EXPLANATION AND APPLICATION — The Most Sacred Heart of Jesus. Where was then the body of Jesus? In the grave. The sufferings of Jesus were all over. When did He shed the last drops of His blood? When His side was opened with a spear. What could be seen through the opening in His side? His Heart. A mother often asks her child: "Where do you love me?" Where does the child point? To his heart. Our father and mother love us more than any one else. But our Saviour loves us infinitely more than they. He loves us so much, that He shed for us the very last drop of blood in His Heart. He wished also to show us His most loving Heart. Therefore He allowed His side to be opened with a spear. In many pictures you can see the Heart of Jesus, and Jesus pointing to it, as if He said to us: "Oh, see this Heart which has loved men so much." What do we owe to our Saviour for His love? We should often say: "Sweet Heart of Jesus, be my love."

Our gratitude to Jesus for His love. I once read of a fight between a lion and a large snake. The snake had enveloped itself around the lion and was squeezing him to death. But a knight passing by, seeing this, pulled out his sword and cut the snake in two, and saved the lion's life. How do you think the lion showed his gratitude to that knight? He followed the knight everywhere, and brought him deer and other game which he caught for him. He never left the knight. Thus you can see how a wild beast showed his gratitude to him who had saved his life. If you do not wish to be less grateful than a wild beast, you must thank our divine Saviour. How can you show your gratitude to Him? When Blessed Margaret Mary was still a child, she also learned that our Saviour had suffered so much on the cross. She therefore had a great love for Jesus. Seeing a crucifix one day she wept and kissed it, saying: " Most beloved Jesus, I will belong entirely to Thee." Whenever after this she saw a crucifix, she would pray before it, and thank Jesus for suffering so much for her. Dear children, accustom yourselves to think on our loving Jesus and His bitter passion, especially when you see a crucifix. Think on it whenever you recite these words of the Creed: " Suffered under Pontius Pilate, died and was buried," and pronounce these words devoutly.

Prayer to the five wounds of Jesus. There is another prayer, by which we venerate the passion of our Saviour; that is the prayer to the five wounds of Jesus, in which we say: " O Lord Jesus Christ, who died for us on the cross, through the wound of Thy right hand, have mercy on us." (Rehearse this with the children, and repeat the prayer for each of the other wounds: of Thy left hand; of Thy right foot; of Thy left foot; of Thy sacred side.)

38. The Soul of Jesus goes down to Limbo. Jesus rises from the dead.

OBJECT. I will tell you to-day where the soul of Jesus went after His death.

RELATION. When the soul of Jesus left His body it went down as fast as lightning to Limbo, where the souls of those were who had already died. They were waiting there for the coming of the Redeemer. The soul of Jesus remained three days with them. He said to them: "I have redeemed mankind. You shall soon go to heaven."

EXPLANATION — *Limbo*. What leaves man's body when he dies? The soul; the spirit. What did Jesus breathe forth at His death? His soul. Where did the soul of Jesus go when He died? It went directly and quickly to Limbo. Limbo was a place under the ground, anciently called hell, that is, a lower region. It was not the hell where the devils and wicked men, who are dead, suffer punishment. In Limbo there were the souls of good, pious men, such as, Adam and Eve, Abel, the pious shepherds, the wise men, who had already died; and also of the Holy Innocents massacred by Herod on account of the Infant Jesus. Also Simeon and Anna were there. And who else? St. Joseph, the foster-father of Jesus. He had not been dead very long. All these persons were good and holy at their death. How do we call them? The souls of the just. Where ought these souls to have gone after their death? To heaven. But why could they not go there? Heaven was then closed. They had to wait in Limbo until heaven would again be opened. Some of those souls had spent already over three thousand years in Limbo. They had no pains to suffer in Limbo, no fire as there is in hell or purgatory. But they were not allowed to see God. You can imagine how these souls longed for heaven. Who was to open heaven for them? They could hardly wait until the Redeemer would come.

Jesus in Limbo. All on a sudden Limbo became very bright, just as it does on earth when the sun rises. The soul of Jesus was there. And His soul was surrounded by very many angels. Jesus was glorious and as bright as the sun. The whole of Limbo was beautifully lit up by Him. Jesus spoke to the just: "I have just died on the cross for all men; now heaven is opened, and you shall all leave this place and go to heaven." You may imagine how those holy souls rejoiced. They all knelt full of joy before Jesus, adored and thanked Him. Where did the soul of Jesus go after His death? Who were in Limbo? The soul of Jesus went, after His death, to Limbo, where were the souls of the just who had died. Therefore we say in the Creed: " He descended into hell." Mention some of the souls that were there. What did Jesus say to them? How long did the soul of Jesus remain there?

OBJECT. On the third day the soul of Jesus returned to His body, and Jesus rose from the dead, as I will now tell you.

RELATION. At dawn of the third day Jesus rose from the dead and came out glorious from the grave. And behold, there took place a great earthquake, and an angel came down from heaven, rolled away the large stone from the grave, and sat on it. His appearance was like lightning, and his garment was as white as snow. The guards trembled for fear, and were like dead. At the same time pious women set out for the grave. They wished to embalm Jesus. When they arrived, they saw the grave open. The angel said to them: " You seek Jesus of Nazareth, who was crucified. He is not here; He is risen. Make haste and tell it to His disciples and Peter."

EXPLANATION — *The body and soul of Jesus again united together*. The third day after the death of Jesus had come. On which day did Jesus die? That was the first day. Which day comes after Good Friday? Holy Saturday. That was the second day. And which is the third day? Easter Sunday. On Easter Sunday the soul of Jesus returned from Limbo. Jesus took the souls of the just along and many angels. They all went to the grave of Jesus. They passed through the large stone into the grave. The body of Jesus lay there as if asleep. And the angels knelt down around it to adore it. Jesus showed the holy souls His wounded and torn body. They all shuddered out of holy fear, and again thanked Jesus for the sufferings He had endured for them. Then the soul of Jesus bent over His body and entered it and entirely penetrated it and thus again became united with His body.

Jesus rises from the dead. In what state was the body of Jesus when His soul had left it? What took place in the body of Jesus, when His soul returned into it? His members began to move. Jesus freed Himself from the sheets around Him and stood up. The sun had not yet risen. What begins with the rising of the sun? The day. But before the sun rises, it begins already to be light. It was just then that Jesus rose from the dead. That time is called the dawn of the day. When did Jesus rise from the dead? At the dawn of the third day, Easter Sunday.

The glorified body of Jesus. The body of Jesus was now a great deal more beautiful than before. It was as bright as the sun at noon on a clear day. The whole grave was filled with a dazzling light. The eyes of Jesus were like two lovely morning stars. Instead of the frightful crown of thorns, there was a bright golden ring around the forehead of Jesus. His hair, like shining gold, covered His neck and shoulders. His garments glittered from light blue, like the sky in sunshine, to the beautiful red of sunrise and sunset. It was a wonderfully pleasing sight. The wounds made by the scourging were no longer visible. Only the five great wounds of the hands, feet and side remained, but they were healed; they were as beautiful as roses, and were shining like the rays of the sun.

Jesus had a new and wonderful life. He no longer needed food and drink, nor to walk slowly on the ground as we do. Just as birds take flight in the air and fly quickly from one place to another, so Jesus could go as fast as lightning from one place to another. His body was as light as air. He was transparent, and passed like an angel through walls and stones. His body was almost like a soul, a spirit. Therefore we say: " The body of Jesus at His resurrection was transfigured and glorified."

In what state was the body of Jesus, when He rose from
the dead? Why do we call a body glorified?

The joy of Jesus risen. Oh, how happy was Jesus in His
glorified state! It was now a joy for Him to be the Redeemer. His sufferings and torments were now over, and
seemed like a dream. He now rejoiced over them, and His
joy has no end. Now our Saviour raises His hands and
eyes towards His heavenly Father. He now wishes to
show Himself to Him in His glory; and in exultation He
exclaims: "I am risen from the dead." And it seems as
if the heavenly Father turns to Jesus and says: "Thou
art My beloved Son." And the holy souls wondering
praise the risen Saviour and sing: "Alleluia. This is the
day which the Lord hath made; let us exult and rejoice
in it. Alleluia. Sing to the Lord a new hymn, for He
hath done wonders." Thus was the resurrection of Jesus
celebrated already in His grave.

Jesus comes forth from the grave. And now Jesus came
out of the grave. With what was the grave closed? What
had the chief priests done to the stone? And whom had
they placed before the grave? But the stone, the seal and
the guards could not keep Jesus in the grave. What happened to the body of Jesus when the soul went back into
it? It became alive again and also glorified. How can
a glorified body come out of a closed grave? Also the
angels and the souls of the just had gone in and out of
the closed grave, and the soldiers had not noticed it. They
were now guarding an empty grave. They would soon
find it empty. Who then came down from heaven? What
did the angel do? Now everybody could look into the
grave. What was the appearance of the angel? What
other wonder took place? How did the guards get frightened at the earthquake and at the appearance of the angel?
The guards after a while regained consciousness. They
got up and looked very frightened at the open grave.
Where did they no longer wish to remain? Where did

they go? They related to the chief priests: "Jesus rose this morning from the dead. The grave is open and empty." The chief priests gave money to the guards, saying to them: "Keep quiet about that, and do not tell any one that Jesus is risen from the dead. Tell the people: We fell asleep at the grave, and the apostles came and stole the body of Jesus." And the guards obeyed them.

The women at the grave. Who went out early in the morning to the grave? What did those pious women intend to do? We lay on the graves of our friends wreaths and flowers; we do this to show our love for them. How did the holy women wish to show their love for Jesus? They wished to embalm Him. They took along ointments, sweet herbs and myrrh. What did they see when they came to the grave? They were frightened. They entered the grave. What did they see there? The angel knew whom they were seeking. What did he say to them? What did he announce to them? To whom should they hasten to deliver the joyful message? You can easily imagine how happy these women felt.

Jesus appears to His Mother. Immediately after His resurrection Jesus went to His Mother. She knew He would rise from the dead. She waited the whole night for Him. She had decorated her little room with flowers and fine plants. Then she put on her feast day dress, and knelt down to pray. Not very long after midnight she heard a sweet hymn sung softly as by heavenly voices, and her room became so full of light, that her lighted lamp seemed as if it was not lighted at all. Our Saviour was there with many angels and the souls of the just from Limbo. Jesus greeted His Mother very affectionately. Mary prostrated herself at His feet, and exclaimed with joy: "Is it Thou, indeed, my dear Son?" Our Saviour replied: "Yes, beloved Mother, it is I. I have risen from the dead, and have come to tell thee." He then embraced her, laid His face on hers, and pressed her to His heart.

Mary then looked at His holy glorified body, His face and His hands. Jesus showed her His wounds, which had been so dreadful, but which now were so shining and so lovely. Mary rejoiced and praised God for giving back her Son to her.

EXPLANATION — *The combat between Jesus and the devil.* To whom did men belong after the sin of our first parents? Our Saviour wished to rescue men from the devil. How did the devil hold them in his power? Jesus fought the devil. Soldiers (in certain countries) wear a helmet to protect their head. What did Jesus allow to be placed on His head? The crown of thorns was His helmet. Soldiers have a sword to fight with. What did Jesus have in His hand? A reed. Soldiers like to fight on horseback. Our Saviour in His fight was hanging on the cross. The soldiers in battle utter their war-cry. What did Jesus do on the cross? He prayed. During a battle when the cavalry mingle in the fight and the cannons roar, the earth trembles. What happened to the earth, when Jesus was combating the devil? There was a great earthquake. The combat was terrible. God the Father looked on attentively from heaven; the angels listened and held their breath. The devils were watching the result of the battle. The terrible battle lasted three hours, and Jesus died. Where was His body laid? People would think: "O misfortune! Jesus is dead, the devil has conquered." And the devil, indeed, cried out, "Hurrah!" He thought: "Jesus is dead and buried; a big stone closes His grave; He can never get out; I have won the fight. All men now belong to me. No one shall escape me. I will drag them all into hell." But the devil rejoiced too soon.

The victory of Jesus over the devil. What did Jesus do on the third day? He rose from the dead. To whom does the victory now belong? What a terror for the devil! Now his head is crushed. How did Jesus restore life to His body? He re-united His soul with His body. He raised Himself from death to life! Which other dead persons did He raise to life? That Jesus raised them to life is a great miracle indeed; but that He raised Himself to life is the greatest of miracles! Who raised Himself to life? What does it prove? That Jesus is God!

The victory of Jesus over death. In the stable of Bethlehem Jesus was born as a little, helpless child. There He received human life, which lasts only for a time. On Easter Sunday Jesus received His new life. What can no longer happen to Jesus? Suffering and death. Jesus rose from the grave glorious and immortal. Because He rose from the dead, we also shall rise one day from the dead. Now death is only a temporary sleep, for Jesus has conquered death.

PICTURE. Let us look at the picture of the resurrection.

The risen Saviour. What do we see on His head? The crown of victory. Why does His body shine so beautifully? His body is glorified. What do you see in the hands and feet of Jesus? Why do you see no other wounds in His body? What does our Saviour hold in His hand? A flag. What is on the flag? This flag shows that Jesus has gained the victory. He who conquers in a difficult battle is called a hero. What, then, is our Saviour? Whom did He overcome? Death and the devil. The cross tells us that Jesus conquered them by His death on the cross.

The angels, the guards. Who else are seen in the picture? How do you recognize the angel? What is he doing with his hands? Why does he kneel with joined hands? In what position are the guards? Why are they lying on the ground? What frightens them? Whom did the guards not see? Only angels and good men were allowed to see the glorious risen Saviour.

The grave. Show me the grave. In what kind of place was it? It is now open and empty. Where is the stone that closed it?

SUMMARY. What did Jesus do on the third day after His death? He rose glorious from the dead. The Creed says: " The third day He rose again from the dead."

APPLICATION. Because Jesus rose from the dead, we celebrate a great feast — Easter Sunday. The church is beautifully adorned. Alleluia is heard during the Mass. " Jesus is risen, alleluia." We thus express our joy that Jesus rose from the dead, triumphing over His enemies, and opening heaven to us. Now Jesus reigns forever. Therefore heaven and earth, angels and men rejoice. Children should also share in the joy. What do they get on Easter Sunday? You surely do not know why children get eggs on Easter Sunday. I will tell you. An egg contains a little bird, a little chicken. When the time of hatching comes, the little chicken breaks the shell with its bill and comes out alive. So also did Jesus come out alive from the closed grave; and so shall our body come out alive from its grave on the last day.

39. Jesus appears to His Disciples. Jesus ascends to Heaven.

OBJECT. I will now relate how Jesus showed Himself to His disciples after His resurrection.

RELATION. After His resurrection Jesus remained forty days on earth. He appeared often to His apostles, and sometimes to His other disciples. Once five hundred of His disciples were present. He wished to show them that He was really risen from the dead. He even ate and drank with them. Moreover, He wished yet to teach many things to His apostles.

EXPLANATION — *The apparitions of Jesus.* After His resurrection Jesus could have immediately returned to heaven. Mankind was already redeemed. But Jesus wished first to show Himself to His apostles. One evening they were all together in a room in Jerusalem. For fear of the Jews they had locked the doors. All at once there was Jesus standing among them. How did He get in? Because He suddenly stood before the apostles, we say: "He appeared to them." The apostles did not know where He came from, or how He got in. But how they rejoiced when they saw Him! They would have liked Him to remain with them. But suddenly He was gone, that is, He disappeared as suddenly as He had come. At one time how many of His disciples were present when He appeared? Over five hundred. On some occasions He sat at table with the apostles. What did they then do? Ate and drank. Our Saviour also showed them His wounds. Once He allowed one of the apostles to touch them, to put his finger into the wounds in His hands, and his hand into His side. In this manner Jesus appeared various times during forty days to His disciples.

Reason of the apparitions of Jesus. If the apostles had not seen Jesus after His resurrection, they would probably not have believed that He was risen from the dead. Why did He appear so often to them? He wished to prove clearly that He was risen from the dead. For the same reason also He ate and drank with them, showed them His wounds, and allowed one of His apostles to touch them. But Jesus did not remain on earth merely to show Himself to His apostles. He also taught them to say Mass, to baptize and many other things, because they would soon have to go to preach to all men in the whole world. At last, the time came for Jesus to return to heaven.

OBJECT. I will now tell you how Jesus ascended into heaven.

RELATION. On the fortieth day after His resurrection Jesus appeared to His apostles for the last time. They were again in Jerusalem, assembled in the Supper Room. Jesus sat down at table with them and explained Holy Scripture to them. Then He commanded them: "Stay in the city until you are endowed with power from above. And then go forth all over the world to preach to Jews and pagans." Then He led them out to Mount of Olives. There He raised His hands over them and blessed them. Whilst He was blessing them He was lifted up heavenward in their presence, entered heaven and sat at the right hand of God.

The apostles adored Jesus and gazed at Him ascending until a cloud concealed Him from their view. Then two angels clothed in white appeared and said: "You men of Galilee, why are you standing here, looking up to heaven? This same Jesus, who has been taken up from among you into heaven, shall come again in like manner, as you have seen Him ascend." And the apostles returned with great joy to Jerusalem.

EXPLANATION — *Jesus appears for the last time.* Before ascending into heaven, Jesus wished to take leave of His apostles. He wished on that occasion to eat once more with them. How many days' after His resurrection did Jesus ascend into heaven? On the fortieth day. It was a Thursday. Where were the apostles assembled? Jesus sat at table with His apostles. He sat in the middle, and His apostles and disciples sat around Him. The holy women also were there, seated at another table. Next to Jesus was His Blessed Mother. She wished to see all that our Saviour did, and hear all that He taught. Jesus first prayed and blessed the food. Then He distributed the food to each one, and to His Blessed Mother and the holy women. Whilst eating, Jesus spoke with His apostles, and said to them: "The time has now come for Me to return to My Father in heaven. I will prepare in heaven a place for you and for all who will believe in Me, so that you may be there with Me."

Jesus promises the Holy Ghost. When the apostles heard that they would not see Jesus any more on earth, they felt very sad. Many of them wept. They would

have liked to keep the Saviour with them. Perhaps they
said: "O dearest Jesus, stay with us. When Thou art
gone, we shall be all alone in the world, like poor orphans
without a father." But our Saviour consoled them, saying: "If I go not to the Father, you shall not be able
to go to Him. Therefore you ought to rejoice, that I go
away from you. Do not be afraid. Do not leave Jerusalem so soon, but remain together waiting and praying."
Where should the apostles remain? And what should they
do? Our Saviour would send them the Holy Ghost. The
Holy Ghost would come down from heaven upon them,
and give them strength. The apostles would then be endowed by Him with strength. Where would the Holy
Ghost come from? From on high. In this way they
would become so strong, as to have no fear of any one.
How long should the apostles remain in Jerusalem? Until
they would be endowed with strength from on high.
What should the apostles then do? Go all over the world
and preach the Gospel to all nations.

On the way to Mount of Olives. After Jesus had said
this, they all rose. Our Saviour took His Mother by the
hand and placed her in the midst of the apostles, saying
to them: "My Mother is henceforth to be your Mother.
Love her very much. She will always pray for you."
Then He ordered Peter to come in the midst of the apostles, and said to them: "When I shall have ascended into
heaven, Peter shall be your chief; and you must obey
him." Then Jesus said to all: "Come to see Me ascending into heaven."

Where did Jesus lead His apostles? Many of the disciples also went along. On Mount of Olives there were
other disciples waiting for Jesus, for they had heard that
He was about to leave the earth. At the foot of the
mountain there were shade trees. In this cool place Jesus
sat down on the grass for a while with the apostles and
conversed with them. The people of Jerusalem had heard

that Jesus was about to leave the earth. When they saw that a number of persons had gathered together on Mount of Olives, they set out in crowds for the Mount. When it was near noon, Jesus stood up with His disciples and went up the Mount with them. The apostles, Mary and the holy women were with Jesus, and people from all sides followed, as in a procession. Whilst going up the Mount, our Saviour's face and body began to shine. He walked always faster and faster, as if He was trying to get away from the apostles.

The last blessing. When Jesus reached the top of Mount of Olives, Jesus was gloriously bright. All stood around Him in a circle. The holy souls of Limbo were also there; but they were invisible and could not be seen. It was noon. Jesus was shining as brightly as the sun, but in various colors, like a grand rainbow. Now Jesus looked once more with infinite love on His Mother, on the apostles, on all present. Now He was going to give them His last blessing. What do we do when the priest gives us his blessing? We kneel down, and make the sign of the cross. Thus did Mary, the apostles and all present. And what did our Saviour do? He turned around towards all, and blessed them and the whole world.

The Ascension. And what happened to our Saviour whilst He was giving His blessing? He was lifted up from the ground. He made Himself light, and His feet left the earth and He rose upward towards heaven. The eyes of all followed Him. Bright and shining He went up higher and higher. Now He is almost up to the clouds. Then there comes a bright cloud from heaven, shining like the sun; but Jesus is still brighter. He enters that cloud, just as if one sun would enter another sun. The souls of Limbo ascended invisibly upward with our Saviour and also entered the bright cloud. When Jesus had reached the top of that cloud, He could no longer be seen from the ground. But others saw Him: the angels.

They looked down from heaven and saw Jesus standing on the cloud. But He soon leaves the cloud and ascends higher and higher. Now the clouds are far below Him. Now He is as high up as the stars, and He still continues to go higher and higher until the stars are far below Him, and He has reached the gate of heaven.

The entry into heaven. Now a voice in heaven is heard saying: "Open the eternal gates of heaven! Open them wide, for the King of glory is about to make His entry into heaven." And now, children, for the first time since the sin of our first parents, the gate of heaven was opened, and the Redeemer of mankind, followed by the countless souls from Limbo, made His glorious entry into heaven. It was a long and grand procession. The angels came to meet our Saviour, singing: "Alleluia, praise the Lord who ascends over the heaven of heavens." And the multitude of the souls from Limbo, who accompanied Jesus, sang: "We rejoiced, when we were told, that we shall go into the house of the Lord. Better is one day in Thy house, O Lord, than a thousand other days." Our Saviour went through heaven, always higher and higher, above all the angels and archangels, and higher till up to the throne of God.

Jesus sits at the right hand of God the Father. There the Father and the Holy Ghost rose from their throne to meet our Saviour. The Father took Him by the hand, looking at Him with unspeakable love, and said to Him: "Because Thou wast obedient to Me unto the death of the cross, now Thou shalt be higher than every one else. Be seated on My throne at My right hand, and rule over the whole world. Every knee shall bend to Thee in heaven and on earth, and all the angels shall adore Thee." At these words all the angels and all the souls in heaven prostrated themselves on their faces and adored our Saviour. He is now seated on the throne at the right hand of God the Father almighty, and rules and governs the whole creation together with the Father and the Holy Ghost forever and ever. What place does our Saviour hold in heaven?

The apparition of the angels. The apostles were still on Mount of Olives. When they saw Jesus rising upwards from the ground, they knelt down in great astonishment. And how did they again venerate our Saviour? What did they do whilst Jesus was ascending heavenward? How long did they gaze at Him? How was He hidden from their view? And even when they could no longer see Him, they kept on looking upward. Who suddenly appeared near them? They came from heaven. How were they clothed? What did they say to the apostles? Why did they say " Men of Galilee "? What question did they ask the apostles? What would you have answered, if you had been there? The apostles probably said the same. What did the angels tell the apostles about Jesus who had just ascended into heaven? Who knows when that will be? The angels then disappeared. The apostles and the crowds remained a good while longer on Mount of Olives, speaking about the Saviour's Ascension.

The return of the apostles. Where did the apostles go after leaving Mount of Olives? We would now naturally think that the apostles grieved and wept, because our Saviour had left them. But no; they returned to Jerusalem full of joy. They had never before seen anything so glorious; and they never forgot it so long as they lived.

EXPLANATION — *Christ ascended into heaven in soul and in body.* If our soul is perfectly pure when we die, it will go straight to heaven. What will be done to our body? What will happen to our body in the grave? What happened to the body of Jesus on the third day after His burial? How did His body become alive again? From that moment His body and His soul remained always united together. And, therefore, Jesus ascended in body and in soul into heaven. After our death which part of us will go to heaven? But how was it with Jesus when He ascended into heaven? How long was it after His resurrection? What feast does the Church celebrate in honor of our Saviour's ascension into heaven.

APPLICATION. Now it is a pleasure for Jesus to be the Redeemer of men. Now He can rest after His labors and sufferings. The wicked Jews can no longer do Him any harm. No enemy can reach Him on His throne. The gate of heaven is now wide open day and night, and every day many holy souls enter it. They all place themselves around His throne. It looks like thousands of wreaths of angels and saints around Him. The saints take off their golden crowns, kneel down, thank our divine Saviour and adore Him. Our Saviour is seated on His beautiful throne. He alone is seated. He is raised above all. He is the Lord of all. How far different is it now from what it was on Good Friday, when Jesus died on the cross! On Good Friday the people in church are sad; many weep. Why? But now we should rejoice the more, because Jesus in heaven is raised above all.

You are destined to go to Jesus in heaven. What has He prepared there? You are to be, as well as the angels and saints, near Jesus forever in heaven. How greatly you should rejoice at this thought! But to go to heaven, you must do like Jesus. He had to deserve His place in heaven. What did the Father say to Him when He led Him to His throne? How did Jesus deserve so high a place? All through obedience. You must, therefore, be obedient like Jesus. When your parents command you to do something, you must do it, even if you would rather go and play. When the food is not to your liking, think: "Like Jesus, I will accept what is bitter and disagreeable." When the teacher gives you a hard lesson, you must cheerfully do your best to learn it well. In this manner you will deserve a high place in heaven.

A certain mother used to call up her boys every morning, saying: "Boys, get up; life is short, you have but little time to deserve heaven. Every minute you oversleep yourselves, you could have employed well to gain greater happiness in heaven. Therefore get up quickly, and go and assist at holy Mass." Dear children, when your mother calls you in the morning, obey at once and get up, dress, say your morning prayers, and go to hear Mass. If you promptly obey your parents and superiors you will surely gain a high place in heaven.

40. The Holy Ghost descends upon the Apostles.

PREPARATION. With what were the apostles to be endowed after our Saviour's Ascension? Whom did Jesus promise He would send them from heaven for this purpose? Where should the apostles remain until then? What should they do?

OBJECT. I will now relate to you how the Holy Ghost came down from the apostles.

RELATION. In Jerusalem the apostles went to the hall where they usually stayed in that city. There they all remained in prayer, and there were with them the Mother of Jesus and other disciples. There were about one hundred and twenty persons in all. On the tenth day there suddenly came a sound from heaven as of a mighty wind, and it filled the whole house where they were assembled. Tongues as of fire appeared and rested on each of them. And they were all filled with the Holy Ghost, and they began to speak in diverse tongues. When the people of Jerusalem heard that great sound, they hastened in great numbers to the house where the apostles were. St. Peter came out, and preached to them that Jesus had risen from the dead, and was now seated in heaven at the right hand of God. Many believed and were baptized. About three thousand persons were admitted into the Church on that day.

EXPLANATION — *Waiting for the coming of the Holy*

Ghost. Where had the apostles returned after the Ascension of Jesus? Where did they stay in Jerusalem? Who were with the apostles? How many were there in all? They were in that large room, or hall, as in a church. What did they do there? Spent the time in prayer. In this manner they remained together for ten days. The tenth day was a Sunday. On this day the Jews celebrated a great feast, Pentecost. On this day Jews from every country came to pray in the temple. Was there any other feast when the Jews had to come to pray in the temple of Jerusalem? The immense temple was filled with people, and the streets were crowded.

The mighty wind. What came up suddenly in Jerusalem on the tenth day? What was the sound like? But this sound was not over the whole city, but only at and around the house where the apostles were assembled. The sound from heaven came always nearer and nearer, till it was all around the house, and at last it entered and filled the house.

The tongues as of fire. Another wonderful thing took place. The room in which the apostles were, became suddenly all bright. What was seen there? They came there suddenly. No one knew where they came from. Therefore we say that they appeared. They were first seen on the ceiling; then they were seen coming down slowly. Where did they place themselves? Over each apostle one fiery tongue placed itself and remained suspended over him. Look at the picture of the descent of the Holy Ghost. Who is sitting in the midst of the apostles? What do you see over the head of the Blessed Virgin? Also there is one over the head of each apostle. These tongues were not of real fire, and therefore did not burn the apostles.

The filling with the Holy Ghost. The Holy Ghost was in the fiery tongue. When the fiery tongues placed themselves over the apostles, the Holy Ghost invisibly came into the apostles by descending from their heads to their hearts, until they were all filled with Him. When a vase is filled with water, we say that it is full of water. With what were the apostles filled? The Holy Ghost descended also on all the disciples present.

The miracle of tongues. How could the people hear that the Holy Ghost had come down upon the apostles? Before that day the apostles could speak and understand only one language — the Jewish language. You yourselves understand and speak only one language. Which is it? In church we hear the priest and the altar boys praying in another language. Which is it? The Latin. Do you understand it? You sometimes hear Germans, Italians, etc., speak. What language do they speak? Almost every country has its own language different from all other languages. If you wish to learn the language of another country, you must study it even for many years. Some persons find it very hard, and even impossible to do so. But after receiving the Holy Ghost, the apostles could understand and speak not only the Jewish language, but also every language in the world, without having studied them. How could this be? The Holy Ghost taught them all at once. That was a great miracle.

The apostles go forth to preach. What did the people of Jerusalem do when they heard that mighty sound? They hastened to the house in which the apostles were, and remained in front of it. They wished to see what had happened there. The door of the house was soon opened, and all the apostles came out. How wonderful! Before this the apostles were so full of fear, that they always kept the door locked for fear of the Jews. Now they no longer feared the Jews.

St. Peter's sermon. St. Peter came forth and preached. What did he preach about? He said to the Jews: " You committed a great sin, when you crucified Jesus. He is the Son of God and the Redeemer. He is risen again from the dead, and has ascended into heaven. There He is seated at the right hand of God. To-day He sent down the Holy Ghost upon us. Be now sorry for your sins, and receive baptism." Among those who heard St. Peter preach there were many strangers from Egypt, Rome, and every country in the world. There were many thousands of people present at his sermon. Why were there so many strangers in Jerusalem? Now think a moment: if there were here, besides yourselves, Germans, Frenchmen, Italians, Chinese, Japanese, who could not understand a word of English, could they now understand every word I say to you? Not at all. But St. Peter's sermon in the Jewish language was understood by Egyptians, Romans, Greeks, Gauls, etc., who did not know a word of Jewish! Who caused this great wonder?

The effect of the sermon. All had listened attentively to St. Peter's sermon and understood it. What was the effect of the sermon? Three thousand persons believed in Jesus Christ and were baptized. These persons were called Christians. Why? Because they became disciples or followers of Jesus Christ. Who were the very first that believed in Jesus Christ? The apostles and disciples who followed Him whilst He was still on earth.

The Church of Jesus. All the Christians together are called the Church of Christ. His Church was small in the beginning. Who first belonged to it? The apostles, disciples and the holy women. And when were there new Christians? How many? There were more than three thousand persons who heard St. Peter's sermon. Why did not all of them become Christians? Because only three thousand believed in Jesus Christ and were baptized. How are people received into the Church? By baptism. How do people go into your house? By the door. How do people enter the Church of Christ? By baptism. Baptism is the door of the Church of Christ. How many were baptized on Pentecost and entered the Church of Christ? When they were baptized, they also received the Holy Ghost.

EXPLANATION — *The enlightening.* The Holy Ghost is like a light. Of what use is a light? It shines and enlightens things. The Holy Ghost shone in the souls of the apostles and enlightened them. After this the apostles understood much better than before what Jesus had done and taught, and clearly remembered what they had already forgotten.

The strengthening. The apostles had to know well all that our Saviour had done and taught, because they had to preach it all over the world. But the apostles had always been afraid of the Jews. How did they act after the Holy Ghost had come upon them? They opened the door and came out to preach publicly. And what did St. Peter do? He reproached the Jews for the great sin they had committed in crucifying the Redeemer, the Son of God. St. Peter no longer had any fear of the Jews. He and the other apostles were full of courage, for the Holy Ghost had endowed them with strength and fortitude; He had strengthened them. How had Jesus foretold this to the apostles? What effects did the Holy Ghost produce in the apostles? He enlightened and strengthened them, and enabled them to speak in different languages.

The Holy Ghost is sent to the Church. How do we call those who received the Holy Ghost on Pentecost? Christians. And, taken all together, what did they form? The Church of Jesus Christ. Therefore we can say also: The Holy Ghost came down upon the Church of Christ. In remembrance of the descent of the Holy Ghost, we celebrate the feast of Pentecost, ten days after the Ascension of Jesus into heaven. How many days after Easter is the Ascension? How many days after Easter is Pentecost?

The Holy Ghost comes to us also in baptism. The Holy Ghost descended not only into the souls of the first Christians, but also into your soul and heart when you were baptized. In whose image and likeness was your soul created? Your soul is an image of God. When you were born, your soul was not pure and beautiful. There was a sin in it. Which sin? Original sin. That sin defiled the image of God in your soul, and made it ugly. God could not then be pleased with your soul. If you had died so, you could not have gone to heaven. Therefore, when you were a little baby, you were brought to the church. For what? And when you were baptized, the Holy Ghost came invisibly into your soul, and washed away from it original sin. Your soul then became so clean and pure that there was not even the slightest stain in it. And then the image of God in your soul became perfectly pure and beautiful. And the Holy Ghost gave your soul a snow-white garment. This garment made your soul holy. How do you call it? The holy garment of sanctifying grace. Your soul then became as beautiful as a little angel. And if you had died then, your soul would have flown directly to God in heaven, and people would have said: " That child is now a beautiful little angel." And at your funeral they would have said: " That is the body of an angel." And your brothers and sisters, and also your parents could have prayed to you as they now pray to the angels and saints in heaven. Who came down into your soul at baptism? What did the Holy Ghost remove from your soul? And what did He bring to your soul? The garment of sanctifying grace, more precious than all the riches of the world. What did it make your soul? Holy. The Holy Ghost made you holy; He sanctified you. Each of the three Divine Persons has benefited you. What benefit has the Father bestowed on you? What benefit has the Son conferred on you? And what has the Holy Ghost done for you? He sanctified you.

The Holy Ghost dwells in the soul. After your baptism, the Holy Ghost remained and dwelt in your soul. How do you call the house in which God dwells? God's house, a church. And what has your soul, your heart, become since the Holy Ghost dwells therein? A house of God, a church, a temple of the Holy Ghost. Sometimes some relatives or friends come to spend a few days at your house. They are called your guests. They usually bring some present for you. In like manner, the Holy Ghost has come to stay in your soul. He brought something for your soul. What has He brought? Therefore you can call Him the guest of your soul.

Mortal sin drives away the Holy Ghost. The Holy Ghost wishes to remain always in your soul. But He can dwell only in a pure and holy soul. That is why He is called the Holy Ghost. So long as Judas was good and pious, the Holy Ghost dwelt in his soul. But when Judas committed a grievous sin, the Holy Ghost left his soul and with Him the garment of grace went away also. And then the devil entered his soul, his heart. The same happens to other men. When does the Holy Ghost leave the soul? How long does the Holy Ghost remain in the soul?

SUMMARY. The Holy Ghost is the Third Person of the Blessed Trinity. He is true God like the Father and the Son. He was sent to the Church on Pentecost. The Holy Ghost came into our soul already at our baptism, and remains in our soul as long as we keep free from mortal sin.

APPLICATION. Suppose you had suddenly become children of a monarch, of a millionaire? How happy would you feel? But since you received in baptism from the Holy Ghost the holy garment of grace, you are more noble, more rich than the children of a monarch, of a millionaire, for you are children of God. Should not this fill you with joy? But be very careful to remain children of God, and do not lose the garment of grace. How could you lose it? By committing a mortal sin, for instance. Rather die than commit a mortal sin. Children are anxious to be beautiful and rich. With the garment of grace our soul is as beautiful as an angel and much richer than any monarch or millionaire. If you are good, the Holy Ghost will make you every day more and more beautiful and rich. Therefore He enlightens you with the light of His grace. Then He inspires you to do good; for instance, He suggests to you to say: " I will pray; I will be devout in church; I will cheerfully obey; I will study diligently; I will be modest." It is the Holy Ghost that sends to you all these good thoughts. Before the sermon, before the instruction we recite a prayer to the Holy Ghost. Then He enlightens us that we may better understand and remember the sermon and the instruction, or the word of God. The Catechism also is the word of God. The Holy Ghost helps you at the instruction in Catechism to understand it better. When you find the Catechism lesson hard to learn, stop awhile and say an Our Father to the Holy Ghost; and then take a new start in studying it, and you will learn it more easily.

When you feel inclined or tempted to do anything bad, for instance, to disobey, to tell lies, to steal, say: " Help me, O Holy Ghost, to avoid that sin." And the Holy Ghost will give you the strength to overcome your evil inclination and avoid that sin.

There are some children who are happy to obey always punctually. They find nothing too much or too hard. Do you know who makes them so willing to obey? It is the Holy Ghost. He strengthens them. And when the Holy Ghost makes a person strong, he finds everything easy and pleasant. And everything a good child does is precious in the sight of God.

On the roof of some churches there are gilt stars. When the sun shines on them, they shine and twinkle like the stars in the heavens. But if the sun does not shine on them, they can hardly be seen. What makes those stars so beautiful? The sun. The Holy Ghost in your heart is also a sun. All you do becomes gilt and bright by His light, and is pleasing to God. And the heavenly wings of your soul grow always more and more. But if the Holy Ghost is not in your heart, all the good you then do, is almost nothing in the sight of God, and heavenly wings are wanting to you. Without the Holy Ghost you can do nothing to deserve heaven.

You now see how much the Holy Ghost benefits you. Is He not a dear sweet guest in your soul? Often pray devoutly to the Holy Ghost, and ask Him often to come to you and enrich you with His grace. Say to Him: "O Holy Ghost, my sweet Guest, who possessest all graces, come to enlighten and strengthen me, and help me to understand the word of God, and cheerfully to fulfil all His commands."

41. The Catholic Church.

CONNECTION. The last time I gave you an explanation of the Church. You know that Jesus preached for three years among the Jews, and that many believed in Him. How were those called who believed in Him? Christians. What did all the Christians together constitute? The Church of Jesus Christ. By the Church of Jesus Christ we do not mean a stone or frame building into which we go to pray. When people see you going together to church, they say: "Here comes the school." They do not mean the school-house, where the teacher teaches, and the children learn and recite their lessons. What do they mean? And when something was said in school, people say: "The whole school laughed." They do not mean that the school building or the school-room laughed. And when we say or speak about the Church of Christ, we do not mean the church building. What, then, do we mean by the Church?

OBJECT. By degrees the number of Christians increased and the Church grew larger, as I will tell you to-day.

DEVELOPMENT — *Spreading of the Church after Pentecost.* Our divine Saviour wished that all men should belong to the Church. Therefore, shortly before ascending to heaven, He said to His apostles: "Go into the whole world and teach all nations, baptizing them in the name of the Father, and of the Son, and of the Holy Ghost." What did Jesus command His apostles? But men spoke many different languages in the world. What did Jesus do to enable all men to understand the apostles? When did the apostles begin to preach? Who preached the first sermon? What was the effect of his sermon? Because they believed in Jesus Christ they were called Christians, or faithful, because they were faithful in believing and becoming Christians. How many new Christians were there on Pentecost? To what did they belong? To the Church.

Just as St. Peter preached on Pentecost, so did the other apostles preach afterwards. They first preached in the Jewish country. The chief Jews did not like it, and therefore they persecuted the apostles as they had persecuted Jesus. They put the apostles in prison and scourged them; but this did not stop their preaching; they preferred to die rather than disobey Jesus. Who gave the apostles such great courage and strength? The apostles also proved the truth of what they preached about Jesus. Soon after Pentecost Peter saw a beggar who was a cripple lying down near one of the gates of the temple. St. Peter took him by the hand, and said: " In the name of Jesus of Nazareth arise and walk." The cripple immediately jumped up, and was able to walk. What did St. Peter do by this? He performed a miracle. Who is alone able to work a miracle? God; Jesus as God. What did St. Peter say when he cured that cripple? The people therefore knew that a miracle had been performed through Jesus, and many believed in Him, five thousand men, besides the women and children.

But the apostles did not all remain in Judea. Where did they afterwards go to preach Jesus Christ and His doctrine? All over the world. One went to Egypt, another to Persia, another to Rome; and so they went to every country. They preached wherever they went, and everywhere many became Christians, and the number of Christians kept on increasing. Jews and pagans, rich and poor, even princes and kings believed in Jesus Christ and were baptized. To what did they all belong? Thus the Church of Christ spread always into more and more countries.

The Christians, a family. All the members of the Church clung together and loved one another very much, just as it is with you at home. The father and mother and the children all belong together and love one another. And when any member of the family goes elsewhere, do you not love him still? Does he not still belong to the family? How do you show your love to the absent ones? By writing, sending little presents as tokens of love. You are all but one family. In like manner, all the Christians belonged together and loved and helped one another. They formed one large family. They did not all live together at Jerusalem. Where else were there Christians? In Egypt, in Greece, in Rome, in every country. They formed an immense family, the Church of Christ.

The Pope, the head of the Church. In every family there must be one at the head who commands and cares for all. Who is it? The father. The father is the head of the family. The Church, a very large family, must have a head. This head is also a father, our Holy Father, the Pope. All the Catholics in the world love and obey him and call him Holy Father, or the Pope. Who is the head of the Church? The Pope.

St. Peter, the first head of the Church, the first Pastor or Pope. St. Peter was the first Holy Father or Pope. Who made him head of the Church? One day Jesus asked St. Peter: "Dost thou love Me?" St. Peter answered: "Lord, Thou knowest that I love Thee." Then Jesus said to him: "Feed My lambs; feed My sheep." What a great meaning in these words! What do you call a man who takes care of sheep and lambs? A shepherd, or a pastor. What did Jesus order St. Peter to do? To feed the lambs and sheep belonging to Jesus. What, then, did

He make St. Peter? A shepherd, or pastor. But the
sheep and lambs of Jesus were not ordinary sheep and
lambs, but all Christians, that is, all the men, women and
children who believed in Jesus and were baptized; these
formed the flock, or the Church of Christ. But the sheep
of Christ's flock, or Church, are not all close together as
sheep and lambs in a flock. They are scattered over the
whole world, in every country, city, town, etc. And St.
Peter was ordered by Jesus to feed them all, to care for
them, to be their shepherd, their pastor. St. Peter was,
therefore, the first head of the Church, or Pope.

The apostles were also all shepherds. But St. Peter could
not care all alone for the immense flock of Jesus. It
needed many shepherds, shepherds in every country and
place. Jesus knew this; therefore, He made the other
apostles shepherds also, as helpers of St. Peter. Each
apostle was to care for a part of the flock, but they all had
to obey St. Peter, the head-shepherd.

Bishops, the successors of the apostles. But St. Peter
and the other apostles did not live always; they all died
in the course of time. To take their places after their
death, the apostles chose and ordained other pious men as
bishops, or shepherds, for this was the will of Jesus Christ.
And these bishops succeeded the apostles after their death.
When a bishop died, another was chosen in his place, and
this has continued until now and will continue as long as
the Church of Christ lasts, and that will be until the end
of the world. There are now even more than one thousand bishops in the world. (Name some cities where bishops reside.)

The Bishop of Rome. Before his death St. Peter lived
in Rome. The bishop who succeeded him, lived also in
Rome; and all his successors lived also in Rome. The
Bishop of Rome is the successor of St. Peter. What was
St. Peter to the whole Church of Jesus Christ? Her head.
The Bishop of Rome has always been the head of the

Church. How is he called? There have been already over
two hundred and sixty Popes.

Priests, the assistants of the bishops. Because the Pope
and the bishops are the successors of the apostles, they
must do what the apostles did. What did Jesus command
the apostles to do? To teach men what He had taught
and baptize those who believed. They have also to say
Mass, to hear confessions, administer the sacraments, etc.
But some bishops have to care for several hundred thousand Christians, scattered in cities, towns, etc. The bishop
cannot alone care for all, hear the confessions of all, baptize all the children, say Mass for all, preach to and instruct
all, prepare all the dying for a good death, etc. He needs
a great deal of help. Who preaches, says Mass for you,
instructs you, etc.? The pastor; his assistant. The bishop
ordains priests and sends them as his help in the parishes
of his diocese. Therefore there are several hundred thousand priests in the world helping the bishops to care for
their share of the flock of Jesus Christ.

The Catholic Church founded by Jesus Christ. Which
bishop is the head of the Church? Who was the first head
of the Church? Who is the successor of St. Peter? Who
are the successors of the other apostles? Who help the bishops in caring for the souls of the faithful? Who willed that
St. Peter and the other apostles should have successors?
Jesus willed also that priests should help the bishops in
caring for souls. Who wills that the Church should be
as it is now? In other words, who founded the Church?
The Church in which the Pope is the head, is called the
Catholic Church, and all the Christians who belong to it,
are called Catholics. Who belong to the Church of Christ?
Catholics. You are also Catholics. How did you become
Catholics?

APPLICATION — *Society of the Holy Childhood.* It is a
great happiness to belong to the Catholic Church. I will
tell you how you can thank God for it. In Asia, in China

there are many millions of pagan children. They are not baptized. They do not belong to the Catholic Church; if they die thus, they cannot go to heaven. And many die thus. The parents often throw their new-born babies into the streets, or into rivers, or into the woods, where they die of hunger, or cold, are drowned or are eaten up by animals. Would you be willing to help to have these children baptized and become Catholics like yourselves? You can help a little. How? By saying daily a Hail Mary that God may grant that those children should be baptized, and giving every month one cent to save these poor little children. The money is sent to pious priests in those countries. They baptize them, save their life, feed and clothe them, bring them up as Catholic children, just as you yourselves are brought up and taught to serve God and save your soul. Sometimes those pious priests buy those children from their parents, and bring them up as good Catholic children. The more money sent to these priests, the more pagan children they can baptize and make good Catholics of them. There are thousands of Catholic children, like yourselves, who daily say a Hail Mary and give one cent every month for those pagan children. They do this in honor of the Holy Child Jesus, and they form a society called Society of the Holy Childhood. What must the members of that society do every day? Every month?

42. The End of the Catholic Church. The Communion of Saints. The Forgiveness of Sins.

OBJECT. I will now show you how great a happiness it is to be a member of the Catholic Church.

DEVELOPMENT — *The shepherds, or pastors lead.* All Catholics together form the Church or flock of Christ. During His life Jesus Himself was the shepherd. He once said of Himself: " I am the Good Shepherd." When Jesus returned to heaven, He did not wish to leave His flock without a shepherd. Whom did Jesus, before ascending into heaven, appoint as the head shepherd of His flock? What did He say to St. Peter? " Feed My lambs, feed My sheep." What did He appoint His apostles to be? Shepherds.

The flock of Jesus is very great. There are now over three hundred millions of Catholics in the world. Who is now the head shepherd of this great flock? The Pope. (Give his name.) That large flock is now divided into more than one thousand smaller flocks. The bishops are the shepherds of these flocks. The flocks of the bishops are still very large; they average one hundred thousand each. Each bishop cannot care by himself for his whole flock. By whom are the bishops helped? By the priests. Each bishop has, on an average, over one hundred priests to help him. The priests also are shepherds, or pastors. I am the pastor or shepherd of   Rev. Father is pastor of   So it is all over the world. Every parish has its shepherd, or pastor. Where does the pastor lead his flock?

The flock follows, obeys. Some of you have perhaps already seen a flock of sheep going somewhere. Where is the shepherd? In front; and the sheep follow him whereever he goes. How beautiful! In like manner, the Rev. pastors lead their flocks to the pastures. The bishop goes ahead, and his priests follow him, each one leading his own little flock. And who is at the head of the whole flock of Jesus Christ? The Pope. Why? Because he is the head-shepherd of the whole flock, and the whole flock follows him.

The end or object of the whole flock and of the head-shepherd is heaven. Do you know where the Pope is leading the flock of Jesus Christ? To heaven. Towards heaven the Pope directs his steps. The sheep in every little flock look to their shepherd or pastor in front; and

THE CATHOLIC CHURCH 211

these shepherds look to the shepherd ahead of them, the bishop; and all the bishops look to and follow the Pope at the head of all of them; and the Pope looks to heaven and walks in the road leading there, and all follow him in that direction.

The Church leads us on the right road. If the Pope would not lead the immense flock of Jesus Christ on the right road, the whole flock would not reach heaven. But the Pope knows the way to heaven. Our divine Saviour showed the way to His apostles. It is true that the apostles did not always understand well what Jesus said, and that they forgot much of it; but later on they remembered and understood all. How? The Holy Ghost enlightened them on Pentecost.

The Holy Ghost directs the Church. Since Pentecost the Holy Ghost has always remained with the Church. He is still with her and enlightens the Pope and the bishops. Therefore the Pope and the bishops now know the way to heaven as well as the apostles did; and they now teach the very same things which Jesus commanded the apostles to teach. Who help the bishops in the care of souls? The priests. The bishop tells his priests what they must teach to their flocks, and the priests teach nothing else than what their bishop teaches; and the bishops teach only what the Pope teaches. Therefore all is true that is taught in the whole Church, and the Church cannot lead us on a wrong road, but leads us always right. Who takes care that the Church should always lead us right? The Holy Ghost. When did Jesus send the Holy Ghost to His Church? Jesus Christ sent the Holy Ghost to His Church on Pentecost.

We must obey the Church. Where will the Church lead us? To heaven. She goes in front. And what must we do, if we wish to go to heaven? If we wish to go to heaven we must follow, that is, obey the Church. To be saved means to go to heaven. What must we do to be saved? If we wish to be saved, we must always obey the Church.

In the Church we receive the forgiveness of our sins. A sheep that does not follow the shepherd, will get always further and further away from the flock, and at last it will no longer see the flock. It does not know then where to go; it runs about in every direction, and gets at last entangled in briars and thorns; and if the shepherd does not come to free it from the briars and thorns, the poor sheep perishes. So it is with the Catholics who do not follow (obey) the Church. They go astray and get entangled in sins, perhaps in mortal sins, and if there were no one to loosen them, they could never go to heaven. But the Church can come and loosen those sheep of hers from their sins. The sheep help along, for they confess their sins to the priest. And then the priest loosens them from their sins, that is, he forgives their sins. What must we do to have our sins forgiven? Each of you have already been forgiven a sin. Which sin was it? Original sin. When was it forgiven you? It is only in the Catholic Church that sins can be forgiven. Therefore we say in the Apostles' Creed: "I believe in the forgiveness of sins." He whose sins are forgiven, can again go to heaven.

Object of the Church. No one is able to find heaven by himself. Who leads us on the right road to heaven? The Church; for it was for this purpose that Jesus founded His Church. Jesus established His Church to lead men by the right road to heaven, to eternal salvation. To what must all men belong, in order to be saved? Therefore Jesus said to His apostles: "Go into the whole world and preach to all nations," etc., etc.

The Catholics, or the Christian faithful on earth. When, in a family, the father earns some money, the mother and the children derive profit from it. And when one of the children earns money, his brothers and sisters and parents share in it. And in the great family of the Catholic Church when a member gains some merit, all the other members share in it. Many of the faithful are pious and holy and do much good. For this they deserve a great reward from God. They do not keep it all for themselves. You and all other Catholics share in it. A girl that goes to the convent, and becomes a Sister, deserves great reward from God. All the faithful share in it. When the Pope, the bishops and priests say Mass, they pray for all the faithful. And as at home the parents pray for the children, and the children for the parents, so all the faithful pray for one another.

The suffering souls in purgatory. When one of the faithful dies in the state of grace, he may not go directly to heaven. Why? Because he may not be perfectly pure at his death; perhaps his soul is then stained with some venial sins. His soul must be entirely purified, before it can enter heaven; therefore it is sent to purgatory, where it will have to suffer until it is perfectly pure. There are many, many souls in purgatory. They must suffer much; they cannot help themselves. Therefore we call them the suffering souls, the poor souls. These souls still belong to us. They are our brothers and sisters of the great Catholic family. In purgatory they think of us, and cry out to us: "Oh, help us! Please help us." And we can help them. How?

The souls in heaven. Where do the souls in purgatory go when they are perfectly pure? The souls that are perfectly pure at death, go directly to heaven. There they see and enjoy God, and are perfectly happy. They are the "blessed" in heaven. There are probably members of your family already in heaven; for instance, your grandparents, a child that died soon after its baptism, etc. Although they are already dead and in heaven, they still belong to your family. They think of you and pray for you. All the souls in heaven belong to the great Catholic family. They think of us, love us and pray for us.

The Communion of saints. Who still belong to the great Catholic family on earth? The souls in purgatory and the souls in heaven. The faithful on earth, the souls in purgatory and the souls in heaven form a society which is called the Communion of saints. The souls in heaven are already holy or saints. The souls in purgatory have the garment of sanctifying grace, and will soon be perfectly holy. The Catholics on earth have been sanctified in baptism, and should daily become more and more holy, for they are destined to be saints in heaven. Therefore the society of the saints in heaven, of the souls in purgatory and of the faithful on earth is called the Communion of saints.

SUMMARY. Who belong to the Communion of saints? What must we do to be saved? Who takes care that the Church will lead us by the right road to heaven? For what purpose did Jesus Christ establish His Church?

APPLICATION. 1. The saints in heaven are willing to help us, that we may succeed in saving our soul on earth and may join them in heaven. Therefore they pray for us, and when we ask God for something, they pray to God to give it to us, that is, they intercede for us. God willingly grants us what the saints beg Him to give us. Let us love to pray to the saints in heaven, and especially to the Blessed Virgin and St. Joseph. They are our patrons. We should, then, pray daily to them. Each of you has a special patron, whose name you bear. What is the name of your patron? Of yours? A good child prays daily to his patron. Often say: " My holy Patron, St. ...., pray for me; protect me." 2. Just as the saints in heaven willingly help us, so should we help the souls in purgatory. Let us often pray for them, saying: " Eternal rest give unto them, O Lord, and let perpetual light shine upon them. May they rest in peace. Amen." Pray especially for the souls of the members of your family, of your benefactors, etc. You now see how all in the Catholic Church help one another to be saved. How happy it should make you, and how grateful to God you should be for it!

43. The Resurrection of the Body and Life everlasting. Amen.

PREPARATION. What becomes of man's body after death? The grave is, indeed, a small, narrow bed. Your bed at home is warm and soft. In it you sleep well and soundly. Children often sleep so soundly, that they do not wish to get awake. What does your mother then do? She awakens you. And then what do you do?

No one is warm and comfortable in the grave; it is a cold, hard and heavy bed. How is it covered? With earth. The dead in the grave sleep continually day and night, summer and winter, and so soundly that there is no awaking them. But the time shall come, when all the dead shall again awake, at the resurrection of the dead.

OBJECT. I will now tell you who will again awake the dead.

RELATION. At the end of the world the sun will be darkened, the moon will give no more light, and the stars will fall from the heavens. Then our Saviour will send His angels, and they will sound their trumpets all over the earth, saying: "Arise, ye dead; and come to judgment." The angels will sound their trumpets so loudly, as to awaken the dead in their graves. And behold! in a moment the dead shall get alive again and come out of their graves. The bodies of the good shall be wonderfully bright and beautiful; but the bodies of the wicked shall be gloomy and horrible. That will be the resurrection of the dead.

EXPLANATION — *The last day.* What will happen to the sun, moon and stars at the end of the world? There will not be any more sun. What begins when the sun rises? The day. And when is the day over? When the sun sets. And when shall the sun not rise any more? How do you call that day on which the sun will rise for the last time at the end of the world? The last day.

The resurrection of the dead. The bodies of the dead will sleep in their graves until the last day. How long then will the bodies of the dead remain in the ground? Until the last day. What shall then happen with all the dead? They shall rise again. What does your mother do to make you get up in the morning? How will the dead be awakened? Our Saviour will awaken the dead. Whom will He send on earth to do this? The angels seated on a hurricane; they will ride quickly all over the world. What will they do at the same time? Blow their trumpets. How powerful will be the sound of their trumpets? Then there will be a stir in every grave. The bones of each dead body come together, flesh grows at once over them, and skin immediately covers the flesh. Each person gets his own bones, flesh, skin, etc., no matter how long before his body rotted and fell to pieces, or how the wind scattered the dust into which the body had fallen. God knows how to bring all together again.

But the soul is still wanting to that body. Where does the soul go after death? The soul is not buried in the grave with the body. How did the body of Jesus get alive again? In like manner it will be with us. God places the soul again into the body, and makes the body and soul one again; that is, He again unites the body and soul together. And now the body gets alive again and comes out of the grave. In this manner all men shall rise again on the last day. Rich and poor, kings and beggars, children and grown up persons, all shall rise at once together. Therefore the last day is called also the day of the general resurrection.

When Jesus was on earth, He raised three dead persons

to life: Lazarus, a young man and a girl. Jesus re-united their souls with their bodies. But these three persons died again. What did their souls do, when they died again? They again left their bodies. But when, at the general resurrection, the souls of all men are again united to their bodies, there shall be no more separation. How long, then, shall they remain united? Forever. How long will our bodies remain in the ground? Until the last day. What will God then do to the body? Raise it up. With what will each body be re-united? With its own soul. For how long? Forever. How do we call the general resurrection on the last day? The resurrection of the body. Therefore we say in the Apostles' Creed: "I believe in the resurrection of the body."

The bodies of the good. But how different will the bodies be, when they shall rise again! They will not be all alike. The bodies of the good will come out of their graves beautiful like flowers, like the stars, bright and shining like the sun, splendid like a rainbow. During their life they made good use of their bodies; of their tongue to pray, of their hands to give alms and to work for God, of their feet to obey and go to church. Their bodies were perhaps often sick and in great pain. Now they are rewarded. Their bodies are no longer sick, or feel pain, or die. They will be as bright and transparent as crystal. They will no longer have to walk slowly and wearily on the ground, but as light and as cheerful as birds, they will go up in the air and more quickly from one place to another. Who has had such a body? What did we call the body of Jesus Christ? The bodies of the just (good) shall also be glorified after the general resurrection.

What kind of body will the just have when they shall rise from their graves? In such a glorified body will the soul dwell forever. Suppose a very rich man would present you with a beautiful house grandly furnished and ornamented, and say to you: " In this grand building you may dwell forever." Oh, how happy you would feel! How much more happy will the just be, when they shall have so wonderful and glorious a body for their soul to dwell in forever!

The bodies of the wicked. During their life the wicked abused their bodies to commit sin; their eyes to look at bad things, their tongues to curse and speak indecently, their feet to go with evil companions. When a child does something wrong, for instance, tells a lie, it can be seen in his face. When he is angry or envious, his face shows it clearly, and betrays his guilt. In like manner, all the sins of each wicked person shall be seen as if they were written on his forehead. How horrible the wicked will look! Suppose you would now see a corpse already corrupt and eaten by worms! Merely to think of it disgusts and shocks us. But how much worse and how ugly will the bodies of the wicked be at the general resurrection! What a horrible sight, what a horrible stench will there be! How disgusting will it be for the souls of the wicked to dwell forever in such bodies! Suppose you were shown a hole full of filth and vermin, and were told you would have to live in it! You would surely say: "I would rather die a thousand times than live there!" In like manner, the souls of the wicked would rather die than dwell in such bodies. But they cannot die, and shall have to dwell forever in those horrible bodies!

The bodies of the good and the wicked, when they rise from the dead shall appear in the same state as were their respective souls at the hour of death. The souls of the good at their death were inconceivably beautiful and grand; therefore their bodies at the resurrection will be glorified and wonderfully beautiful! But the souls of the wicked at death were fearfully ugly and hideous; and so shall their bodies also be at the resurrection. The more horrible was the soul at death, also the more horrible shall the body be at the resurrection. (In like manner, the same similarity between the souls and bodies of the just.)

APPLICATION. Now children, what kind of body would you wish yours to be at the general resurrection? If you wish your body to be then beautiful and glorious, you must take care to have a beautiful soul during your life and at your death. Not all children can now be beautiful in body, but every child that wishes it earnestly, can become wonderfully beautiful in soul. How? By taking great care to be punctually obedient, patient in suffering, devout at prayer, pure in thought, word and deed, truthful, honest and charitable towards all. Your body shall then be wonderfully beautiful at the resurrection, and forever remain so.

44. Death; Judgment; Purgatory; Heaven; Hell.

PREPARATION. God said to our first parents: " You shall not eat of the tree in the middle of paradise, or else you shall die." Our first parents broke the commandment of God; and now all men must die.

OBJECT. Let us now see how a man dies.

RELATION. A father of family is about to die. The mother and the children stand around his bed and weep. They light the blessed candle. The dying man is in his agony. There is a cold perspiration all over his body. His hands and feet grow cold. His sight grows dim; he hears the weeping of his wife and children; he hears also the prayers for the departing soul. Soon he can hear no longer. His heart still beats, but slower and slower, weaker and weaker; it stops a moment, and then beats once more; another longer stop; and it beats once more, then comes His last gasp, and his soul has left his body; his heart is still; he is dead.

Soon his corpse is prepared for burial; it is cold and

stiff; it is laid in the coffin. The priest comes and prays over him; then he is brought to the church; and thence to the graveyard, followed by his wife and children, relatives, friends praying for him. Whilst the coffin is laid in the grave the priest prays and blesses the corpse with holy water and incense. The grave is then filled up, and all go home. Now the dead man is alone in his grave, night and day among the dead in their graves. The corpse soon begins to corrupt, and continues to do so until only a handful of dust is left.

EXPLANATION — *The soul leaves the body.* Each of us shall die sooner or later. Relate what happens at death. What happens to the hands and feet? To the eyes and the ears? To the heart? What finally leaves the body? The soul leaves the body. When God created man, the soul was not at first in the body. In what state was the body then? Lifeless. What is the body now without the soul? Dead. At death the body becomes cold and stiff as at the creation of the first man.

The body returns to earth. Where is a dead body brought? What happens to it there? What remains of it? Out of what was the body of the first man made? Of earth. And what becomes of the body in the end? It returns to earth. After death the body returns to that from which it was taken; for it returns to earth. What happens to the soul at death? At death the soul leaves the body, and the body returns to earth.

OBJECT. I will now relate to you what becomes of the soul immediately after death.

DEVELOPMENT. When the soul is breathed out (leaves the body), she looks at herself, and she sees whether she is in the state of grace, or in the state of sin, also whether she is perfectly pure or stained with venial sins.

The judgment. The soul then flies to God. God examines the good and bad deeds of the soul, that is, He judges the soul. Where does the soul go immediately after death? Before God. What does God do with the soul? God judges the soul.

Hell. If a man who has committed a mortal sin dies in it, his soul has no longer sanctifying grace, but is fearfully defiled by sin, and is frightfully ugly. God cannot bear the sight of her. He says: "Depart from Me, into the everlasting fire of hell with the devils." And that soul is at once cast into hell. But not all those who commit mortal sin are cast into hell. Only he who is not sorry for his mortal sin and does not confess it sincerely, shall be cast into hell. He who dies with two mortal sins will be cast deeper into hell, than if he had committed only one. He who dies with even only one mortal sin, shall surely be cast into hell, whether he is rich or poor, young or old, a monarch or a beggar. Who are cast into hell? All who die in mortal sin. This happened to Judas. What enormous sin had he committed? What was the last thing he did? Hanged himself; and that was another grievous sin. Where was he cast?

(When time is wanting, the following in [] may be omitted.)

[God holds a pair of scales in His hand; before Him are two books; one of gold, and the other all black. In these books are written what each man did during his life. In the golden book is written all the good a man has performed: all his good thoughts, all his good words are written in it; none are left out. Also all the good he did, such as: how a child liked to pray, how he was always punctually obedient, always truthful, etc. All this is written in the golden book. But in the black book is written all the evil a man has committed. How many thoughts a child has every day! And some are perhaps not good. When a child has a wilful bad thought, a thought of anger, etc., it is written in the black book. In that book are found also all his bad words, his lies, curses, etc. Every bad word is marked down. In it are found also all the evil things he did, such as: praying without attention, neglect of prayer and study, disobedience, stealing, striking others, missing Mass on Sundays, eating meat on Fridays. All the evil deeds he committed are written in it.

Every sin is to be punished. What is the punishment for a mortal sin? For a venial sin? Also in the black book the punishments a man deserved for each sin is marked down. But if he was sorry for his sins and confessed them, his guardian angel effaced them. You may imagine how large those two books are! They contain all the good and all the evil done by all mankind.

Let us see how God judges a soul. First, a soul that has not the garment of sanctifying grace. There is a large ugly stain on her that makes her look horrible. God opens the golden book, in which it is written that that soul during life went to Mass, prayed and obeyed, etc. Then He looks into the black book, and finds written in it that that soul committed mortal sin, was not sorry for it, did not confess it, and died in it. Now God will show which weighs more, the good she did, or the mortal sin she committed. He places in one end of the scales all the good she did, and in the other end the mortal sin she committed. The end on which the mortal sin is placed is much heavier, for it sinks very deep. Which then weighs more before God, all the good a man did, or one mortal sin which he committed? And therefore God condemns that soul, saying: "Depart from Me into the everlasting fire of hell with the devils." And that soul is at once cast into hell.]

Heaven. When at the hour of death a soul has the garment of sanctifying grace, and comes to be judged by God, God examines her very closely, to see whether she is as bright as the sun and as white as snow that has just fallen. And if she has some stains, or even only one, she cannot yet enter heaven, for nothing defiled can enter there.

Only he who is perfectly pure and free from the slightest stain of sin, can be admitted into heaven immediately after death. Who, then, goes directly to heaven immediately after death? Only he who is perfectly free from all sin. Perhaps such a one committed even many sins. But he confessed them all, and God, like a good father, forgave him, because he was sorry for his sins. But the father sometimes says: " I forgive you, but as a punishment, you shall not go out and play," etc. God acts in like manner. When He forgives a man's sins, He often gives him a punishment for them; sometimes it is some suffering, some sickness, some misfortune, some disappointment. Every one can also impose on himself some penance or punishment for his sin; for instance; to say some prayers, to hear a Mass on a week day, to abstain from eating or drinking between meals, etc. Such punishments last only for a time; they are called temporal punishments. If a man bears such punishments with patience, he will be, sooner or later, free from all punishment for his sins. And then he is fit to enter heaven. To be allowed to enter heaven we must be free from all sin whatever, and also from all punishment due to our sins. So long as we still owe temporal punishment for our sins, we cannot yet enter heaven, although all our sins may have already been forgiven. The Blessed Virgin at her death went straight to heaven, because she had never in her life committed the slightest sin. She had no stain of sin; she had never deserved any temporal punishment; therefore she was perfectly fit to enter heaven immediately after her death.

Purgatory. Now reflect on this: A soul appears before the throne of God; she wears the garment of sanctifying grace; she is very dear to God. But she is not yet free from every sin. There are yet some little stains of sin on her. Where can that soul not go yet? To heaven. But she will not be cast into hell, for she is holy. Where will that soul be sent? To purgatory. Why? Because she is not yet free from every sin. Or else: A soul at death is free from all sin, but not yet from all the temporal punishment which she owes for her forgiven sins. Where can that soul not yet enter? Heaven. She cannot be cast into hell, for she is free from sin. She also is sent to purgatory. And why? Because she has not yet paid all the temporal punishment she owes. Therefore two kinds of souls go to purgatory. Which are they?

What happens to the souls in purgatory? How long must they remain there? Until they are perfectly free from sin and from all temporal punishment due for sin. Then and then only can they be admitted into heaven. That may be a long, long time. And in purgatory they suffer terrible pains. And they cannot help themselves. What are these souls called?

The Particular Judgment. Therefore every soul after this life is brought to God to be judged. Men die every day. Some will die to-day, others will die to-morrow. As soon as a man dies, his soul is at once brought before the throne of God to be judged. Each man is then judged in particular; that is, separately from all others, and this at the very moment of his death. He who dies first is judged first; he who dies later, is judged later. Because each man is judged in particular after his death, this judgment is called the particular judgment.

SUMMARY. Where does the soul go immediately after death? What is the judgment called which every soul then undergoes? Where does the soul go after the particular judgment? Who is cast into hell? Who goes directly to heaven? Who is sent to purgatory?

APPLICATION. Suppose you would die now, and your soul would have to appear now before the judgment-seat of God. God would show you all the evil you have done in your whole life. All your envious, angry and bad thoughts; all your bad, lying, abusive words and curses; your prayers omitted or badly said, and the evil things you have done. Your guardian angel will accuse you of not having listened to him. O woe, woe! What would then happen to you? Where would you be cast, if your soul was stained with a mortal sin? What a terrible misfortune this would be for you! You would be cast into hell with all the devils and wicked men. In hell a terrible fire burns forever. The pains of hell are most horrible.

Therefore, dear children, be sure never to commit a mortal sin. Rather suffer everything, even death itself, than commit a mortal sin. If necessary, rather suffer a great sickness and even die a painful death, in order to avoid mortal sin, for you shall then surely go to heaven. Sickness and death cannot injure you; but one mortal sin suffices to send you to hell, where you would be forever miserable. Therefore, children, no mortal sin!

Take care also not to be obliged to stay long in purgatory. What sins will bring you to purgatory? For instance, praying carelessly, disobedience, telling lies, quarreling, stealing little things. Many children make no account of little faults. They say: "Oh, I shall not go to hell for that." How foolish to say that! If you shall not go to hell for that, you shall go to purgatory, where the sufferings are greater than any suffering in this world. Suppose a man steals a dollar, saying: "I shall not be hanged for that, but I shall have to go to the penitentiary for some months at least." Does he act reasonably? How much more foolish is the light-minded child, who is not afraid to commit venial sin. Purgatory is a thousand times more to be feared than the penitentiary.

Be therefore on your guard against little faults. Many a child is now burning in purgatory, weeping and thinking: "Oh, had I prayed better, been more obedient, never told lies, etc., I would not have to suffer such terrible pains; but I would now be already in heaven happy with God." But that child has to continue to suffer perhaps for weeks and months, and even longer! Therefore, children, be reasonable, and avoid all that would later on cause you fearful pains in purgatory. And when you suffer some pain, or are sick, be patient and think: "I will suffer these pains for my sins, that I may not suffer so much in purgatory."

45. The General Judgment.

PREPARATION. After the general resurrection Jesus Christ will come again upon earth. When did He come the first time? When did He leave the earth? When He ascended into heaven. Where is He now? What place has He in heaven? He is seated at the right hand of God the Father Almighty. From thence He will come after the general resurrection again on earth. What did the two angels say about this to the apostles at the Ascension of our Saviour? Which coming of Jesus will that be? The second.

OBJECT. I will tell you to-day what will happen when Jesus Christ will come again on earth.

RELATION. Jesus told His apostles what would happen at His second coming. He said: "The Son of man shall come in His glory, and all the angels with Him. Then He shall sit on the throne of His glory. All the nations of the earth shall be assembled before Him. And He shall separate them as a shepherd separates the sheep from the goats. He shall place the sheep on His right hand, and the goats on His left. Then the King shall say to those on His right hand: Come, ye blessed of My Father, and possess the kingdom prepared for you from the beginning of the world. But to those on His left the King shall say: Depart from Me, ye cursed, into the everlasting fire which was prepared for the devil and his angels. And these shall go into everlasting punishment, but the others into life everlasting."

EXPLANATION — *The first and the second coming of*

Jesus. The second coming of Jesus will be very different from the first. Jesus came the first time as a lovely, poor, helpless infant, for He was born in a stable at Bethlehem. For the love of us He there made Himself little and poor. Many thought that they needed not to follow Him, and that they could mock Him. But how will Jesus, the Son of man, come upon earth the second time? He shall come in His glory, seated upon the clouds, and the clouds around Him shall shine as the dawn of day, and our Saviour's body will be as bright as the sun, and a large fiery cross shall be placed before Him.

The first time Jesus came quietly during the night; only a few knew of His birth. Who will be with Jesus when He shall come the second time upon earth? All the angels of heaven shall come with Him. All the angels that came and appeared near Bethlehem and sang their joyful hymn, and millions and millions of other angels shall come with our Saviour. These countless angels are called a great host, a great power. Hence Jesus shall come with great power.

At His first coming Jesus lay in a manger (crib). Where shall He be placed at His second coming? He shall sit on the throne of His glory, that is, on a glorious throne. In what capacity will He come, since He is seated on a throne? As King of heaven and earth. A king's throne is surrounded by many noblemen and many noble ladies, who form his court. Who form the court of the heavenly King? The angels. When our Saviour is seated on his throne, the wounds of His hands, feet and side shall be seen by all men. They will be as beautiful as roses in full bloom, and will shine as bright as the stars.

At our Lord's first coming only a few shepherds and wise men came to venerate Him. Who shall be assembled before Him at His second coming? All the nations of the earth shall be assembled before Jesus. Americans, Europeans, etc.; that is, all the men who shall have lived on earth from Adam to the end of the world, shall be assembled before Jesus. All of us shall be there also. From every direction men in great numbers shall come there. The good with their glorified bodies shall fly there swiftly, full of joy. It will be a long procession, almost without end, for there will be so many. Their angels also shall joyfully accompany them. When the just shall see our Saviour so bright and resplendent, seated on the throne of His glory, they shall wonder greatly, and shall begin to praise Him, singing beautiful canticles. In the Apostles' Creed the just are called " the living," and the wicked are called " the dead."

But the wicked with their heavy, swollen, ugly bodies, will be unwilling to approach our divine Saviour. He will appear terrible to them. Woe to them! This Jesus, in whom they would not believe, whom they reviled, whom they offended and outraged by their sins, is now seated on His glorious throne as King and Judge of all men. When Jesus was an infant, He had to flee from Herod into Egypt. And now Herod and all the wicked would wish to flee away from the Saviour. Oh, if they could only crawl into the ground! They would be only too glad, if they could only die and cease to exist! Therefore they shall call upon the hills and mountains: " Ye mountains fall over us; ye hills cover and hide us." But that is not possible. The wicked can die no more. They must appear before the Saviour on His throne. The devils drive and push them forward, as a herd of unclean animals, to the judgment-seat of the Saviour.

Why did the Saviour come the first time upon earth? To redeem all men. The second time He shall come to judge all men. After the general resurrection He shall come to judge the living and the dead, the just and the wicked.

On what day will Jesus come to judge all men? On the last day; the day of the general judgment. You have heard of another judgment in which our Saviour judges each man. What is it called? The particular judgment. When does it take place? In it each one is judged alone. But at the general judgment how shall men be judged? All men together. How is this judgment called? The last judgment, the general judgment.

The manifestation of the consciences. All men that have ever lived up to the end of the world are assembled before the throne of the Son of God to be judged. What shall be seen on the bodies of the wicked? Their sins. All the sins committed by each man during his whole life shall be clearly seen on his body. Even those sins children committed when alone, when they thought: " Nobody sees me." How untrue! God saw it, and at the general judgment all men shall see it. Suppose a child, all alone, committed some sin, something shameful; and then everybody would find it out! How ashamed he would feel! But it will be a much greater shame for him at the last day, when all mankind shall know all the shameful things he did! Known to his parents, brothers and sisters, to the priest, etc., who always believed that child to be good and pure! And now they find out how bad and deceitful he was! What a shame for him! But if that child was sorry for his sins and made a good confession, those sins will not harm him.

Also all the good each one has done during his whole life shall be manifested to all mankind. For instance, that child's piety, his hearing Mass on week days also, his obedience, his modesty, truthfulness, patience, etc., shall be known to all men. Oh, what an honor, what a joy for that child!

The separation. At first all men will be mingled together before the Saviour's throne; the beautiful bright bodies of the just (the living) shall be mixed up among the horrible disgusting bodies of the wicked (the dead). But they do not fit together. What will our Saviour do?

He shall separate them as a shepherd separates the sheep from the goats. The goats are stubborn; they will not follow the shepherd, and give no peace to the sheep. Therefore the shepherd removes the quarrelsome goats from the peaceful and obedient sheep; in other words: The shepherd separates the goats from the sheep. In like manner, at the general judgment our Saviour shall separate the disobedient, wicked sinners from the good and obedient just. On which side will He place the good? On His right. And the wicked? On His left.

The sentence. The reward of the just. What shall the King say to those who are on His right hand? "Come, ye blessed of My Father, and possess the kingdom prepared for you since the foundation of the world. Come to Me, into My arms, to My Heart! You shall be blessed and happy. You have been good, pious children of the heavenly Father. Come now to your Father in heaven; possess that kingdom of happiness; it is yours; it has been prepared for you since the beginning of the world, for in the beginning God created heaven and earth. So dear were you to the Father Almighty in heaven, that when He created the world, He already created the beautiful heaven for you." Oh, how the good will rejoice when hearing these welcome words of our divine Saviour!

The punishment of the wicked. What will the King say to those on His left hand? "Depart from Me, ye cursed, into everlasting fire, which was prepared for the devil and his angels. Depart from Me; away with you; I do not wish to see you any more, you wicked; you are cursed; no more shall you see Me. And yet how good I have been to you! For you I suffered; for you I died, that you might all come with Me to heaven. But you would not. You were so wicked; you would not be sorry for your sins. Therefore away with you into the everlasting fire of hell." Who is in that fire? And who else? And the other wicked angels. Therefore, "away with you into the everlasting fire prepared for the devil and his angels." Now the wicked utter terrible screams. They would wish to implore God for mercy. But now it is of no use. Then the earth shall be opened, and the wicked shall be cast down into hell! Where shall the wicked go after the general judgment? Into hell! But the good shall accompany Jesus, Mary and the angels into heaven. What a glorious procession! Where shall the good go after the general judgment? To heaven.

The last judgment and the harvest. At the general judgment the same will happen as at the harvest. The chaff shall be separated from the wheat, and be put aside. What shall be done with it? It shall be burnt. And what is done with the wheat? It is placed in the granary. This is what happens at the harvest. Which kind of men are like the chaff? What shall be done with the wicked after the general judgment? They are cast into the fire of hell. And where shall the good be placed? In heaven. And how long shall heaven and hell last? For all eternity.

The heaven of the good. All joy. Oh, how beautiful is heaven? In heaven there are millions and millions of beautiful angels. There you shall see your good guardian angel. How you will rejoice with him! He will feel happy, because he helped you to go to heaven. You shall see also an immense number of beautiful saints in heaven. I feel confident that you shall find among them your parents, brothers and sisters, relatives, etc. How happy you will be to meet them and never more to be separated from them! In heaven you shall see also the Blessed Virgin very near the throne of God. How glad you will be to go to her, to thank her, to kiss her hand and to be allowed to call her your Mother! But your greatest joy in heaven shall be to see God in His infinite beauty, and to love Him with your whole heart. You shall never tire seeing His beauty, which will enrapture you as it will enrapture all the saints and angels in heaven for all eternity. You shall have in heaven everything you can wish for. In heaven all is pleasure and joy.

No suffering. On earth you may have often wept. In heaven God Himself will wipe away all your tears. There shall be no pain, no suffering there; no grief, no sorrow, no troubles; but perfect happiness, which lasts forever, and is called life everlasting. Therefore we say in the Apostles' Creed: "I believe in life everlasting."

The hell of the damned; nothing but pain and suffering. How much you dread fire! You cry even when you burn your finger a little. How you would cry and scream, if your whole hand would burn for some minutes in the stove! How frightful it would be, if you were thrown into a large fire or a furnace. The pain would be horrible. (St. Laurence roasted by slow fire on a gridiron.) But all that would not be the fire, the torments of hell! And in hell the whole body of a damned person is always burning, and never burnt up!

No joy, no pleasure. No matter how unhappy is a person on earth, he always has something that gives him pleasure. His parents, relatives or friends console him; or there is the thought that he will soon get well, get out of his troubles. Or he thinks: "If I die, I shall have peace, or rest." He can pray God to take him soon to heaven. But in hell there is nothing that can give him the least pleasure. There is no one to cast on him a look of love or sympathy. No one to speak a kind word to him, or to encourage him; no one to give him the least hope. There is no heart that loves him or cares for him. Those that loved him in life, have forgotten him, or curse him, whenever they think of him. Who can live without love or sympathy?

For all eternity. The damned know that never shall there be any change or improvement in their state. Their bodies are always burning, but are never consumed. Thousands and millions of years shall come and pass away, and they shall burn all that time, and shall continue to burn forever after that!

Have you ever seen a canary bird sharpening his bill on the wire of his cage? Now listen. In a country far from here, there is a large mountain. It is about five miles long, five miles wide and five miles high, and is all of hard stone. To this mountain a bird flies once every thousand years and rubs his bill on it. Now how many thousands of years will it take that bird to wear out that mountain with his bill? No one can tell. But if the damned in hell were told: "When that bird shall have worn out that large mountain with his bill, you shall come out of hell," they would cheer so loud as to be heard in heaven! But, dear children, when that bird would have worn out that mountain with his bill, the damned would not have one minute less to suffer in hell! They turn about in the flames of hell in horrible pains; they groan, they weep, they howl and curse! And this shall continue for all eternity, and eternity has no end.

SUMMARY. At the general judgment Jesus Christ will come again upon earth to judge all men. Therefore we say in the Apostles' Creed: "From thence He shall come to judge the living and the dead." The judgment at the end of the world is called the last or general judgment. When the judgment shall be over, the wicked shall be cast into hell, and the good shall be taken up to heaven. In heaven there is no pain, no suffering, but all pleasure and joy forever! This is called life everlasting. Therefore we say in the Apostles' Creed: "I believe in life everlasting. Amen." But in hell there is nothing but pain and suffering, and not the least joy or pleasure; hell lasts forever.

APPLICATION. Dear children, do you wish to be cast into hell? What a terrible misfortune that would be! But if you were to commit one mortal sin, and should die before you repent of it, you shall be surely cast into the everlasting fire of hell! Therefore, children, never commit a mortal sin. Rather suffer all, rather die immediately than commit a mortal sin and deserve to be cast into hell!

Where do you all wish to go? But what must you do to go to heaven? Is not heaven worth doing all that? To gain heaven you ought to find nothing too great or too difficult. So many other children have done it all, and why should not you also be able to do it? Therefore avoid sin, always do your duty, and often say to yourselves: "I will do my best to get a high place in heaven!"

PART II
THE COMMANDMENTS OF GOD.

1. The Commandment of the Love of God.

1. OBJECT. I will teach you to-day why we should love God, and how much we should love Him. One day a lawyer came to Jesus and asked Him: "Master, what must I do to gain heaven?" Jesus answered: "Thou shalt love the Lord thy God with all thy heart, with all thy soul, with all thy mind and with all thy strength."

2. EXPLANATION. a. PATERNAL GOODNESS — *Body.* It is so easy and so beautiful to love God. For God is our good Father. He created us; otherwise we should not be in this world. God gave us a beautiful body. Our body has two eyes to see. Whence do they come? How unfortunate should we not be, if we were blind. God gave us also two ears, that we may willingly listen to our parents and teachers. What else has God given us in our body? A mouth, hands and feet. A mouth and tongue that we may ask questions, express our thoughts, laugh and sing, pray and praise the God in heaven whom we love.

God has given you hands to work diligently, and feet to go where duty directs. You have also in your breast a heart, though small, which beats joyfully. Do you know where your heart is? Our good God gave you a heart to love and life itself.

What do all these good gifts prove? That God loves us. And every day God, like a good father, loves you and cares for you. From the highest heaven, where the angels dwell, God looks down upon every child with pleasure. He gives it its daily bread, and helps it in all its troubles and wants. Through whom does He give you your daily bread? Through your parents. He gave you your parents also, that, in His stead, they may care for you. And that they may do this well, He has placed in their heart a great love for you. No one on earth loves you as much as your parents. Enumerate all the good God has done for your body. Every corporal good we have comes from God.

Soul. And what did God breathe into your body? An immortal soul. In whose image did God create your soul? How beautiful was your soul then! Who entered your heart when you were baptized? And what did He bring to your soul? Your soul became then much more beautiful; she became holy. And God wills that your soul should remain beautiful and holy. And whom did He place by your side to guard and protect you? Your guardian angel accompanies you at every step, at every motion. Where is your guardian angel to bring you after your death? There you shall always be happy. You see now all the good God has done for your soul. Enumerate it all. All good comes from God.

Heart. What does a child feel for his father and mother, because they give him so many good things? Love. From whom do we receive all that is good? From God. What do we owe to God for it? Love. Therefore we must love God, because all good things come from Him. We love God in the same way as we love our parents. When your mother says to you: "Show me where you love me," you show her your heart. We love with our heart. We love God also with our heart. Therefore God says to each one of you: "My child, give Me thy heart." And our Saviour commands us: "Thou shalt love the Lord thy God with thy whole heart."

b. LOVE OF THE SON. I will now tell you why God still more deserves our love. God the Father has given us what was dearest to Him. He sent His Son upon the earth; and God the Son bestowed on us all His love. What was God the Son going to do for us? To suffer and die. Which of you would be willing to suffer and die for some one else? But what none of you would be willing to do for some one else, our divine Saviour did for the love of us. For the love of us our Saviour underwent a death-agony and sweat blood. For the love of us He allowed Himself to be fearfully scourged. For the love of us He allowed a crown of sharp thorns to be pressed down on His head. For the love of us He carried a heavy cross and allowed Himself to be nailed to it. On what day did our loving Saviour suffer and die for us? On Good Friday. On that day the crucifix is placed on a black cloth spread out on the floor, and the faithful, and the children likewise, kneel down before it to venerate our Saviour.

Sorrow. And when we consider our loving Saviour's pale features, His head crowned with thorns, his eyes covered with blood, his bloodless lips, and the cruel wounds in His hands and feet and in His side, we feel compelled to say: "O Jesus, Thou didst suffer too much for me, a poor child; it pains too much even my sinful heart." And then we feel our heart moved, deeply moved. This feeling of sorrow sometimes increases so as to cause many to shed tears, and even to sob aloud. And then they bend over to kiss tenderly the Saviour's wounds in His hands, feet and side.

When we kiss some one, what do we intend to show? What do we intend to show to our Saviour by kissing His wounds? That we love Him. And wherefrom did our love and sorrow arise? From our heart; from our feelings. But it is the consideration of our mind that causes various feelings to arise, spring up in our heart, that causes us to compassionate with our suffering Saviour, and to resolve never again to displease Him by committing sin.

Joy. Where will our soul go after our death? To heaven. In heaven you will see our divine Saviour in His glorified body. He will look lovingly at you, and

His five wounds will shine as bright blooming roses. How beautiful will that be? What will then be your feelings? Feelings of love and joy, like those of the angels. We rejoice also on earth over our Lord. How do the angels express their joy? They sing. What beautiful hymn do they sing continually? " Holy, holy," etc. And how can we express our joy with regard to God? We can rejoice in our mind, in our feelings. Where are our feelings? When we rejoice very much, our heart begins to beat. Yes, our heart leaps, as it were, for joy. Love and joy warm up our heart, and even cause it to grow hot, for people say: " My heart burns with love and joy." And thus we observe our Saviour's commandment: " Thou shalt love the Lord thy God with all thy mind." How should we love God? What commandment did our Saviour give us?

c. SUPREME GOOD — *The highest, the best.* How good must God be, since He loves men so excessively! How good is a mother towards her child! It cannot be expressed. The angels are far better than a mother, than all men. Who is the best among all angels and all men? Oh, how good is Mary! But God is infinitely better than Mary and all angels and men. Mary and the angels and saints are not so good and holy of themselves. Who was with Mary, when the angel saluted her? And who came down over Mary. God helped also all the other saints to be good and holy. But does any one help God to be so good and so holy? No; God is good in Himself; God possesses all good in Himself. Whatever good there is in men, in the angels, in Mary and in all the saints, they received it all from God. And God has infinitely more in Himself. There is nothing in heaven and on earth that is so good as God. Therefore our Saviour said: " God alone is good." Hence we call God the highest and the best good.

Beautiful. If I could only tell you how beautiful is

God. How beautiful is the sun! And how do the stars twinkle so friendly at night! And are not the flowers beautiful? What is there beautiful in the sun, in the stars? And what pleases us so much in the flowers? How beautiful must not God be, who has made them all? What there is bright in the sun, what twinkles in the stars, what is beautiful in the flowers, in Mary, in all the angels and saints, they have all received it from God. And all that is infinitely more beautiful in God. There is nothing more beautiful than God; hence we say: "God is the most beautiful good."

Most lovely. What should we feel towards God on account of His unsurpassable beauty and goodness? Love and joy. You love your mother very much, and why? Your mother deserves your love, for she is lovable or lovely. But Mary is much better and more beautiful than your mother and all the angels and saints. And what does she deserve much more than they? She is much more lovely and deserving of love than they. Who is the best and most beautiful of all in heaven and on earth? God. What, then, does He deserve more than every one else? He deserves our love more than any one else. He is, therefore, the most lovely of all. (Repetition of the highest, the best, the most beautiful, the most lovely.) We must love God because He is the highest (supreme), the best, the most beautiful, the most lovely good.

Soul. He who loves God is often with God in his thoughts and takes pleasure in God. With what do we think? Who is it that thinks with the mind? The soul. Which part of yourselves must be with God in loving Him? Our soul. Therefore our Saviour commands us: "Thou shalt love the Lord thy God with thy whole soul." With what else must we also love God? With our heart, with our mind.

Whole. We must, then, love God with our heart, with our mind, with our soul. What other word does our

Saviour place before heart, mind and soul? The word *whole*. We should love God with our whole heart, that is, we should love God with our whole heart more than anything else, as much as we can. We should love God with our whole soul, that is, we should think on God more than on anything else, as often as we can. We should love God with our whole mind, that is, we should rejoice about God more than about anything else, as much as we can. But with our little heart and our soul and our mind, we are far from loving God as much as He deserves. Would that we had thousands of hearts more wherewith to love God, and thousands of souls to think on Him, and thousands of minds to rejoice over Him.

All our strength. We should love God with all that we are and with all that we have, our eyes, ears, mouth, tongue, hands and feet, with all that is within and without us; in a word, we should love God our Lord with all our strength, for our Saviour commands: " Thou shalt love the Lord thy God with all thy strength."

3. SUMMARY. Tell me again with what we should love God. With our heart, our soul, our mind, all our strength. How did our Saviour command this to us? " Thou shalt love the Lord thy God with thy whole heart, with thy whole soul, with thy whole mind and with all thy strength." This is called the commandment of the love of God. (Repeat questions on this.) Why should we love God? We should love God, because He is the highest (supreme) Good, and everything good comes from Him.

4. APPLICATION. " FOR THE LOVE OF GOD." a. Do GOOD — *Pray.* How does a good child show that it loves God with its whole soul? By often thinking of Him. Of whom does it at once think when awaking in the morning? Of whom does it think at night before going to sleep? Your first thoughts in the morning should be about God, and your last thoughts at night before falling asleep should be about God also.

Prayer of thanksgiving. Why should we give to God our first thoughts on awaking in the morning, and also our last thoughts before falling asleep at night? Because He bestows so many good things on us. What do you say to your father, when he gives you something good? But every day God gives you far more good things than your father and mother. How do we thank God? By praying to Him. How do you thank God at night? "O my God, I thank Thee for all the benefits Thou hast bestowed on me this day." During the night God, like a good father, watches over you, gives you a quiet, refreshing sleep and keeps you in good health. Therefore you should thank Him in the morning: "I thank Thee, O my God, for all Thou hast done for me, and for having watched over me and preserved me this night." You should also thank Him after each meal, and why?

Devout prayer. You also pray before your meals. But when your mother has prepared something you like, or you are very hungry, you say the prayer before meals with hands joined, but your thoughts and your heart are directed to the eatables on the table, but not to God, to whom you are speaking. On whom should you think when you are praying? When you think on God in your prayer, your soul is with God. And when you pray devoutly, the love of God and joy about God are awakened in you. And then what else is with God? Your heart and your mind, and not merely your tongue and your lips, and your prayer is devout. This kind of prayer pleases God very much, for He then sees that you really love Him. How must you pray to show God that you really love Him?

Awaking love. You should often tell God that you love Him: "O my God, I love Thee with all my heart, because Thou art the highest (chief, supreme) Good." Whenever you thus awake in you the love of God, your heart and your mind ascend to God.

To please God. If you love God where will you like

to go? To church. For instance, you hear the church bell ringing in the morning, and the thought strikes you, that you would please God, if you went to church to hear Mass. But it is so cold outdoors, and it is so nice and warm in your bed. But you, nevertheless, get up immediately; for what? For the love of God, to please God. In church your knees sometimes pain you, and you would like to sit down. But the thought presents itself: " It will please God, if I remain kneeling; " and you remain kneeling. Why? To please God. Another time you are engaged in playing a very interesting game, and you hear your mother calling: " John, come home." It is very hard for you to stop playing at once; but the thought presents itself: " Obey to please God," or " for God's sake," and obedience becomes easier. What we do out of love becomes easy. Everything we do to please God is easy.

Why should you willingly obey? To please God, and not in order to be praised. Why should you go to church? To please God, and not perhaps to get a picture as a reward. Why should you willingly and devoutly say your prayers? Mention other things we should do to please God. Study, work. To study, work, pray, obey, go to church, are all good things. What should we do to please God? We should do all that is good to please God. To please God you should rise in the morning, say your prayers, study, obey, help your father and mother. What do we show when we do good to please God? We show that we love Him.

b. AVOID EVIL. What should you avoid doing, if you love God? Telling lies, stealing, cursing, etc., for lying, stealing, cursing are evil, are sinful. We should, therefore, do no evil, avoid evil. For instance, you are kneeling down in church. Your companion would like to talk with you, and you are on the point of doing the same. But the reflection comes: " That would be wrong, sinful.

I would offend God by doing so." What would you then do? Not talk. To please whom would you have kept from talking? Another time you hear somebody walking out of the church, and you at once feel like looking around to see who it is. But the thought strikes you: "It is wrong to look around in church," and you keep looking at the altar. And why did you not look around? On account of God, to please God. Sometimes even ill-behaved children behave well in church and do not talk or look around, but they avoid doing these things not to please God, but for what? Because they are afraid of being punished. Perhaps you are passing a fine orchard with plenty of fine ripe fruit. You feel like taking some, for there is nobody near. What good thought can keep you from stealing? "God sees me." Also: "to please God I'll keep from stealing."

You have hitherto perhaps often avoided evil for fear of punishment. This did not please God much. Henceforth you should do better. Why should we avoid evil? We should avoid evil, in order to please God. You should then resolve: "To please God I will not curse, I will not tell lies, I will not steal, I will not disobey, I will not misbehave in church." What does it prove if you avoid doing evil, in order to please God? It proves that we love God. In what other way can we prove that we love God? If we do good in order to please God. Therefore we show that we really love God, if, to please Him (for His sake), we do good and avoid evil.

2. The Commandment of the Love of our Neighbor.

OBJECT. I will show you to-day that we must love all men.

I. EXPLANATION — *Neighbor*. Who created all men? God. According to what? According to (or after) His own image. God is, therefore, the Father of all men. If

God is our Father, what are we? His children. And
what are we, if God created us in (or after) His own
image? We are images of God. All men are God's children and images. What do father (mother) and children
form? A family. What do God and all men form? A
family. That is a very large family. It is God's family.
To God's family all men on earth belong. How many
fathers in a family? Charles and Rose have together but
one father. What is the relation between Charles and
Rose, since they have the same father? Brother and sister?
They are the nearest relatives to each other. In like manner all men are related to each other; they are brethren
to one another; they are one another's neighbor. All
the children in school are neighbor to one another; all the
people in our town, in our State, in our country, in the
whole world are our neighbor, for we all are children of one
and the same Father, God. Every man, woman and child
in the whole world, without exception, are our neighbor.
And why? Where does the Father of us all dwell? In
heaven. Therefore, all men in the world, without exception, are our neighbor, because we are all children of the
same Father in heaven.

Our divine Saviour taught us this. One day, as you
know, a lawyer asked Him: " Master, what must I do
to go to heaven?" How did Jesus answer him? " Thou
shalt love the Lord thy God," etc. And then Jesus added:
" Thou shalt love thy neighbor as thyself." Then the lawyer asked Him: " And who is my neighbor? " And
Jesus related to him the following parable:

II. RELATION. A man was traveling from Jerusalem to
Jericho. On the way he was attacked by robbers who beat
him, stole all he had and left him half dead. A Jewish
priest passing by saw him and left him lie there. Then a
levite coming that way saw him and also left him lie there.
Finally, there came a Samaritan along that way; he saw
the poor traveler, went to him, dressed his wounds, took

him to an inn and had him cared for till he was cured. Now our Saviour asked the lawyer: "Which of these three acted as neighbor towards that unfortunate man?" The lawyer replied: "He who showed compassion (mercy) towards him." Then Jesus said: "Go thou and do likewise."

EXPLANATION. Who asked a question of Jesus? The lawyers were men learned in the Jewish (Mosaic) law and in the Scriptures; sometimes they were called scribes. They read and studied constantly the Holy Scriptures. Who remembers on what occasion King Herod called the Jewish priests and scribes together? What question did he put to them? Now one of these lawyers or scribes asked Jesus: "Who is my neighbor?" What would you have answered him? Our Saviour instead of that, related an anecdote, or a parable.

A man was going from Jerusalem to Jericho. You already know all about Jerusalem. Jericho is a city in Palestine about twenty miles from Jerusalem. The road lays across mountains, where there were highway robbers. What misfortune happened to that man on his way? The robbers attacked him. What did they take from him? Money, clothing and everything he had. They robbed him. And they also so cruelly beat him, that he was covered with wounds. The robbers then escaped. In what state did they leave that man? Half dead. It was a wicked thing for those robbers to attack, rob and so badly wound that man who was going his way peaceably. The hot sun shining on his wounds caused him great pain. He was every moment growing weaker, and he knew that, if some one did not come soon to his assistance, he should die. He heard steps coming nearer and nearer. Who was coming? The poor wounded man was glad, for he thought that he would get some help. The Jewish priest saw the unfortunate man. What did he do? He passed on. Who came along soon after the priest? The levites had to assist the priests in the temple. What did the wounded man desire that the levite should do? But the levite, like the priest, passed on. Now a third man was coming along the same way; he was riding on a mule. He was a Samaritan, that is, he was a native of Samaria. The wounded man thought: " I hope that man will not pass on as the others did, and leave me here to die." And the Samaritan took compassion on him, and came to his assistance. He first washed his wounds. And what did he pour into them? Oil is cooling and curing. How much good it did to the poor man! Then he bound up his wounds, and lifted him up. But he could not walk. How did the Samaritan bring him away? He lifted him up on his mule and brought him to an inn (hotel), and said to the innkeeper: " Take care of this wounded man until he is cured, and I will pay all the expenses." Now repeat how the Samaritan helped the unfortunate man. He, therefore, not only had compassion on him, but he also helped him. He who has pity on the unfortunate and helps them, is merciful, is charitable. What did the Samaritan show towards the wounded man? Charity. He is, therefore, called the Charitable Samaritan.

III. Explanation — *To love as ourselves.* Who treated that traveler so cruelly? The robbers. What evil had he done to them? None. Suppose some one would come in here and, without any provocation, would tear off your clothing, and beat you till your blood would flow. How would you like it? Not at all. You would not like to be thus treated. It would be equally wrong and cruel to treat others in that way. Our Lord commands us to act quite differently, for He says: " Whatsoever you would wish others to do unto you, do ye unto them." If you were lying on the ground all covered with wounds, and would see people passing by, what would you wish them to do for you? What did that wounded man wish the passers-by to do for him? What would that priest and that levite have wished, if they had been in the place of that unfortunate man? That very thing they should have done for him. But they thought: "That man is a stranger. I do not know him. It is none of my business." Is it true that a stranger's misfortune is none of our business? What is every man to us, even if he is a stranger to us? What was that wounded stranger to that priest and that levite? Because he was the child and the image of God. What we do to God's child and image, we do to God Himself. If the priest and the levite had cared for that wounded man, God would have considered it as done to Himself.

This must have been the thought of the good Samaritan, that he should do unto that unfortunate man what he would wish him to do to himself, if he were in his place. And he actually did it. Which of our Saviour's commandments did he thereby fulfil? "Whatever you wish others to do unto you, do ye unto them." He who does to another what he would wish another to do unto him, loves him as he loves himself. How did the good Samaritan love his neighbor? As himself. Which of our Saviour's commandments did he fulfil? The commandment of the love of our neighbor.

Now you can answer the question our Saviour asked of that lawyer. What did He ask him? Which three did our Saviour mean? How would you answer our Saviour's question? The good (charitable) Samaritan. Why? Because he had compassion on the wounded man and assisted him. In other words, he showed mercy (charity) to him. What answer did the lawyer give? "He that showed mercy to him."

IV. SUMMARY. The commandment of the love of our neighbor is: "Thou shalt love thy neighbor as thyself." All men without exception are our neighbor, because all men are children of one Father in heaven. We love our neighbor as ourselves when we observe this commandment of our divine Saviour: "Whatever you wish that others should do unto you, do ye also unto them."

V. APPLICATION. What were Christ's concluding words to the lawyer: "Go thou and do likewise." Our Lord meant by these words: "Act like the Samaritan." Our Lord practised what He commanded the lawyer to do.

1. When our divine Saviour was going through Palestine preaching the Gospel, people were wont to bring Him after His preaching, sick people to cure, such as the blind, the deaf and dumb, the lame. How did our Lord help the blind? the deaf and dumb, the lame? How glad and happy were those He cured! On one occasion there was an immense crowd of people with Jesus. They had had nothing to eat for a long time, some even for three days. Our Saviour fed them all by a miracle. On another day He met the funeral procession of a young man; He saw the mother of the deceased, a poor widow, weeping; He said to her: "Do not weep," and He went to those who were carrying the corpse, and raised the dead young man to life. Thus did Jesus help many others also. What did our Saviour show by helping so many? That He loved them. How did He best show that He loved all men? By dying for all men. Our Saviour loved even His enemies. How did He show, when He was arrested, that He still loved Judas? He allowed Judas to kiss Him. How did He show that He loved Malchus, who was one of those who came to arrest Him? How did He show, when He was hanging on the cross that He loved even those who put Him to death? He prayed for them.

2. You see how Jesus acted like the good Samaritan. He is Himself the Good Samaritan. He helped all. And we also will help our neighbor, when in need. Hence Jesus says to us also: "Go and do likewise." There is Rose N., who comes to our school. She rides to school every morning, for she can hardly walk. She cannot go up the steps by herself. What do most of you do? You go away

and let her help herself as well as she can. What do you care for Rose? You act like that priest and that levite towards the poor wounded man. But not all act in that way. What do some do to help Rose to go up the steps? Rose cannot run and jump and play like the other children. If you were in her place, how would you wish the other children to act towards you? Remain near us. Thus should you act towards Rose. A few of you could remain with her and speak kindly to her. That would do Rose good. What does it prove?

There is an old hunchback. When he crosses a street, he is always surrounded by a number of bad children who make fun of him and mimic him. This always hurts the poor old man's feelings; it is as if he received a wound in his heart. It has often so pained him, as to make him weep. Who inflicted so painful a wound on the poor old man? Those rough, ill-bred, uncharitable children, who, like the robbers in the parable, fell upon him and badly wounded him in his feelings. What would you, N. N., have done, had you seen those bad children acting so cruelly? Reported them in school. That would have been right. Perhaps you would also have said to those children: " Stop that; let the poor man be in peace." That would have been even better. Why is it wrong to pain that old man? He is our neighbor, a child of God. Other good children have thought of this, and therefore saluted him in a friendly manner, and when they saw him sitting in front of his little home, they went to him and tried to entertain him. This always made him very glad.

Children sometimes mock and ridicule their schoolmates. As soon as a child gives a wrong answer, the others begin to laugh at him. That is ugly and uncharitable; the child then gets so timid, as no longer to have the courage to answer a question. How would you like to be treated thus by the others? What ought we to refrain from, when others make a mistake? On what saying should we then think? "Whatever thou wishest others to do unto thee, do thou also unto them."

3. When you undertake to help your little sister to perform her task, and she is rather awkward, you at once scold her, abuse her. Is not that rather rough conduct? Will that make your sister smarter? How would you take being treated in such a way? Therefore "whatever," etc. You have brought to school a fine large apple, and you are just going to bite into it and eat; but you see near you a pair of hungry, longing eyes, those of a schoolmate who is very poor. You can give him half, or even the whole apple, and you do so. What does he see in this act of yours? You have won his love and even his friendship. You have two pencils, and he has none. What can you do? You meet a young child in the street that has lost its way, and is far from home. What can you do? There is another poor child sent to the grocery, that has lost the money for bread, and is crying. What can you do? Help to look for it. There is an automobile coming; a little child in the street will surely be run over by it, if you do not carry it out of danger. What should you do? How many other cases in which you can all show that you love your neighbor!

ON THE COMMANDMENTS.

3. God gave the ten Commandments.

Which are the two principal commandments? You have already learned many beautiful things about them. God Himself told us more clearly how we should love Him and our neighbor, by giving the ten commandments to the Jews. These ten commandments oblige all men.

OBJECT. I will relate to-day how God gave the ten commandments,

I. Relation. The Israelites dwelt many years in Egypt. There they worshiped the true God. The Egyptians worshiped false gods. There was a pious and learned man among the Israelites called Moses. God spoke to him: "Lead the Israelites out of Egypt; I will give them a beautiful country to live in." The Israelites departed. They had a long way to go. In the beginning of the third month they came to Mount Sinai. There they put up their tents. Moses went up the mountain, and there the Lord spoke to him: "Go down and order them to sanctify themselves to-day and to-morrow, and to wash their garments, and to be ready on the third day. And when they hear the blast of the trumpets, they shall come to the mountain." Moses did what God had commanded him. The morning of the third day came. And it began to lighten and thunder. A dark cloud covered Mount Sinai, and gave it a terrible aspect; it began to quake, to smoke and to emit flames. The blast of the trumpets became louder and louder, and the Israelites were terrified. Moses led them to the foot of the mountain, and God spoke from the midst of the flames, saying:

1. I am the Lord thy God. Thou shalt not have strange gods before Me; thou shalt not make to thyself any graven thing to adore it.

2. Thou shalt not take the name of the Lord thy God in vain.

3. Remember that thou keep holy the Sabbath day.

4. Honor thy father and thy mother, that it may be well with thee, and thou mayst live long on the earth.

5. Thou shalt not kill.

6. Thou shalt not commit adultery.

7. Thou shalt not steal.

8. Thou shalt not bear false witness against thy neighbor.

9. Thou shalt not covet thy neighbor's wife.

10. Thou shalt not covet thy neighbor's house, nor his field, nor his servant, nor his handmaid, nor his ox, nor his ass, nor anything that is his.

Full of dread, the people said: " We shall do all that the Lord has commanded." After this Moses again went up the mountain, and remained there forty days and forty nights. All that time he ate no bread and drank no water. God gave him two tables of stone, on which His finger had engraved the ten commandments.

II. EXPLANATION. Where did the Israelites dwell? There they were obliged to work very hard for the Egyptians, without receiving any pay. If they did not perform enough work, or took a little rest, they were beaten by the Egyptians. The Israelites were thus very badly treated in Egypt. But there was something else that was much worse. The Egyptians worshiped cats, crocodiles, storks and a calf. They said: " These are our gods." What kind of gods were those animals? False gods. Whom did the Israelites worship? But they gradually began to worship false gods besides the true God. From whom had they learnt this? It could have easily happened in the course of time, that they would at last no longer believe in the true God. Therefore God willed that the Israelites should leave Egypt. Who was to lead them out of Egypt? What did God say to Moses about this? By what way were the Israelites to go? It was on that way that God gave them the ten commandments. From what mountain? How long had the Israelites already traveled? Here they stayed for a long time. They could not build solid houses, because they were not to remain there always. And they could not live without shelter. In what did they live? In tents. They carried along all the parts of tents. And when they came to a place where they were to stop, they put up their tents. Where did Moses go? He went up the mountain. God wished to proclaim His commandments on the third day. That was a matter of great importance. Therefore that day was to be a great feast day for the Israelites. What kind of clothes do you put on on feast days? What would your mother do, if your clothes were not clean? Suppose you were to go and see the president on a certain day; how careful you would be to be neat and clean in your whole appearance! But there is no one greater than God, and the Israelites were to appear before God! What were they ordered to do? They were required to be outwardly neat and clean. But God does not see merely the exterior, but even into our inmost heart. How should our heart be, when we go before God? Free from sin; it should be pure and holy. What were the Israelites to be free from in their soul? From sin. Therefore they had to make a twofold preparation. What was the outward preparation to consist in? And the inward? How long were they given to prepare themselves? What order did God send them through Moses?

The morning of the third day came. It was a terrible day. What did the Israelites see on the mountain? In what was the mountain enveloped? In a dark cloud. In the cloud there were constant flashes of lightning, as if the mountain was on fire. The thunder pealed so fearfully, as to cause the mountain to quake and totter. Who was in the cloud and in the fire? God Himself. What did the people feel when they beheld the dazzling flashes of lightning and heard the terrible peals of thunder? Fear and terror. Where did Moses lead the Israelites? To the foot of the mountain. When they reached it, God spoke to them from the midst of the fire: "I am," etc. The people were greatly frightened when God, with a voice of thunder, proclaimed the ten commandments, and they trembled as they listened. What did the Israelites promise after hearing the commandments God gave them? Where did Moses then betake himself? How long did he remain there? During all that time he took neither food nor drink, that is, he fasted. Can you tell me why Moses remained so long on the mountain? During that time God explained to him the ten commandments. The Israelites might have forgotten the commandments. But God would not permit it. What do I often do when I wish you not to forget what I teach you? Write it on the board. Therefore what did God do with regard to the ten commandments?

III. and IV. EXPLANATION AND APPLICATION. On what do I write? On the blackboard. With what? That can be easily rubbed out. On what did God write the ten commandments? On two tables of stone. They were very large. Who has already seen writing on stone? Where? On tombs, monuments. The writing cannot be rubbed out. Why? It is cut into the stone, and will last as long as the stone itself. The ten commandments are to last always; as long as the world lasts. Wherefore God engraved them deeply in the tables of stone. How? With His finger, just as if they had been carved in the stone. Who gave the ten commandments? Where? To whom? On what were they written? God gave to Moses the ten commandments written on two tables of stone. How are these tables of stone represented? One with numbers I, II and III, meaning the first, second and third commandments, which concern our duties towards God. The other with the following seven numbers up to X, meaning the seven remaining commandments, which concern our duties towards our neighbor. The first three commandments teach us how we must love God; and the other seven teach us how we must love our neighbor.

V. APPLICATION. 1. What did the Israelites see and hear when God gave the ten commandments? God was angry with the Israelites because they disobeyed Him and adored also false gods. Therefore he said: " I am the Lord thy God; thou shalt not have strange gods before Me; thou shalt adore none but Me." And thus He spoke ten consecutive times to them, telling them what they should do, and what they should not do. Three times He said: "Thou shalt;" and seven times: "Thou shalt not."

2. When God spoke thus to the Israelites, His voice was as terrible as the rolling of thunder, and His eyes shone through the cloud as the most vivid lightning. You can see from this that God was very severe when He gave the ten commandments, and He is very strict in requiring their observance. He who breaks one of the commandments, commits a sin, and will be punished by God. We have examples of this in Adam and Eve, in Cain, in the angels who rebelled against God. How did He punish Adam and Eve? Cain? God will punish us also, if we break any of His commandments. He can cause us to fall dead whilst we are committing a sin. And if we die in mortal sin, God must, in His justice, condemn us to hell. We shall all die once, and then shall have to appear before God to be judged. How terrible will it then be for us, if we have not kept the commandments and fallen into mortal sin! God will then say to us: "Depart from Me, you accursed, into everlasting fire, which was prepared for the devil and his angels." How unhappy you would then be! What must you do to avoid such a misfortune? Keep the commandments. But a good child needs not to be threatened with punishment to make him keep the commandments of God. Only lately I taught you why you ought to obey, to pray, to study. To please God. Why should you also keep the commandments? What do we show when, to please God, we keep His commandments? Our divine Saviour says: "He that loveth Me, keepeth My commandments."

3. The Israelites had to appear at the foot of Mount Sinai before God. You appear every morning during holy Mass before God. What had the Israelites to do before appearing before God? You should not come to church without washing your face, your hands, and combing your hair, and your clothes and shoes should be clean. But

God looks further than your dress; He sees into your inmost heart. How should your heart especially be, when you appear before God? Pure. But you cannot purify your heart all alone. Who has to help you? God. Hence when you enter the church, take holy water devoutly, and whilst making the sign of the cross with it, say: "O Lord, cleanse (purify) me of my sins." If you do this devoutly, God will forgive you your sins.

FIRST COMMANDMENT OF GOD.
4. The Worship of God. A.

I. PREPARATION. What do you do when I come into the school? We stand up and salute you. By doing so, you honor me. What do you do when you meet me on the street? We take off our hats and salute you. By doing so, you also honor me. When the bishop comes to our church, all turn out in procession to receive him, in their best clothes, and the church bells ring joyfully, and the church is beautifully decorated. By all this the clergy and faithful wish to show due honor to the bishop. But there is One who deserves far greater honor than the bishop, than the Pope himself. Who is it? God. We must honor God far more than all else.

OBJECT. I will show by the history of the three wise men how we should honor God. Who can relate their history?

II. RELATION. When Jesus was born at Bethlehem, there came wise men from the East to Jerusalem. They asked: "Where is the new-born king of the Jews? We have seen His Star in the East and have come to adore Him." When Herod heard this, he was afraid. He summoned the priests and the scribes, and asked them where the Christ (Messiah) was to be born. They answered: "At Bethlehem in the tribe of Juda." Then Herod sent the wise men to Bethlehem, saying: "Go there and seek diligently for the Child; and when you have found Him, tell me, and I also will go to adore Him." The wise men set out at once for Bethlehem. And the star appeared and led them to the place where the Child was. When they saw the Star, they rejoiced very much. They entered the place and found the Child with Mary, His Mother. They prostrated themselves and adored the Child. They offered Him gold, frankincense and myrrh. During the night God commanded the wise men not to go back to Herod; therefore they returned by another way to their country.

A. THE ADORATION OF THE THREE WISE MEN.

III. DEVELOPMENT — *Hope.* How did the wise men learn the birth of the Redeemer? From a Star. The prophets had foretold that a special Star would appear at the birth of the Redeemer, and that the Redeemer would be king in Judea. Who had told this to the prophets? God. But what God says is true. Therefore the wise men firmly believed it. And they wished to see the Redeemer. They went to Judea. In what city did they first seek the Redeemer? What did they inquire about Him? Who had called the Redeemer a king? Why did the wise men seek the new-born King in Jerusalem? Because King Herod lived there. They therefore believed they would surely find the Redeemer in the royal city of Jerusalem. Therefore they said: "They hoped surely to find the Redeemer." But they did not find Him in Jerusalem. But through King Herod they found out that the Redeemer was to be born at Bethlehem. They at once started for Bethlehem. And as they left Jerusalem, the Star again appeared to them. What were their feelings at this sight? Why? They felt sure of finding the Redeemer. They followed the Star. Where did the Star stop?

Faith. Naturally a king's son is born in a palace; but the wise men stood in front of a miserable stable. They go in. They seek a king's child in a costly decorated cradle. And they find a Child in a manger lying on straw. A royal child is usually surrounded by many noble attendants. And whom do they find with the Infant Jesus? Others would have probably thought: " And is this Infant lying on straw in a manger in this wretched stable really the King of the Jews?" But the wise men believed in this Infant King. They believe Him to be the promised Redeemer, because the Star indicated Him. They believe Him to be the King of the Jews. They believe that poor Infant to be the infinite, great, rich and almighty God. By their faith they honor and worship the divine Infant. The wise men believed in the Infant Jesus.

Adoration. The wise men had already said in Jerusalem why they were seeking that Infant. In order to adore Him. Adoration is due to God alone. What did the wise men believe the new-born King of the Jews to be? God. And how, on this account, did they worship that Infant, when they had entered the stable? They prostrated themselves before the Infant Jesus and adored Him. Therefore they took off their crowns, for they knew that that Child was a far greater king than they. Where is His throne? This Child is the King and Lord of heaven and earth. Before Him they are very little, as a mere nothing. All that they are and have, come from Him, for He is their Lord and their God.

King and Lord. People willingly make presents to the great; they wish to honor them by so doing. In like manner, the wise men brought gifts to the divine Child. Each of them had brought the best his country produced. What was the gift of the first of these wise men? Gold. A king wears a golden crown. Therefore gold is the gift for a king. The head of the Infant Jesus should be decorated with the most beautiful crown of gold. Why? In what capacity did the wise men present gold to the Infant Jesus? They intended to honor him as a king.

God. What gift did the second of the wise men offer to the Infant Jesus? Incense is placed in a censer, that its sweet fragrance should ascend to God. Incense is offered to God. By offering incense the wise men worshiped the Infant Jesus as God. Hence by their gifts they honored the Infant Jesus as King and as God.

To love above all. What do we show when we make a present to some one? That we love him. What did the wise men show to the Infant Jesus by their beautiful gifts? That they loved Him. That Child was dearer to them than their gold and silver, than their parents, than their own children, than everything in the whole world. How much did the wise men love the Infant Jesus? The wise men loved the Infant Jesus above all things. They worshiped the Infant Jesus by their great love.

To hope. The wise men would have liked to remain with the Infant Jesus. But they had to return to their own country. They wept when taking leave of the Infant Jesus. They knew they would again see Him. Why did the Infant Jesus come upon earth? To redeem us from sin. Where then again can men go? To heaven. The wise men believed that the Infant Jesus would enable them to go to heaven. Where, then, did the wise men expect to see again the Infant Jesus? The wise men, therefore, hoped in the Infant Jesus. By their hope they honored and worshiped the Infant Jesus.

How, then, did the wise men honor the Infant Jesus? 1, They believed in Him; 2, they hoped in Him; 3, they loved Him above all things; 4, they adored the Infant Jesus. How did they consider the Infant Jesus? The wise men considered and honored the Infant Jesus as King and God.

B. OUR ADORATION OF GOD.

IV. *Faith.* The first commandment is: " I am the Lord thy God; thou shalt not have strange gods before Me." Which people adored strange gods besides God? The

Israelites. The Israelites, therefore, believed in many gods. That was a grievous sin. There is only one God. God is a spirit. We cannot see Him. But we must believe in Him. God Himself has said: " I am God, and there is no God besides Me." What God says is true. He is the eternal Truth. What do we then owe to God? We are bound to believe in God. By this faith we honor and worship God.

To awaken our faith. Every child of God received this faith in baptism. This faith is always in the child that is baptized. But the child does not always think on it. This faith, is, as it were, asleep in the child's soul. But it needs to be awakened. That takes place when we say it to ourselves, when we say it to God, that we firmly believe in Him. We can do it with these words: " My God, I believe in Thee, the eternal Truth." You ought daily to say that little prayer. You know another prayer in which we express our belief in God. Name it. The Apostles' Creed. How does it begin?

Hope. He who believes in God and keeps His commandments, will go to heaven. God promised it. Suppose a person commits a mortal sin after baptism; can he yet go to heaven, if he dies in that state? He would be cast by God into hell, to burn forever in its fire. But God does not wish the sinner to be lost. He has compassion on him, and will willingly forgive him, if the sinner is sorry for his sins and confesses them. God promised this. God is infinitely merciful. What may he hope for, who dies without sin? To go to heaven. What may the greatest sinner hope for, if he is sorry for his sins? He may hope to go to heaven. Why? God promised it; God is merciful. We must, therefore, hope in God.

To awaken hope. He who hopes in God's mercy, honors God. And that is what God demands of us. How should we honor God on account of His mercy? We must hope in God. Every child of God possesses this hope after his baptism. But it sleeps in him, like faith. What must we do to awaken this hope? We must awaken it, by saying: "O my God, I hope in Thee, as the infinite Mercy." Henceforth daily awaken your hope in that way.

Love. How to awaken it. What have you just been told to awaken every day? Faith. What did you learn some time ago that you should daily awaken in your heart? Love. What do you say when you awaken in your heart love for God? "O my God, I love Thee as the chief (supreme) Good." With what do we love God? With our heart, soul and mind. When we say these words, our heart, soul and mind should be with God. How much should we love God? With our whole heart, our whole soul, our whole mind, and with all our strength; in a word, we must love God above all things. How do we show that we love God? When, to please Him, we do good and avoid evil. Why should we love God? Because He is the chief (supreme) Good. He who loves God as the chief and most beautiful Good, honors God. This God demands of us. How should we honor God, because He is the chief Good? We should love God above all things. Why should we honor (worship) God? 1, Because He is the eternal Truth; 2, because He is infinitely merciful; 3, because He is the chief Good.

Divine worship in the Blessed Sacrament. How did the wise men worship the divine Infant, when they entered the stable? They prostrated themselves before Him and adored Him. Where do we find the Infant Jesus? In the church. He dwells in the tabernacle. The tabernacle is His crib. We cannot see the Infant Jesus as the wise men saw Him. He is concealed in the Sacred Host. The wonderful Star is there also. It is the lamp constantly burning before the tabernacle. It is like a fiery little tongue saying to us: "Here Jesus dwells." Therefore whenever we enter the church we come like the wise men, into the presence of the Infant Jesus. How should we honor Jesus? We should adore Him. Therefore on entering the church we at once look towards the tabernacle, and genuflect before entering a pew. What do we say when we take our place? "In the name of the Father, etc. O Jesus to Thee I live, to Thee I die, Thine I am in life and in death. Amen. In the name of the Father," etc. Thus we adore our Saviour. We should adore God alone. To Him alone is due this act of worship. We adore in the Blessed Sacrament Jesus as God.

Divine worship in the Holy Sacrifice of the Mass. Our loving Saviour every day comes down from heaven upon the altar. This takes place at the Consecration of the Mass. The priest raises Him in the Sacred Host, that we may see and adore Him. It is then that the altar boys ring the bell, and the faithful, in profound adoration, say in their heart: "O Jesus, my Lord and my God. O Sacrament most holy, O Sacrament divine, all praise and thanksgiving be forever Thine." The same happens when the priest raises the chalice containing the precious blood of our Lord. We should then say: "Eternal Father, I offer Thee the precious blood of Jesus Christ in satisfaction for my sins and for the Holy Church."

The Offertory. You should not merely adore the Infant Jesus, but should also, like the wise men, make an offering to Him. He does not ask of you gold, or incense, or myrrh. He wishes something more valuable. You should during the Mass offer yourselves to the Infant Jesus. What is the name of that part of the Mass when this should be done? And how will you make that offering? By saying: "O my Jesus, I give Thee my body and my soul and my whole heart, and all that I am and all that I have. Make me all Thine." Who gave you your body and your soul, and your heart, and all you are and all you have? To whom, then, do you belong? Who is your Lord and Master? And our Saviour especially is our Lord. And how did He become so? Therefore let us, at the Offertory, give ourselves freely to our dear Saviour; our heart, our body, our soul, our whole being. By doing so we honor and worship Him as our Lord. He especially desires our heart, our love, He who suffered and died to gain our heart, our love. Will you not give Him your heart? You have already been taught how to do it.

When the priest raises the host upon the little golden plate, you should in your thoughts place your heart upon that little plate, saying: "Dearest Infant Jesus, I offer Thee my heart; deign to accept it and preserve it pure from all sin." But not every heart is pleasing to Jesus. What kind of heart pleases Him?

The Communion. Jesus loves to enter a pure heart. During every Mass the Infant Jesus comes into the heart of the priest. Before receiving Him into his heart the priest strikes his breast three times, saying: "Lord, I am not worthy," etc. This part of the Mass is called the Communion. It comes shortly after the Consecration. You can easily tell when the priest is at the Communion, for the altar boy rings the bell each time the priest says: "Lord, I am not worthy," etc. You should then do like the priest, and strike your breast at each ringing of the bell, saying: "Lord, I am not worthy," etc. Then add: "Jesus, Jesus, come to me; my heart longs for Thee; I desire to receive Thee. Make me good and pure; keep me from sin." And Jesus will gladly come spiritually into your soul. (Questions for repetition appropriate to the foregoing on the Consecration, etc.) Children should each have a prayer book and bring it with them to church, and during Mass they should make use of the prayers in it for hearing Mass. You should pray not only in the church, but also at home. What prayers should you say in the morning? At the ringing of the Angelus? Before and after meals? And at night? All these prayers make up what we call the daily prayers. He who wilfully neglects his daily prayers, especially for some time, cannot be excused from sin. Some children hardly ever say a prayer; others usually say their night prayers, but never their morning prayers, or any other. That shows they do not love prayer.

Of whom do pious children think, when they say their prayers? Of God. They pray devoutly, and their prayer is pleasing to God. Other children say their prayers, but usually think of something else than God, when they are praying. Some even laugh, look around when they are saying their prayers. In the morning they think of their play or their breakfast when saying their morning prayers. Even in church, whilst they are praying, they think of almost everything else, except of God. Wilfully to think of other things, to gaze around or to laugh during prayer is sinful, for it is a want of respect for God. When therefore you go to confession, accuse yourself of being wilfully distracted during prayer in this way: " I accuse myself of being wilfully distracted during prayer "; then add whether it is always, every day, or only a few times. You pray well, if you try your best to think of God all the time you are praying.

As to those who wilfully neglect their daily prayers, they should confess: " I neglected my prayers "; then say if it was often, or only a few times; or even if it was for weeks and months. To neglect all prayer for about two months is surely a mortal sin, and must be confessed.

Table of sins against the first commandment: I neglected my daily prayers. I did not pray devoutly.

5. The Worship of God by Sacrifice.

OBJECT. I will tell you to-day how the first men worshiped God.

I. PREPARATION. When we wish to worship God right well, we go to the church. The first men had no churches, no altars. When they wished to worship God, they built an altar of stones. On it they placed wood, and on the wood they laid ears of corn, apples, cherries and other fruits, or a lamb, intending to give these things to God. They set fire to the wood in order to burn everything on it as an offering to God. This was a sacrifice. Whilst those things were burning, they would kneel and pray thus: " Thou art, O God, our supreme Lord and Master. All that we are and all that we have comes from Thee. Thou hast also given us life. We would willingly give Thee all that we are and all that we have, and even our very life; but Thou dost not wish it. We, therefore, give Thee the finest things we have, our best fruits, our most beautiful lamb. Deign favorably to accept these our gifts." And if the smoke from the burning gifts rose beautifully upwards, they believed God to have graciously accepted their sacrifice. I will also relate to you how the sons of Adam and Eve worshiped by sacrifice.

II. RELATION. Adam and Eve had two sons; Cain was the first, and Abel the second. Cain was a farmer and Abel, a shepherd. Abel was good, and Cain was wicked. One day each offered a sacrifice to God. Abel offered the finest lambs of his flock, and Cain offered fruits of the earth. God was pleased with Abel and his sacrifice; but did not regard Cain and his sacrifice. Cain was very angry, and looked very gloomy. The Lord spoke to Cain. " Why art thou angry and dost look gloomy? If thou actest right, thou shalt be rewarded; but if thou dost evil, punishment shall await thee. Repress thy evil inclinations, otherwise they shall rule over thee." Cain did not heed God's warning. One day he said to his brother: " Let us go out into the field." When they had gone out, Cain fell upon his brother Abel and killed him. God asked Cain: " Where is Abel, thy brother? " Cain replied: " I do not know; am I my brother's keeper? " God said to him: " What hast thou done? The voice of thy brother's blood crieth to Me from the earth. Be thou, therefore, cursed upon the earth. When thou shalt till it, it shall not yield to thee its fruit. A fugitive and a vagabond shalt thou be upon the earth." And Cain went out from the face of the Lord, and became a' fugitive, and found no rest.

CONSIDERATION — *The sacrifices of Cain and Abel.* How were the two sons of Adam and Eve called? Who was the elder son? Who was the younger? What was Cain? What was Abel? The brothers were very different in their hearts from each other. What kind of a heart had Cain? What kind had Abel? Abel did what was right before God. He was just. What did they one day offer to God? For what purpose did they do this? To worship God as the supreme Lord of all things. They built each an altar. What did they put first on the altar? What did they place on the wood? What was Cain's offering? What was Abel's? Each one offered the best he had; Cain offered the finest fruits (products) of the earth, and Abel, his finest lamb. Each of them set fire to his sacrifice. Then both knelt down, and besought God to accept their offerings. Abel's offering burnt beautifully; the flames and smoke ascended beautifully heavenward. The smoke of Cain's sacrifice fell to the ground. Whose sacrifice was pleasing to God? God regarded it with pleasure. Whose sacrifice God did not regard? What could Cain learn therefrom?

Abel. Let us see why God was pleased with Abel's sacrifice. Each of the two brothers built a beautiful altar, and offered thereon the best he had. Each knelt down nicely and prayed to God to accept his sacrifice. Of whom must we think when we pray? When we think of God in our prayer, our soul is with God. We have devotion, and the love of God is awakened in us. This was the case with Abel when he was praying near his sacrifice. He forgot everything else around him; he thought only of God, and his heart was inflamed with the love of God.

Cain. It was entirely different with Cain. Whilst he was praying, his thoughts were directed to his crops on his farm (enumerate). These were his greatest joy. To whom ought Cain to have directed his thoughts and his soul during his prayer? What would then have been awakened in his heart? What was wanting to his prayer? Devotion and love of God.

The heart. In what did the two brothers appear to have acted well alike in their sacrifice? In all that was outward. In what were they entirely different? In what was inward; in their heart. Let us take a look into their hearts. What did God see in Abel's heart? Love of God and devotion. What was wanting in Cain's heart? Therefore only Abel's sacrifice was pleasing to God. Even if we perform very nicely all that is outward, make a fine genuflection, join our hands in a devout manner, that is not sufficient. What does God consider the most? The heart. God looks upon the heart as the most essential.

Envy and anger. Cain would have God to take pleasure in his sacrifice. What would he have been obliged to change in his conduct to obtain God's pleasure? He should have thought: " I must endeavor to have as good a heart as Abel, so that I may have in prayer devotion and love of God. I will henceforth think oftener on God, that God may be pleased with my sacrifice." But unfortunately Cain did not do this. What were his feelings towards Abel, because God had been pleased with his sacrifice? His heart was burning with envy and anger towards Abel. His anger was very visible in his countenance, which expressed both envy and anger. Whose fault was it that God did not love him as much as Abel? His own. It was very unjust for Cain to be full of envy and anger against Abel. God saw the envy and anger in Cain's heart, and reproached him for his injustice towards Abel. What did God say to Cain? " Why art thou angry," etc. In which case would Cain be rewarded by God? What would happen to him if he did evil? Perhaps Cain had already thought of putting Abel out of the way. How did God admonish him for this? " Repress thy evil inclinations."

The crime. Cain did not heed God's admonition. What did he say one day to Abel? What a crime did he commit in the field on that day? So far had his envy and anger led him as to commit murder.

The punishment. God knew what Cain had done. What did He ask Cain? Cain should have acknowledged that he had killed his brother, and said to God: " Dear Lord, I am sorry for my terrible crime. Deign to forgive me." Cain could then have hoped for God's forgiveness; for God is most merciful. He forgives even the most heinous crimes. He would have forgiven Cain's crime, if Cain had been sorry for it. But Cain was obdurate. What answer did he give God? Then God reproached him with his crime. What did He say to him? The blood of his brother which he had shed seemed to have a voice crying out to God in heaven: " Punish him! Punish him!" What punishment did God lay on Cain? Cain should have no more happiness on earth. What should the earth no longer produce for him? Fruit. And he should nowhere find peace, but flee like a fugitive and a vagabond from place to place. And so it came to pass. Cain's heart was always full of dread. A voice always said to him: " Thou art a murderer, and shalt be cast into hell." Cain was afraid of that voice. He ran hither and thither, and would hide himself out of fear. That voice always cried out to him: " Thou art a murderer." At times he seemed to hear Abel saying to him: " O dear brother, let me go; I have done thee no harm." And Cain would then cry out: " O my sin, my sin; it is too great; God will not forgive me."

III. APPLICATION AND PICTURE. The catechist shows the children for some moments a picture of Cain and Abel. Then he asks them to point out Cain and Abel;

their respective altars in the background with their sacrifices. How did they build their altars? Which is Cain's? Which Abel's? How do you distinguish them from one another? How does the smoke of Abel's sacrifice ascend?

Our Sacrifice. We have also an altar in our church. Every day a sacrifice is offered on it to God. The Holy Sacrifice of the Mass. The Infant Jesus is offered in it. You also should offer something to God. What? Our heart. What did Cain and Abel do, whilst the sacrifices were burning? They knelt down and prayed with joined hands. They both knelt and joined their hands very nicely. You should imitate them in this. In church you should kneel straight, join your hands and look towards the altar, and make the sign of the cross correctly whilst pronouncing the words slowly and distinctly. God pays attention to this. But that is not yet the chief thing. What did God principally consider in the sacrifices of the two brothers? Their hearts. What did God perceive in Abel's heart? And therefore He was pleased with his sacrifice. And why was He not pleased with Cain's? His heart was bad, destitute of love and devotion. The same takes place with your offering and prayers during Mass. However beautifully you would act exteriorly, if your heart is evil and full of sin, neither your offering nor your prayers would please God. To enable your offering and your prayers to please God, your heart must be good and pure, and you must exert yourselves to have in your heart during Mass devotion and love of God.

B.

6. Honoring the Saints.

OBJECT. Last time you heard how we must honor and worship God; who can repeat it? To-day I will tell how we are allowed to honor the saints.

I. Development — *All the Saints.* This is now the month of May. Every evening we have devotion in church. How do we call it? The May devotion. How beautiful is it then in the church! Where does the priest kneel during this devotion? At the Blessed Virgin's altar. What special things do you see during May on her altar? It is adorned with flowers, and there are many lighted candles on her altar. We intend to honor the Blessed Virgin with those flowers and candles. What is done during the devotion? Hymns are sung. Can you mention some of them? Not only are hymns sung, but also prayers are recited. What prayers? The litany of the Blessed Virgin. By these hymns and prayers we also honor the Blessed Virgin. Let us again repeat how we honor the Blessed Virgin. How is her altar adorned? With flowers and candles. How do we honor her during the devotion? With hymns and prayers.

But we sometimes place flowers and lighted candles before the pictures of saints. Tell me which pictures of saints are thus honored in our church. Have you also pious pictures at home? Which ones have you? and you? Do you pray before them? In some Catholic countries the pictures or statues of the Blessed Virgin and of the saints, and crucifixes are placed along roads, near houses, and people are seen on their knees praying before them. Some have little lamps always lit before them. These pictures, statues, etc., were placed there long ago by pious people to honor the saints and to excite devotion in the hearts of those who pass by them. We honor the saints whenever we read or relate something about them. We venerate them by singing hymns in their honor, by praying to them, and also by adorning their images with flowers and lighted candles.

Mary. Mary, the Mother of God, was honored already when she was living on earth. One day when she was kneeling and praying in her little room, the angel Gabriel came to her. Who had sent that angel? How did he address Mary? "Hail, Mary, full of grace." It was God who thus saluted her through His angel. That was a great honor for her. God never saluted any one else in so beautiful a manner. He wished to show her how dear she was to Him. Why was Mary so dear to Him? Because she was so pious. She did not commit even the least sin. She even never was stained by what sin? Original sin. Her soul was as resplendently white and pure as a lily, and even much more so. Mary is the most beautiful, the most pious, the most holy among women and virgins. How is she called on this account? The most Blessed Virgin Mary. What message did God send to Mary by the angel? That she would have a son, and that the Son of God would be her Son. How do we call Mary on this account? Mother of God. For what did God choose Mary? To be the Mother of His Son. That was a still greater honor for her. Thus did God honor Mary whilst she was on earth. Where is Mary now? God honors her still more in heaven. He placed a throne for her in the highest heaven near His own throne. The Son of God placed His Mother on that throne. He clothed her in a magnificent garment and placed on her head a crown of twelve bright stars. (Show a picture of Mary crowned with twelve stars.) Who wears a crown on her head? What is Mary, because she wears a crown? A queen. Yes, God made her the Queen of heaven; she is the Queen of the angels and the saints. God has honored her, therefore, above every one else.

A good thing. God honors and loves the other saints in heaven. He has adorned them with wonderful glory. Some wear white garments, others red, and others violet. Some carry palms in their hands, others carry lilies. All are as bright as the sun, wear crowns and are seated on thrones. Thus does God honor the saints in heaven. They are His friends and favorites. He is pleased when we honor the saints; He even wills that we should do so. Therefore the Pope and the bishops teach: "It is a good thing to venerate the saints." How do we call the Pope together with the bishops? The Catholic Church. We, therefore, say also: "The Catholic Church teaches that it is a good thing to venerate the saints."

A useful thing. How do we venerate the saints? Chiefly by praying to them. Which litany do we recite in the May devotions? The leader calls Mary beautiful names, such as, "Mother of God, Virgin of virgins." What do all answer? Pray for us. In the month of March the litany of St. Joseph is usually said. There is also the litany of the Saints. The leader mentions (invokes) the name of some one of the saints in heaven, such as: "Holy Mary, Mother of God, St. Joseph, St. Peter, all the apostles, all the angels, the Holy Innocents." When you call your mother, she knows that you want something from her. And when we call on Mary and the saints, what do they know from this? That we want something from them. And how do you answer the leader? To whom should the saints pray for us? To God. Therefore we say to the Blessed Virgin: "Pray for me to Jesus, thy Son." Why do we not pray directly to God? Sometimes you need something, such as a book, an article of clothing, which you should ask from your father. But you are afraid to ask your father, for he is displeased with you. To whom do you make your wants known? To mother. And mother asks father for you, and father procures it for you. In the same manner we act with God, when we wish to obtain something from Him. We have committed many sins, and are afraid God may not give it to us; and we go to our heavenly Mother, and beg her to help us. How do we ask her? "Holy Mary, pray for me." Or we go to St. Joseph, and say: "St. Joseph, pray for us." Or to some other saint, saying: "Pray for me to God to grant me the favor —" And the saints consent, and pray to God for us. And God is pleased to grant their prayers, their requests for us, for He loves them as His friends. He then helps us sooner, than if we prayed directly to Him. Once I had lost my watch, and I could not find it. I prayed to St. Antony very devoutly to help me to find it. And I soon found it in the street all in good order. Thus St. Antony helped me by his intercession. And whom does not the Blessed Virgin help? How many very sick persons have prayed to her to cure them, and have got well! But did Mary herself cure them? No. Who cured them? God, for He alone can do so, since He is almighty. What then had Mary to do with their cure? She prayed God to cure them. She helped to cure them by her prayers (intercession). In like manner, the saints have helped many by their intercession. It is, therefore, useful to honor and venerate the saints.

Imitation. He who thus honors the saints delights to hear them spoken of and to read anecdotes about them. He thus finds out always more and more how holy the saints were. The same thing happens to him that once happened to many children. They were often with a holy boy, called Stanislaus. Stanislaus was fond of staying in church. His favorite place there was before the tabernacle. There he often knelt for hours, with his hands joined and his eyes cast modestly down, and looked like an angel. Every one liked Stanislaus. All the children sought his company. When he was praying in church, every child wished to kneel behind him; every one wished to see how piously and devoutly he prayed. All wished: "O if I were only as pious as Stanislaus!" They tried to imitate him. These children soon became much better and more pious, so that their parents were greatly astonished thereat.

The same will happen to you, if you read or hear much about the lives of the saints, such as St. Aloysius and St. Stanislaus. What will you then also wish for? To become pious like these saints. The veneration of the saints

would then be very useful and profitable to you. Therefore the Church teaches: "It is useful to honor the saints."
What did we say a few moments ago about honoring the
saints? Therefore the Church teaches: "It is good and
useful to honor the saints."

Mary. Which saint does God honor the most? Mary,
the most Blessed Virgin. Why? Because she is the
Mother of God. Mary is our Mother also. We are all
her children. She looks upon us from heaven and cares
for us. She can help us more than all the other saints in
heaven together. For she is the Mother of God. If she
intercedes for us with the heavenly Father or her divine
Son, we are sure of being heard. Mary is more willing
than the other saints in heaven to help us. She is our
Mother. It has never been heard that any one invoking
her, has not been heard.

II. Connection. To whom must Mary pray when she
wishes to help us? To God. Who is, then, far above
Mary and all the saints? Must God intercede with any
one when He wishes to help us? No, for He is almighty.
He depends on no one and can do all He wishes. How
do Mary and the saints help us? They help us by inter-
ceding for us with God. Therefore we only pray to them.
What do we say when we pray to the saints? Pray for
us. But we do not adore Mary and the saints. We may
adore only God. What would we consider Mary and the
saints to be, if we adored them? As God. But there is
only one God. And God said from Mount Sinai: "Thou
shalt not have strange gods before Me." Against which
commandment would we sin, if we adored the saints?
Against the first commandment.

III. Summary. What does the Church teach about
venerating the saints? The Catholic Church teaches that
it is good and useful to venerate the saints. Whom should
we venerate (honor) the most among the saints? The
Blessed Virgin Mary. Why do we venerate the Blessed

Virgin Mary in a special manner? We venerate the Blessed Virgin Mary in a special manner, because she is the Mother of God and our Mother also.

IV. APPLICATION. 1. We celebrate feasts to honor the Blessed Virgin. Can you mention one of Mary's feasts? The Assumption, the Purification, or Candlemas-day. Pious persons honor the Blessed Virgin daily. You also should pray to Mary every morning and every evening. Which of you prays to her morning and evening? You should every morning and evening say three Hail Marys in honor of her purity, that she may keep you pure. When you are in danger, when you are tempted, say: " Mary, my dear Mother, help me; protect me." If your father or your mother is sick, if you are in great want or in trouble, go to the church and kneel before the Blessed Virgin's altar, and pray earnestly to Mary to help you. She can obtain from God everything conducive to our welfare. Never forget to say the Angelus morning, noon and evening.

2. We celebrate feasts to honor other saints. Mention some of them. The feasts of St. Joseph, Sts. Peter and Paul, St. Aloysius. We celebrate a feast day, a Holyday of obligation, to honor all the saints together. Name it. All Saints on Nov. 1st.

3. You should pray daily also to St. Joseph, saying: " St. Joseph, Protector of the Church, protect me against temptation, make me good, and help me to lead a holy life."

4. Mary and St. Joseph are our patrons. Besides them every child has his own patron. The saint whose name he bears. Who is your patron? Who is yours? A good child prays daily to his patron. Say at least to him both morning and evening: " My holy patron, St. ....., pray for me." There are three patrons to whom every one should pray daily. Two of them, Mary and St. Joseph are for all children. The third one is the saint after whom

each one has been named. You should ask your parents to relate to you something of the life of your patron. You should strive to become as good and as pious as your patron. You should at least know what he did to become a saint; and then try to imitate him. You cannot give him greater pleasure than by trying to be good and holy like him.

SECOND COMMANDMENT.

A.

7. Reverence for the Name of God.

OBJECT. I will teach you to-day how to pronounce the name of God.

I. PREPARATION. Each of you has a name. What is your name? By what name are you called? Charles. The name Charles has been given you, that you may be called by it. For yourself, for your own use, you need no name. When you, Bernard, wish to say that you were at church this morning, you do not say: " Bernard was at church"; but you say: " I was at church." How do the other children call you? Whom do they mean when they call for Bernard? Me. Your name Bernard means yourself. Whom does he mean who says, President? The President. Whom does he mean who says, God? The name God means God Himself.

OBJECT. I will teach you to-day how to pronounce the name of God.

II. RELATION. A certain prophet was permitted to take a look into heaven. He saw God seated on His golden throne; and there knelt around Him the angels and saints. They bowed their heads, adored God and constantly sang a wonderfully beautiful hymn. " Holy, holy, holy, Lord God of hosts. Heaven and earth are full of Thy glory. Glory be to the Father, and to the Son, and to the Holy

Ghost." And when the Son of God was born at Bethlehem, the angels joyfully came down upon earth, praising God and singing: " Glory be to God on high."

CONSIDERATION — *God is holy*. Where did the prophet see God sitting in heaven? On a golden throne. God is the Most High; therefore He is seated on the throne. Who are around Him? The angels and saints. What beautiful hymn are they constantly singing? Why do they continually sing, Holy, etc.? In what position do they sing. They kneel and bow their heads. They do this out of reverence for God. What were the Israelites required to do when they had to appear before God on Mount Sinai? How had they to prepare themselves? Because God is holy, and he who appears before God, must be holy.

The name of God is holy. When we speak with God, we call Him by His name. What does the name God stand for? For God Himself. In pronouncing His name we think of how great, how holy, how beautiful, how mighty God is. There is nothing higher, more mighty, or more holy than God. Therefore the name of God is the most holy of names. The name of God is the most holy word we can think of. The first commandment obliges us to worship and adore God.

Revere the name of God. What do we owe to the name of God on this account? That we should show it reverence. What do the angels in heaven sing to revere the name of God? " Glory be to the Father," etc. With what hymn did the angels honor the name of God when the Redeemer was born? " Glory be to God on high." God wills that men should also revere His name. Therefore He proclaimed from Mount Sinai the second commandment in these words: " Thou shalt not take the name of the Lord thy God in vain." There are several names that mean God: Lord God, Lord, Creator, heavenly Father, Jesus Christ, Saviour, Redeemer.

1, *In prayer.* We pronounce the name of God in all our

prayers. Many begin with: "O my God." What name do we give to God in the Lord's Prayer? Father. In the Hail Mary? Lord; Jesus. We revere God's name by devoutly pronouncing it in prayer.

2. *In our wants.* Many pronounce the name of God even when they are not saying their prayers. A child, for instance, has just fallen into the water and is already sinking; his mother in great fear exclaims: "Good God, help me!" What will happen to that child, if no one comes to help him out? He will drown. The child is in great danger, in great need of help. What name did his mother pronounce? When we call some one by his name, we wish to obtain something from him. Why did the child's mother in her great need pronounce (call upon) the name of God? That God might help her. It is a beautiful thing to pronounce and invoke the name of God in our need. It pleases God. By doing so, we show that we believe God is almighty and can help us. We thereby honor His name. God wills that we should call upon Him in our wants, for He says: "Call upon Me in Thy need, and I will save thee."

People invoke even the names of the saints in their wants. For instance, a fire suddenly breaks out in a house. Some one of the family sees it, and exclaims: "Jesus, Mary and Joseph, help me." A sick person in his pains cries out: "Jesus, Mary and Joseph, deign to help me." A child is troubled with evil temptations; when aware of them, the child says: "Jesus, help me"; or, "Mary, pray for me." All these three persons were in need. Whom did they invoke in their need? Why did they invoke them? For help. What did they show to those holy names? Honor. Hence we honor, or revere, the name of God, when we invoke it in our wants, and also in prayer.

3. *In vows.* The name of God can be honored in another way. A child is dangerously ill. His mother greatly fears he will die. Therefore, she says: "Dear

Lord, if Thou restorest my child to health, I promise Thee
a pilgrimage to   ., and to offer Thee   I bind myself, under pain of sin, to do so." And God heard her
prayer, and her child got well again. What promise did the
child's mother make? To whom did she make it? And
now that her child is cured, what must she do? Make the
pilgrimage and the offering promised. A promise made
to God must be kept. How is such a promise called? A
vow. What name did the child's mother invoke? By her
vow she honored the name of God.

Breaking a vow. Now suppose that child's mother
would not keep her vow. Would she act right? God
helped her, because she invoked His name and made Him
a promise. Now she must keep her promise. If she does
not keep, but breaks her vow, it is just as wicked, as if
she had invoked God's name out of mockery. And instead
of honoring the name of God, she dishonored it. But
God forbids this in the second commandment. Recite the
second commandment. It is, therefore, a sin to break a
vow.

III. SUMMARY. We honor the name of God 1, when
we pronounce it in prayer; 2, when we invoke it in our
needs; 3, when we make a vow. We dishonor the name
of God when we break a vow.

IV. APPLICATION. You have just learned how we may
honor the name of God. You can do it many times a day,
for instance, by repeating a short prayer, such as: "My
God, I believe in Thee; My God, I hope in Thee; My God,
I love Thee with all my heart. My Jesus, have mercy on
me; My Jesus, all for Thee; Jesus, help me; Mary, help
me." But you must pronounce the holy name of God with
devotion, otherwise you will not please God. We should
do so especially when we pray, for God wishes us to honor
and revere His name as the angels and saints do in heaven.
Our divine Saviour taught us in the Our Father to say:
"Hallowed be Thy name." This means: "Our Father,

grant that I and all men may always honor and revere Thy holy name as the angels and saints do in heaven."

B.

8. Taking God's Name in vain.

OBJECT. I will teach you to-day, that we are not allowed to take God's name in vain.

I. RELATION. When Jesus was arrested on Mount of Olives by His enemies, He was brought that very night to the highest court of the Jews. Peter and John followed Him from a distance. Peter went into the court (front yard) of the high priest, to see what would happen to Jesus. There one of the maid servants recognized him and said to him: " Thou art also one of the disciples of Jesus." Peter said: " No, I am not; I do not know that man." And then he swore. Soon one of the men servants came to Peter, and said to him: " Yes, thou art one of the disciples of Jesus." Peter swore again and wished all kinds of evil to himself, if he were even acquainted with that man. When Jesus later on was hanging on the cross and suffered such terrible pains, the Jews mocked Him, saying: " He helped others, and He cannot help Himself. If Thou art the Son of God, come down from the cross."

CONSIDERATION — *Swearing.* Where was Jesus led after His arrest? Which two of His disciples followed Him? Peter wished to see what would become of Jesus. Where did he betake himself? The night was chilly. The soldiers, the men and maid servants of the high priest had lighted a fire in the front yard of the high priest. They all stood around it warming themselves. Peter stood among them. Who recognized him? What did she say to him? " Thou also art a disciple of Jesus." This was really so. Peter feared lest the soldiers would do him harm, would at last arrest him as they had arrested Jesus. What was his answer? " I do not know the man." But the maid servant would not believe him. Suppose, Charles, you went yesterday with your brother from school directly to N. (the next town), far away from any orchard; and some one points you out to the teacher as having yesterday after school stolen fruit in an orchard near by. What would you answer to your teacher? " No; I did not steal fruit in that orchard; I went with my brother directly after school to N." How would you make the teacher believe you? I would call my brother. Your brother would be your witness; he could say (testify) that you were telling the truth.

Peter would have wished he had a witness to testify that he (Peter) did not know Jesus. But there was no one around that he could call as a witness. Who knows all things? God. Who, then, could have told whether Peter knew Jesus? God. And now Peter called God as a witness. He who calls God as a witness of his telling the truth, swears (takes an oath). And this was what Peter did as an answer to the maid servant. Peter swore. In swearing people say: " God is my witness, that I am telling the truth." " As true as there is a God in heaven, what I say is true." Or: " God knows I am telling the truth." Peter used an expression like these, when he swore.

People often have to swear in court. For this, in Catholic countries, there is in the court on a table a crucifix between two lighted candles. He who swears, raises his right hand, and says: " I swear by almighty God, that I am telling (will tell) the truth. May God help me and His Holy Gospel." In the United States, the Judge (notary) reads the formula of the oath in the form of a question: " Do you swear that you will tell the truth, the whole truth and nothing but the truth? So help you God?" During this time the witness raises his right hand, says, " Yes," and then is expected to kiss the Bible. Swearing (taking an oath) means: " O God, Thou knowest all things; Thou knowest that I am speaking the truth. Thou art my witness." By these words we honor the name of God. We are not allowed to swear to anything, unless we are perfectly sure that it is true, so that God, who is Truth itself, can testify that we are telling the truth.

Swearing falsely. Peter swore that he did not know our Saviour. Could God have said to him: " That is true; you are telling the truth "? No. Why not? Peter knew our Saviour. He had always been with him. In swearing Peter did not tell the truth. He who swears to what he knows is not true, swears falsely. How did Peter swear? Peter swore falsely. He who swears falsely, lies; and he wishes God to say that he is telling the truth; he wishes God to help him to lie! By swearing to what is true we honor the name of God. But what does swearing falsely do to the name of God? It dishonors, it profanes the name of God. It is just like invoking the name of God in mockery. To swear falsely is a mortal sin. Swearing falsely is called perjury.

Moreover, a person may swear to something that is true, and yet commit a sin by doing so. For instance, a woman, speaking to her neighbor about the doings of her six-year-old Johnny, says: " I cannot tell you how smart my Johnny is; he can count from one to one hundred, and from one hundred backwards to one." But her neighbor does not believe that. But Johnny's mother replies: " What I say is as true as there is a God in heaven." That woman has sworn. Why did she swear? Because her neighbor would not believe that Johnny was so smart. But Johnny's smartness is a matter of no importance whatever. Hence it matters not, if her neighbor will not believe it. God is too holy for any one 'to call Him to witness things of no consequence. To swear is permitted only in matters of real importance and when it is necessary to testify in court, or when the law requires it. When is it not permitted? He who swears about trifles, without necessity, without a good reason, commits a sin. How did Johnny's mother swear? Unnecessarily. What did she commit in doing so? To swear without necessity is not a mortal sin in itself. Who commits a mortal sin by swearing? Why? Who commits sin by swearing? First, he who swears falsely, and secondly, he who swears without necessity. Children should not swear at all.

Cursing. Peter committed also other sins in the courtyard of the high priest. Who else, besides the maid servant, recognized Peter? What did he say to Peter? " Yes, thou art one of the disciples of Jesus." What did Peter answer? As the servant would not believe him, Peter grew angry. And what sin did he commit a second time? And besides that, Peter also cursed. You have probably heard people cursing; for instance, teamsters cursing their horses or their mules; also persons getting angry and quarreling with each other, cursing each other. You have perhaps sometimes heard a man cursing himself, calling on God to damn not only other people, but even his own soul! Peter was angry; he began to curse, and to curse himself, if what he said about not knowing Jesus, was not true! Cursing is sinful, and the sin is in proportion to the evil wished; the greater the evil wished in a curse, the greater also is the sin. Peter in cursing used the name of God; he dishonored it; he profaned it. He committed a very grievous sin by doing so. How must we use, or pronounce, the name of God? With the greatest reverence and respect. He who curses uses it to insult and wish evil. He profanes the holy name of God. Some people curse very often; some even can hardly speak without uttering a curse. We sometimes hear even little boys curse; some little boys curse, because they think it is a smart thing to curse. Good people on earth and the saints and angels in heaven pronounce the name of God with the greatest reverence and respect. In hell the devils and the damned are always cursing; cursing themselves, cursing others, cursing God. Hence cursing is the language of hell. And those persons, those children that curse are like the devils and the damned in hell; and if they do not amend, they will go to hell after their death, to curse for all eternity in the flames of hell! How ungrateful are those who curse almighty God! They abuse their tongue to profane the holy name of God, that tongue which God gave them with which to praise Him. They vent their stupid anger on the holy name of the best of fathers, of their greatest Benefactor, of their Redeemer, who died to save them. O dear children, do not ever use that abominable language of hell!

Pronounced with levity. Suppose a man going through our town, would hear his name called out by everybody. This indicates that no one wishes to have anything to do with him. How will he feel about it? Angry. No one likes to have people halloo his name everywhere. It would make you angry or cause you to weep. And your name is not a holy name. But what is the name of God? Not only a holy name, but the most holy of names. And yet how many persons there are who frequently, and that daily, say: " My God, O God, my Lord, O Lord, Jesus," as a mere common-place exclamation, just as if this holy name were only a common, insignificant word! Does this show any respect, any reverence for God Himself to pronounce His holy name with such levity? But as those who act thus, do not intend thereby to offend or dishonor God, they do not thereby commit a mortal sin, but only a venial sin. In like manner, many, who are addicted to cursing, curse without reflection, without meaning what they say; they do not commit a mortal sin thereby, but they are obliged to do all they can to get rid of such an evil habit.

Blasphemy. Whilst our divine Saviour was hanging on

the cross many Jews sinned grievously. Jesus suffered terrible pains; it was of His free-will that He suffered them for the sins of mankind. But how did the Jews cry out to Jesus? They meant to say: "Thou hast said that Thou art God; but Thou hast no power; Thou canst not help Thyself." They profaned, mocked and made fun of the name of God. They committed thereby the horrible sin of blasphemy. This takes place continually in hell, where the name of God is blasphemed day and night. This grievous, horrible sin is the sin of the devils. Sometimes men blaspheme God, when some misfortune happens to them, or when they get very sick. They charge God with being unjust, cruel, with not hearing their prayers, with not caring for them. How terrible!

II. CONNECTION. Let us examine the ways in which the name of God is dishonored, or profaned. Who pronounce the name of God with levity? Those who utter (pronounce) it without reflection. Who pronounce it in anger? Those who curse. Who profane or mock the name of God? Those who blaspheme, those who commit perjury, those who break a vow. Which of these usually commit only a venial sin thereby? Which of them sin grievously? What do they all do to the name of God? They dishonor it.

III. SUMMARY. The second commandment is: "Thou shalt not take the name of the Lord thy God in vain." Who sins against this commandment? 1, He who pronounces the name of God with levity; 2, he who abuses it by cursing; 3, he who swears falsely or unnecessarily; 4, he who breaks a vow; 5, he who blasphemes God.

IV. APPLICATION. 1. Let us again examine which sins Peter committed in the front yard of the high priest. What did the maid servant ask Peter? What did Peter answer? And what did he do besides? He swore that he did not know Jesus. How did Peter swear? What did the man servant say to Peter? What did Peter answer? And what else did he do again? And what else besides? Cursed himself. How did Peter sin against the name of God in speaking to the man servant? Now suppose Peter would go to confession; how must he confess his sins? " I cursed once, and swore falsely twice."

2. Johnny, on his way to school, stumbled, fell down and hurt himself. He got angry and cried out, calling on God to damn those who put that thing there, which he stumbled against. When writing, he knocked his inkstand and spilled ink over his paper; then came another curse in his anger. How must he confess his sins? " Twice I got angry and cursed." Robert tells that he got a present from his uncle of ten dollars. Albert says: " I do not believe it." " It is true, as true as there is a God in heaven; may God strike me dead, if it is not true." How did Robert sin? By unnecessary swearing. How must he confess his sin? " I swore once without necessity."

God sometimes immediately punishes those who profane His name. One day the tongue of a terrible curser began to swell as soon as he had uttered a terrible curse, so that it hung out of his mouth, and he could no longer draw it in, and thus he died. Dear children, never laugh, if you hear any one cursing; say then in your heart: " Dear Lord, forgive him. Hallowed be Thy name. Blessed be the holy name of God."

4. Some children have accustomed themselves to pronounce the name of God with levity. These children should from this moment make this resolution every morning: " O my God, I am resolved not to pronounce on this day Thy holy name with levity. Help me to keep this resolution." And try to think of this resolution sometimes during the day. And in case you have again pronounced the name of God with levity, say: " O my God, hallowed be Thy name; blessed be Thy holy name."

How to confess sins against the second commandment;

I pronounced the name of God with levity. I cursed.—
I swore without necessity.

9. Third Commandment of God; First Commandment of the Church. Sanctification of the Sunday and of the Holydays of obligation.

I. PREPARATION. In how many days did God create the world? What did God do on the seventh day? And God willed also that men also should rest on that day. The seventh day is, then, a day of rest. The word sabbath means, day of rest. Which is the first holy day in the world? God willed that this day should belong to Him. God is our Lord and Master. What was the Sabbath called? The Lord's day. The day men should spend in a holy manner. How? By worshiping God in a special manner. Adam and Eve did this already in the earthly paradise. But men gradually neglected to keep the Sabbath holy. Even the Israelites in Egypt often did not observe it. Therefore, when God gave the ten commandments on Mount Sinai, He strictly commanded the Israelites: " Remember, that thou keep holy the Sabbath-day." That is: " Already in paradise I commanded that the Sabbath should be kept holy. Think on it. Do not forget it."

The Sabbath, or day of rest, was for the Israelites Saturday. But our divine Saviour did not wish that the Christians should have their day of rest on Saturday. On what day of the week did Jesus Christ rise from the dead? On a Sunday. By His resurrection the Son of God sanctified the Sunday. Therefore our Saviour wills that we should have our day of rest on Sunday. Moreover, it was also on a Sunday that the Holy Ghost came down upon the apostles. On which Sunday? The Holy Ghost also sanctified the Sunday. We should think of this on Sundays. Sunday is thrice holy for us. God the Father, God the Son and God the Holy Ghost sanctified it. How did God the Father sanctify it? How did God the Son? How did God the Holy Ghost? Therefore Sunday is the day of God, of the Lord. In Catholic countries each one has also a day, which he calls his day. Which day is it? Each one's name day, the feast day of his patron. How is it celebrated in the family? Sunday, the Lord's day, is to be observed, celebrated, by all men. "Remember," etc.

OBJECT. I will tell how we should keep Sunday holy.

II. RELATION. Suppose this day was Sunday. How glad you feel on Sundays. The whole week before you rejoice when you think on Sunday. Why? Because there is no school on Sunday. People do not need to work on Sunday. On Sundays we wear our best clothes, and hear the bells ringing, and go to church. People go to church from every direction. Those who live the furthest away are generally the first in church. Holy Mass begins. There is a sermon, and all the faithful listen to it attentively. All keep their eyes fixed on the priest at the altar during Mass. Mass over, all go home, and the whole family have dinner together. And usually there are sweetmeats, or fruit, for the children. In the evening there is divine service with Benediction. Is not the Sunday a beautiful day? It is the day of the Lord.

CONSIDERATION — *Abstaining from servile works.* How many working days in the week? What do people do on those days? What does the farmer? The carpenter? The merchant? How many days do people work in a week? This God has commanded. In giving the ten commandments on Mount Sinai God said: "Six days shalt thou labor, and shalt do all thy works. But on the seventh day is the Sabbath of the Lord thy God. Thou shalt do no work on it, thou, nor thy son, nor thy daughter, nor thy man servant, nor thy maid servant, nor thy beast."

Therefore people rejoice about Sunday the whole week in advance. They are then allowed to rest. What kind of work is forbidden on Sundays? Farming, working at a trade; hard work, manual labor, sewing, ironing, laundry work and the like. These kinds of work are called servile works. From what kinds of work must we abstain on Sundays? The servile works profane the Sunday, and are sinful. How do we profane the Sunday? Some kinds of work are not forbidden on Sundays, such as, preparing the meals, getting water, feeding the cattle, and the like. Also we are allowed to read, write, study, draw, play musical instruments, play.

Works of devotion; Mass and Sermon. We must serve God on Sunday. Where is divine service held? In the church. The church bells ring and call the faithful to church. They come from every direction to church. All are dressed in their best clothes. They carry prayer books in their hands. Mass begins and all look towards the altar to follow the priest in the different parts of the Mass. After the Gospel is the sermon; all listen to it attentively. After the sermon the priest continues the Mass. Who comes down on the altar at the Consecration? Our divine Saviour is now in our midst; He prays on the altar with us and for us to His heavenly Father. For this reason the Church commands us to assist at holy Mass on Sundays. He who assists at Mass on Sundays, performs a pious work, and sanctifies the Sunday. He who, through his own fault, does not assist at (misses) Mass on a Sunday, commits a mortal sin. Those who cannot go to Mass on Sunday, such as the sick, those who have to wait on the sick, who live too far from church, who on account of necessary work cannot come to church, are excused from assisting at Mass. When are children bound to go to Mass on Sundays? When they have reached the age of discretion, which is about the seventh year.

There are children who go, indeed, to Mass, but look

around, talk and laugh during Mass. This is bad behavior; it is a sin. How can a person, a child commit sin during Mass? By misbehaving. Where should we look devoutly during Mass? Towards the altar, to be able to follow the priest in the different parts of the Mass. How should we honor our divine Saviour when He comes down on the altar at the Consecration? We should adore Him. What should you offer to our Saviour during Mass? Our heart. In which part of the Mass? At the Offertory. And in which part should you ask our Saviour to come into your heart? At the Communion. He who does these things well, assists devoutly at Mass. That is the principal thing. This is what the Church commands: " Thou shalt hear Mass devoutly on Sundays and Holydays of obligation."

Evening Service. Pious Christians assist also at the evening service on Sundays. It consists of Vespers, or of some special devotions of confraternities, sodalities, and exposition and Benediction of the Blessed Sacrament. There is no strict obligation to assist at the evening service, but to neglect doing so is to deprive ourselves of many special graces, and especially of the blessing of Jesus Christ Himself. But it is a strict obligation to assist at Mass on Sundays and Holydays of obligation; and it is a mortal sin to neglect this through our fault.

Holydays of obligation. Besides the Sundays, there are six Holydays of obligation, which the Church commands us to observe just like Sundays. What are we commanded to do on Sundays? To hear Mass devoutly. And what are we forbidden on Sundays? To perform servile works without necessity. The six Holydays of obligation usually fall on week days. They are: 1, Christmas, Dec. 25th, the day on which Jesus Christ was born; 2, the feast of the Circumcision of our Lord, Jan. 1st.; 3, the Ascension of our divine Saviour into heaven, the sixth Thursday after Easter Sunday; 4, the

Assumption of the Blessed Virgin Mary into heaven, on Aug. 15th; 5, All Saints, Nov. 1st; and 6, the Immaculate Conception of the Blessed Virgin Mary, Dec. 8th. Who can tell me what is the meaning of the Immaculate Conception? It means that Mary alone of all the descendants of our first parents was conceived immaculate, that is, without the stain of original sin, because she was destined by God to become the Mother of the Redeemer. What does the Church command us to do on those six Holydays? To hear Mass, just as on Sundays. What does she forbid us to do on those six Holydays? To perform unnecessary servile work. What kind of sin does he commit who neglects, through his own fault, to hear Mass on any of those days? A mortal sin. And what kind of sin does he commit who performs unnecessary servile work for hours on any of those days? A mortal sin. (On these six feasts and other great feasts that come on a Sunday, such as, Easter and Pentecost, the altars and the church are usually grandly adorned with lights, flowers, etc., and the priest wears the finest vestments at Mass and the other services.)

III. SUMMARY. How must we keep the Sundays? How must we keep the Holydays of obligation? Who are dispensed from hearing Mass on Sundays and Holydays of obligation? What kind of works are forbidden on those days? May necessary servile work be performed on those days? How must children behave in church, especially during Mass? Is it a sin to come in late during Mass on Sundays and Holydays of obligation? What would you say of him who, through his own fault, comes to Mass only at or after the Offertory? What must he do who comes late to Mass, that is, after the Offertory has commenced? He must, if possible, hear another Mass, for the obligation of hearing Mass requires us to hear a whole Mass, to be present at least at the three principal parts of the Mass: the Offertory, the Consecration and the Communion. (Insist firmly on this, on the necessity of being already in church when the Mass begins.) Do those children hear Mass who do not pay any attention to the Mass, but spend the whole time of the Mass in looking around, talking and laughing? What kind of sin do they commit? (Impress deeply on the minds of the children to behave well during Mass, to use their prayer books and follow the priest especially when the children are not with their parents during Mass.)

IV. *Connection of the first three commandments with the commandment of the love of God.* Which are the two greatest commandments? Why must we love God above all things? What ought we to be, since God is so good a father to us? Let us see how a child shows that he loves his father. On whom does that child often think, who really loves his father and mother. On whom should a child love to think, who dearly loves his Father in heaven? With whom must a child like to speak, who dearly loves his Father in heaven? What is the meaning of speaking with God? When should we pray? How do we call the prayers we should recite every day? How should we pray? Which commandment of God requires us to worship God by love and prayer? Which is the first commandment of God? What does God see when we love to pray? When does God see from our prayers, that we do not love Him dearly? When we do not pray at all, or pray without devotion. In which commandment of God is the commandment of the love of God more fully explained?

The child that loves his father and mother, likes to pronounce the names of father and mother. What name should that child pronounce, who loves God? God is holy; how then, should we pronounce His name? In which two cases ought we to pronounce the name of God? What do we then do to the name of God? What does God see from our pronouncing His name with reverence in prayer and in our wants? But what does He see, if we pronounce His name without respect? Who dishonors and profanes the name of God? Which commandment forbids the profanation of the name of God? Which is the second commandment? Therefore the second commandment gives a fuller explanation of the commandment of the love of God.

Where does a child, who loves his parents, like to be? At home with his parents. We are children of God. In whose house do we, therefore, like to be? On which day especially should we like to go to God's house? What should we do in God's house? Which divine service should we attend? From which works should we abstain on the Lord's day? What does God see when we thus sanctify His day? Which commandment requires us to keep the Lord's day holy? Which commandment, therefore, further explains the commandment of the love of God?

V. APPLICATION. 1. Let us again consider which sins are committed on Sundays. Which kinds of work are not permitted on Sundays? Servile works. For instance, a tailor says on Sunday morning: " Those clothes must be finished." Hence he worked the whole forenoon. At noon he goes to a saloon. How did he keep the Sunday? Why? Because he performed servile works and missed Mass. How must he confess his sins? " I neglected to hear Mass on Sunday; and I worked all forenoon on Sunday." There was fine weather for a whole week. The weather on Sunday was also fine. A farmer said Sunday afternoon: " I will bring in the hay." His neighbor was already bringing in his hay with his two servants during Mass on Sunday morning. What kind of sin did the first farmer commit? How many sins did the second commit? And his servants also missed Mass and worked. Whose fault was that? The farmer's. How should each servant confess his sins?

Robert intends to go to Mass on Sunday; but Antony

says to him: "Let us go into the woods and get birds' nests." At noon they return home from the woods. What do you say about them? How must they confess their sin in confession? And what must Antony confess besides?

A certain boy usually missed Mass on Sunday once a month. How must he confess his sins? Another boy heard Mass twice a month. How often did he miss Mass? How must he make his confession? A boy did not go to Mass for two Sundays, because he was sick? Did he commit any sin on account of it? Frank was not at Mass last Sunday; he had not yet finished his breakfast when the last bell rang. What do you say about this? Rose did not hear Mass last Sunday, for she had to get something in the grocery. Johnny was not at Mass either, for he could not find his shoe; everybody helped him to look for it. Bertha and Louise were not at Mass either, because their dresses were torn. What do you say about these cases?

Anna could not go to Mass, because she had to mind the baby, in order to let her mother go. Did she commit any sin? Fanny could not go to Mass, because she had to go at once to the drug-store to get medicine for her sick father. Did she commit any sin? Lena was not at Mass on Sunday, because it was raining hard, and the church was three miles distant, and the road was very bad. Was that a sin for her? Andrew was in church. He first looked till he had seen everybody. Then he said foolish things to the boy next to him; he would at times punch the boy at his left in the ribs; then he took out his knife and cut the pew in several places. Then he took out the marbles from his pocket, and counted them several times over. One of them fell down and ran over the floor; this made the other boys titter and laugh. He said no prayers at all. What sins did he commit? How must he confess them? I misbehaved in church, and talked and laughed and disturbed others. And if it was during Mass on Sunday, he also missed Mass: a mortal sin.

2. Dear children, never miss Mass on Sundays and Holydays through your own fault. Mass is the most beautiful thing on Sunday. A Sunday without holy Mass is not a real Sunday, not a real Lord's day. He who devoutly hears Mass on Sunday, feels happier during the week; he feels that God loves and blesses him. And if during your whole life you hear Mass devoutly every Sunday, God will bless your whole life. He will protect you, and you will be sure at the end of your life to go to heaven. He who neglects to hear Mass on Sunday, will not pray well to God during the week, and there is reason to fear he will not go to heaven. When you are grown up, avoid working on Sunday without necessity. On Sunday rest and pray well, for Sunday is the Lord's day.

How to confess sins against the third commandment. I neglected, through my own fault to hear Mass on Sundays and Holydays.— I misbehaved in church.

FOURTH COMMANDMENT.

A.

10. Duties of Children towards their Parents.

I. PREPARATION. Which are the two greatest commandments? Which is the commandment of the love of our neighbor? Who is our neighbor? Which persons are the most nearly related to us? Our parents and our brothers and sisters. Which is the fourth commandment of God?

OBJECT. I will teach you to-day that we must respect, love and obey our parents.

II. RELATION AND CONSIDERATION. 1. We must respect our parents.

Our invisible and our visible father. Look at a little child. God created that child. God is that child's father. You were once as small as that child. Who created you? Who, then, is your father? Can you see God? What is He then? Invisible. Where does He dwell? God is, therefore, our invisible heavenly Father. When God gave life to you little children, you were helpless. A little child, an infant, can do nothing but cry and struggle. It needs some one to care for it. Therefore God gave you a visible father and a visible mother, your parents, to take care of you.

Parents and superiors, God's representatives. After your baptism God placed you in the arms of your mother, saying: "Here is a dear little infant. I created it. It is Mine. It has an innocent heart and a wonderfully beautiful soul. The angels and saints in heaven rejoice over that little child. And I Myself love it as the apple of My eye. Take care of that child in My place; see that it keeps alive and grows strong. Feed it, clothe it, give it a home. Bring it up, teach it to pray, to love Me, to obey and to be pious. Preserve it from sin, so that it may one day come to Me in heaven. It is destined to be a great saint in heaven, and to shine there like a bright star. That is its right." Who, then, is your kind, almighty, invisible Father? Whom did God, your invisible Father, appoint as His visible representatives in your regard? In whose stead do your visible parents care for you? What, then, are your parents? Our parents are God's visible representatives towards us. (Parents, who die when the children are yet young, are replaced by foster-parents, stepfather, stepmother, adopted parents.)

Superiors. Parents are not always able to train, to educate the child themselves; they need the help of others, such as the teacher in school, the priest, etc. These persons are the child's superiors, each in his own place, and represent or replace the child's parents, and are likewise representatives of God.

Honor and respect due to the representatives of God. God is our almighty Lord and Master. What do we owe Him? Honor and respect. How do you show Him honor and respect when you enter the church? When you pronounce His name? On Sundays? Your parents and superiors are God's representatives. What, then, do you owe to them? And when you show them honor and respect, you honor and respect God Himself, whose place they hold towards you. Therefore God says to you: "Honor thy father and thy mother, that it may be well with thee and that thou mayst live long upon earth."

Example: Joseph of Egypt. Let us consider how Joseph honored and respected his aged father. Joseph's brothers were shepherds. What was his father also? What high office had the king of Egypt given to Joseph? Joseph was a great lord, and his father was only a shepherd. Nevertheless Joseph was not ashamed of his old father. What did Joseph send to bring his father to Egypt? Chariots. What did Joseph do, when he heard his father was coming? He drove in his chariot to meet him. Joseph paid such honor in Egypt only to the King, for he was next to the King. All the people in Egypt were obliged to honor and respect Joseph. Hence Joseph went to meet his father with as much honor as he would have gone out to meet the king himself. What did Joseph do when he perceived his father? He came out of his chariot, and, like a good son, went directly to his father to welcome him and embrace him. Then he took him with him in the royal chariot. Then leading him to the king, he said: "This is my father." For Joseph knew: "However high up I am in the world, my father is above me." What was his father to Joseph? God's representative. What, then, did Joseph do to his father? He honored his father.

Therefore you also should honor your parents. Why? Because they are God's representatives. What do you say to them every morning and every night? How should you speak to them? Respectfully. You must not speak to them as you would to your playmates, who are your equals. How should you speak to your superiors?

2. We should love our parents.

Our parents love us. Because God is your Father, He loves you as a father loves his children. With what do we love? God has for you, His children, a father's heart full of love. His heart, with which He loves you, is like a fiery sun full of love. Now God wills that your parents should in His stead, rear you for Him. They must have love to do this properly. Therefore God let a spark of love fall from His loving fatherly heart into the hearts of your parents. Therefore, your parents love you as if with divine love. How beautiful was it when you were yet an infant. Your mother would herself put you to bed at night, and sing and rock you to sleep, whilst sewing or knitting something for you. In the morning your mother, when you awoke, would take you out of your little bed, kiss you, press you to her heart. Oh, how good does the little child feel in its mother's arms, and near its mother's heart! Oh, how beautiful it finds the world when mamma is near! A mother's love watched near you, a mother's love cared for you, a mother's love protected you. Mother follows you everywhere, laughs and smiles when you laugh and smile, weeps when you weep, relieves you of pain, when you hurt yourself; warms your body in her arms, and your soul in her heart. And when the child is sick, mother sits and weeps and watches day and night near its little bed, and leaves nothing undone to allay its pain, to effect its cure. In a certain house the mother has a child that is a cripple. Oh, poor, dear little child! Perhaps others do not like you; but your mother loves you so much the more. Therefore, the greater the marks of her affection, the greater and the more ingenious is her care for that child.

The father also dearly loves his children. He works hard from morning till night to earn a living for his child, to enable the mother to procure all the child needs. For his child he undergoes fatigue, exposes his health, wears out his strength, and sometimes must put up with humiliations and harsh treatment, or has to engage in dangerous work. No one in this world so greatly benefits a child as its parents. How do we call those who do us good? What are our parents in our regard? Our benefactors. The greater the good a person does to us, the greater benefactor he is to us. Who, in this world, does us the most good? Therefore our parents are our greatest benefactors.

In God's stead. From whom have our parents the means to do us good? In whose stead do they provide for our wants? Through whose hands do we receive God's greatest benefits? Through the hands of our parents.

We must also love our parents. What do we owe to our parents for their great love and their many benefits? We must love our parents. If we love our parents, we love also Him, in whose stead they bestow benefits upon us. Whom, then, do we love when we love our parents?

Example of Joseph of Egypt. How beautifully did not Joseph of Egypt show how he loved his father! What did he send to his father and his brothers when there was a famine? Why? What was his first question when his brothers came the second time to Egypt? Why? Joseph had become a powerful and rich lord. But he had not lost his childlike love for his father. Which were his first words after making himself known to his brothers? What does that prove? Afterwards he said to his brothers: " Hasten to my father." And where were they to bring his father? And for what? And what did Joseph do when he again saw his father? He embraced and kissed him amid a flood of tears. What does this prove? Joseph cared for his father and his brothers. Which part of the country did he give them? And what did Joseph do when his father died? He wept over him. What do you conclude from all this? How a grateful child should love his parents.

You are not able to do as much for your parents, as Joseph did for his father. But in how many things you can help them! Get water for them, mind the baby and the little ones, carry messages go out on errands, put things in order. What can you not do for them, if they are sick! Give them to drink, hand them their medicine, their food, avoid making noise; remain near them, to attend to their wants; pray for them. And when you are bigger, how can you show that you love them? Help them in their work.

3. We must obey our parents.

The parents command. Where do children wish to go after their death? There our heavenly Father dwells. Which children will go to heaven? Only the good and pious. But it is the duty of parents to see to it that their children should be good and pious. That is why God entrusts the children to them. Every mother wishes that her children should be the best and the most pious. How often does not a good mother kneel at night alongside her baby's cradle, earnestly praying God to bless and sanctify her child and protect it against all evil! "Bless, O Lord, and protect my child against all that is evil." Or on a Sunday afternoon the mother brings her baby to church and kneeling before the tabernacle, beseeches our divine Saviour to place her child in the wound in His Sacred Heart, that it may be always good and free from sin. Thence she goes before the altar of the Blessed Virgin, and consecrates her child to the Mother of God, praying

Mary to protect her child, to keep it pure and be a mother to it. At night before putting her child to sleep, she makes it lisp a few prayers to Jesus and Mary, and then making the sign of the cross on its forehead, she kisses it good night, and does not leave till the child is asleep.

During the day the mother, tenderly holding her child in her lap, speaks to it of God, of the Child Jesus, of His birth and life, of His passion, etc., and teaches it the daily prayers. She tells the child of the beautiful heaven and its joys, what is to be done to go there.

Obedience. What must children do when their parents command them to do something or forbid them to do certain things? Children must obey their parents. Whose place do the parents take with regard to their children? For whom must parents bring up their children? Whom do children obey when they obey their parents? What do children cause to their parents and to God when they obey? Suppose a mother has seven or eight children as large as you, or even larger, who are all obedient to her. They are like a beautiful crown of flowers around her. They all pray together with her. Such a mother is a thousand times more beautiful than a blooming rosebush amid thorns. God looks down graciously on such a mother and her children. And how proud is that mother of her well brought up and obedient children! What is the greatest monarch to your mother in comparison with her obedient child? The monarch may be more beautiful, but the mother loves her obedient child best; the monarch is richer; but her obedient child is far dearer to her than the richest monarch. The mother knows only her child, she sees him only, loves him only, for he is her obedient child. And he who would tell you that he loves you more than do your father and mother, believe him not. You should, then, be glad when you have a chance to obey your parents, and you should never wait till they repeat the command. A good child obeys promptly. Sometimes it may be hard to obey. But what will make it easy? To do it for the love of God.

Consider the dear Child Jesus in the house of His parents at Nazareth. It was all the same to Him, if they commanded Him to do something easy or something difficult. Nothing was too much for Him. As soon as He received a command, He thought: "My Father in heaven wills this." And He would do it cheerfully. His parents saw that nothing pleased Him more than to be told to do something. There were then other persons on earth who did good, but the heavenly Father had no greater pleasure in any of them, than in the quiet obedience of His Son. The Son of God wished to teach obedience to children. He wished to show them how beautiful obedience is in the sight of God. Therefore you should not always wish to do only what pleases you. You must, before all, do what your parents command you. The child that does what his parents and teachers command, does enough, for he does what God wills. Hence all you do is beautiful and holy in the sight of God. Not every child can be rich, beautiful and smart. That is not necessary, in order to please God. But every child can obey; and that is worth more before God than to be rich and smart. No matter how stupid and incapable a child is, he can do much, for " he can obey." When you find it hard to obey consider: " Jesus, my Saviour, was obedient; for His sake I also will obey." And the more you advance in age, the more obedient you should be to your parents. It is a sad thing when parents must say of their children: " The older they grow, the more lazy and wicked they become." Our end on earth is to grow better every moment.

Joseph's example. You have a beautiful example of an obedient son in Joseph of Egypt. His brothers were usually away from home. Whom did their father send to them? For what reason? This was no easy matter for

Joseph, for he had to walk fully sixty miles where there were no roads and many wild beasts. Joseph knew also how ill-disposed his brothers were towards him. What did Joseph do? He obeyed. His father did not need to repeat his command or to threaten or coax Joseph. He always obeyed at once.

THE REWARD.

1. *Joseph in his father's tent.* Therefore his father loved him more than his other sons. How did he show this? How did Joseph get along with his father? Well. What is the fourth commandment? What promise did God add to it? " That it may be well with thee." What did God promise to the children who obey their parents? Why was it well with Joseph in his father's tent?

2. *Joseph in Putiphar's house.* Who bought Joseph in Egypt? Who was with Joseph in Egypt? That is: " God protected Him." What did God cause to happen with everything Joseph did? " God blessed all that Joseph did." How did his master feel towards Joseph? What did he do to Joseph? What did God bestow on Joseph in Putiphar's house? Protection and blessing. How was it there with Joseph? Well. What promise was fulfilled in him?

3. *Joseph in prison.* What happened to Joseph on account of Putiphar's wife? In prison people are usually unhappy. Who was also with Joseph in the prison? How did God so arrange things that it was well with Joseph even in the prison? How did the jailer show his love for Joseph? What else did God bestow on Joseph in the prison? His protection. The chief baker and the chief butler of the King each had a dream. Who explained their dreams? From whom does the explanation of dreams come? Who enabled Joseph to explain their dreams? Thus God blessed Joseph. What did God bestow on Joseph

in the prison? What promise was fulfilled in Joseph also in the prison?

4. *Joseph is exalted.* Whose dreams did Joseph explain later on? How was the king pleased with his explanation? How did he reward Joseph? What did the king do before all the people to honor Joseph? What did he order to be proclaimed? See how wonderful; in the morning Joseph was yet in jail, and now! Now the whole country obeys him. Who brought all this about? How did God reward Joseph in Egypt for his obedience to his parents and superiors? What promise was fulfilled in Joseph? The same promise will be fulfilled also in all good children. This does not mean that every good child will be a king, or a king's prime-minister. What may all children who obey their parents, expect in this life? God's protection and blessing. How long did Joseph live after the death of his father? Was his life a long life? Who gives men a long life? To which children did God promise a long life? Why did God grant to Joseph a long life? Nevertheless good children may also die young, because God wishes to have them in heaven with Him. And where is Joseph now? He is exceedingly happy there. What did God give to Joseph in the next life? Everlasting happiness. He does the same to all good children. What, then, have good children the right to expect in the next life? Everlasting happiness.

III. CONNECTION — *Jesus.* With whom do good children like most to be? Who was the most holy Child that ever lived on earth? With whom did the Child Jesus like to be? How did he always speak to His parents? What did He do, when His parents wished for anything? And what did He do, when they commanded Him something? What did the Child show to His parents? Respect, love and obedience. What was Jesus from all eternity? What were Joseph and Mary? Men. To whom, then, did the Son of God show respect, love and obedience? The Son

DUTIES OF CHILDREN

of God was obedient to His parents for thirty years. Why did the Son of God wish to be subject? Obedience is necessary for all men; no one can be saved without it. Who sent the Son of God upon the earth? What was He to do for us? What did Jesus show also to His heavenly Father? How did He pray in the Garden of Olives? How many times did He pray in that manner? Why did He pray thus? What (condition) did He add each time to His prayer? How was He disposed towards His heavenly Father? And what did He do in the end? He was obedient unto death.

Sem and Japhet. Which of Noe's sons honored their father? On what occasion? What did Noe say concerning them? And what happened? Who imparts blessing to children? God.

Joseph. About whom have we related that God bestowed on him His protection and blessing? How did God bless Joseph in his father's tent? In Putiphar's house? In prison? With the king? Joseph had then a happy life. Was his life long or short? And what did God bestow on him in the next life? Everlasting happiness.

IV. SUMMARY. "Honor thy father and thy mother, that it may be well with thee, and that thou mayst live long on earth." In the fourth commandment God requires us to respect, love and obey our parents (and superiors), because they are God's representatives in our regard, and because our parents are our greatest benefactors. The children who fulfil their duties towards their parents have the right to expect in this life God's protection and blessing, and everlasting happiness in the next.

V. APPLICATION. 1. Dear children, engrave this resolution so deeply in your heart, that you shall never forget it during your whole life: "I will respect, love and obey my father and my mother, because they are God's representatives toward me, and my greatest benefactors."

Blessed Thomas More held the office of Chancellor, one of the highest in England. Every morning he would go to kiss his aged father and ask his blessing. His father would then make the sign of the cross over him and say: "May God almighty, the Father, and the Son, and the Holy Ghost bless thee." When Thomas More would enter a room where his father was, he would go directly to his father and salute him with a reverential bow. Thus should children honor their parents. The honor you pay to your parents God will never forget.

2. Love your parents tenderly, and love to be with them. You cannot appreciate the happiness of a child who still has his father and his mother. If you could realize this, no one on earth would be so dear to you as your father and mother. The most beautiful place in the world for a child is the heart of his mother. The best place on earth for him is also at the table of his father. Oh, how poor, how greatly to be pitied the child who no longer has his father and mother. Strive to cause much joy to your parents. Therefore, be pious, and be fond of reciting those prayers you learned at your mother's knee from her lips. For the love of your mother you should never omit a single day to recite them. Always behave properly; a child that is ever modest and friendly, is like an angel. All who see him, love him. God and the angels in heaven look on that child with pleasure and joy. And people say to one another: "How happy are the parents in having so well behaved, so good and so pious a child!" Such a child is an honor and a joy to his parents.

3. I know one thing especially, which you can all do for your parents; a thing which you ought to do for them every day. What is it? To pray for your parents. You should never forget it. Every time you hear Mass, you should pray for your parents. You should pray also at home for them both morning and night. Have you prayed already to-day for your parents? Pray that God may

bless and protect them and preserve them from misfortune, sickness and every evil. You cannot during your life ever repay them for all they have done for you. Therefore pray to God to reward them for it all during their life, and finally in heaven forever.

4. Never forget the admonitions of your father and mother. Consider their teachings as something sacred. They seek only your welfare. And no matter what others may promise or offer you, heed them not, if your parents forbid you. Strictly do what they tell you. Tell them: "My dear father, my dear mother, I will willingly do as you tell me." A child, however much he may pray and work, if he does not obey his parents, is not a good child. If you fulfil your duty towards your parents, "it shall be well with you, and you shall live long upon earth."

B.

11. The Sins of Children against their parents.

I. OBJECT. I will tell you to-day about a king's ungrateful son, who endeavored to dethrone his father.

RELATION. Absalom was his name; he was the son of King David. Absalom was very wicked. He ordered his servants to kill his brother. David was so irritated by this crime, that Absalom had to flee. He was allowed to return only after three years. Absalom was large and handsome. His hair was exceedingly beautiful and long. He became proud and would no longer obey his father. He was anxious to be the King. Therefore he at length undertook to dethrone and kill his father. See now, how he went to work to gain his end. He went around among the people and spoke ill of his father, saying: "My father does not care for you. If I were king, I would care better for you, and help every one." By degrees the people joined his party, and at last revolted against David, and chose Absalom as their king. Now Absalom with a

large army marched against his father to capture and kill
him. David had to flee barefooted, in order to escape.
David wept, and all who were with him wept also. At
last a battle was fought between the faithful soldiers of
David and the big army of Absalom. Absalom's army was
defeated. Absalom had to flee on his mule. Passing
under an oak tree, his fine long hair got caught in one
of the branches and he could no longer loosen it, so that
the mule went on and left him hanging to the tree by his
hair, and dangling in the air. A soldier came and drove
three javelins through Absalom's bad heart. So he died.
The soldiers cast his dead body into a deep hole, and covered it with a big heap of stones. Absalom's grave can
yet be seen, and every one that passes it, stops, spits upon
it and throws a stone upon it. This means: " Here lies
one who deserved to be stoned to death." God says:
" Cursed be he who does not honor his father and mother."

CONSIDERATION — *Unfriendly.* What was the name of
that King's son of whom I have just spoken to you? Who
was his father? Why was Absalom obliged to flee from
his father's house? How did his father feel over it? How
many years after that he was allowed to return home?
Oh, if he had never come back home! He gave no joy
to his father. Other children are glad to be with their
parents. Their faces brighten when they speak with them.
They feel happy to be able to help their parents. They
are satisfied with all that their parents say and do. They
are loving, friendly children. But Absalom was not pleased
with what his father said and did. When his father gave
him a command, Absalom looked cross, and murmured interiorly. When his father was out of sight, Absalom
would laugh at him and ridicule him. How do we call
those children whose faces are bright and pleasant towards
their parents? Friendly children. How was Absalom towards his father? Unfriendly.

Impertinent and stubborn. When his father admonished him, Absalom acted like bad children towards their parents. They say: "Shut up; that is none of your business; I do as I please; I am old enough; I do not need you." Or they wish their parents were dead. That is impertinence. It is sinful. How did Absalom probably behave towards his father? He was impertinent towards him. What does an impertinent child deserve from his parents? When the mother wishes to punish such a child, he resists; and after that, stamping his foot, he says: "No, I will not do it; I would rather be killed than do it." It is a sin to be stubborn towards one's parents.

Evil language. I have not related anything to you about Absalom's stubbornness towards his father; but what is far worse. What was Absalom's father? What did Absalom wish to be? What should then become of his father? He should be dethroned and killed. How did Absalom begin to execute his design? He went among the people, saying: "My father does not care for you; if I were king, I would care better for you, I would help you all." Thus did Absalom speak ill of his father. It is a sin for us to speak ill of our parents. How did Absalom sin against his father? Absalom spoke ill of his father. How does a good child speak to others about his parents? What duty did Absalom transgress by speaking ill of his father? He did not honor him. And what effect did his talk have among the people? It made them lose their respect for the king.

Disobedience. Subjects must not merely respect their sovereign. They owe him also obedience. But Absalom wished to be king. Whom, then, should the people obey? Whom should they no longer obey? Whom did Absalom no longer wish to obey? And he often disobeyed him. And bad children do the same. They disobey their parents. Other children require to be commanded several times before they obey their parents, or they do what they are commanded very carelessly. These children do not exactly disobey their parents; but what do they do? They obey badly. Whose place do parents hold towards their children? Whose place does the sovereign hold towards his subjects? Whom do children obey, when they obey their parents? Whom do the subjects obey, when they obey their sovereign? Whom do children honor, when they honor their parents? Whom do children disobey, when they disobey their parents? To whom do children show disrespect, when they show disrespect to their parents? (The same questions concerning subjects.) Therefore it is a sin for children to be disrespectful, impertinent and stubborn towards their parents and to obey them only partly or not at all. (Apply to subjects.)

To grieve. Absalom succeeded in causing very many to revolt with him against his father, King David. When Absalom arrived on his splendid chariot, the people assembled, waved their hands and hats and shouted: "Hurrah for Absalom." People looked at him seated in his chariot with his fine head of hair covering his shoulders and breast, bowing to all around him. "How fine he looks," some said. Others remarked: "What beautiful hair he has!" "O would he were already our king!" And Absalom looked so friendly, smiling to every one, so anxious was he to be king. At last the people were so full of enthusiasm, that they proclaimed him king. But what was to be done with King David, Absalom's father? He was to be captured and put to death. Absalom's party, well armed, marched with him against King David; and David had to flee from his son, and this so fast, that he was barefoot. How must David have then felt in his heart? Sad and grieved. How do you know these were his feelings? Because he wept. All with him saw him weep; and they all wept with him. Woe to those children who by their bad conduct cause their parents to weep for grief over them!

Whose place do parents hold towards their children?

And the parents, in God's stead, supply all their children's wants. What are parents on this account towards their children? Their greatest benefactors. How do we feel towards those who do us good? What should have been Absalom's feelings towards his father? Our father and mother should be what is dearest to us on earth. Hence Absalom should have given joy to his father. But what did he cause his father? Grief. Whom do we grieve when we grieve our parents? Therefore it is a sin to grieve our parents; a sin against the love we owe them.

Absalom's punishment. Absalom was severely punished for this by God. The soldiers of David fought against the big army of Absalom. Absalom was defeated. What did Absalom do to escape capture? What happened to him in his flight? His hair got caught in the branch of a tree and he was caught hanging and dangling in the air. He had wished to dethrone his father, and to sit high on his throne. And he was lifted high up; but not on a throne, but like on a scaffold, for he there suffered death. How did it happen? That was a frightful death. Did not Absalom deserve it? That was a punishment from God. What overtook Absalom for not honoring his father? The punishment of God. What did the soldiers do with Absalom's corpse? How do we bury our dead? And what do we put over their graves? That is an honor for the dead. How was Absalom's grave covered? That was a disgrace for Absalom. What do people do to Absalom's grave when they pass by it? They spit on it, and throw a stone on it. That is a sign of contempt. What happened to Absalom in this life, because he did not honor his father? Disgrace before men. And what must have happened to him in the next life from God Himself? Everlasting punishment in hell. Such is the lot of bad children. Already in this life God sends them all kinds of misfortune; people will have nothing to do with them and ridicule and despise them. And if they do not amend, they at last become reprobates in hell! What did God say concerning them? " Cursed is he who does not honor his father and mother." What must bad children expect in this life? God's punishment and disgrace before men. And in the next life? Eternal damnation.

II. CONNECTION. You have already heard of a bad son, who was cursed by his father. Who was it? Cham. Why did his father curse him? How did Cham sin against his father? Cham had mocked his father. You have also learned how some other sons grieved their father. Who were they? The brothers of Joseph. How did they grieve their father? How great was their father's grief? But see now their punishment. What happened to them the first time they went to Joseph in Egypt? Where did Joseph order them to be put? And what happened to Simeon? Thus God punished them through Joseph. What did Juda offer to do when, at their second journey into Egypt, Joseph wished to keep back Benjamin? Why? You see from this. that his brothers had mended their ways. And what happened after this to Joseph's brothers? And why did everything after this succeed with them, although they had so greatly grieved their father? But why did Absalom meet with such a terrible end on account of his father?

III. SUMMARY. Wicked children must therefore expect in this life to receive punishment from God and disgrace from men, and eternal damnation in the next. Children sin against their parents, 1, by unfriendliness and impertinence; 2, by grieving their parents; 3, by obeying them badly, and by disobedience.

IV. APPLICATION. 1. Let us enumerate all the sins Absalom committed against his father. How did Absalom speak to the people against his father? How should he confess that sin? " I spoke ill of my father." How grieved in heart was David when he had to flee barefooted from Absalom? How did Absalom sin thereby against his father? How should he confess this sin? "I have greatly grieved my father." How did Absalom sin against his father by disobedience? How should he tell this sin? "I have disobeyed my father." How must he tell all the sins he committed against his father?

2. How did Cham sin against his father? He mocked him. How did his father feel, when he was told of it? How should Cham tell his sin? "I mocked my father." How should Joseph's brothers tell the sins they committed against their father? "We have greatly grieved our father."

3. Fred easily gets angry. His mother said: "Fred, get me some wood." Fred replied: "I will do so, when I feel like it." His mother duly punished him for this. But Fred got red in his face, made a fist, stamped the floor with his foot, and said: "No, I will not do it now." How did Fred sin against his mother? By disobeying her. How else? He was impertinent and stubborn. How must he confess these sins? "I disobeyed my mother. I was impertinent and stubborn towards her."

Rose's mother is sick. She tells Rose: "Child, make the fire." But Rose acts as if she had not heard her mother. Her mother tells her again. Rose answers: "Immediately;" and she plays with the cat. Now her mother begins to scold her. Rose at last obeys. But how did she obey her mother? How should she confess her sin. "I did not obey my mother properly." The church bell rings for Mass. Bertha's mother tells her: "Go to church to hear Mass." But Bertha remains wandering about outside of the house. Another time her mother said: "Bertha, study your lesson." Bertha replies: "There is plenty of time yet for that." How did Bertha sin against her mother? She was disobedient to her. How should she confess her faults? "I disobeyed my mother twice."

Johnny was lazy and ill-mannered towards his mother.

When his father came home, he did not spare the rod, and Johnny had besides to go to bed without his supper. When leaving the room Johnny curses his father and wishes he were dead. How did Johnny sin against his father? How must he confess his sins? "I cursed my father; I wished for his death."

Do you always respect your parents? Are you never unfriendly towards them, and do you not murmur against them? Have you never caused your mother to weep on account of your disobedience? Do you obey your parents promptly? How beautiful would it be, if your mother could thus pray to God: "O my God, I thank Thee for having given me so good a child; he has always loved me, and never grieved me."

How to confess sins against the fourth commandment. 1. I was impertinent and stubborn towards my parents and superiors. 2. I grieved them by my bad conduct. 3. I obeyed badly; or, I disobeyed them.

FIFTH COMMANDMENT.

A.

12. Sins against the Life of the Body.

I. PREPARATION. Who is our neighbor? Every man. Your relatives, all your schoolmates, all the people dwelling in this place, in this country, all mankind are our neighbor. Why are they all our neighbor? Because all men are children of one Father in heaven. They were all created by God the Father, redeemed by God the Son and sanctified by God the Holy Ghost. God loves all men. And what does God will us to do to all men? Therefore He commanded us: "Thou shalt love thy neighbor as thyself." (Whom do we love, when we love our neighbor?) How do we show that we love our neighbor? Do we really love him, if we do him any harm?

No. Dear children, God has told us in the fifth and the following commandments what we must avoid in order not to injure or harm our neighbor.

OBJECT. I will show you to-day that we must not injure our neighbor in his body.

II. DEVELOPMENT — *Envy.* You remember the history of Joseph of Egypt. Who was Joseph's father? How many sons had Jacob? Which son did Jacob love most? Why did he love Joseph more than his other sons? Joseph was a good, pious son. How did Jacob show that he loved Joseph more than his other sons? He gave Joseph a fine coat of many colors, made from costly material. It resembled the coats worn by the sons of kings. Whom did Joseph resemble with this coat? The coats of Joseph's brothers were not so beautiful, nor so costly. Jacob loved his other sons also. But why did they not get so fine a coat as Joseph? Joseph must have been very much pleased with his coat. But who were not pleased on account of it? They thought: "Joseph is no better than we are; if we cannot get such fine coats, Joseph does not need or deserve any either." They envied him his fine coat. He who is jealous of what another has and cannot bear to see him have it, is envious, is guilty of envy. What were Joseph's brothers on account of his coat? They were envious of Joseph. Envy was deep-seated in their hearts. It burned therein like a little furnace. Their envy was not so very dangerous, but it was evil, it was a venial sin. But was it not foolish for them to be envious of Joseph? Was it not their fault, if their father did not love them as much as Joseph? They should have resolved: "Let us be as good and as pious as Joseph, and father will love us as much as Joseph." That would have put the fire of envy out of their hearts, and their hearts would have become pure, and God would have been pleased with them. But they made no such resolution, and the fire of envy burned fiercer in their hearts.

Hatred. Once whilst watching their flocks they did a very wicked thing; but Joseph did not join in. This irritated them. But matters grew worse. Joseph told his father what his brothers had done. He did not do this because he liked to see them punished, but because he wished them to amend, to do better. He wished them no harm. But his brothers did not amend. They got very mad against Joseph. They would no longer go with him, or hear anything about him, or even speak to him. And whenever they said anything to him, they showed thereby that they were very mad with him. How? Because they never said anything kind to him. You see now that the evil fire had grown fiercer in their hearts; it was no longer mere envy, but downright hatred. They knew very well how sinful it was for them to envy and hate their brother. But they did not care. If when you came home and would find your house beginning to burn, you would be frightened. And what would you do at once? If you wait until the fire has grown large and has spread, you cannot put it out, and the whole house will burn down. What should Joseph's brothers have done with the fire of envy and hatred in their hearts against their brother? They should have put it out. But they did not do so.

Insult and mockery. The fire in the hearts of Joseph's brothers continued to burn and spread. This was occasioned by the dreams of Joseph. What were his dreams? He related his dreams to them. Where were they with him? And what were all doing together? They were gathering and putting up their sheaves. What was remarkable with Joseph's sheaf? It stood erect. And what happened to his brothers' sheaves? They were all bowing to that of Joseph. Come here, James, and make a bow. Thus it is customary to bow before people in high positions; also for servants before their masters. If the president were to enter now, we should all stand up and bow to him as a mark of respect for his high office. When

Joseph related his dream, his brothers judged that he meant to be their sovereign, or their master, and considered them as only his servants. What effect had this dream on his brothers? It only increased their envy and hatred of him. Henceforth they called him only, the dreamer. " The dreamer said so and so, the dreamer wills so and so, the dreamer did so and so." Do you remember one occasion when they so expressed themselves? When his father sent him to Sichem. What did they say, when they saw him coming? They also probably called him, " Father's pet," out of derision and mockery. Insult and mockery are sharp painful thorns stuck into persons one does not like. Children thus treated begin to weep. It is, therefore, sinful to insult and mock any one. Therefore Joseph's brothers sinned against Joseph.

You see how the fire in the hearts of Joseph's brothers grew worse and worse. Envy, hatred, insult and mockery spread on every side into great flames. It is no longer a little envy; it is a great envy. It is no longer a dislike, but a real hatred. It is no longer a little fun, but a serious insult. The whole day is turned into a constant quarrel and enmity against their brother. Joseph may do what he will, he can no longer please his brothers. And oh, where will all that lead to? You know how far it led Cain. God warned Cain. God surely often warned Joseph's brothers in their hearts. What did God say to Cain? " Why art thou angry, etc. Repress and rule thy evil inclinations." How must not God have spoken to Joseph's brothers? Just as if He said to them: " Put out of your hearts that evil fire of envy and hatred. Crush it out." But how could they do that? When a horse is at full gallop, and there is a precipice ahead, it would seem that nothing could save him and his rider; but the rider has only to draw in the reins, and the horse stops at once! Man's will is strong. When he wills a thing earnestly, he can do much; when he wills earnestly to crush out evil feelings or thoughts, he can do it, for God will help him. Hence Cain and Joseph's brothers could have crushed and put out of their hearts the evil fire of envy and hatred. And they would have been happy. But neither Cain nor Joseph's brothers had the earnest will to do so. The envy and hatred in their hearts grew stronger and stronger. Already his brothers said to one another: "Would that we should never more see Joseph! Would that he were not here any more! If only something would happen to him!" At last the thought came to them: "Let us get rid of him!" So you see how high rose the flames of their hatred. They will soon break out from every side.

Anger. His brothers see him coming from a distance. He was sent to them by his father. They cry out to one another: "Look, there comes the dreamer! The dreamer is coming!" And that evil fire now breaks out in their eyes, in their faces, in their tongues and takes possession of all their members. Their faces are as red as fire, their eyes are fiery, their fists are clenched, and their bodies tremble with rage. What is their feeling against Joseph? A feeling of unrestrained anger. What does their anger prompt them to say?

Striking. When Joseph arrived, they fell upon him, struck him and threw him down, saying: "We have caught you at last, you dreamer, you tell-tale. We are going to drive all dreams out of you! Take off that coat quick." They pulled off his coat, which had so often excited their envy. They strike and beat him, causing him great pain. To strike and ill-treat any one in that way is sinful. Hence Joseph's brothers sinned by injuring the body of their brother.

Wounding. He who is very angry does not care how he strikes and beats the one he does not like, nor how great an injury he does him, nor if he makes him bleed or wounds him seriously. When you wound a person you commit a greater sin than if you merely strike him. He who wounds his neighbor commits a sin against his neighbor's life.

Thoughts of murder. Where did they put Joseph after pulling off his coat and ill-treating him? Into a pit. What did they then do? Joseph had walked a very long distance, and he was very hungry. But his brothers gave him nothing to eat. You may imagine why. They would have either killed him or left him to die of hunger in the pit. What do we call a man who takes away the life of another? A murderer. What did Joseph's brothers intend to be? Murderers. They intended to murder their own brother! What a great crime! So far had their wickedness gone! How did they first feel against Joseph? They envied him, because their father loved him more than them. Their envy was followed by hatred, hatred by anger, and anger by designs of murder. At first there was in their hearts a few sparks of the fire of envy; then hatred blew them into a flame, and anger spread it on all sides, and caused it to break out. But they did not actually murder him. Which of the brothers kept them from murdering him? What advice did he give them when the merchants were passing by? To sell their brother. Why? That their hands should not be stained with their brother's blood. What did they do with Joseph? Sold him as a slave.

Murder. But you know some one who actually murdered his brother. Who is it? What did Cain become? The murderer of his brother. God says in the fifth commandment: "Thou shalt not kill." Cain sinned against this commandment. It was a grievous, horrible sin. He who robs a man of his life, robs him of all he has. A man who is no longer alive, has no use for all that belonged to him. Only He has the right to take a man's life, who has given it to him. Who gives life to every man? Life is like a spark from God Himself. Who has, then, the right to take a man's life? God. Therefore the blood of a murdered person has a voice, and every drop of his blood has a tongue, crying heavenward: "Punish my murderer! Punish my murderer!" And God hears the voice of the blood that has been shed. How did He punish Cain for murdering his brother? This shows you what a horrible sin it is to commit murder.

Suicide. In like manner, he who kills himself, commits also a terrible sin. Which one of the apostles committed it? When Judas found out that Jesus was condemned to death, he was exceedingly sorry. His crime seemed so dreadful that he thought he could no longer live. Therefore he killed himself, committed suicide. How? By his suicide Judas precipitated his soul into hell. And after the last judgment where shall his body also be? A man cannot commit a greater sin than this against his body. Cain sinned against his body in some other way. What effect had his envy and hatred on his body? His face looked frightfully haggard and pale and his body exceedingly lean.

Endangered by levity. Children also are apt to sin in various ways against their own life; for instance, climbing trees, etc., swimming in deep, dangerous places, playing with fire-arms, trying to show their skill, their courage, etc. How many children are daily seriously hurt, and even killed by rashly exposing themselves to great dangers! All this is sinful; it is a sin against the fifth commandment.

III. CONNECTION. God did not forbid in the fifth commandment only the sins against our own life, but also the sins against the life of our neighbor. How did Joseph's brothers first sin against their brother's life? You have heard also of some one else who was envious of his brother. That was Cain. Who was envious of the happiness of our first parents? Who were envious of Jesus? What sin was caused by Cain's envy? By the envy of Joseph's brothers? By the envy of the Jews against Jesus?

What name did Joseph's brothers give him? When did

the Jews mock our divine Saviour? What other sin did Joseph's brothers commit against him, when they pulled off his coat? They pushed him about and beat him. When did the Jews strike our Saviour? With what? With what was the body of Jesus covered by the scourging? What was done to our Saviour's head by the crown of thorns? When did the executioners inflict the largest wounds on Jesus? How many large wounds did Jesus receive when He was nailed to the cross? Therefore Jesus was put to death on the cross. Who were crucified with Jesus? What crimes had they committed? What had Jesus done? The two thieves had therefore deserved death. Who had not deserved death? Who were justly put to death? Who was unjustly put to death? Of whose death were the Jews guilty? What kind of sin would the death of Joseph by his brothers have been? What children were murdered? Who was murdered by his brother? Whom did the murderers of all these injure? Their neighbor. How? They sinned against the body of their neighbor. Whom else did Cain injure besides Abel? Himself. Who injured his own life? All these sinned against the fifth commandment.

IV. SUMMARY. What does God forbid by the fifth commandment? All sins against our neighbor's life and against our own life. Against their neighbor's life all who unjustly kill, wound or strike their neighbor. Against one's own life, whoever kills himself or rashly exposes his life to danger.

V. APPLICATION. 1. Suppose the brothers of Joseph would confess their sins against him; how did they sin at home against him? By envy and hatred. How at Sichem? Insult, anger, pushed and beat him, wished to kill him, sold him. "We have envied and hated our brother, insulted, pushed and struck him; wished first to kill him, and then to let him starve; and finally we sold him." Enumerate the sins of the Jews against our divine

Saviour. They envied Him, hated Him, mocked Him, struck Him, wounded and killed Him. How should Cain tell his sins against his brother? "I was angry with my brother, and I beat him to death." How should he tell his sin against his own life? "I injured my life (health) by my envy."

2. Philip and Antony in playing bumped their heads together, and Philip besides stepped on Antony's foot, but not on purpose. But Antony got mad and began to abuse Philip with harsh names. Philip cried out: "If you do not stop, I will tell father." Now Antony got fearfully mad, knocked Philip down and beat him till his strength gave way. How must Antony tell his sins? "I had a quarrel with my companion, I called him harsh names and badly beat him." Fred told the teacher that Frank had struck him. The teacher punished Frank for it. But Frank got mad against Fred, and said: "Wait, and I'll give you something to think about; you shall never again tell on me." Afterwards, when he sees Fred, he thinks: "If I could only kill him." So he picks up a stone, throws it at Fred, hits him in the head and makes in it a large bleeding gash. How should he tell his sins? "I struck my schoolmate; I was long mad with him; I said: If I could only kill him. Then I hit him in the head with a stone and made a large bleeding gash in it."

3. Dear children, the first sin on earth was the envy of the devil. Cain's first sin against Abel was envy. Envy was also the first sin of Joseph's brothers against him. How unhappy did envy make our first parents! Through the devil's envy sin came into the world, and through sin death. How unhappy Cain made himself by his envy! How much evil was caused by the envy of Joseph's brothers! Therefore, dear children, take care not to become envious of others. When one of your sisters gets a finer dress than you, and envy endeavors to enter your heart, say: "I will not be envious. Sweet Heart of

Mary, be my salvation." And at once reject every envious thought. Thus you will suppress envy. If your big brother gets a larger slice of bread (piece of cake) than you, little one, the fire of envy at once tries to be enkindled in your heart. At once throw it out. Rather say: " Sweet Heart of Jesus, grant that I may ever love Thee more and more." Your schoolmate is praised either for knowing more or for being more diligent than you. Envy threatens to force an entrance into your heart; at once do all you can to keep it out, otherwise the same will happen to you as to Joseph's brothers. Hatred and anger will take possession of your heart, and impel you to call harsh and insulting names, and then to quarrel, to ill-treat and strike your neighbor. Resolve to-day: " I will never hurt my neighbor in his body; I will never call any one harsh or insulting names." If you have hurt or pained any one, show yourself afterwards very friendly to him, assist him whenever you can, and thus atone for your fault.

4. And now, dear children, one thing more: Be not cruel towards animals, towards living beings. Children usually take delight in killing or tormenting what they see. It is fun for them, but torture and pain for the animals. Let these enjoy the short life God has given them. He who torments or kills such beings, shows that his heart is cruel and devoid of feeling for others; such a one delights also in seeing his companions punished or in suffering.

B.

13. Seduction, or leading astray.

I. PREPARATION. What sin stains the soul of a child from its very birth? Original sin. His soul is dead (spiritually). Suppose a child dies in original sin. Where is it that that child's soul cannot go? How is original sin removed from the souls of children? By baptism. In baptism the Holy Ghost enters the soul of the child, and gives it spiritual life. And so long as the Holy Ghost remains in that soul, it remains spiritually alive. Suppose that child later on commits a mortal sin. Who then enters its soul? The devil. Who leaves that soul? The Holy Ghost. How is the soul after the Holy Ghost leaves it? That soul can now no longer do anything to gain heaven. Where would that soul go, if the child would die? What life it would not obtain in heaven? Where does the soul go that is in mortal sin? You see now what injury a person does to the life of his soul by a mortal sin. In like manner, we can do the same injury to the soul of our neighbor. Last time you heard how injury is done to another's life.

OBJECT. To-day you shall learn how the life of another's soul can be injured.

II. DEVELOPMENT — *The devil seduces our first parents.* How did our first parents live in the beginning? How were they in the earthly paradise? What did God forbid them? What punishment did God threaten them with, if they would transgress His commandment? What did He promise them, if they would observe it? For a time our first parents obeyed God, and they were happy. But who envied their happiness? Therefore he sought to ruin their happiness. In which animal did the devil conceal himself? Where was the serpent? Who came one day near the forbidden tree? Eve stopped in front of it and saw the serpent on it. The devil did not at first show what he intended, but showed himself very friendly to her. What did he ask Eve? He meant by this: "Is it true that God said that to you? I can hardly believe that God forbade you to eat of this fine fruit." Eve could have remarked from these words that an evil spirit was speaking through the serpent, for an angel would not have spoken in that way. Angels are always pleased with what God wills. Eve should, therefore, have gone away at once. But what did she do? And what answer did she give to the serpent?

It was as if she had said: "Yes, so it is." Now the devil became still more friendly towards her. What did he say to her? "You shall not die." He meant by this: "It is not true that you shall die. God is only frightening you, to keep you from eating of that fruit, for He does not wish you to be happy." What else did the devil say? "If you eat of this fruit, your eyes shall be opened, and you shall be like God; but God does not wish that, and therefore He said: You shall not eat of the fruit of this tree." The nice words of the serpent already pleased Eve more than the commandment of God. What did she now examine more closely? And what did she see about the fruit? What happens to many children happened to her also. When you pass a confectionery or a fruit store and look at the cakes, at the delicious fruit, your mouth waters, and you would like to eat some; you long for some. The same happened to Eve. Looking at the fruit, she longed for some; and the longer she looked, the more she longed to eat some. And the nearer she came to the tree, the finer the fruit seemed to her, and her longing grew stronger and stronger. She put out her hand, and what did she do? To whom did she give some? and what did Adam do?

How the seducer acts. Who had resolved to induce our first parents to eat of the forbidden fruit? Let us examine how he went to work. How did he induce Eve to stop before the forbidden tree? How did he call Eve's attention to himself? In answer to his question Eve told him what punishment God had threatened, if they would eat of the forbidden fruit. How did he succeed in removing Eve's fear of the threatened punishment? The devil had won half of the victory. And he no longer asked her any questions. How did he excite in Eve a longing for the forbidden fruit? How did Eve's longing grow stronger? What finally happened? Eve yielded to the temptor and ate of the forbidden fruit, and gave some to Adam. Whose commandment did our first parents transgress? What did they commit by so doing? Who induced them to do so? The devil seduced our first parents.

The devil is a murderer of souls. How he rejoiced in making our first parents unhappy! Now their souls belonged to him, and he went into them. Who was expelled from their souls? In what state were their souls after the Holy Ghost had left them? What do we call him who kills a man's body? Murderer. He who kills another's soul is also a murderer. Who killed the soul of Eve? What, then, is the devil? The devil is a murderer of souls from the beginning. The devil does all he can to murder souls. "He goes around like a roaring lion, seeking whom he may devour."

Every seducer is an accomplice of the devil. Who seduced Adam to sin? Eve. Whose accomplice (helper) was Eve, when she seduced Adam to sin? She was the devil's accomplice, and so is every one who leads others into sin. The devil has many accomplices in the world. Fred goes every Sunday to Mass. But Frank says to him: "Steal a dollar from your mother, and we shall not go to church to-day; but we can buy cakes and candy and go to the park, etc., and have a fine time." They carried out that plan. What did Fred steal at home? Where did they go during the Mass? What did he commit thereby? And who induced him to commit those sins? The devil led our first parents into sin. And what did Frank do? Into what sins did he lead Fred?

Every seducer to mortal sin is a murderer of his neighbor's soul. What happens to a soul that is seduced to commit mortal sin? How frightful it is for a man to plunge a dagger into his neighbor's heart and thus kill him! It is equally dreadful to murder the soul of our neighbor. What kind of murderer was Frank? Whose accomplice was he? Consider the value of a soul. Whose image is it? How did our Saviour redeem it? There hangs to each soul a drop of Christ's infinitely precious blood. Oh, how excruciating sufferings had our dear Saviour to undergo, in order to redeem our souls! Do you know what it is to be a seducer and murderer of souls? What a terrible judgment will such a seducer undergo! Our divine Saviour will say to him at the general judgment: "Depart from Me, accursed seducer, into everlasting fire." The seducer murders souls, which cost so much to our Saviour to redeem. He who leads others into sin, is a devil.

III. CONNECTION. Who seduced Eve into sin? Who tried to lead Joseph of Egypt into sin? What did Joseph do? What should Eve have also done? What would, then, not have happened? Eve was also guilty in being seduced into sin. Whom did Eve seduce into sin? What should Adam also have done? Whom would Eve not have seduced, if she had not first been seduced by the devil? Who is the cause of the sin of both Eve and Adam? Whom did Cham intend to lead into sin? To commit what sin? Whom did Absalom seduce? To commit what sin? Which of all these persons remained faithful, when others tried to lead them into sin? Who were those that yielded to seduction (fell into sin)? Whom should you imitate when some one tries to seduce you? What would your soul be, if you allowed yourself to be led into a grievous sin? How is he called who kills the body? How is he called who seduces another into committing mortal sin? Suppose a person is without sin, and is killed, where does his soul go? Suppose a person who has been led into a mortal sin, and dies in it, where does his soul go? Where shall his body go later? A person, who has been led into mortal sin, lives after that; what can he still do concerning his sin? His soul will then again become spiritually alive. Which life can be regained? Which life cannot be regained, if it is once lost?

IV. SUMMARY. He injures his neighbor's soul, who leads (seduces) him into sin. He who unjustly strikes, wounds or kills his neighbor's body. The fifth commandment forbids all the sins which may prove injurious to the bodily or spiritual life of ourselves and of our neighbor.

V. APPLICATION. 1. Let us have another example of seduction. A mother calls out: "Johnny, come home." But Johnny is now playing. Frank says: "Stay here, Johnny, don't go." Johnny stays. Another time Frank says to Johnny: "I know where there are fine strawberries. Let us go and get some." Johnny goes along. They enter a neighbor's garden, and help themselves; but the owner sees them and comes after them; Frank escapes, but Johnny is caught and gets a beating. After this Frank tells Johnny: "That is a mean man; get even with him by throwing stones into his windows." And Johnny breaks that man's windows by throwing stones into them. How should Frank tell his sins? "I led my companion into sin, once into disobedience, another time into stealing, and then into breaking a neighbor's windows."

2. Dear children, beware of leading others into sin. He who does so, acts like the devil. He must then think: "I am a devil." Our divine Saviour says: "He who leads others into sin, deserves to have a millstone hung about his neck and to be thus thrown to the bottom of the sea, that the world may get rid of him."

3. Beware of bad companions. Better no companion at all, than a bad one. A bad companion, who leads one into sin, is like a devil. He seeks to kill a soul. Seducers appear to be kind and friendly, as if they were innocent lambs; but in their hearts they are wolves. When one of them comes to you, and says "let us do so and so;" and you know that such a thing is sinful, leave him at once, and never go with him again. Make this resolution: "I will not, for the whole world, commit a sin and offend God."

How to confess sins against the fifth commandment: I

was envious; I was angry; I insulted and mocked others; I struck others; I led others into sin (mention the sin).

THE SIXTH AND NINTH COMMANDMENTS.

A.

14. Impurity.

I. PREPARATION. When God created the first man He said: "Let us make man in our own image and likeness." Relate what God then did. The bodies of our first parents were beautiful; but far more beautiful were their souls, which were adorned with a wonderfully beautiful garment. What is that garment called? The pure white garment of sanctifying grace. It imparted a dazzling splendor to their souls, like that of the sun. This splendor of their souls penetrated their bodies and made them very bright, and this brightness served as a garment to their bodies. For this reason their bodies needed no clothing to cover them. How good and happy were Adam and Eve in paradise!

Did they always remain good and happy? What loss did Adam and Eve suffer in their souls through their sin? The pure white garment of sanctifying grace. Their souls did no longer shine like the sun, and the brightness of their bodies vanished. And their eyes were opened, and they saw on themselves what they had never before seen. They saw that they were naked. And this made them ashamed, and they blushed. Their bodies were covered with a wonderful brightness before their sin; but were covered with shame after their sin. To cover their shame they made and put on aprons of fig-leaves. Thus they remained partially covered until God clothed them with garments made from the skins of animals, for God does not will that men should be without clothing. There are still savages in certain parts of the world that go naked with the exception of some clothing below the waist to cover what decency requires not to remain uncovered. Natural modesty induces every one to keep those parts of the body covered. He who uncovers them unnecessarily is shameless, immodest.

OBJECT. I will teach you to-day that a child should not be immodest.

II. RELATION. Noe had three sons, Sem, Cham and Japhet. After the deluge Noe began to cultivate the ground again. He planted a vineyard. But he did not know that wine can make a person drunk. The first time he drank wine, he drank too much of it. He got drunk and lay down naked in his tent. Cham saw his father there, and began to ridicule and mock him. He ran out and told his brothers. But Sem and Japhet were better behaved. They would not listen to all he said, but they took a cloak and went backwards in their father's tent, and, without looking at him, they covered him with the cloak. When Noe awoke, they related to him what had happened. Then Noe said: " A curse on Cham; evil shall happen to him; but a blessing over Sem and Japhet, and they shall prosper." And thus it happened. His father's curse came upon wicked Cham, and Sem and Japhet met with blessing and prosperity.

CONSIDERATION — *Noe's drunkenness.* What did Noe plant after the deluge? What did he not know about wine? What happened when he first drank wine? He who is entirely drunk, does not know what he does. How was he lying down in his tent? That part of his body which requires to be always covered, was uncovered. Who saw him in that state? Cham went out to tell it to his brothers. These blushed hearing this, for they were much better than Cham. They refused to speak about it with Cham. What did they do at once? And how modestly did they do so? What did they afterwards tell their father?

Man's body should be holy. This is the will of God. We should not gaze at any immodest part of man's body. Who creates man's body? To whom does man's body belong? The Holy Ghost has come into the hearts of those who are baptized, and remains therein so long as they do not commit mortal sin. What do we call the place where God dwells? The house of God, a church. Our body is the temple of the Holy Ghost. You see how holy God has made your body. On the last day your body shall rise from the grave. In what state will the bodies of the just then be? More bright and resplendent than the bodies of our first parents before their sin. And where are our bodies destined to go? There they will shine as the sun. Therefore, we are bound to keep our body holy.

Sinning in the body through impurity. When a modest child dresses or undresses, bathes or does anything necessary, when it is alone or with others, a modest child never looks at the parts of its body that should always be covered as God directs. A modest child turns away from the sight of even little children uncovered, and makes them cover themselves. How should Cham have acted when he saw his father in the tent? But what did he do? (Immodest = impure. Immodesty = impurity. Modest, modesty = pure, purity.) God says to us in the sixth commandment, that we should not do anything impure. Cham sinned against it by impure looks. But he did even more; for he could not keep to himself what he had seen, but related it to his brothers. He sinned also by impure talk or speech. Sem and Japhet heard the impure talk of Cham. Now suppose they had remained standing with Cham to hear him talk impurely and laugh at what he said; what sin would they have committed? Wilfully listened to impure talk. That also is a sin.

He who has seen or heard anything impure, often remembers it a long time. Although he may not think of it all the time, it comes back to his mind from time to time. When Cham went out of his father's tent, he was still thinking of the impure things he had seen. To reflect on things impure is a sin against the ninth commandment. Cham by reflecting on impure things, sinned against the ninth commandment. Those who reflect on such things, will soon follow Eve's example. What happened to Eve the longer she looked at the forbidden fruit? She longed for it. He who reflects on what is impure, will easily long for it, desire it. But impure desires are forbidden by the ninth commandment, and are therefore sinful. What did Eve do at last when her longing, her desire for the forbidden fruit became stronger? She took and ate some. Thus also act the impure. First, such a one hears or sees something impure, then he thinks of it, and speaks of it, takes pleasure therein, then gets a desire for it, and touches what is impure on himself or others. He commits an impure act, and that is very sinful, and forbidden by the sixth commandment.

With pleasure or wilfully; not wilfully. Let us return to Noe. What effect had the wine on him? How was it that he drank too much? What would he have done, if he had known that the wine was so strong? Hence Noe did not wilfully get drunk. Therefore Noe's drunkenness was not sinful. How did the drunken Noe lie down in his tent? He did not purposely or wilfully do what was impure, for he was a good man. He did not know what he was doing, and, besides, he was asleep. He therefore committed no sin. A child uncovers itself, lifts up its dress, looks at itself, etc. It realizes that it is doing something bad or impure, and takes pleasure in it. What does that child commit? Why? And why did Noe not commit a sin by doing as he did? Why was it no sin for Sem and Japhet to hear what Cham told them about their father? There is no sin of impurity committed unless it is done wilfully, with pleasure. He only who wilfully, or with pleasure, thinks, sees, listens to or does what is impure, is guilty of sin.

How to avoid sins of impurity. You must watch over your eyes and your ears. You should restrain your curiosity, and not wish to see all that is going on, to see the shows and their pictures, or to hear everything that is said, to read every novel or story book. Hence, if you chance to see, hear or read something that is not pure or modest, restrain your wish to look again, to hear more, to read further. When you hear some one talking impurely, do not stay and laugh, but go away at once. In like manner, if you happen to see anything impure, turn your eyes away, and, if necessary, go to some other place. Thus do good children act. Be careful not to expose your person to others.

It happens not very seldom that when children have seen or heard anything impure, the thoughts of these things come back to them. If you then do not want such thoughts, and try to drive them away, you do not commit any sin, for they are not wilful. Sometimes after you drive them away several times, they come back. Keep driving them away every time, and try to think of other things. The best would be to pray at once, as soon as you remark such thoughts in your mind, by saying: " My Jesus, help me; Mary, help me. Jesus and Mary, help me." If you do this every time, you may be sure that those thoughts were not wilful, and that you did not commit any sin. On the contrary, you gained a victory over the temptation, and deserved greater reward and glory in heaven. Endeavor to be as pure as an angel; never touch or look at your person or another's without real necessity, and never out of pleasure. If other children expose themselves, or speak of impure things, it may be necessary for you to report them to the teacher or to their parents.

Impure, unbecoming. Not everything that is unbecoming is also impure. It is unbecoming to call names, queer and harsh names, funny names; but these names are not impure. Impure talk is far worse. Moreover, some games, especially of boys, have certain unbecoming features, but are not impure. It would be better not to engage in them, but they may mostly be engaged in without sin.

III. CONNECTION. The worst sin against the sixth commandment is the sin of action, committed in secret with one's self or with others. How are sins of impurity committed with the eyes? With the ears? With the tongue? What is the difference between impure words and unbecoming words? How is impurity in thought committed? Into what sin of impurity do they fall who take pleasure (indulge) in impure thoughts? Into impure desires, or the wish to commit impurity? Impure desires and wilful impure thoughts are forbidden by the ninth commandment. When are impure thoughts not sinful? When does he who sees or hears impure things, commit no sin? What should we do with a companion who speaks or acts impurely? What should we do with those houses or shows where impure things are to be seen? What must we then avoid? Everything that leads to impurity.

IV. SUMMARY. The sixth commandment forbids all impure words and actions (including seeing, hearing, reading); and also everything that leads to impurity. The ninth commandment forbids impure thoughts and desires.

V. APPLICATION. 1. Let us see which sins of impurity Cham committed. How did he sin with his eyes? In thought? With his tongue? How should he tell his sins? "I saw something impure with pleasure; I took pleasure in thinking on it; I spoke about it to others." Albert passing along heard some young fellows talking obscenely (about impure things); he stopped and listened to them, talked and laughed with them. What sins did he commit? How should he confess them? "I took pleasure in listening to obscene language (impure talk); I spoke obscenely (about impure things)."

2. Dear children, God hates and detests every sin, but more especially the sins of impurity. Therefore He so severely punishes sins of impurity. The deluge. The beautiful cities of Sodom and Gomorrha were destroyed by fire from heaven, because their inhabitants were very impure; where those cities were, there is now a large lake of sulphurous, stinking water, wherein no fish can live; it is called the Dead Sea.

3. Therefore, be on your guard against impurity. When you are with others, or are alone, when no person sees you, He is present who sees and knows all things, our very thoughts and desires, even in the darkest night, and who will severely punish those who sin. Remember also that your guardian angel is always with you and witnesses all you do. Avoid bad company. And when bad thoughts come to your mind, say at once: " Jesus and Mary, help me! Keep me from sin."

How to confess sins against the sixth and ninth commandments. I took wilful pleasure in impure thoughts; I looked with wilful pleasure on impure things (or pictures) ; I read an impure book; I listened wilfully to impure talk; I spoke of (or said, or sung) impure words; I did an impure thing (by myself, or with others).

B.

15. Chastity, or Purity.

" Oh, how beautiful is the chaste generation with glory; for the memory thereof is immortal: because it is known both with God and with men. When it is present, they imitate it; and they desire it, when it hath withdrawn itself; and it triumpheth crowned forever, winning the reward of undefiled conflicts." (Wisd. 4. 1, 2.)

I. Transition. The last time I spoke to you on impurity. In how many ways are sins of impurity committed? Impurity is abominable and detestable. To-day you will hear how beautiful is the virtue of purity.

OBJECT. I will tell you about a boy, who was modest and pure and became thereby most happy.

II. RELATION. His name was Stanislaus Kostka. Already in his childhood Stanislaus was very modest and chaste (pure). When he heard any impure words, he blushed very deeply, and his eyes were filled with tears, and he would immediately go away. If he could not do so, he would get so frightened and so horrified at the impure language, that he would tremble all over, and sometimes even faint. He never defiled his pure soul with the slightest impure sin. The very sight of his face shining with innocence showed how pure and chaste he was. He was therefore called by everybody an angel. Being so pure and chaste, he would never go with impure children; he never looked around curiously; he always kept his eyes modestly cast down. Wherever he was, he remembered that God was near him, and saw and knew all he thought and did.

Prayer was his sweetest joy. Already as a little child, he used to say in one of his prayers: "Dear Lord, I will be all Thine." He daily heard one or more Masses with real devotion. With a bright and joyful countenance, joined hands and eyes cast down in church, he looked like an angel. When praying he forgot everything around him. Those who then saw him, would say: "The little saint is praying." His favorite place in church was before the tabernacle. He would kneel there for hours without leaning on or against anything. Many a time a shining light, like that seen in pictures around the head of a saint, would issue from his face. Stanislaus took delight not only in being near our divine Saviour in church, but especially in having Jesus in his heart. He knew: "When our dear Saviour is in my heart, the devil cannot lead me into sin." Therefore he went every week to confession and Holy Communion. Stanislaus had also a tender love for the Blessed Virgin Mary. He would say: "God is my Father, and the Blessed Virgin Mary is my Mother." He took delight in speaking of Mary. He could never speak enough of her. When he would see one of her pictures or statues, he would kneel down before it, and say a prayer to his beloved Mother. He recited daily the rosary in her honor. Mary rewarded him by making him very pure and chaste.

When Stanislaus was not praying, he was either working or studying. He was never idle. When tired of working or studying, he would join other children in innocent games. He was never seen with a dissatisfied or angry face. He always looked cheerful and contented, and smiling. His eyes were shining with innocence and were like two stars, through which the purity of his heart could be seen. Those who had once seen him, could never forget him. Seldom had a more lovely and graceful boy been seen. All were enchanted at his aspect and could never look enough at him, and there arose in them the thought: "Would that I were so innocent and pure as he!" Therefore, everybody liked him. Every child wished to be in his company and play with him. When Stanislaus was praying in church, each one would try to kneel right behind him, for they wished to see how piously and devoutly he prayed. Many imitated him, and when these children returned home, their parents were astonished to find them far better and more pious than they had been before.

Even the angels and saints loved and honored Stanislaus. Once a whole army of angels came to him, and one of them gave him Holy Communion. When Stanislaus was dangerously sick, St. Barbara came with two angels to him, and one of them gave him Holy Communion. One night when Stanislaus thought he was about to die, the Blessed Virgin holding the Infant Jesus in her arms suddenly stood before his bed. Mary laid the divine Infant on his bed, so that Stanislaus could take Him in his arms and press Him to his heart. Stanislaus did so, and was immediately perfectly cured. He would afterwards often think on this, and wish: " O would that I were now near Jesus and Mary in heaven, and could see them again ! "

St. Stanislaus therefore wrote a letter to his dear Mother Mary in heaven, in which he said: " My dearest Mother Mary, obtain for me that I may die on the feast of thy Assumption. I am longing to see thee and to tell thee how I love thee." Five days before the Assumption he placed that letter next to his heart and received Holy Communion. The following day he fell sick, and said: " I shall die in five days." He got worse, and he received the last sacraments on the eve of the Assumption. When the priest came with the Blessed Sacrament, as soon as Stanislaus saw our Lord, he knelt on his bed; his eyes shone brightly, and his face was like transfigured. All present wept to see him so. He continued to pray as long as he could. All at once his face shone with heavenly joy. He beheld his dear Mother Mary surrounded with a multitude of virgin saints. They had come to take Stanislaus to heaven with them. He died on the feast of the Assumption, as he had prayed for.

Stanislaus was eighteen years old when he died. Quietly with a pleasant smile he passed away. And after his death, his face became more and more bright and pleasant. He had the appearance of an angel. People now came from all directions, in order to behold Stanislaus once more. They kissed his feet, and spoke of how piously and innocently Stanislaus had lived. After two years his body was still incorrupt, and later on the odor of sweet-scented violets issued from his grave. From near and from afar people came to his parents to congratulate them on having had so holy a son. His parents rejoiced greatly. And what a sweet joy must Stanislaus have had, when he came in heaven to the feet of Jesus and His holy Mother! There he received a glorious crown from God.

I. STANISLAUS WAS CHASTE.

CONSIDERATION. 1. *A chaste generation.* How was that boy called about whom I have just spoken to you? What kind of talk Stanislaus would not listen to already when he was only a little child? What was he then? What happened to him when impure language was used, and he was not able to go away? So greatly did he abhor (detest) impurity in others. Much less did he say or do anything impure. From what did he always preserve his soul pure? How could this be seen in him? What did people call him on that account? Which of you have seen the picture of an angel? How beautiful are the angels! Modest and chaste children are like angels God sends upon earth. How many beautiful flowers there are in spring! And what a fine bouquet you can make with them! But much more beautiful is the modest, chaste soul of a pure child! Even the earthly paradise was not so beautiful.

Means of practising chastity. 1. Watchfulness. Stanislaus was very modest. With what children would he not associate? His brother was rude and unrefined. Often he wished to bring Stanislaus with him into bad company. But Stanislaus preferred to be scolded and beaten than to go with him. Once his brother even knocked him down and kicked him around; but Stanislaus would not go with him. For into what would those evil companions have led him, if he had associated with them? Stanislaus always watched over himself. How did he watch over his eyes?

2. THE FEAR OF GOD. And of whom did Stanislaus think wherever he was? He was always careful to avoid the slightest fault. For who knows and sees all things? Why does God know all things? Therefore Stanislaus thought of God everywhere. What does a child avoid, that reflects

that God is everywhere? Who constantly watches at your side? Your guardian angel also sees constantly the face of our Father in heaven. When therefore the devil suggests anything impure to you, think at once: "God and my guardian angel see me; I will not do anything to displease them."

3. PRAYER. Stanislaus was very fond of prayer. What is he who is fond of prayer? What was Stanislaus? A pious child does not become impure. But a child that does not like to pray, does not long remain pure. God does not love an impure child. But Stanislaus wished to belong entirely to God. How did he express this wish in prayer? Stanislaus was always willing to pray. When should you pray at home? Morning and night. Ask your mother, before you go to bed, to sprinkle you and your bed with holy water. A child, when in bed, should join its hands and recite an Our Father and a Hail Mary before falling asleep, and the devil will not be able to do it any harm. What should you do, when the devil suggests any evil to you, in order to lead you into sin? Pray. To whom would you call for help, if a strong man would try to do you harm? "Father and mother, help me!" In like manner, when the devil suggests some evil to you, in order to murder your soul, you should say: "Jesus, help me! Mary, help me! Jesus, do not forsake me! Mary, my Mother, protect me!" Where should you go every morning to pray? And on whom should you think, when you are praying? If you do so, you will pray devoutly. What did St. Stanislaus do every day about holy Mass? On whom only did he think during Mass? On what did he not then think? He forgot everything else during Mass. How did he kneel down in church? What then can you learn from his behavior in church? Whom did St. Stanislaus resemble when he was in church? What did people therefore say about him?

4. DEVOTION TO THE BLESSED SACRAMENT. Where is

our divine Saviour in the church? Where should we kneel to get very near to him? He who truly loves Him, finds pleasure in His company. St. Stanislaus loved our Saviour above all. Where then was his favorite place in church? Every morning he would go to church very early, look towards the tabernacle and ask our Saviour's blessing. What can you tell me about his prayer before the tabernacle? People could see what a great pleasure it was for him to pray before the tabernacle. What was there remarkable on his face? O how many children should be ashamed of themselves before St. Stanislaus? They can hardly stay still for a moment in church. They do not wish to pray, and they soon grow tired of being in church.

5. FREQUENT RECEPTION OF HOLY COMMUNION. It was not enough for Stanislaus to be able to be near our divine Saviour. His love for Jesus was much greater. He wished to have Jesus in his heart also. How does Jesus come into our hearts? How often did Stanislaus receive Holy Communion? The devil can do no harm to him who possesses Jesus. What does the devil try to lead us into? Stanislaus knew that; therefore he often received our Saviour in Holy Communion.

6. DEVOTION TO THE BLESSED VIRGIN MARY. Whom did Stanislaus love next to Jesus? His heart was all aglow with love for her. How could this be seen from his conversations? How did he call her, when he spoke of her? During the day he often prayed: " My Jesus and my dear Mother Mary." What did he daily do to honor her? How did he act when he came across a picture or statue of Mary? How did Mary reward Stanislaus? Dear children, if you wish to be pure and chaste and always to overcome impure temptations, consecrate yourselves to the Blessed Virgin, and say every morning and every night three Hail Marys in honor of the immaculate purity of the Blessed Virgin, and when tempted, say: " Jesus and Mary, help me, protect me." (St. Alphonsus.)

7. WORK AND STUDY. St. Stanislaus prayed often during the day. What did Stanislaus do, when he was not praying? But work and study make one tired. Therefore you cannot study all the time. What do you do in the schoolyard during recess? What did Stanislaus do when he was tired of working and studying? He was very diligent and industrious. He who is always busy had no time for evil thoughts. But alas! not all children are diligent. How do you call such children as are not diligent? Behind every lazy child there stands a devil to suggest to him all kinds of evil and impure thoughts; and the devil does not rest, until he has led that child into sin. Hence the saying: "Idleness is the devil's pillow and the beginning of every vice."

II. CHASTITY MADE STANISLAUS EXCEEDINGLY HAPPY.

1. Oh, how beautiful is the chaste generation with glory. Gracefulness and cheerfulness. Stanislaus always kept busy. He was never out of humor or disagreeable. How was he disposed? What can you say about his face? About his eyes? What could be learnt therefrom? Parents desire beautiful children, and children desire to be beautiful. Chastity makes a child's face bright and cheerful, and the appearance of innocence makes children very happy. A chaste child is as light and as happy as a bird that sings.

2. The chaste are in honor with both God and men. So long as they are on earth, they serve as models for imitation. Chastity adorned Stanislaus so much, that people had never seen a more graceful boy. What were the feelings of those who saw him? How did they also wish to be? The children were especially fond of him. How could this be seen at play? How when kneeling in church? What effect did his good conduct produce on his companions? Who often wondered at this? You see from this that an innocent and pure child is a source of pleasure and joy to every one. He who sees such a child feels

his heart soften, and he thus thinks of that child: " Thou art like a fragrant flower, so nice, so beautiful, so pure. And I feel inclined to lay my hands on thy head and to pray God to preserve thee so pure, so beautiful, so graceful."

3. The chaste are honored by the angels and saints! How did the angels honor St. Stanislaus? How did St. Barbara honor him? Stanislaus was very sick in a boarding house. And no one would call the priest for him. Stanislaus thought he was going to die. Then he prayed to St. Barbara, who helps people to die well. He said: " St. Barbara, deign to help me, that I may not die without receiving Holy Communion." And how did St. Barbara help him? It was about midnight, when Stanislaus sat up in bed, and shaking his sick nurse, whispered: " Kneel down; St. Barbara with two angels are coming to bring me Holy Communion." And so it was.

4. The chaste are in honor with Mary and with God. The Blessed Virgin also honored St. Stanislaus. Mary looks so lovingly on the children who are chaste, as a good mother on her beloved children. And Mary prays to God for them. God also looks as a good father on innocent and pure children. You cannot imagine how greatly God is pleased with them. Look at the heavens on a clear, bright night. How many stars shine and twinkle there. They would seem like angels' eyes looking down so kindly and friendly upon us. What a pleasant sight! In like manner, the innocent and chaste children shine just as pleasantly and as lovely in the eyes of God. God, therefore, loves dearly the pure and chaste.

When the Son of God came upon earth, He chose as His Mother the most pure and chaste Virgin Mary. The disciple He most loved was the pure and chaste John, whom He allowed to rest his head on His Sacred Heart. Therefore Jesus so dearly loved innocent children He said: " Suffer little children to come to Me, and forbid them not,

346 SIXTH COMMANDMENT

for theirs is the Kingdom of heaven." Because St. Stanislaus was pure and chaste the Infant Jesus also came to him. When did this happen? Relate. What was he allowed to do with the divine Infant? Stanislaus could never forget this. Where did he, therefore, long to go? For what? On what feast did St. Stanislaus wish to die? Who was to come to take him to heaven? How did he make known his wish to the Blessed Virgin? How many days was it before the Assumption? And what happened during the following night? What did Stanislaus say as soon as he got sick? He grew always worse and worse, and during the night preceding the Assumption he received the last sacraments. How did he act when the priest brought the Blessed Sacrament? What was the appearance of his face? What were the feelings of all who then saw him? His death came nearer and nearer. What prayers were then said for him? And what did Stanislaus do during those prayers? Whom did Stanislaus expect to come for him? How did the Blessed Virgin fulfil his expectation? Who came with her? What happened to his face when he beheld his heavenly Mother? Then he conversed silently with her until he died. On what feast did he die? Thus did Mary fulfil his prayer. How beautiful and happy was the life of St. Stanislaus! But his death is almost more beautiful. Oh, how happy it is, indeed, to be innocent and chaste!

" And when the chaste generation hath withdrawn itself, men desire it. Its memory is immortal." How old was Stanislaus when he died? What was the appearance of his face when he was dying? And after his death? People from all directions to see him. How did they show that they dearly loved him? Of what did they speak? Thus it happens to the innocent. Long after their death people think of them, speak well of them, praise them and rejoice over them.

Stanislaus was buried. What miracle took place in his body when in the grave? People from near and from afar went to the parents of St. Stanislaus. For what reason? Why did they wish them happiness? Thus do chaste children give joy to their parents even after their death.

"And the chaste generation triumpheth crowned forever, winning the reward of undefiled conflicts."

Where did the soul of St. Stanislaus go when he died? What must have been his feelings when he was admitted to see Jesus and Mary? And how did God reward him for his purity and chastity? When such a pure soul comes before the throne of God, Oh, with what joy she is received by our divine Saviour! And Mary places her among the great multitude of the pure and chaste souls; and she receives a crown more brilliant than that of the other saints, and she accompanies the Saviour wherever He goes, and sings a hymn which other saints cannot sing. How happy must St. Stanislaus have felt in heaven for having so courageously watched over himself and remained so pious and so chaste.

III. CONNECTION. How did people call St. Stanislaus? The little saint, the angel. Whom did he resemble when at prayer? Angels are innocent and pure. How was his soul? And how are the souls of all chaste children? The angels are pictured like beautiful, graceful youths. What effect has the chastity of Stanislaus on his countenance? All chaste children are beautiful and lovely. Because the angels are innocent and pure, God takes delight in them. Why did God take delight in Stanislaus? In which children does God take delight. And who else took delight in Stanislaus? And also in all chaste children?

In whom did Stanislaus take the greatest delight? In whom do the angels? And likewise all chaste children. With whom do the angels prefer to be? Where did Stanislaus like so much to be? And where do chaste children like to go? What do the angels in heaven do near God? They kneel before God's throne and adore Him. What did St. Stanislaus take delight in doing? And before whom he loved so much to kneel? What do all chaste children love to do? Whom did St. Stanislaus love the most after God? To whom do chaste children love to pray? Even the angels in heaven honor and revere the Blessed Virgin Mary, for she is their Queen.

IV. SUMMARY. "Oh, how beautiful is the chaste generation with glory!" Chastity beautifies the bodies and souls of children, and imparts happiness to them. Men cannot forget chaste children. They are beloved by men, by the angels and saints, by the Blessed Virgin and by God Himself. During their life they serve as models to others; their death is beautiful, and after their death people long for them. In heaven they are crowned and receive a special reward, because they struggled so faithfully during their life and remained so pure.

V. APPLICATION. 1. Dear children, from the example of St. Stanislaus you perceive how happy are the children who are pure and chaste. You can all become happy also. Listen and hear how good men encourage you: "Oh, how beautiful are the chaste children with glory. They are honored by God and by men." All are fond of them. If you wish to be happy and be loved by all, be chaste and pure. And what do the angels in heaven say to you? "Oh, how beautiful are chaste children with glory!" Shun all evil companions and all curious looks. Be pure and chaste, and you are already angels on earth, soon to be angels in heaven. Never forget that you have always an angel at your side in order to bring you to heaven. Pray to him and follow his inspirations. And what does the Blessed Virgin Mary, from far above the angels, say to you: "Oh, how beautiful are chaste children with glory!" "Do you sincerely wish to be my children, love me dearly and pray earnestly to me. And I, your Mother, will help you to remain pure and chaste, so that roses will bloom on your cheeks and lilies in your hearts."

And what does our divine Saviour say to you? "Oh, how beautiful are chaste children with glory!" He that loves chastity has the King of heaven as his friend. Do you not wish to be the favorites of the King of heaven and allow Him to draw and press you to His heart? If you do, take pleasure in going to Jesus in the church, and pray to Him before His tabernacle, that He may help you remain pure and chaste. And what does the Blessed Trinity say to you? "Oh, how beautiful are chaste children with glory!" The Father says to you: "I created you in My image. Remain pure and chaste." The Son says: "I redeemed you and gave My life for you. Remain pure and chaste." The Holy Ghost says: "I sanctified you in baptism and made My dwelling in you. Remain pure and chaste." Oh, how beautiful, therefore, are chaste and pure children in the glory of their virtue! Already on earth they are loved and honored by God, and all good men. And when they go before God's throne in their purity and chastity, they obtain honor and happiness without end.

2. Therefore, dear children, when sin entices you, Oh, do not follow it. Remain pure and innocent! The innocence of your soul should be dearer to you than everything in this world. It is your most precious treasure on earth and your greatest honor. Stand up, all of you, look at the crucifix, look at Jesus! See how He hangs on the cross, He who shed His blood to the last drop for your soul, that you may not be lost! Look at Him well! Let each one say: "My dearest Saviour, I promise Thee, that I will not for the whole world, commit a mortal sin through impurity; that I prefer death to mortal sin."

SEVENTH COMMANDMENT.
16. Our Neighbor's Property.

I. PREPARATION. How many brothers and sisters have you, Bertha? One brother and one sister. What are their names? Martin and Rose. Now your father gives you and them clothes and books. To whom do the clothes and books belong which your father gave you? To me. Yes, they are your property. To whom belong those he gave to Martin? To Martin. They are his property. To whom belong those he gave to Rose? To Rose. They are her property. Wherefrom did your father get all that he has, his house, his farm? He bought them; he inherited them. And his horses and cows? He raised them; he bought them. All these things belong to your father; they are his property. Who are those that own a great many things? The rich. Who are those that own but few things? The poor. The poor own something, however little it may be. It is their property. Wherefrom have all men their property? Everything in the world belongs to God. Why? Whose property are all things in the world? God's. Now, Martin, suppose you would take away from Rose the things father gave her. What would your father say? "That is not right, you must give them back to Rose. They belong to her, and not to you." Now, Bertha, suppose you would take away from Martin the things father gave him; what would father say again? Now who is the Father of all men? Therefore God says to each man: "Thou shalt not take away any one's property"; or briefly: "Thou shalt not steal."

OBJECT. I will now speak about a boy who never took away the property of another.

II. RELATION —(*Copied from Rev. Valentine Eschenlohr.* St. Paschal Baylon, when still a boy, was hired out to strangers by his very needy parents. His employers set him to keeping their flock of sheep. He took great care that the sheep should not trespass on or injure the property of others. Nevertheless it sometimes happened that some lambs and sheep would go into the neighbors' fields and there eat the seeds and the clover. As soon as Paschal would notice it he drove his trespassing sheep out of those fields, and then he would examine the amount of the damage they had done, and then note it down in his memorandum, which he had always with him. In the evening he would go to the owner of the field and pay out of his earnings for the damage done by his master's flock. "You are too anxious," others used to say to him; "if you do this every time, you shall have to pay more than you earn." "Oh," said Paschal, "I do not want any unjust goods; I will rather restore my neighbor's property during my life, than later on go to hell." In the summer months he always took a sickle along to help the servants in cutting the wheat, etc. But he would take no pay for that, saying: "I will thereby make up for the damage I may unknowingly have done to these people." Often the other shepherds wished him to go along with them to get fruit; but he never allowed himself to be persuaded to go along with them; and he would never touch or eat any of the stolen fruit. During the vintage a big shepherd wished to compel him to go with him into a vineyard to steal grapes. The shepherd was rough and strong, and was greatly feared by the other shepherds. But Paschal said: "I will not go with you, for that is a sin." The rough shepherd got angry, and pulled Paschal as far as the vineyard, and said: "Either come along with me, or I will kill you." "You can kill me," replied Paschal, "but you cannot compel me to take what does not belong to me." When the impudent man returned, he held the stolen grapes before Paschal's face, saying in mockery: "They are sweet; but you shall not get a single one of them." "I do not want any," replied Paschal;

"when I wish to eat grapes, I will buy them with my own money." Another shepherd was not so good as Paschal; he went along into the vineyard, stole and ate plenty of grapes; but they made him very sick. Paschal said to him: " You now see that stolen things do not profit you." The other shepherds, however much they said and tried, could never persuade Paschal to transgress the seventh commandment. To him his neighbor's property was sacred.

CONSIDERATION — *Injuring another's property*. About whom have I been speaking? Where did he go, when he was yet a boy? What were his parents? What kind of work was given him? Paschal would take out his sheep into meadows and fields, that they might feed on the grass. About what was he very watchful? About his sheep not feeding in the fields of strangers, and keeping them only where they had a right to be, that is, in uncultivated fields, lying between and near cultivated fields. Where did the pilfering sheep sometimes trespass? What would they do there? They would eat the seeds and the young and tender clover, which tasted very good. If those fields had belonged to Paschal, there would not have been anything wrong in that. But whose property were they? They belonged to his neighbor, to others. The owners underwent a loss of a part of their property in the seeds and clover eaten by the sheep. They were injured in their property by Paschal's sheep. It was Paschal's duty to watch over his sheep. Who then was the cause of the damage caused by the sheep? But Paschal did not will it; he did not wish to see his sheep in cultivated fields. What would he do when he saw them there? What would he do to remember it? What had he always with him?

Examples. Children can also injure their neighbor's property. How so? By running through planted fields and gardens, injuring the plants, the trees; killing fowls; marking and scratching walls, throwing stones and breaking windows; in a word, by injuring the property of others. Children sometimes tear or soil the books and hats and other articles of clothing of their schoolmates. That is damaging another's property, and is sinful. Paschal's sheep had enough to eat where he brought them; but when the sheep saw young clover and other tender plants in other fields, they would go there to eat some, because such things tasted better. In like manner, there are children, who, although they have enough to eat, will pilfer, wherever they can, cakes, candy, fruit, jams, preserves, because they taste nicer. These children imitate Paschal's sheep and the other shepherds. How? Children that pilfer at home, will also steal from strangers. Great thieves began by pilfering, by stealing little things at home, in school. Great thieves, when caught, are sent to the penitentiary for months and years. And whenever they are let out, most of them steal more than before.

Robbery, burglary and murder. Almost every day the papers relate robberies that took place the day or the night before in the street, or in dwellings, or in banks, or in business places. People are publicly attacked and threatened with death, if they do not give up their money, their valuables; their purses, etc., are sometimes publicly snatched out of their hands, or their pockets; buildings are entered into at night and all the money and jewelry in them carried away; often if the robbers and burglars meet with opposition, they kill the owners. Bands of boys 11, 12, 13 or more years old, have in large cities turned robbers and stolen thousands of dollars' worth of property by night and by day, and even committed murder. All these thieves and robbers began by pilfering little things at home.

When you find something, such as a knife, a pocketbook, etc., you must give it to the owner, if you know to whom it belongs. If the article you found is valuable, you must try and find out the owner; for you are not allowed to keep what does not belong to you. In that case your parents will do it for you. To keep for yourself what you find, although you know to whom it belongs, is real stealing. It is also stealing to cheat others. If when you buy something and get back too much change through mistake, you must not keep what was given to you over and above the right change, but give it back to the owner. Some children when they are sent to buy something, keep a part of the money given them by their parents, for candy, etc., and tell their parents the article they bought cost more than it really did. That is cheating your parents. It is also cheating to take advantage of the wants of our neighbor, to get a thing from him for much less than it is worth. For instance, a man who is in great need of money for his family, for his business, comes to you asking you to buy his watch, which is worth over one hundred dollars; he offers it to you for fifty dollars; you take advantage of his wants and offer him only twenty-five dollars for it, and at last the poor man gives it to you for twenty-five dollars, for he is in very great need. You have cheated him by this transaction out of twenty-five dollars. That is sinful and cruel on your part.

Restitution and compensation. Let us return to Paschal. His sheep had not done any great damage. To whom did Paschal go in the evening each time that his sheep had caused some damage? What did he do concerning the damage? He paid the owners the amount of the damage his sheep had caused; in other words he indemnified them for the damage. Where did he take the money from in order to do this? His neighbor then recovered what belonged to him, just as God wills it should be. God does not forgive the sin of him who caused damage to his neighbor by stealing, cheating, injuring his property, unless he makes restitution for, or repairs the damage done by him. What must we do to obtain God's forgiveness when we have injured our neighbor in his property?

Although Paschal had committed no sin against his

neighbor in his property, he made restitution for the damage done. Who were displeased at this? What did they say to him about it? What was Paschal's reply? Where do unjustly acquired goods bring us to? He who has injured his neighbor in his property and made no restitution or compensation, shall forever burn in hell. (That is, if the matter of the injustice or injury is grievous; for only a grievous matter can induce a grievous obligation.) Which did Paschal prefer, to make restitution, or to burn in hell? What did Paschal take along with him in summer? For what? Did he ask or take pay for his work? What reason did he give? He wished also to compensate the injury he might have done to others without knowing it.

You see, children, from this, that you are bound to compensate (make restitution for) the injury you have done your neighbor. You cannot always or easily do it with money. Why not? But you can do it like Paschal. How? By helping him; for instance, minding his children, going on messages for him without renumeration.

Helping; concealing stolen goods. To what sins did the other shepherds try to lead Paschal? They were very earnest in this. Did they gain their object? He would not go with them. They also tried to make him eat of the stolen fruit. But what did Paschal do? Why would he not eat of such fruit? He who accepts stolen things, is no better than the thief. What does he commit, who accepts stolen things? What did a big shepherd try to force Paschal to do during the vintage? The other shepherds were greatly afraid of that man. Why? What did Paschal answer him? Why did he not go along with him? How did that bad shepherd take Paschal's answer. He wished to bring Paschal by force with him to steal grapes. Where did he drag Paschal along? How did he threaten him? But Paschal remained firm. What would he have preferred to undergo rather than steal? He was right; for a good child should always say: " I would rather die than steal and commit sin." The impudent man tried another way to overcome Paschal. What did he hold up before Paschal's face, when he came back from stealing grapes? The grapes must have looked very nice and delicious. What did the shepherd say in mockery to Paschal? He expected that it would excite in him the desire to go and steal grapes for himself. What effect did that have on Paschal? Paschal paid no attention to the seducer, although he naturally would have liked to eat such fine grapes. But what kind of grapes he did not wish for? Therefore, what answer did he give that shepherd? But Paschal's companion was not so good. To what did he allow himself to be seduced? What was the effect of eating those grapes? They made him sick. What did Paschal then say to him? This shows that stolen things do not profit, do not bring luck. The shepherds often again tried to induce him to go along with them to steal. Did they gain anything by doing so? Which commandment forbids stealing? Which commandment Paschal did not transgress? In what does he who breaks this commandment injure his neighbor? From whom have men their property? Therefore his neighbor's property was sacred to Paschal.

III. CONNECTION. Let us examine and compare the different ways in which we can injure our neighbor in his property. When a child wishes to pilfer at home, he waits till his mother has gone out. Why? The child pilfers in secret. Who is it that does not wish to be seen taking other people's things? The thief. How does the thief act? In secret. In like manner, did the child act, who kept back a nickel or a dime for candy, for he did not wish mother to know it. Also the child who got too much change at the grocery, and kept it for himself, did this secretly also. A burglar also enters houses and buildings to steal in secret, especially when every one is asleep. The robber steals things by force. He who takes advantage of others in bargains, in buying and selling, of their poverty, ignorance or simplicity, is as bad as the robber. What do all these persons commit? Sin. There is another kind of sin against the seventh commandment. Which is it? To cause damage wilfully to our neighbor's property. If the damage is not caused wilfully, it is no sin. Why? Was the damage done by Paschal's sheep to the property of others, a sin for Paschal? What did he, nevertheless, do about it? Made restitution or compensation. What must they do who have injured their neighbor in his property? They must make restitution, restore what they have taken or its value. (If the stolen or damaged object was valuable, the obligation of restitution binds under pain of mortal sin; so that if the thief, etc., is able to make restitution and does not do it, he cannot have any of his sins forgiven. Hence to such a one St. Augustine says: " Restitution or damnation.")

IV. SUMMARY. The seventh commandment, " Thou shalt not steal," forbids doing unjustly every kind of injury to our neighbor in his property, such as by pilfering, stealing, cheating, robbery, or keeping what belongs to another (things found).

V. APPLICATION. 1. Let us see once more what sins are committed against the seventh commandment. Charles is fond of pilfering. As soon as his mother is out of sight, he looks everywhere for sweetmeats. From one place he steals sugar, from another some cake, or some fruit. This he does almost every day. How should he tell his sins? " I stole sweetmeats almost every day." One day Mark's mother left the key in the drawer. Mark opened it, and took two dimes out of it. How must he tell his sin? " I stole two dimes " (or twenty cents). Another day when making a purchase in a grocery, he saw some nickels on the counter, and when the clerk's eyes were turned in another direction, he took three nickels. Passing near a fruit-stand he took a peach and an orange. He took a knife from another boy. How must he confess his sins? "I stole from a store three nickels, and a peach and an orange from a stand and a knife from a boy." Johnny entered the neighbor's orchard at least twenty times, and stole plums, pears and other fruits each time. How should he tell his sins? "I stole fruit at least twenty times from a neighbor's orchard." John got five cents too much change in a store, and more than thirty times he kept five cents each time from the money his mother gave him to pay for things he brought from different stores. How must he tell his sins? "I kept five cents given me too much in change, and more than thirty times I kept back five cents from the money mother gave me to pay for things bought." Frank found a purse on the sidewalk containing five dollars. He knew to whom it belonged, for he had seen a man drop it; but he kept it; he did the same with a knife a schoolmate had left on his desk in school, and with a silk handkerchief of the priest which he had found on the steps outside of the church. How must he tell his sins? "I found a pocket-book containing five dollars; and I found also a knife and a silk handkerchief. I have kept all these things, although I knew who had lost them." Robert quarreled with a companion on Sunday, and threw him into a gutter, and ruined thereby his fine new suit of clothes. The next day at school he spoiled a schoolmate's Bible History by tearing a good many leaves out of it. How must he tell his sins? "I ruined a companion's fine new suit of clothes, and spoiled a school book of one of my schoolmates."

2. Dear children, beware of taking eatables and sweetmeats and other little things at home, for you will thereby acquire the habit of stealing. Never take even the smallest thing belonging to your neighbor. Rather suffer hunger than steal; rather be always poor and needy and honest, than become rich by stealing or cheating. A thief disgraces himself before God and men. Never destroy or

damage your neighbor's property. The devil is fond of destroying things out of sheer malice. He who injures his neighbor's property, has something devilish in him. If you have stolen anything or done injury to your neighbor in his property, be sure to make restitution or compensation. Otherwise, according to the amount of the injury you have done, you shall have to burn for a time in purgatory or in hell forever!

How to confess sins against the seventh commandment. I have pilfered or stolen eatables at home; I have stolen money at home (from my parents); I have stolen from others; I have cheated others; I have kept things I found; I have injured or destroyed the property of others. When the amount stolen or the damage done is great, it should also be mentioned.

EIGHTH COMMANDMENT.

17. Lying and Falsehood.

I. Preparation. In the earthly paradise God said to Adam and Eve: " If you eat of the tree in the middle of paradise, you shall die." But they ate of it. And what happened to them later on? Therefore what God had said was true. After their sin God promised them a Redeemer. When did the promised Redeemer come? Therefore what God had said was true. What God says is always true. Whose Son from all eternity was the promised Redeemer? The Redeemer also spoke to men. What did Jesus foretell that Judas would do against Him? And what really happened? What were the things that Jesus foretold? True. What did Jesus foretell to Peter? And what really took place? And all that Jesus said and taught was true; for Jesus is God. All that God says is true; for God is Truth itself.

Whose children are all men? According to what did

God create men? Whom do children resemble? Whom should all men resemble? But God always tells the truth; He is the Father of truth. How should all men speak always? Men should, therefore, say nothing false or untrue. Therefore God says in the eighth commandment: "Thou shalt not bear false witness against thy neighbor."

OBJECT. I will show you from the conversation of the devil with Eve, how wicked and ugly it is to bear false witness.

II. DEVELOPMENT.

1. HYPOCRISY. How did the devil show himself towards Eve, when she came near the forbidden tree? Very friendly. But he had no good intentions towards her. To what did he wish to seduce her? What effect was that to produce on our first parents? To make them unhappy. What kind of intention has he who seeks to make another person unhappy? An evil intention. What did the devil intend in his heart towards Adam and Eve? But how did he outwardly show himself? Very friendly. The devil represented himself better disposed towards Adam and Eve than he really was. He who represents himself better disposed towards another than he is really, is said to dissemble, to play the hypocrite. Who is a hypocrite? What was the devil when he spoke to Eve? Wicked men often do likewise.

There is a beggar begging at a corner, or near a church. When he sees a priest or a pious person coming his way, he takes out his beads, makes the sign of the cross, and makes out he is praying, and why? To make the priest, etc., believe he is a pious, holy man. And what for? To get an alms. He plays the hypocrite; he is a hypocrite. Why? He represents himself, he tries to make people believe that he is far better than he is really. How does that beggar act? Through hypocrisy which is an ugly, hateful sin. Who was the first hypocrite? The devil. A hypocrite is false, deceitful like the devil. And so is a false, deceitful child. How some mischievous, wicked children, when they do wrong, try to appear innocent in order to throw the blame on others who are innocent!

2. LIES. The devil, with all his hypocrisy, would probably not have succeeded in seducing Eve, if he had not also used other means. He asked her a question. What was it? What was Eve's answer? And what did the devil then say to Eve? "By no means shall you die"; that is, you shall certainly not die. Did not the devil know what would happen, if our first parents would eat of the forbidden fruit? And yet what did he say? Therefore he spoke to Eve differently from what he knew, differently from the truth. What was the truth? Therefore the devil said to Eve what was not true. He said not only: "You shall not die," but added something else. What did he add? "You shall be like God." The devil knew very well that Adam and Eve could not become like God. Therefore he again asserted what he knew was not true. What do we call it, when a person says something which he knows is not true? A lie. What did the devil do in speaking to Eve? He tried to deceive her by telling lies. Telling a lie is a sin. What sin did the devil commit? Here is another example. Rose was kept in after school for missing her lesson. She came home late. Her mother asked her: "What kept you so late?" Rose answered: "I was playing with some of the school girls." Did Rose tell the truth? She knew very well that it was not true. What sin did she commit?

What do you call those who tell lies? Liars. Who told the first lie? Who was, then, the first liar? Lying comes from the devil, and the devil is called "the father of lies." Everything the devil said to Eve was a lie from the beginning to the end. He can tell only lies, and seeks to deceive every one by his lies.

Who cannot lie? What is everything that God says? Why? Because He is Truth itself. Therefore God intensely hates lies. Why is the devil called "the father of lies"? Since God can tell only what is true, how may we call Him? The Father of truth.

Whose children are all men? Whom should they resemble? But God is Truth itself and says only what is true. What should all men say, if they wish to resemble God, their Father? Whom does the liar resemble? Every lie he tells is as an ugly stain which the devil makes in his soul. The more lies a man tells, the more he is like the devil. Who is the father of the liar? Who is a child of the devil? The liar. What a disgrace to have the devil as one's father! The devil hates God with a terrible hatred. He is thoroughly wicked, and God's greatest enemy. And since the liar is a child of the devil, and resembles the devil, God hates the liar and all lying. And therefore God so severely punishes lying; and this, even in this life. A child, telling his first lie, blushes. And when his lie is found out, he is ashamed. No one wishes to have anything to do with a lying child. When he wishes to say something, usually some one says to him: "Keep still, you are a liar." People do not believe him any more, who has been found out telling a lie. This is a punishment God sends him. It is a great disgrace to be a liar, for lying is the sin of the devil. The Roman emperor Claudius had forbidden liars to be buried after their death; their bodies were to remain exposed in the fields either to rot or to be devoured by wild beasts, and their houses were to be torn down.

But God punishes lies in the next life. How many children are now burning in purgatory to expiate their lies. Some who lied in matters of importance, and thus did great harm to their neighbor, are even burning forever in hell! Dear children, never tell a lie, even if you could, by doing so, acquire millions of dollars! We must never tell a lie, however small, were we able thereby to save all men from death. For every lie is a sin, and we are never allowed wilfully to commit the least sin, for we would offend God thereby. He who is fond of telling lies, will also easily steal and become a thief.

3. SLANDER. The liar is wicked. He would like that others should be looked upon as wicked. Therefore he tells lies on them. In this manner the devil, speaking to Eve, acted against God. What punishment did God threaten against our first parents, if they would eat of the forbidden tree? What did the devil say about it? " By no means." This meant: " It is not true; you shall not die." But who had said it to Adam and Eve? Did not the devil then mean that God had told them a lie? Was not that the same as calling God a liar? But God cannot lie, and does not lie. Therefore the devil slandered God; that is, he told a lie about Him. Calumny or slander is telling a lie or lies about some one; or falsely accusing some one of a sin he did not commit. It is a sin. It is the devil's sin. The slanderer is a child of the devil; nay, he is himself a devil, for only he who is very wicked can accuse of something bad, wicked, sinful, him who is perfectly innocent. Have not some of you told lies on your brothers and sisters, on your schoolmates? Have you not sometimes accused others of the evil you yourselves had committed? What kind of sin did you commit thereby?

4. DETRACTION OR BACKBITING. Who knows of a boy mentioned in Bible History, who told his father of a sin his brothers had really committed? Joseph of Egypt. Why did Joseph tell his father about his brothers' sin? He wished that their father should admonish them: " That is a sin; you must never do it again." Had he also another reason? He wished that they should never do it again, and that they should behave better. What were Joseph's intentions in this? Good. For what purpose are we allowed to tell the faults of our neighbor? Who have the care of bringing up the children properly and of pre-

serving them from sin? Who have that care in the school. To which person did Joseph make known the fault of his brothers? To whom are you allowed and even obliged to tell the faults of your brothers and sisters? And the faults of your schoolmates? For what purpose? Therefore you must tell the truth, when your parents ask you concerning the behavior or misbehavior of your brothers and sisters. In like manner, a school boy or a school girl must tell the truth to the teacher, when the teacher inquires about the behavior of their schoolmates.

Charles had stolen money from his parents. His parents found it out; but no one else knew anything about it. Charles is punished for it by his father. Whilst punishing Charles, his father says very loud: "Oh, that I should live to be disgraced by my boy, who has become a thief! You ought to be put in jail, for thieves belong there, or should be hanged. Are you going to steal again? I am going to knock stealing out of you, you thief! Shame on you!" But Charles cries aloud, and repeats several times: "O pa, let me go, I will never do it again! I will never steal again in all my life." At last Charles' father stops whipping him. But Frank, who lived next door, heard the blows and all that Charles and his father had said. Frank was so glad, for he was mad with Charles; Frank was also a gossip (talker). And so he went around to all other boys and related with great pleasure all he had heard. Now to whom would Frank have been allowed to tell the fault of Charles? And for what? That Charles should amend. But there was no necessity for Frank doing this. Why? What were his intentions concerning Charles? What did Charles' fault concern strangers? Why should other people know anything about it? There was, then, no necessity for Frank to make known to strangers that Charles had been guilty of stealing. Now when Charles goes along, the other children cry out: "The thief is coming!" And no one will go with him. Many say to him: "Get out of here, you thief." That is a great disgrace for Charles.

Suppose Bertha had beautiful long hair; she would let it hang down her back in fine tresses tied with a red ribbon. It enhanced her beauty. But one day Bertha was asleep on a bench in the garden. A wicked man sneaked in and suddenly cut off her hair. When Bertha re-entered her house and looked into the mirror, she began to cry, because her beautiful tresses were gone, and she looked so changed, and almost ugly. Who caused such a change in her? How? By cutting off her hair. Now let us go back to Charles. He had previously been very much liked by everybody. Other children had been fond of his company, for they looked upon him as a good, honest boy. That was an honor for Charles. But how did they afterwards look upon him? How they blame and abuse him! What do they now do when he comes near them? They no longer have any regard for him. He has lost his good name (reputation) with them. How must he feel about it? What will he probably do at home on this account? Whose fault is it, if Charles has lost his good name? Frank took away (cut away) his good name. How? There was no need for Frank to make known the fault of Charles to everybody, and thus rob him of his good name by backbiting him. Detraction (backbiting) is sinful. How did Frank sin against Charles? How would Frank like it, if some one would publish his faults everywhere? Remember: "What you do not wish to be done to you, you should not do to your neighbor."

III. CONNECTION. Johnny is the last in his class. He says: "Two times two are three." Is that true? Does he commit a sin by saying so? Why not? Rose, as we have heard, who was kept in after school and came home late, gave her mother as an excuse: "I was playing." She, therefore, told a falsehood. What did Rose commit? Why? When is a falsehood sinful? Who is a liar, Johnny or Rose? Who was the first liar? How did the devil behave outwardly towards Eve? But what design had he in his heart? Who was outwardly friendly towards his brother? Cain. What design had he in his heart against him? What do we call those who outwardly show themselves much better than they are in their heart? Hypocrites. What, then, was Cain? How did Herod act the hypocrite in presence of the wise men? Relate. When Jesus was arrested Judas kissed Him. How does a person feel towards the one he kisses? And what are his intentions towards those he loves? Good. But what did Judas feel in his heart towards Jesus? But he acted as if he loved Jesus and wished Him well. What, then, was Judas? What were the brothers of Joseph when they showed their father Joseph's bloody coat? Who was the first hypocrite? He pretended to be good. Of whom did he speak evil? He therefore slandered God Himself. How did Putiphar's wife slander Joseph? She accused him to her husband of a crime he had not committed. Whom did Joseph accuse of a fault which they really had committed? To whom Joseph did not tell it? Why did he tell it to his father? Why did he not tell it to strangers? What would you say, if Joseph had told the fault of his brothers to his father, in order to get them punished? What sin would Joseph have committed, if he had related the fault of his brothers to other persons? To whom should children make known the faults of their brothers and sisters? The faults of their schoolmates? What should children do when their parents and teachers question them about the faults of their companions? What would they commit, if they would then not tell the truth? They would tell a lie.

IV. SUMMARY. When does a person sin by lying, hypocrisy, slander and detraction? Which is the eighth commandment? What does it forbid? Lies and hypocrisy, detraction and slander.

V. Application. 1. Let us learn how the sins against the eighth commandment should be told. Let us begin with the sins of the devil. What sin did he commit when he pretended to be so friendly towards Eve? Hypocrisy. What sin did he commit when he said: "You shall not die?" He told a lie. What sin, when he said: "You shall be like God"? Another lie. He also made believe that God had lied to our first parents. What sin was that? Slander. How should the devil tell his sins? "I once acted the hypocrite, told two lies, and slandered once." James said to Henry: "Go and see in your neighbor's stable a young calf with two heads." That was not true, but it was said as a joke. What sin did James commit? How must he tell that sin? "I once told a lie in a joke" (or a jocose lie). It is not allowed to tell jocose lies. We should detest even the smallest lie. Michael, instead of studying his lessons at home, was full of mischief. The result was that he broke a pitcher. Afraid of being punished, he said to his mother: "The cat has knocked the pitcher down and broken it." What sin did he commit by saying that? He told a lie. How must he tell that sin? "I told a lie to escape punishment." Bertha in church pretends to be praying. She holds her hands joined before her face; but in reality she is talking to the girl next to her. In what did she commit sin? How must she tell it? "I once acted the hypocrite." Rose is envious of Jane; she says to the teacher: "Jane has stolen." But that is not true. But the teacher believes it and punishes Jane. What sin did Rose commit? How must she tell it? "I slandered my schoolmate." What sin did Frank commit in telling everybody that Charles had stolen? How must he tell it? "I have been guilty of backbiting."

2. Dear children, promise almighty God: "I will always tell the truth, and I will never tell a lie." If you have done something deserving of punishment, you should resolve in your mind: "No, I will not tell a lie about it,

however great the punishment that may be given me." It is better to tell the truth, and be punished by your parents or your teachers, than to lie about it, and be punished by God for your lie. If you have committed a fault, admit it openly and honorably: "Yes, I did it." A child that acts thus, acts right, and is more easily forgiven, and either will not be punished at all, or only slightly. A child that committed a fault and lies about it, deserves a double punishment. Never tell a lie, even when no one can find it out. But God knows it. If any of you have the bad habit of telling lies, you should resolve every morning (at prayer); "I will not tell a lie to-day. My dear Saviour, help me." And whenever you catch yourself lying, say: "My God forgive me, and help me never again to tell a lie." You may add also an Our Father and a Hail Mary.

How to confess sins against the eighth commandment: I told lies; I acted the hypocrite; I was guilty of backbiting.

THE TENTH COMMANDMENT.

18. Unjust Desires of our Neighbor's Property.

I. PREPARATION. Mention some things belonging to you. What do you call the things that belong to you? My property. Mention some things that belong to our neighbor? Money, houses, stores, farms, cattle, etc. How do you call those things? Our neighbor's property. Which is the seventh commandment? What does the seventh commandment forbid?

OBJECT. I will show you to-day that it is already a sin to wish or to try to take our neighbor's property.

II. RELATION. A certain boy entered a house to fetch a boy to school. He could see no one in the room, but he saw a basket of apples on the window-sill. "What fine apples," he thought; and drew near to them very eagerly. He would very willingly have taken one. But, said he aloud, "No; that would not be right; I am not allowed to do so. Although nobody sees me, God sees me, for He sees all things." The boy leaving the apples alone was about to go away, when he heard a voice saying: "Stop! Remain here!" He was frightened, hearing this, and more so yet by seeing an old man coming to him. The old man said to him: "Be not afraid; you are a good boy. Because you think of God, take as many apples as you like. And remember as long as you live this saying: 'Even when alone, never do anything wrong.'"

CONSIDERATION — *The temptation.* Where did that boy go? What for? Did he see any person in the room? What did he see on the window-sill? Beautiful rosy apples that made his mouth water. The boy thought: "Would that they would give me one!" But it seemed that no one was there to give him one. Then an evil thought came to him. What was it? He approached the basket; and the apples looked still more beautiful. Has any one of you already seen such fine apples? How do such apples appear the longer you look at them? What happened to Eve the longer she looked at the forbidden fruit? The more she desired it; the greater was her longing for it. The same happened to that boy. How did he look at the apples? Eagerly. And what did the devil suggest to him? Steal some. If those apples had belonged to his father, would he have done right if he had taken some? But to whom did they belong? What then was it wrong for him to do? Which commandment forbids the taking of another's property? The seventh commandment makes it unlawful (forbids) to take another's property. What does he commit who takes another's property? A sin.

The Victory. The boy had not yet thought of that. All at once he reflects: "Stop; that would be stealing, a sin; and it would be wrong for me to do it." But the devil suggested: "But nobody sees you!" But his guardian angel suggests something else to him; and the boy says it to himself half aloud. Who knows what he said? Then what was the boy about to do? What words did he suddenly hear spoken behind him? The boy thought there was nobody in the room. Where had that old man (grandfather) been? Therefore the boy had not seen him. In the meantime the old man had watched to see what the boy would do.

The reward. How greatly must the boy have been frightened when the old man addressed him! What especially frightened him? The thought that the old man thought he had intended to steal. Tell me what the old man said to him. Why did he call the boy a good child? What thought kept the boy from stealing? How did the old man reward him? How glad did the boy then feel?

III. CONNECTION. That boy deserved the reward he received. What did he deserve it for? How did it happen that he did not take any apples, although he eagerly desired some? He thought that God forbade it. Who had once a great longing for a forbidden fruit? Eve also remembered that God had forbidden her to eat of it. From which of her words do we know that? But what did the devil say to her? And what did the devil suggest to the boy? But how did the boy overcome his suggestion? And what was the boy about to do? But Eve was not so much afraid. And what did she do? She remained, and continued to look at the fruit. And what effect did that have on her? It increased her desire for the fruit, and made her think: "How fine is that fruit; I will just take one, even if it is forbidden." And what did she then do? The evil deed followed the evil desire. Evil or bad desires are therefore forbidden and sinful.

Did our first parents commit sin by eating of the fruits of the other trees? Why not? Therefore they were allowed also to desire them. What should we say about that boy's desire, had he wished to take apples from his father's tree? Why? If he had desired that some of his neighbors would give him some of their apples, would his desire have been good or bad? But if he had wished for a chance to steal apples from his neighbor? Why? He would have sinned against the tenth commandment: "Thou shalt not covet thy neighbor's goods." What do you say about desires or the intention to get our neighbor's goods by stealing, robbery, or cheating? When are desires of our neighbor's goods sinful and forbidden? When are they allowed and not sinful?

IV. SUMMARY. The tenth commandment, "Thou shalt not covet thy neighbor's goods," forbids all sinful desires of our neighbor's goods. Summary of the last seven commandments. What is forbidden by the tenth commandment? To desire or try to take away any of our neighbor's property. Which commandment forbids the unjust taking away of our neighbor's property? Which commandment forbids the taking away of our neighbor's honor? Which commandment forbids the taking away of the life of our neighbor's body and of his soul? What does he lack who robs his neighbor of his good name, chastity, life, etc.? He lacks love for his neighbor. What does he possess who never injures his neighbor in his good name, life, chastity and property? Who are our nearest neighbor? Our parents, brothers and sisters. What do children owe to their parents? What do children prove, who perform all they owe to their parents? Which commandment prescribes these duties to children? What do all the commandments from the fourth to the tenth inclusive concern? Our duties towards our neighbor. These commandments tell us what the love of our neighbor requires us to do and to avoid. Which commandment briefly commands us to love our neighbor? In which commandment, therefore, are the seven commandments included? In the commandment of the love of our neighbor.

V. APPLICATION. 1. Let us hear something about a few

other boys who coveted their neighbor's goods. Paul would like to get cherries from his neighbor's cherry tree. But the watchman is near, and therefore he is afraid to climb the tree. What kind of desire has he? How must he tell his sin? "I had a desire to steal my neighbor's fruit." Frank would like to steal money from his mother. He looked everywhere for the key of the money-drawer, but could not find it. Did he commit a sin? How should he tell it? "I intended to steal money from my mother." Fred was looking at his neighbor's beautiful pears. He said: "If I were only allowed to go in and get some." What do you say about his desire? Henry looking at a pile of fine apples in his neighbor's house, thought to himself: "If those apples were ours, I would eat my fill of them." What do you say about his desire? Jane saw Mary with a handsome new dress. She said: "Oh, if I only had that dress!" What do you think of her desire? John has a fine gold watch, a birthday present from his rich uncle. He is proud of it and shows it to all his companions; and every one of them says in his heart: "I wish I had that watch." But Henry says: "I wish I had one like it." What do you think of these desires?

2. Dear children, the devil many a time comes to you, and suggests some evil to you; he does this especially when you are alone. You should then remember the old man's saying to the boy. What is that saying? Who is everywhere with you? When you commit a sin, you offend God, and God will punish you for it. When the devil tries to lead you into sin, imitate the boy I told you about. What did the devil suggest to the boy? "Only take one; no one sees you." What did the boy then do? You should do the same. You may also say a prayer, or sing a hymn.

3. You should not even make such wishes as these: "If I only had as fine a hat as N.; if I only had as much money as N.; if I should only get as costly presents as N."

Be good; obey your parents faithfully; be diligent;

be honest; say well your daily prayers, be pure and chaste, be patient and kind towards all, keep from grievous sin, then God will love you, and everybody will love you. You shall then be useful everywhere, and all will be well with you on earth, and in heaven all your desires will be fully satisfied.

How to confess sins against the tenth commandment: I desired, intended, tried to steal.

PART III
THE SACRAMENTS

THE SACRAMENTS

1. The Sacraments in general.

1. OBJECT. I will relate to you to-day what Jesus did, in order to enable men to go to heaven.

2. RELATION. In the beginning of the world there flowed from the heart of God the Father a fountain of graces. God caused those graces to flow into the hearts of Adam and Eve. Grace surrounded the souls of our first parents like a white garment and made them holy. It was the white garment of sanctifying grace. By means of this white garment Adam and Eve became children of God. They lived good and happy in the earthly paradise, and were never to die.

But Adam and Eve sinned. Then God closed the fountain of grace in His heart, and grace ceased to flow into the hearts of our first parents. Therefore Adam and Eve lost the white garment of sanctifying grace; and sin entered their souls, and defiled their souls and made them horrible. Now Adam and Eve were no longer children of God. And because all men are children of Adam and Eve, they all have lost the garment of santifying grace and inherited sin. Heaven was closed against them, and remained so for four thousand years.

Then God sent His Son from heaven upon the earth to take away sin from us and to open again the fountain of grace. To effect this the Son of God had to suffer more than we can tell during His whole life. Already in the stable of Bethlehem He began to suffer for us. Finally our Saviour was arrested. The soldiers mocked Him, spit upon Him, beat Him in the face with their fists. Then they scourged Him with whips so cruelly that they tore not only His skin, but even His very flesh to the bones. Jesus wept for pain, and His tears and blood flowed down together to the ground. Then they placed on His sacred head a frightful crown of long, sharp and stiff thorns, like nails, and beat it with sticks to drive the thorns deep into His head; and much blood ran down His face. Jesus suffered the most on Mount Calvary. The executioners drove through His hands and feet thick nails. And Jesus hung on the cross by His hands and feet for three hours until His death. Finally, a soldier, with his spear, pierced the side of Jesus into His very heart, and from the wound there flowed out all the blood that was left in Him. And when His precious blood flowed out of His pierced hands, feet and side, the fountain of grace was again opened.

CONSIDERATION. a. *The flowing of grace.* What was it that flowed in the beginning of the world from the heart of God the Father? Grace sanctifies, and, therefore, how is it called? Santifying grace. Where did God cause His grace to flow? What effects did it produce in the souls of our first parents? This grace penetrated their souls through and through and surrounded them as with a spotless white garment. How is this garment called? The white garment of sanctifying grace.

b. *The closed fountain of grace.* This fountain of grace did not flow continually. What happened to it when Adam and Eve sinned? God the Father closed the fountain of grace in His heart. Where then did it cease flowing? What did Adam and Eve lose in their souls? And what entered their souls instead? What did their souls become through sin? Whose children did they then cease to be? What then happened to heaven? Who inherited the sin of Adam and Eve? What garment is therefore wanting to the soul of every man? Where could no man enter? How long did this last?

c. *Jesus suffering for us.* Whom did God send after this

on earth to our help? His Son. What had the Son of God
to do for us? When did He begin to suffer for us? What
did Jesus suffer for us? He suffered more than we can
tell for us during His whole life. Finally, He was arrested,
mocked, spit upon, cruelly scourged, crowned with thorns
and finally nailed to a cross. On what was our Saviour
laid at His crucifixion? That was a hard bed indeed. And
hard it must have been for Jesus to lie on it, for His back
had been torn by the scourging. What was then done to
Jesus? What fearful pains He must have felt when those
dreadful nails were driven through His hands and feet into
the cross! Blood flowed from His back, blood flowed over
His face. What caused the blood to flow over his face?
And blood flowed from His hands and feet. How long did
Jesus hang on the cross? Then His soul left His body;
our Saviour was dead. What fresh wound did a soldier
then inflict on His body? It was then that our Saviour shed
the last drop of His blood for us.

d. *The fountain of grace opened again.* At that moment
God the Father opened again the fountain of grace from
His heart, and grace again began to flow. Jesus had deserved this by His bitter passion and death. Grace flowed
from the heart of God the Father into the heart of His
Son, and flowed from the heart of the Son together with
His blood. This blood flows with grace in seven streamlets
from the cross. These seven little streams are the seven
holy sacraments.

e. *Grace is distributed in the seven sacraments by the
Holy Ghost.* Our Saviour has commanded that grace
should be dispensed to men through the seven sacraments.
Therefore we say that our Saviour instituted seven sacraments. From these seven sacraments the Holy Ghost
directs the blood of Jesus Christ into our soul. What did
I say is contained in the blood of Jesus? Grace. What,
then, does the Holy Ghost direct into our soul by means of
the seven sacraments? Grace. Who has deserved grace'

for us? Jesus Christ. He is God. What, then, is grace called, as coming from God? Divine Grace. And this grace again enables us to go to heaven.

3. CONNECTION. Which of the three divine persons closed the fountain of grace? God the Father. When? When Adam and Eve sinned. Who opened again the fountain of grace? God the Son. When? When He suffered and died for us on the cross. Who distributes grace? The Holy Ghost? By what means? Through the seven sacraments.

4. SUMMARY. Who, then, has deserved grace for us? Jesus Christ. By what means? By His passion and death. Whence does grace flow? From the heart of Jesus. In what is grace contained? In the blood of Jesus. In how many streamlets does the blood of Jesus flow from the cross? In seven little streams. Which are these seven little streams? The seven sacraments. Who instituted the sacraments? Jesus Christ. Who distributes grace? The Holy Ghost? By what means? By means of the seven sacraments.

5. APPLICATION. 1. Never forget what our Saviour did for you. After the sin of our first parents the devil rejoiced and prepared for each of you a little place in hell. But the Son of God came down upon the earth to redeem you. Do not forget how much this cost Him. He had to suffer cruelly and die for you. Think on this when you recite the sorrowful mysteries of the rosary that Jesus sweat blood for us, that He was scourged for us, crowned with thorns for us, carried His cross for us, and was nailed to it and died on it for us. Let each one think that Jesus suffered all this for him. 2. On Good Friday a large cross with the image of Jesus on it is laid down before the altar in the church. The faithful come to venerate it; they kneel down, pray to Jesus crucified for us, and kiss the wounds of His hands, feet and side. They do this on Good Friday, the day on which He died for us. Often the mother takes

her little children with her to teach them this act of veneration towards Jesus crucified. As you are now big enough,
you are able to go by yourselves to adore our Lord and
lovingly to kiss His sacred wounds. You should then say:
" O Lord Jesus Christ, I thank Thee for having deigned to
die for me. *Do not, I beseech Thee,* let Thy blood and
Thy suffering be lost for me."

2. Baptism.

OBJECT. I will show you to-day, how a man becomes a
child of God.

1. PREPARATION. What do you call a child, whose father
and mother are dead? An orphan. Who is an orphan
here? Orphans usually get strangers as parents. What
are these parents called? Foster-parents. A certain king
once found an orphan in his travels. The orphan was
dirty, its clothes were torn, and it was crying bitterly. Out
of compassion the king took the orphan child along into his
palace. What was done first with that dirty child? What
did the washing remove from that child? The dirt. And
it could not keep its torn clothes. What kind of clothes
was given to it by the king? That child now looked like a
king's child, so nice it was. And the king was so pleased
with it, that he took it to be like his child. But the king
had a child of his own; that was his own real child. But
the king, as I said, took that orphan child as his own child.
What kind of child was the orphan child to the king? An
adopted child. What were the two children in relation to
the king? One was his real child, and the other was his
adopted child. Whose children were our first parents before their sin? God's children. After their sin? The
devil's. Whose children are all men so long as they are
stained with original sin? I will now tell you how men
become God's children by means of baptism.

2. RELATION. When you were born your soul was de-

filed by original sin. It was dirty and ugly. God would not look at your soul and could have no love for you.

He who wishes to be cleansed from original sin, must be baptized. For our Saviour said to His apostles: " Go into the whole world, teach all nations, baptizing them in the name of the Father, and of the Son, and of the Holy Ghost." Therefore your parents sought for you a godfather and a godmother, and these took you to the church. The priest came to meet you already at the door. Then he took you to the baptistery; there he poured water on your head, saying: " I baptize thee in the name of the Father, and of the Son, and of the Holy Ghost." And whilst the priest was pouring water on your head, a wonderful thing took place in your soul. The Holy Ghost came into your soul, washed away from it original sin, and purified and adorned your soul with the white garment of sanctifying grace. Now your soul was beautiful and bright, and you became children of God. The angels, full of joy, looked upon you, saying: " See how bright is the soul of that child! She now wears the garment of the children of God." Other angels said: " It is a pity that this child is not in heaven with us." Others also said: " Do you not see what God intends to do? Because this child has become also a child of God, our good God wishes to take it at once into heaven."

So beautiful was your soul after baptism! It is true, that this could not be seen from your body. But in order that there might be some external mark of this, the priest, after baptizing you, laid over you a white garment, saying: " Take this white garment and bring it unstained to the judgment-seat of God." You were then joyfully brought home to your parents delighted at your being cleansed from sin and being made children of God. The day of your baptism was indeed beautiful!

CONSIDERATION. a. *What baptism removes.* With what was your soul defiled when you were born? With original sin. What did the king order to be done to the orphan child that was covered with dirt? What did the washing remove? As your soul was defiled with original sin when you were born, your soul had to be washed. Who commanded it? To whom did He say it? With what words? Therefore your parents procured godparents for you. Whither did they take you? Who came to meet you at the door of the Church? Where did he bring you to? And tell me what did the priest do there? What words did he say in doing so? Your head was washed by the water the priest poured on it. But the child that is baptized has not its body dirty, but where is it dirty? The soul of the child must be cleansed. Therefore the Holy Ghost descended into your soul at baptism. And whilst the priest externally washed your head, the Holy Ghost washed your soul internally. With what was your soul defiled. The Holy Ghost washed it away. And now in what state is your soul? Pure, cleansed.

Many grown up people are not yet baptized. With what is their soul still defiled? With original sin. And probably such a grown up person has committed actual sins, for instance, by lying, getting angry, detraction, etc. How can his soul be cleansed from original sin? His actual sins also are forgiven by baptism. Which sins does baptism wash away? Original sin and all actual sins previously committed. By baptism we are cleansed from every sin.

b. *What baptism confers, or gives.* 1. After the orphan child was cleansed, it could no longer wear its torn clothes. With what kind of clothes did the king present it? In baptism your soul received from God the Holy Ghost a beautiful white garment. To whom did God for the first time give for their souls such a beautiful white garment? And all men through their sin lost the beautiful white garment of sanctifying grace. Who has deserved this grace again for us? By what means do we receive grace? By the sacraments. Who dispenses, or imparts, grace?

Wherefore the Holy Ghost brought in baptism grace into your soul. And grace enveloped your soul like a beautiful white garment. How is this garment called? What does baptism impart to the soul? Baptism imparts to the soul sanctifying grace. This garment makes the soul as beautiful and as holy as an angel. It shines as bright as the sun. Therefore God is delighted with it. Also that orphan child in its new dress greatly pleased the king. How did the king show his pleasure therein? He adopted the orphan as his child. God does the same to you, when your soul is adorned with sanctifying grace. God adopts you as His children. What may we call Him, since we are His children? Father. Whose children do we become by baptism? By baptism we become children of God.

c. *Where does God dwell?* Our soul is destined to go there after our death. With what must it then be adorned? With what it should not be defiled? Which souls are not admitted into heaven? By what means is the soul cleansed from original sin? Which sacrament is then necessary for all men in order to go to heaven? Which sacrament must, therefore, be received first? Baptism is the first and most necessary sacrament.

3. CONNECTION. What does baptism remove from our soul? What does baptism impart to our soul? Whose children do we thereby become? How may we then call God? Before baptism you have only one father. How many fathers have you now? Name them. An earthly father and a heavenly Father. Which is your real father? Which Father has adopted you as His children? God the Father has also a real Son. Of whom did God the Father say: "This is My well-beloved Son." When? And what did Jesus say on the Mount of Olives when He began to pray to God? "Father." How then may you with Jesus address God in heaven? In which prayer do you call God Father? In the Our Father. What are those children to each other who have one and the same father? Brothers

and sisters. What is therefore Jesus to you? Our Brother.

4. The summary may be expressed thus: The first and most necessary sacrament is baptism, which cleanses us from all sins and makes us children of God. With what words did Jesus command baptism to be given?

5. APPLICATION. 1. How happy were Adam and Eve as long as they preserved the white garment of grace! God was pleased with them, and everything went on well with them. But they ate the forbidden fruit. By this sin they lost the white garment of grace and ceased to be children of God. They were expelled from paradise. Weeping, Adam and Eve looked back towards paradise, and they could no more return to it. 2. It was not difficult to lose the white garment of grace, for they had only to commit one sin. But to regain it was very difficult. For this the Son of God had to come upon the earth. You know how painfully and bitterly He had to suffer and die for us.

But now we are again children of God. Have you ever thought how rich and happy you are in being children of God? How happy was that orphan child in becoming the king's child! But which is it happier to be, a king's child or God's child? A child of God is far more happy and rich than a king's child. But be careful to remain children of God and to preserve the white garment of grace. How easily you could lose it. How did Adam and Eve lose it? Yes, by only one mortal sin you could lose it. Who caused Adam and Eve to lose it? The devil will also try to lead you to sin. Often does he suggest to you to do evil, to disobey, to get angry, to lie, to steal, to be immodest and impure. Do not listen to him. Remember the boy near the basket of apples. What saying did he remember? Remember it also. Who also saw Adam and Eve sinning? Who saw Cain sinning, killing his brother? Who sees you also? Pray to your guardian angel to help you to keep out of sin. 3. If you are thus on your guard against sin, and pray well every day, study diligently, obey and help your parents at home, then the garment of your soul will grow daily more beautiful and bright, and you will always please God more and more. And when death comes, your soul adorned with sanctifying grace shall take its flight to heaven.

3. Confirmation.

OBJECT. I will teach you to-day how we are strengthened by the Holy Ghost in the sacrament of Confirmation.

I. PREPARATION. 1. Our divine Saviour taught all that we must know and do to reach heaven. Why is it that our Saviour can tell it to us best of all? Because He is God. But what God says is true. Therefore we believe it. But God wills that we should show our faith to men. Suppose you knew a certain thing and wished that your teacher also should know it. How would you act? Tell it to him. Now you wish others to know what you believe about God. What must you do? How can people find out what you believe about God? I must tell them. When you tell what you believe, then you make known your faith to others, that is, you profess your faith. When, therefore, can people say to you: " You profess your faith "? I profess my faith when I tell what I believe. In what prayer do you say or profess what you believe about God; for instance, that God is the Creator of heaven and earth? In the Apostles' Creed. Why is it thus called? Because it is a profession of the faith preached by the apostles according to the command of our divine Saviour. Is there not a sign whereby we profess our faith?

2. It is not enough to profess our faith with our words, we must so live as our faith directs. A certain child does nothing but good. He prays, goes to church, is always obedient. What kind of life does he lead? A good life. Another child does much evil; he curses, lies and steals. What kind of life does he lead? A bad life. Who teaches

us that we must lead a good life to go to heaven? He, therefore, who does good, leads the life that faith directs or prescribes, that is, a life in accordance with faith, or a life of faith. When do you lead a life of faith?

3. Who first believed in our Saviour? But the apostles did not always believe firmly. Which of the apostles had once to answer whether he knew Jesus? Who can relate this? What did the maid servant ask him? What did Peter answer? What was it that he did not profess? His faith. Why did he not profess his faith, and told the maid servant a lie? Why did the apostles run away when Jesus was arrested? Why had they locked the doors after the resurrection of Jesus? What were the apostles when they were so afraid? Timid.

Object. I will tell you to-day how the apostles were strengthened by the Holy Ghost.

II. Relation. On the tenth day after the Ascension of Jesus to heaven the apostles were assembled in Jerusalem in the Supper-room praying. The doors were closed. Suddenly there came a sound from heaven as of a mighty wind. And there appeared tongues as of fire over the heads of the apostles. And they were all filled with the Holy Ghost, and they began to speak in various languages. At the sound of that mighty wind people hastened from all directions to the house where the apostles were. The apostles at once opened the door and went out. And St. Peter began to preach, saying: " Jesus, whom you crucified, is risen from the dead, and is seated at the right hand of God." Many believed and were baptized. The chief priests forbade St. Peter and the other apostles to preach again about Jesus. But St. Peter preached again, and said firmly: " Jesus commanded us to preach; and we are bound to obey God rather than men." And he preached again. Then Peter and the other apostles were put into prison. The judges ordered them to be scourged, and most severely forbade them to preach any more about Jesus. But the apostles paid no attention to the prohibition, and rejoiced at being thought worthy to suffer for Jesus. And when they were released, they preached again, saying: " Jesus Christ is truly the Son of God." And they lived faithfully according to their faith. Wherefore all of them, except one, suffered martyrdom for their faith in Jesus Christ.

CONSIDERATION — *The Holy Ghost comes down upon the apostles.* Where were the apostles assembled on the tenth day after the Ascension of Jesus? Who then came down upon them? Relate what was then heard. What did the people do on hearing it? In what manner did the Holy Ghost come down upon the apostles? Where did the fiery tongues place themselves? That was the exterior. At the same time the Holy Ghost entered interiorly the hearts of the apostles, and they were all filled with the Holy Ghost. Whom did the apostles receive on Pentecost? What did the Holy Ghost bring along into the hearts of the apostles? He brought His grace into the hearts of the apostles.

The apostles profess their faith. Relate what the apostles did after receiving the Holy Ghost. What did St. Peter preach about Jesus? Who is Jesus, since by His own power He rose from the dead and ascended into heaven? The apostles believed it firmly and preached it to the people. To whom had St. Peter previously said that he did not know Jesus? What did he thereby fail to profess? His faith. Now Peter firmly believes that Jesus is the Son of God, and he tells the people so. What does he do in saying that? He professes his faith. The other apostles did likewise. What then did they do? They professed their faith.

They profess their faith with constancy. How did many of the Jews show that they also believed what St. Peter preached? They received baptism. This displeased the chief priests. What did they then forbid the apostles? But the apostles remained firm and were not afraid. And what did St. Peter answer? What did the apostles continue to do? How did the judges then punish the apostles for disobeying them. But what was the effect of the punishment on the apostles? They rejoiced. The apostles did not yield; wherefore we say: They remained constant. How do you know this? They continued to preach. What, then, did they again profess? The apostles professed their faith with constancy.

The apostles lived according to their faith. The apostles professed their faith not only by preaching. St. Peter never again told a lie. The apostles carefully kept themselves from every sin. They prayed much and obeyed our divine Saviour in all things. What, for instance, had Jesus commanded them? To go into the whole world to preach, baptize, etc. They did all this. What kind of life did they lead? Who teaches that we must lead a good life? They, therefore, live as faith directs or prescribes. In other words, the apostles lived faithfully in accordance with holy faith.

The Holy Ghost strengthened the apostles. The apostles were quite different from what they had previously been. They had no more fear. When did they cease fearing? How could you easily find out that already on Pentecost the apostles showed no more fear? They opened the door and came out of the house. Who then enabled them to give up all fear? What did He place in their souls? What effect had it in their souls? Who, then, made the apostles strong? The Holy Ghost. The Holy Ghost strengthened the apostles.

We also are strengthened in Confirmation by the Holy Ghost. We may use the word confirm instead of strengthen. You will be confirmed one day. Who will come to confirm you? When you are confirmed, you receive the Holy Ghost into your soul. But you cannot see Him. In Confirmation you shall be strengthened by the Holy Ghost.

III. CONNECTION. When were the apostles strengthened

by the Holy Ghost? When will you be strengthened by
the Holy Ghost? You always wish to grow big and strong.
But you cannot at once become big and strong in body.
How do you grow thus? By degrees. By what means do
you grown big and strong in body? How did the apostles
become strong at once? By what means will your soul become strong at once? What are soldiers for? Against
whom must they fight? What must they do rather than
run away? You also have an enemy, not of your body,
but of your soul; he tries to kill your soul. Who is it?
What must you do against the devil? What may you be
called, since you have to fight? What do the soldiers need
to fight and to protect themselves? What do you receive
in Confirmation from the Holy Ghost, that you may protect yourselves against the devil? What happens to your
soul in baptism? What beautiful garment does it receive?
Whose child are you when you have this garment? What
happens to your soul in Confirmation? And against whom
must you then fight? And what are you called on this
account? What then do you become through Confirmation? What do you become through baptism?

IV. SUMMARY. Which grace does the Christian receive
in the sacrament of Confirmation? He is strengthened by
the Holy Ghost, that he may profess his faith with constancy and live up to it faithfully.

V. APPLICATION. 1. Like the apostles, dear children,
you must also profess your faith with constancy. What
ought you to answer, when somebody asks you whether you
are a Catholic? You must never, out of fear or shame,
reply: " I'm not a Catholic." What would you thereby
commit? Yes, for, like St. Peter, you would have denied
your faith.

2. In which prayer do we profess our Catholic faith?
In the Apostles' Creed. By what sign can we profess our
faith without saying a word? By the sign of the cross.
Usually we say something when we make the sign of the

cross. What do we then say? At the beginning of the Gospel during Mass we make the sign of the cross differently. Who knows how it is then made? With the right thumb on our forehead, then over our lips, and finally on our breast. What does this manner of making the sign of the cross mean? When I make it on my forehead, it means: " I am not ashamed of the Gospel," that is, of my faith. When I make it over my lips, it means: " I profess it with my words." And when I make it on my breast, it means: " I bear it in my heart."

3. When do you make the usual or large sign of the cross? Before and after prayer. What do you know about a man that takes off his hat, and about a woman that bows her head when passing before a church or a cross? I know that they are Catholics. If they do the same when meeting a priest?

4. The Most Holy Sacrament of the Altar.

OBJECT. I will relate to you to-day how our loving Saviour gave to His apostles His flesh to eat and His blood to drink.

I. The evening before His death Jesus was in the Supper-room with His apostles in order to eat the paschal lamb with them. It was the last time before His death that He ate with them. The supper over, our Saviour took bread in His sacred hands, and raised His eyes heavenward to God, His Almighty Father, gave thanks, blessed the bread, broke and gave to His disciples, saying: " Take and eat, for this is My body, which shall be delivered for you." With great devotion the apostles ate what Jesus gave them.

Then, in like manner, Jesus took the chalice containing wine; again gave thanks, blessed it and gave it to His disciples, saying: " Drink ye all of this, for it is My blood which shall be shed for you and for many unto the for-

giveness of sins. Do this in remembrance of Me." He
then passed the chalice to each apostle in turn, first to
Peter, then to John, then to James, and so on until all had
drunk out of it.

CONSIDERATION — *The Last Supper.* When did Jesus
eat with His apostles for the last time before His death?
Where? How is this meal called, since it took place in
the evening? What did Jesus do the day following for
us? That day was Good Friday. The Last Supper took
place the previous evening. That was Holy Thursday
evening. After the supper our Saviour looked very affectionately on His apostles, for He wished to show them that
He loved them dearly.

The changing, or transubstantiation of the bread. What
did Jesus first take in His hands after the supper? It was
a fine, white thin loaf of wheaten bread. It was not to be
cut, but broken. Then Jesus looked up to His heavenly
Father and thanked Him. Then what did He do to the
bread? He made the sign of the cross over it. Who has
seen the priest making the sign of the cross over beads, a
cross or a medal? Then what do you call those articles?
Blessed beads, a blessed cross, or medal. What would you
call the bread over which Jesus made the sign of the cross?
What did Jesus then do with it? He broke it in twelve
parts, and gave one part to each of the twelve apostles. But
what words did Jesus pronounce when He gave it to His
apostles? Now just reflect, children. When Jesus pronounced over the bread these words: " This is My body,"
a great wonder took place; the bread was no bread any
more, but was turned into the living body of Jesus Himself. Therefore we say: The bread was changed into the
true living body of Jesus. (Repeat.) What did the
apostles then do with the living body of Jesus? The apostles ate the real living body of Jesus. But in a living body
there is also its blood. Therefore, in the body into which

the bread had been changed and which the apostles ate, there was also its blood.

What was on the table before Jesus said: "This is My body"? Bread. What was no more there after Jesus had pronounced these words: "This is My body"? No bread any more. What was really there? What, then, had become of the bread? Therefore we say: The bread was changed into the true body of Jesus. With what words was this change made? What words did Jesus speak in changing the bread into His body? With the words: "This is My body," Jesus changed bread into His true body.

The changing or transubstantiation of the wine. Jesus took the chalice in His hands. What did the chalice contain? Jesus did the same with the chalice as He had done with the bread. What did He first do with the bread? What did He first do also with the chalice? What kind of wine was in the chalice? Jesus then passed the chalice to His apostles. What did He say in doing so? This is etc. (as given above). Then a great wonder took place in the chalice. The wine, by the words of Jesus, was changed into the true blood of Jesus Christ. And it was His real blood that Jesus gave His apostles to drink. Therefore, the apostles drank the true blood of Jesus.

What did the chalice contain before Jesus said those words? What was there in the chalice after He had said those words? What, then, had happened to the wine? How was it changed? By the words of Jesus, "This is My blood," the wine was changed into the true blood of Jesus. Into what did Jesus change bread and wine at the Last Supper? At the Last Supper Jesus changed bread and wine into His body and blood. How did He do this?

The body and blood of Jesus under the species of bread and wine. You must not imagine that the living body of Jesus, which the apostles ate, looked like our dear Lord sitting at table among the apostles. Jesus with the apostles looked like a man, had all the appearance of a man. How did Jesus look when He was born? Like an infant. How did He look when, at the age of twelve years, He was among the doctors in the Temple? Like a twelve-year-old boy. How did Jesus look when, at the age of thirty years, He began to preach? Like a man of the same age. It was the same when His body was nailed to the cross and hung on it for three hours. The crucifix here shows us Jesus in the appearance of a man. What is the difference between the appearance of Jesus on Mount Calvary and on this cross? On this cross Jesus is represented in wood; on Calvary He was there with His body of flesh and blood. Which of the two is the true body of Christ? The Christ on this cross is only a picture or representation of Jesus, but not His true living body.

The body of Jesus which the apostles ate at the Last Supper, was the true living body of Jesus, but it had not the appearance of a man, or of the little Infant Jesus. It looked like bread, and tasted like bread. It looked no bigger than the bread before it was changed, and no one could see that it was alive in the appearance of bread. It had the complete appearance of bread. Therefore the apostles could not see with their eyes the body of Jesus, nor could they taste Him when eating, for the body of Jesus was concealed under the appearances of bread. But the apostles believed that it was the real living body of Jesus, for Jesus had said: " This is My body." And all that Jesus says is true. In what appearance did the apostles eat the body of Jesus? And what was contained in this body of Jesus under the appearance of bread?

In like manner, the blood of Jesus, which the apostles drank, did not resemble the blood in the body of Jesus. What is the color of the blood in the body of a man? Is it cold or warm? The blood of Jesus which the apostles drank was not red, was not warm and did not taste like blood. It looked and tasted like wine. What was the ap-

pearance of the blood of Jesus in the chalice? It had all
the appearance of wine. Under what appearance did the
apostles drink the blood of Jesus? Under the appearance
of wine. Under which appearances was the true body of
Jesus, which the apostles ate, and the true blood of Jesus,
which the apostles drank? They were concealed under
the appearances of bread and wine.

Our Saviour's love. You have already seen how a
mother acts with her child when she wishes to show him
how much she loves him? She takes him in her arms and
presses him to her breast so tightly, that it would seem as
if she intended to press him into her heart, and she kisses
him, saying: "I love you so much that I could eat you
up." But the love of Jesus for His apostles was much
greater than a mother's love for her child. On Holy
Thursday our Saviour knew that on the following day He
would die. Hence He said: "Since I shall die to-morrow, I shall no longer be as man on earth with the apostles."
But our Saviour loved His apostles so much, that He
wished to be always with them. For this reason He
changed Himself into food and drink, that He might enter
the hearts of the apostles and be always with them. How
happy did the apostles become on this account! For they
bore in their hearts our divine Saviour, who is all love.
And how full of love must their hearts have been!

The apostles received the power of consecrating. Jesus
wished, out of love for all men, to be in the hearts of all
of them, in order to remain with us. Therefore, He willed
that the apostles also should have the power of changing
bread and wine into His sacred body and blood. Wherefore, after He had, at the Last Supper, changed bread and
wine into His body and blood, He said to them: "Do
this in remembrance of Me." What should the apostles do?
They should do what He had done, as He had done.
What had Jesus just done? He had changed bread and
wine into His body and blood, and distributed them as food.

He, therefore, gave His apostles the power to change, in remembrance of Him, bread and wine into His body and blood, when He said to them: " Do this in remembrance of Me." What power, then, did Jesus give to His apostles at the Last Supper?

This power has been transmitted to the bishops and priests. Christ wished to enter the hearts of men under the appearances of bread and wine until the end of the world. For how long must, then, bread and wine continue to be changed into our Saviour's body and blood? But the apostles themselves could not live until the end of the world, and do that until then. Our Saviour, therefore, willed that they should transmit that power to others. For this reason the apostles laid hands on other pious men and ordained them bishops and priests with the power of changing bread and wine into the body and blood of Jesus, and ordaining other men to do the same.

This power is exercised in holy Mass. Bishops and priests exercise this power whenever they say Mass. The bishops and priests, therefore, in holy Mass change bread and wine into the true body and the true blood of Jesus Christ. To whom, then, did the apostles transmit their power? How did they do this? When do bishops and priests exercise this power?

The Sacrament of the Altar. Where does the priest say Mass? At the altar. Where, then, are bread and wine changed into the true body and the true blood of Jesus? At the altar. Therefore the body and the blood of Christ under the appearances of bread and wine are called the Sacrament of the Altar. (Repeat.)

The most holy Sacrament. What is contained in every sacrament? Grace. Whence does grace flow? From the heart of Jesus. In the Sacrament of the Altar we receive not merely graces. Whom do we receive in the Sacrament of the Altar? Jesus. He who receives Jesus, possesses all graces. Therefore the Sacrament of the Altar is more holy than the other sacraments. How, then, is it called? The most holy Sacrament. Hoẃ is the little place on the altar called, where our Saviour dwells in the most holy Sacrament? The tabernacle.

The institution of the most holy Sacrament of the Altar. Who was the first to prepare the most holy Sacrament of the Altar? Jesus. When? At the Last Supper. When did He eat the Last Supper with His apostles? On the eve of His sorrowful passion. It was then that He instituted the most holy Sacrament of the Altar. When did Jesus institute the most holy Sacrament of the Altar? He instituted it at the Last Supper on the eve of His passion. How did He institute it? Jesus took bread, blessed, broke and gave to His disciples, saying: " Take ye and eat, for this is My body." Then He took the chalice with wine, blessed and gave to His disciples, saying: " Drink ye all of this, for this is My blood. Do this in remembrance of Me."

II. CONNECTION. What did our Saviour have in His hands in order to change it into His body? From what did God make the body of the first man? Into what did God then change slime? Into what did Jesus change bread and wine? How did God give life to the body He had formed from the slime of the earth? How did Jesus cause bread to become His living body? What was there before God breathed a living soul into that body? What was there after God had breathed a living soul into it? What was there on the table before Jesus said: " This is My body, this is My blood "? What was there after Jesus had pronounced those words? What appearance had Adam's body after the change? The appearance of a living man made of flesh and blood. What appearance had the body and blood of Jesus after the change? The appearances of bread and wine. There were no signs of life therein.

III. SUMMARY. The most holy Sacrament of the Altar

is the true body and the true blood of our Lord Jesus Christ under the appearances of bread and wine. Our Saviour instituted it at the Last Supper on the eve of His passion. Jesus took bread, blessed, broke and gave to His disciples, saying: "Take ye and eat, for this is My body." Then He took the chalice with wine, blessed and gave to His disciples, saying: "Drink ye all of this, for this is My blood. Do this in remembrance of Me." Jesus gave to His apostles also the power to change bread and wine into His body and blood, saying: "Do this in remembrance of Me." The apostles transmitted this power to bishops and priests. The bishops and priests exercise this power in the Mass.

IV. APPLICATION. 1. You have learnt that our Saviour is present on the altar under the appearances of bread and wine. Where does He dwell? In the tabernacle. When entering a church, we can see at once whether our Saviour dwells in the tabernacle. How do we know it? When the lamp before the altar is lit. Our Saviour dwells there, because He loves us so much and wishes to be always near us. In the tabernacle our Saviour constantly watches day and night over us, prays for us and blesses us. Sometimes during the day you see people kneeling, looking towards the tabernacle and praying. Very often Jesus is all alone. Should you not also sometimes visit our dear Saviour in the church? For instance, during the day, after school, or when you are passing by, you could easily go into the church to visit our Lord for a few moments. On such occasions kneel down, adore our Lord, and tell Him how much you love Him, that you will try to behave well, and ask Him for all that you need. This will please our Saviour and bring you blessing and success. After doing this, you may go out quietly to your work or your play.

2. I will now tell you an anecdote about our Lord showing Himself in the Blessed Sacrament in His real figure to a pious boy. Little Antony used to feel happy every time he served Father Peter's Mass. One day Antony saw

during Mass how Father Peter was holding a little child in his hands, and then putting the child into his mouth and eating it. Antony got frightened and told it to his mother, saying: " Dear mother, I have always liked to serve Father Peter's Mass, but now I am afraid to do so. Shall I continue to serve his Mass?" His mother surprised said to him: " My child, what are you thinking of? It should be a great pleasure to serve the Mass of so holy a priest." But Antony replied: " Yes, dear mother, Father Peter has until now been kind and good; but guess what he is now doing. Just think of it; this morning during his Mass, Father held in his hands a beautiful little child, then he put that child into his mouth till it disappeared. Father has such friendly eyes and such a nice face; but I never knew before that he ate little children. Could he not some time do with me what he did to that little child? It is true that little child made no resistance at all. Will you not, dear mother, tell me not to serve Mass any more?" But Antony's mother, weeping for joy, said to him: " Dear child, continue to serve Father Peter's Mass. That little child you saw him eating, was the dear little Infant Jesus. Later on you will say: When I was yet an innocent child, I served the Mass of a saint."

5. The Holy Sacrifice of the Mass.

OBJECT. We shall hear how we can offer a sacrifice to the good God.

I. PREPARATION — *The sacrifices of Cain and Abel.* Which of you has already offered something to God? What offering did you make to Him? Which two men once offered sacrifice to God, as the Bible History relates? What did they offer? Fruits of the earth and lambs. Relate how they offered these sacrifices. What did they do, whilst their offerings were burning? They knelt and prayed, saying: " Dear Lord, Thou hast created all things.

All that we have comes from Thee. The lambs, the fruits
of the earth, our bodies, our souls, our very life are gifts of
Thine, dearest Lord. We would wish to offer them all to
Thee in return for Thy goodness; and we would willingly
die for the love of Thee. But this we cannot do. Therefore, we offer the best and the most beautiful of what we
have. Deign graciously to accept our offerings." (Repeat.) What did Cain offer in sacrifice? And what did
Abel offer?

Our offer or sacrifice is Jesus Christ. We also and all
men have received all we have from God. What ought we,
then, to do with all of it? What should we even offer to
God? Our very life. Yea, we have even, on account of
our sins, deserved death. To whom did God say in the beginning that men deserved death on account of their sin?
What did God say?

Who died for our sins? Where did He die? There-
fore we say: Jesus sacrificed Himself for us on the cross.
What did Jesus sacrifice for us on the cross? His life;
Himself. Jesus Himself was the victim. To whom did
Jesus sacrifice Himself? To God, His heavenly Father.
And for whom did Jesus sacrifice Himself? For us; for
our sins. Upon what did Cain and Abel lay their sacri-
fices? Which was the altar on which our Saviour sacrificed
Himself? On the altar of the cross.

The bloody Sacrifice. In sacrificing his lamb Abel killed
it. He let the blood flow out of it until it was dead. What
happened on the cross also to the blood of Jesus? Whither
did the blood of Jesus flow? Where was the body of
Jesus? What became of Jesus, when all the blood had
flowed out of His body? The sacrifice was consummated.
Because the blood of Jesus flowed in His sacrifice on the
cross, His was a bloody sacrifice. The sacrifice of Jesus is
now offered daily. Do you know when this happens?

OBJECT. I am going to tell you beautiful things about
holy Mass.

I.

RELATION — *The Relation is first given entire. Before developing each of the principal parts, one of the respective divisions of the Relation is to be repeated.*

When the priest is about to say Mass, he puts on beautiful vestments. Over all of them is the chasuble. On it is the image of the cross. Thus dressed the priest, preceded by the server, or servers, goes to the altar. In his hands he carries a chalice covered with a cloth. On the middle of the altar the priest spreads a fine white cloth, and places the chalice upon it. Then the priest comes down the steps of the altar and recites prayers alternately with the server. The people in the church pray, and, if it is a high Mass, the choir sings. The priest then again goes up to the altar praying. He prays or sings first on the right side of the altar, and then on the left. Finally, he comes to the middle and uncovers the chalice, and the server rings the bell. On the chalice is a gilt little plate holding a host. The priest takes it with the host on it in his hands and raises it up whilst saying: " O heavenly Father, almighty God, bless and graciously accept this spotless offering. To Thee I offer it for my sins, for the sins of all now present and for the sins of all Christians, both living and dead." Then the priest puts the host down on the white cloth. After this the priest takes the chalice in his hand and pours into it wine and a few drops of water. He next holds up the chalice praying God also to bless and graciously accept the offering in the chalice for the salvation of the whole world. Finally, he places the chalice on the white cloth and covers it.

II.

After this the priest prays or sings for a short while, and then everything becomes quiet and still in the church and everybody looks towards the altar. The priest takes the host in his hands, looks heavenward and blesses it. Then bowing forward he pronounces over the host our divine Saviour's words: "Take ye and eat, for this is My body." By these words the bread is changed into the true living body of Jesus. Out of reverence for our Saviour the priest bends his right knee to the floor, adoring Jesus. Rising he holds our Saviour up high, that the people in church may see and adore Him. During this time the server rings the bell three times. The priest then lays our dear Lord on the white cloth, and makes another genuflexion.

After this the priest takes the chalice with the wine in his hands; then bowing forward he pronounces over the chalice the words of our Saviour: "Take and drink ye all of this, for this is My blood." There is now in the chalice the precious blood of Jesus Christ. Therefore the priest again genuflects and adores the blood of Jesus. Then he raises the chalice with the blood of Jesus upward, so that the people may see and adore it. At the same time the server again rings the bell three times. The priest next lays the chalice down on the white cloth, covers it, and then genuflects, adoring our Saviour.

III.

Having done this, the priest prays for some minutes, and finally takes the gilt little plate with the host on it in his left hand, and with his right strikes his breast three times, saying each time: "O Lord, I am not worthy that Thou shouldst enter under my roof; but say only the word, and my soul shall be healed." Each time the server rings the bell. The priest then takes the sacred Host in his right hand, and with it makes the sign of the cross over himself, saying: "May the body of our Lord Jesus Christ keep my soul unto life everlasting. Amen." Now the priest places the sacred Host on his tongue and receives our Lord

Jesus Christ. He remains still for a while, adoring Jesus in his heart.

After this the priest takes the chalice with the precious blood of Jesus Christ in his right hand and with it makes the sign of the cross over himself, saying: " May the blood of our Lord Jesus Christ keep my soul unto life everlasting. Amen." Then he most reverently drinks the precious blood of Jesus Christ.

If there are in church persons who also wish to receive our divine Saviour, they kneel at the communion railing, and the priest takes the cup or ciborium containing the body of our Lord Jesus Christ under the appearances of bread, in his left hand. Turning to those persons and holding our dear Lord in his right hand over the ciborium, so that all may see it, he says once: " Behold the Lamb of God; behold Him who takes away the sins of the world." Then he repeats three times: " O Lord, I am not worthy," etc. The people repeat the same words, each time striking their breast. The priest then goes down to the communion railing, and gives to each one there our divine Saviour, making the sign of the cross over him with the Sacred Host and saying: " May the body of our Lord Jesus Christ keep thy soul unto life everlasting. Amen." After this the priest returns to the altar. Finally, after he has said or sung some prayers the Mass is over.

I. THE OFFERTORY.

(Repeat I of Relation.) *Jesus goes to sacrifice Himself for us.* What does the priest put on when he is about to say Mass? Which vestment does he put over the others? What is pictured on this vestment? A cross. Who carried a wooden cross on His back? Therefore the priest going to say Mass represents Jesus Christ going to sacrifice Himself. What does the priest hold in his hands when going to the altar? The altar is covered with a white cloth, and looks like a table that is set. What does the priest first unfold and lay on the altar? What does he place on that fine little white cloth?

What is done in the Mass before the Offertory. Where does the priest go again? What does he do below the altar steps? Who prays with him? And what are the people in the church doing? Where does the priest go when he is through the prayers at the foot of the altar? On which side of the altar does he first pray? Where does he pray next? Where does he at last stand? There he prays a moment. What does he then do? How do the people in church know this? The server rings the bell.

The offering of the bread. What lays on the chalice? And what is on the little plate? The host is made of the finest wheat flour. Under the appearance of bread in the host and under the appearance of wine our Saviour will sacrifice Himself to His heavenly Father. Where did Jesus first sacrifice Himself to His heavenly Father? In what appearance did He sacrifice Himself to his heavenly Father on the cross? But in the Mass our Saviour does not sacrifice Himself to His heavenly Father in His appearance as man. Under what appearance does He sacrifice Himself therein?

The spotless Sacrifice. The priest takes in his hands the little plate with the host. What prayer does he recite in so doing? What does the priest call the host on the little plate? "Spotless Offering." What does he ask the heavenly Father to do to it? To bless it. What does the bread then become? Blessed bread. This offering will later on be changed into the true living body of Jesus. The body of Jesus was perfectly pure and free from every sin. Wherefore what does the priest call the offering which is to be afterwards changed into the body of Jesus? Whom does the priest ask to accept it graciously?

Why is the Sacrifice offered. In his prayer the priest said why the heavenly Father should accept this spotless Sacrifice. How did he express himself? "For my sins, for the sins of all who are present, and for the sins of all the faithful living and dead." First for what? Second, and third? Where does the priest now place the host?

The offering of the wine. The priest then takes the chalice in his hands. What does he pour into it? Wine. The wine is to be afterwards changed into the precious blood of Jesus Christ. When Jesus sacrificed Himself on the cross, a soldier opened His heart with a spear. What flowed out of His heart? Blood and water. Therefore the priest puts into the chalice also a few drops of water. How does the priest then raise the chalice? What prayer does he say in doing so? He prays that God the Father in heaven may bless and graciously accept that sacrifice. What does the priest call the wine in the chalice? Sacrifice. To whom does the priest offer this Sacrifice? What does he ask God the Father to do to the wine? What kind of wine does it then become? Blessed wine. Into what will it afterwards be changed? Where does the priest then place the chalice with the blessed wine?

SUMMARY. Which are the gifts the priest offers to God? For what does the priest offer them to the heavenly Father? That He would bless them. Therefore this part of the Mass is called the Offertory. It is the first principal part of the Mass.

II. THE CONSECRATION.

(Repeat the second (II) part of the Relation.)

The consecration of the bread. Immediately after the Offertory the priest prays or sings for a time. What suddenly takes place after this in the church? Where do all then look? What does the priest take in his hands? The host. Tell me what the priest does then? He raises his eyes heavenward and blesses the host. In what position does he place himself? What words does he pronounce over the bread? Who was the first to pronounce those words over bread? When was that? What happened when our Lord said those words? The same thing takes place also when the priest pronounces over the bread those words of our Saviour. What takes place then? After those words what does the priest hold in his hands?

The adoration. Who on earth first carried our Saviour in her arms? When was that? Who else came that night to the Infant Jesus? How did the shepherds venerate the Infant Jesus? Who came from heaven to venerate Him? How did they joyfully sing, because the Infant Jesus had come upon the earth?

Behold now at the consecration the same thing happens as in the stable of Bethlehem. The same Saviour comes from heaven upon the altar. And just as our Saviour in the stable of Bethlehem was wrapped in swaddling clothes, so does He in the Mass lie upon a fine white little cloth. How did our Saviour appear in the stable of Bethlehem? And what is His appearance during Mass? We do not see our Saviour; what do we see? Only the appearances of bread. And just as the angels at Bethlehem sang a joyful hymn when Jesus was born, now the altar boys ring the bell, and angels come down from heaven invisibly and surround the altar and adore our Saviour. What does the priest do? He bends his knee to the floor and adores our Saviour, and then raises our Saviour towards heaven. And why? How are the people present reminded of this? Where does the priest then place our Saviour? How does the priest again venerate our Saviour?

The consecration of the wine. What does the priest after this take in his hands? In what position does he now place himself? What words does he pronounce over the wine in the chalice? Who was the first to pronounce those words over a chalice containing wine? What then happened to the wine? The wine was changed into the blood of Jesus. The same thing takes place also when the priest pronounces these words of our Saviour over the wine in the chalice. What does the chalice contain after this?

The adoration of the precious blood of Jesus. How does the priest venerate the precious blood of Jesus? What does he then do with the chalice? What do the servers do at the same time? Why? Where does the priest then place the chalice containing the blood of Jesus? How does he again venerate it?

SUMMARY. What happened to the bread and wine when the priest pronounced over them these words: " This is My body, this is My blood "? The bread was changed into the true body of Jesus, and the wine into His true blood. This part of the Mass is called the Consecration. It is the second part of the Mass.

The Victim. Dear children, at the Consecration our divine Saviour comes down from heaven to us on the altar. In heaven He is seated at the right hand of God the Father Almighty. His body is wonderfully beautiful and shines as brightly as the sun, and His five wounds are like blooming roses. He can no longer suffer, no longer die. He is glorified, and exceedingly happy. In this shining, glorified body He comes at the consecration from heaven upon the altar. But no one sees that brightness and splendor. Why? What appearance does our Saviour take at the Consecration? He does not move; He allows Himself to be lifted, to be handled and treated just as the priest wills. No one can see that He is alive; He is as if dead. He is like a victim. So great is our Saviour's love for us.

III. THE COMMUNION.

(Repeat part III of the Relation.)

I. *The partaking of the body of Jesus.* Which parts of the Mass have you already learnt? After the Consecration the priest prays for some time. Then he takes the gilt little plate with the sacred Host in his left hand. What does he do with his right hand? What does he say each time? And what does the server do? Why does he ring the bell?

Then the priest takes the sacred Host in his right hand, and with it makes the sign of the cross over himself. What does he say at the same time? Where does the priest place the sacred Host? Why? That he may receive holy Communion, that is, receive the body of our Saviour.

The soul's food. If the heavenly Father would ask the priest: "What hast thou done with My Son?" The priest would answer: "I have eaten Him as the food of my soul, for Thou gavest Him to me." Our divine Saviour under the appearance of bread has entered, like a food, into the soul, the heart of the priest.

Why do the parents give their children bread to eat? That they may grow and get strong. But our Saviour under the appearance of bread is not food for the body. For what is He the food? Our Saviour under the appearance of bread is a food for the soul. This food should keep the soul healthy and make it strong.

The adoration. Our divine Saviour is now in the priest's heart. What do you call that little place in the church in which our Saviour dwells? What may we now call the heart of the priest, since our Lord dwells in it? The ciborium in which our Saviour is kept, is holy. The chalice which contains His precious blood is holy. The tabernacle in which He dwells is holy. What is the heart of the priest, when Jesus dwells therein? What do you do when you pass in front of the tabernacle? People often kneel before the tabernacle, wherein Jesus dwells. What do they do there? What does the priest do after Jesus enters his heart and remains therein?

The drinking of the precious blood. What does the priest take in his hand after receiving our Lord's body? What does he do over himself with the chalice? What does he say then? What does he do with the blood of Jesus?

The union. Now Jesus lives in the priest's heart. The priest and our Saviour are one; they are most intimately united. This part of the Mass in which our Saviour most intimately unites Himself with the priest, is called the Communion. It is the third part of the Mass.

The Communion of the faithful. Often there are some persons who also wish to receive our divine Saviour. Where do they kneel? With what is the communion railing, or table, covered? It is covered with a white cloth, like a table prepared for a meal. The priest now takes the ciborium in his left hand and turns towards the people. There are sacred Hosts in the ciborium. These he changed at the Consecration together with the large Host into the living body of Jesus. The priest takes one of these Hosts in his right hand and holds it over the ciborium, saying: " Behold the Lamb of God, behold Him who takes away the sins of the world." Then he says three times: " Lord, I am not worthy," etc. What do the people do at the same time? Then where does the priest go? What does he do with the sacred Host over each of the communicants? What does he say when doing so? Where does he place the sacred Host? After this the priest places the ciborium with the sacred Hosts in the tabernacle. The communicants swallow the sacred Host and go to their places.

II. SUMMARY. What is our Saviour for their soul? Food for their soul. Who previously already had our Saviour for the food of his soul? To whom does our Saviour give Himself in holy Communion as the food of their souls? In holy Communion our Saviour gives Himself to the priest and to the faithful as food of their souls.

The heart a tabernacle. Jesus lives in the hearts of all who receive Him. The heart of each is like a tabernacle. When they return from the Communion table devoutly with joined hands and eyes cast down and our dear Saviour in their hearts, we can say of each one: " Here Jesus dwells."

What does the priest do after holy Communion? He says some prayers; and when he has said them, and given his blessing to the faithful, the holy Sacrifice of the Mass is over.

III. CONNECTION — *The unbloody sacrifice of Jesus.* In what appearance does Jesus give Himself in holy Communion as food of the soul? In which part of the Mass did He assume (put on) that appearance? What was the appearance of Jesus, when He sacrificed Himself for us on the cross? Where was His body when His sacrifice was accomplished? And where was His blood when His sacrifice was accomplished? In the sacrifice of the cross the body and the blood of Jesus were separated.

What kind of appearance did the body of Jesus put on at the Consecration? What kind of appearance did His blood then put on? It seems, then, as if the body and the blood of Jesus were separated from each other in the Mass. And Jesus appears to us as if dead. Jesus sacrifices Himself in the Mass as He did in the sacrifice of the cross. How do we call the sacrifice of the cross, because in it His blood flowed? A bloody sacrifice. In the Mass Jesus dies no more, there is no real shedding of blood. Therefore the Mass is the unbloody sacrifice of Jesus Christ.

IV. SUMMARY. Who sacrifices Himself in the Mass? What kind of sacrifice is the Mass? The Mass is the unbloody sacrifice of our Lord and Saviour Jesus Christ. The principal parts of the Mass are: 1, the Offertory; 2, the Consecration; 3, the Communion. At the Offertory the priest offers to God bread and wine, that God may bless them. At the Consecration bread and wine are changed into the true body and the true blood of our Lord Jesus Christ. At the holy Communion our Saviour gives Himself to the priest and the faithful as the food of their souls.

APPLICATION. 1. When our divine Saviour lived on earth, He was very kind and friendly towards children. He loved them dearly and was fond of their company. Now suppose you were all alone at home engaged in some work, and all at once the door opens, and in comes to you our dear Saviour, our God. What would you do? Would you not stop working, and go to meet our Saviour, kneel down before Him and adore Him? What would you say to Him? Would you not bid Him welcome, thank Him for coming to you, and tell Him how much you love Him?

In the holy Mass the same kind, loving Saviour daily comes at the Consecration from heaven in order to visit you. Should you not, therefore, when the bell rings for Mass, put everything aside and joyfully hasten to the church? Will you not, in order to visit our Saviour at Mass, rise daily half an hour earlier? It is not very nice when we must force the children to go to Mass.

At the Consecration the little bell at the altar rings so clearly. You hear its fine voice three times. You should rejoice when you hear its sound. But each time you should think on what your Lord and God says to you by means of that bell: " It is I, your Lord and God, who now come to you. Kneel down and adore Me." And all in church, young and old, are already on their knees, bowing their heads, beating their breast and adoring our divine Saviour.

2. Johnny was a pious little boy, five years old. One day with his mother he visited the superioress of a convent. The superioress was preparing hosts. As soon as little Johnny saw the hosts, he became very serious. Then he cautiously took one of the hosts in his hand and kissed it so devoutly. Then the superioress said: " Johnny, our Saviour is not yet in it." " Oh," replied Johnny, " I know this quite well; but to-morrow during Mass Jesus will come into it, and he will find my kiss there." So you see that Johnny already kissed that host devoutly, because it was to be changed next day into the Saviour's body. How much more devoutly must you, then, venerate at the Consecration the Host, which is Jesus Himself!

6. Hearing Mass.

OBJECT. To-day I will speak again about the Mass, and will teach you how you must behave during Mass.

I. THE OFFERTORY.

DEVELOPMENT — *Our Saviour's gift.* What is represented on the vestment worn by the priest when he says Mass? Who really carried a cross on his back? Our Saviour then sacrificed Himself for us on the cross. Where does the Saviour always renew this sacrifice for us? But here Jesus offers Himself through the hands of the priest. Whose place does the priest take at the altar, in order to offer up the sacrifice of the Mass? For whom does our Saviour offer this sacrifice? For all Christians, but especially for those who are present. When the priest dressed in the vestments for Mass goes to the altar to say Mass, our Saviour thus addresses you: " Now, My child, I go to offer Myself for thee through the hands of the priest." To whom does our Saviour offer Himself during Mass through the hands of the priest? To His heavenly Father. What does He offer? Himself. Which is then our Saviour's offering? Our Saviour Himself. Under what appearances? When does the offering or sacrifice become our Saviour Himself? At the Consecration. At the Offertory it is only bread and wine. At the Offertory the priest already speaks of the bread and wine, as if they were the true body and the true blood of Jesus. What does he call the offering? Spotless. Why a spotless offering?

The offering of Christians. But you also should offer along during Mass. What do you need for this? An offering. What did Cain offer? What was Abel's offering? Which lamb and which fruits did Cain and Abel offer? The finest and the best. What could you offer to God? Money; a candle. But at Mass God does not seek money or candles as an offering. God desires something of your own selves. This you have already learned (see Part on the Commandments). What does He say to you? "My child, give Me thy heart." You should, therefore, offer Him your heart. You should offer Him your thoughts, words and actions, all that you have, and all that you are, your whole self.

The precious gift. But God is so great, so rich, so powerful, so beautiful. Therefore, the offering we make to God ought to be precious. What kind of offering, or gift, should you make to God? But you are only poor, sinful children. Your thoughts, words and actions, all that you have, and all that you are, are not precious in the sight of God. Now our loving Saviour comes and says to you: "Take Me under the appearances of bread and wine, and offer Me to the heavenly Father. I wish to be Myself your offering." But there is nothing in the whole world so good and so precious as this offering. Even the heavenly Father has nothing better. Because this offering is His own only-begotten and well-beloved Son under the appearances of bread and wine. How much is this offering worth in the sight of God? God is most pleased with this offering.

The offerings combined. Wherefore when the priest, at the Offertory, offers to the heavenly Father His divine Son under the appearances of bread and wine, that is also your offering. Where has the priest placed the offering? Also in what? Place there also all your thoughts, words and actions, and all that you have and are, and especially your heart. By doing so your offering and our Saviour's offering will be united into one offering. Now how much is your offering worth in the sight of God? Wherefore, when the priest at the Offertory, holds upward the little gilt plate and the chalice to God Almighty, imagine you are standing alongside the priest at the altar and are offering in your hands with the priest the little gilt plate and the chalice to the heavenly Father. At the same time you should say: "My God, with the priest at the altar, I offer

Thee all my thoughts, words and actions, all that I have, all that I am, all that I do and suffer; and especially I offer Thee my heart. Deign graciously to accept this my offering. I unite it with the unbloody sacrifice of Thy Divine Son, which the priest offers Thee on the altar." (Rehearse.)

The heavenly Father's pleasure in our offering. The heavenly Father will consider, not so much you and your offering, as the offering of His Son, whom you hold with your own on the little gilt plate. And the heavenly Father cannot but graciously and willingly accept your offering, as He did the offering of the innocent Abel.

APPLICATION. 1. In giving your heart to God, you give Him little indeed. But since our Saviour deigns to join Himself to your offering, your offering becomes very precious. Should you not then be fond of going to hear Mass? Would it be too much for you daily to rise half an hour earlier than you do now, in order to go to Mass? Could any one believe that there are Catholic children who talk during Mass? Should you not always assist devoutly at Mass?

2. When Cain and Abel made their offerings to God, they both gave the best they had. Both of them knelt down, with their hands joined in prayer. And yet God was pleased with only one of the offerings. Which one was that? And with which one was He not pleased? Why did Abel's offering please God? Because he had a good heart; because there was love and devotion in his heart. Why did not Cain's offering please God? Because his heart was wicked; because there was no love, no devotion in it. What did God consider in their offerings? God pays attention to the heart; a good heart is the chief thing in our offerings to God.

You should then during Mass give your heart to our Saviour that He may offer it to His heavenly Father. But if your heart is worthless, because of the sins that fill it!

Would it not be a shame for our Saviour to offer such a heart to His heavenly Father? Would it be right to bring to Mass a heart that is envious, immodest, impure, disobedient and angry, or that lies, curses, or steals? No! We may offer to God only good thoughts, good words, and good actions, that is, a good heart.

Wherefore when you pray thus at the Offertory: " My God, I offer Thee all my thoughts, words and actions," you should resolve to have no envious, impure, angry thought, not to lie, curse, speak impurely, not to steal or do anything immodest. When you pray: " I especially offer Thee my heart," you must resolve: " I will do my best to have a heart free from sin, and I will love God with my whole heart." Only then is your prayer at the Offertory true: " My God, I offer Thee all my thoughts and especially my heart."

II. THE CONSECRATION.

OBJECT. Which principal part of the Mass follows the Offertory? I will now tell you what you should do at the Consecration.

The reception of the King. Who comes from heaven on the altar at the Consecration? Our Saviour is the King of heaven and earth. When the king visits a place, he is received solemnly by his subjects. The streets are decorated with triumphal arches, flags, etc. Old and young in their Sunday clothes, girls dressed in white, all go to meet him, to show him their joy and affection. And when the king makes his appearance, there is an outburst of cheers almost without end.

Our Saviour's reception in Jerusalem. The Jews once received Jesus in the same way. When, on Palm-Sunday, Jesus entered Jerusalem as a king, children and grown persons turned out in their fine clothes to meet Him. They carried palm and olive branches in their hands and cheered Him, repeating: " Hosanna in the highest! Blessed is He that cometh in the name of the Lord. Hosanna in the highest."

Our Saviour's reception in holy Mass. Which King comes down upon the altar at the Consecration? It is the King of kings, the greatest of lords, the very Son of God, our Lord Jesus Christ. 1. Therefore, when the priest comes near the Consecration, he bows his head, saying three times: " Holy, holy, holy, Lord God of hosts; heaven and earth are full of Thy glory. Hosanna in the highest." Then standing upright, he makes the sign of the cross, saying: " Blessed is He that cometh in the name of the Lord. Hosanna in the highest." 2. And when the choir sings the same words, repeat also the same words in your heart. 3. But when Jesus is about to come really upon the altar to put on the appearance of bread, the choir and every one in the church is silent. The priest bows forward and pronounces in a whisper the words of consecration first over the bread, then over the wine in the chalice, and bends his knee to the floor to adore our Saviour, and then raises Him heavenward. At this very moment the heavenly Father looks down from heaven on the altar. There He sees the most lovely, beautiful and holy of all things in the hands of the priest. He sees His well-beloved, only-begotten Son under the appearances of bread and wine offering Himself to Him on the altar. No human eye has ever so joyfully looked upon a human being, as the heavenly Father's eye looks down upon His well-beloved Son offering Himself in sacrifice under the appearances of bread and wine. 4. In the meantime the server rings the little bell, and all in church are kneeling, bowing their heads, striking their breast and adoring. Whom are they adoring? Our Saviour, the King of heaven and earth, our God. All this is to tell us that our God is now with us, and to welcome Him in our midst.

The adoration of the Sacred Host at the consecration. What happens to the bread and wine at the Consecration?

The bread is changed into the true living body of Jesus. Jesus, at the Consecration, comes down, for the love of us, on the altar, in order to live for us under the appearance of bread. If you offer all your thoughts, words, actions and sufferings to please God, you also live for God. This is what you resolved at the Offertory; you should, therefore, keep that resolution. Wherefore, at the elevation (raising up) of the sacred Host, say: "O Jesus, my Lord and my God, I wish to live for Thee." When saying this, strike your breast (*thus*).

But we cannot see Jesus living under the appearance of bread; He does not move; He allows Himself to be laid down, lifted up and carried; He allows His priests to do what they will with Him. He appears now as He did when He sacrificed Himself on the cross for us. He is as if He were dead. Also there is something in you which should be as if it were dead. In your heart there is as an effect of original sin, an inclination to evil. It tries to make you take pleasure in evil thoughts, to listen to evil words, to look at evil things, to speak and do evil. When this inclination to evil seeks to induce you to look on others with envy, your eyes should be as if blind and dead, so that you may not look upon others with envy. When you feel inclined to tell lies, let your tongue, for the love of God, be as if dead, so that you may not tell lies. When you feel inclined to steal, let your hands, for God's sake, be as if dead, so that you may not be able to touch the property of (what belongs to) others. In this way all that is evil will be rooted out of your thoughts, words and actions. You shall then die for Jesus. Hence say also at the elevation of the sacred Host: "O Jesus, my Lord and my God, I wish to die for Thee." If you try hard to do away with everything evil in you and to do only what is good, for the love of God, you can then truly say: "O Jesus, my Lord and my God, I am Thine, both in life and in death." (Repeat.)

The adoration at the elevation of the chalice. At the

elevation of the chalice you may recite this prayer: " O Jesus, may Thy blood purify me! O Jesus, may Thy blood sanctify me! O Jesus, may Thy blood lead me to life ever- lasting! Amen."

What is the meaning of " O Jesus, may Thy blood purify me "? From what should our Saviour's blood pur- ify you? Where are your sins? Therefore the blood of Jesus should wash away the sins in your soul. What is the meaning of " O Jesus, may Thy blood sanctify me "? Where did Jesus shed His blood for us? What did Jesus deserve for us by His blood? Grace. We pray that grace may enter our soul. What does grace do to our soul? Grace makes our soul holy. Therefore we pray, etc.? Where does a holy soul go after death? How long does the soul live in heaven? Forever. Jesus deserved life everlasting for us by shedding all His blood. Therefore we pray, etc. (Repeat.)

The priest extends his arms in prayer. After the Con- secration the priest continues to pray devoutly. Have you remarked how the priest then holds his arms? Extended. Where did our Saviour extend His arms? On the cross. Whom does the priest personate (represent) at the altar? What does he do when he extends his arms?

Our Saviour prays with extended arms. It is just as if our Saviour prayed with extended arms. Where is Jesus represented with extended arms? On the cross. At every procession the cross is carried in front. On the feast of St. Mark, April 25, and on the three days before the Ascen- sion, called Rogation days, or days of prayer, there are pro- cessions with the singing of the Litany of the Saints, to beseech God to bless the newly planted fields, that they may produce good crops. Now suppose that instead of the cross, our divine Saviour Himself would go at the head of the procession and pray with extended arms for us and with us to His heavenly Father. Would you not feel sure that God the Father would grant our prayers?

Our Saviour prays for us and with us. At the Consecration our Saviour comes really on the altar and places Himself at our head and prays with extended arms with us and for us. By doing this He reminds His Father how, when He was hanging on the cross with extended arms, He sacrificed Himself for us and prayed for us. Our Saviour knows all our wants. He knows when we wish to praise God; He knows when we wish to thank God for His benefits; He knows also when we wish to ask God for something. And Jesus takes all our prayers into His heart, and offers them with His prayer to the heavenly Father as an offering.

Our Saviour's prayer is heard by His Father. You surely have no fear of not being heard by the heavenly Father. Because you know that His well-beloved Son prays with you and for you. God the Father cannot refuse to grant you what you pray for.

The prayers said during Mass are the most efficacious. Therefore, all the prayers you say during Mass are worth a great deal more than all your prayers at other times. When you say at home your morning and night prayers, when you pray for your parents, or to your guardian angel, or to the Blessed Virgin Mary, those are only your prayers, for you pray alone. But when you pray during holy Mass, Jesus Christ unites His prayer and offering with your prayer and offering. When you make your offering, Jesus offers it with you; when you pray, Jesus prays with you; when you sing, Jesus sings with you and offers all to His heavenly Father. Therefore by your prayers during Mass you obtain far more graces and blessings than when you pray at other times.

We must also pray devoutly. But there is one thing necessary in all this. You must pray devoutly during Mass, in order that your prayer may please our Saviour, and that He may let it enter His heart. On this condition holy Mass becomes a real happy hour for you, and you will surely receive all the good you pray for.

APPLICATION. 1. You know who comes during Mass upon the altar. It is our Saviour Himself who sacrifices Himself and prays for us. Wherefore, if you wish to obtain some favor from God, for instance, that your sick father or mother should get well, or that some one may help you in your poverty or distress, go to hear Mass, and pray devoutly therein. And after the Consecration, beseech our Saviour to place your prayer in His sacred heart, and offer it with His prayer and sacrifice to His heavenly Father. Such a prayer will please the heavenly Father, and He will surely grant it.

2. On some other occasion, you may wish to thank God for the cure of your mother, or you wish God to help you to be more obedient, to be less inclined to impatience, to anger, etc. Go to hear Mass, and at the Offertory place your request on the little gilt place, and beg our Saviour to offer it with His offering to His heavenly Father. You will thereby greatly please our Saviour and His heavenly Father.

3. During Mass the smallest gift you offer to God has infinite value. Suppose, you wish to offer a nickel to God during Mass. That, surely, is not much. Now a rich man comes to you and gives you $100,000, that you may offer that sum to God. To that big sum you add your nickel and make an offering of it all to God during Mass. The heavenly Father is surely pleased with that offering. But you ought to offer your heart to God during Mass. But you are a poor sinful child, and your heart, in God's estimation, is worth scarcely a nickel. But there is a gift, an offering worth far more than $100,000. What gift is that? Our divine Saviour Himself. Our Saviour gives Himself to you in holy Mass as a gift which you are to offer to God. That is what is represented by the $100,000. And which is your nickel? Your heart. Now add your

nickel, that is, your heart, to the $100,000, that is, our Saviour, and make out a gift, an offering, out of them, and bring it during Mass to the heavenly Father. How much is your offering worth in His estimation? What does it cause Him?

4. Suppose you were to hear that a rich man was going to distribute $100,000 among the people. How you would hasten to him! During every Mass our divine Saviour distributes a great deal more than $100,000. He gives more than all the money in the world. He sacrifices Himself to His heavenly Father, and distributes the immense graces which He deserved for us on the cross. Then hasten to church to hear Mass, in order to obtain as many graces as possible, as you would to that rich man to get as much money as possible.

5. I will now relate to you another anecdote. There was once a pious farmer who went every day to Mass. He had become accustomed to do so when he was a school-boy. He continued to do so even when he was old. When working in the field he would hear the bell ringing for Mass, he left everything lie and went to church. On a certain day he was in the field when he heard the bell ringing for Mass. The distance to the church was great, and he was already tired from his work. On his way to church he thought by himself: "I am already old and walking is hard for me. From now I will go to hear Mass only when I am at home. From the field I will not go to Mass in future. God will surely not be displeased with me for this." As he was thinking over this in his mind, he heard some one walking behind him. He turned around to see who it was, and what does he see? A bright angel. The angel said to him: "Do not do that, I advise you, but go every day to hear Mass, as you have been accustomed to do. Because at each step you take on the way to church, a rose springs up from your footstep. Therefore as many roses grow as you take steps to go to church. See, here are the roses I culled

to-day." And the angel showed a large pile of roses. The angel continued speaking: "If you go to Mass every day until you die, I will place on your head in heaven a splendid wreath of roses." After saying this, the angel disappeared. You may imagine that the pious farmer continued fervently and cheerfully to go to Mass every day.

What the angel said to the farmer, is applicable to you also. By devoutly hearing Mass you receive each time many graces from God. Each of these graces is like a blooming rose. If you wish to wear a wreath of such roses, be sure to go daily to church and devoutly hear Mass.

III. THE COMMUNION.

OBJECT. Which is the third principal part of the Mass? What takes place at holy Communion? I will now tell you how you should act at holy Communion.

Our Saviour gave His body and blood to the apostles as the food of their soul. What did our Saviour at the Last Supper give to His apostles to eat and drink? Under what appearances? What kind of food is our divine Saviour under the appearances of bread and wine? Food of the soul. Which are the words our Saviour said when He gave this food of the soul to His apostles?

You need food for your body. Your mother also gives you to eat and drink. But that food is not for your soul. What is it for? For the body. Why does your mother give you to eat and drink? To make me grow, to make me strong and healthy. What would become of you, if you would get no food? I would get sick and die.

You need food for your soul also. Your soul also can get sick. How? When I commit a sin. And how could your soul also die with regard to heaven? By committing a mortal sin. To remain healthy, your soul also needs food.

The food of your soul is our divine Saviour in holy Communion. You know already which is the food of your soul.

You know that our Saviour said to the apostles: "Take and eat, for this is My body." He says the same to you also: "Take ye and eat, for this is My body." Is not that a precious food? It is a sweet heavenly bread. Your mother rejoices when you greatly relish your food. In like manner, our Saviour rejoices, when Christians relish the food of their soul.

Through our divine Saviour your heart becomes in holy Communion a house of God. Where does our Saviour enter as our food? Into our heart. Therefore our living Saviour lives in your heart. What do you call the place where God dwells? The house of God, a church. What is your heart when Jesus dwells in it? The house of God.

The house of God in your heart should be pure and holy. The house in which God dwells, is holy. How should your heart be as a place in which God dwells? Holy. From what should it be cleansed? From sin.

TRANSITION. If your soul is not pure, you are not fit nor worthy that our Saviour should enter it.

OBJECT. I will now relate to you an anecdote of a prominent man. That man did not believe himself worthy that our Saviour should go to him.

RELATION. The servant of a Roman officer at Capharnaum was very sick. He was already very near death. The officer loved his servant and was anxious for his cure. Therefore he sent some of his friends to Jesus to ask Him: "Lord, be so good as to cure my servant." Jesus at once went along with the messengers. When he got near the officer's house, the officer himself came out, and said to Jesus: "Lord, I am not worthy that Thou shouldst enter under my roof; but say only one word, and my servant shall be healed." Jesus replied to the officer: "Go, and as thou hast believed, be it done to thee." At that very moment the servant was cured.

CONSIDERATION — *The sick servant of the officer.* Where did that man live, about whom I have been speaking? Capharnaum is a town in the Jewish country. What was that man? A Roman officer. He was, then, a prominent man. What did I relate about his servant? The officer was very sorry, and was very anxious that his servant should get well. The physicians in the city could do nothing more for him.

The officer's confidence. The officer had heard that Jesus had cured many sick persons. Therefore he hoped that Jesus would cure his servant also. Whom did he send to Jesus? What did he wish them to say to Jesus? Jesus was immediately ready to go and cure the servant. How do you know that?

The officer's humility. Jesus was already near the officer's house. The officer saw that Jesus Himself was coming. He almost got frightened. The officer had not expected that Jesus Himself would do him so great an honor as to come to him. He thought in himself: " How then can I be worthy to receive Jesus into my own house? I am too mean to be so greatly honored, for I am such a sinner. I do not deserve the honor." But the officer was a prominent man; he had many soldiers under him who had to strictly obey his every command, and also servants to wait on him. And yet he felt so little and so mean in comparison with Jesus. He believed he was of no account in comparison with the Saviour. In a word, the officer was humble.

The officer's faith. The officer also believed that Jesus could cure his servant without seeing him, and did not need to come to his house to do so. He knew that Jesus had only to say one word, and his servant would be healed. What did the officer do, when he saw Jesus coming to his house? What did he say to Jesus? Of what does the officer consider himself not worthy? The word roof here means house. He could have said, into my house, instead of under my roof. Why did he consider himself unworthy of receiving our Saviour into his house? What made the officer believe that our Saviour could cure his servant?

The officer's reward. What did Jesus answer him? What happened at that very moment? The servant was cured. Why was our Saviour able to cure the servant by a single word?

Our Saviour loves to give Himself in holy Communion to us, if we are humble. The almighty Saviour who would go into the house of the officer of Capharnaum, wishes to come to us also in holy Communion. Where does our Saviour wish to dwell when He comes to us? What should our heart then be for our Saviour? But no human heart is pure enough for our Saviour. Therefore no man is worthy enough to receive Jesus into his heart. Every one, even the greatest saint, must think: "How little and how mean I am in comparison with our divine Saviour! How unfit I am to receive my Saviour into my heart!" But who can make our heart so pure and so beautiful, as to make us worthy? Our Saviour Himself. He would need only to do what sufficed to cure the officer's servant, that is, to say only a word.

The priest humbles himself before holy Communion. Wherefore when the priest saying Mass comes to the Communion, in which our Saviour is to come to him, the priest uses the very words of the Roman officer: "Lord, I am not worthy that Thou shouldst enter under my roof." By the word roof, the priest means the house or dwelling of his heart. What else did the officer say? The priest, however, says: "But say only the word, and my soul shall be healed." Repeat now all that the priest says before holy Communion. This he says three times, striking his breast each time. And you should do the same. (Repeat all.) Then the priest receives our Saviour with great reverence. And with the same reverence he drinks our Saviour's precious blood from the chalice.

The real or sacramental Communion. After Communion our dear living Saviour dwells in the priest's heart as God and man, with soul and body, flesh and blood. The soul of the priest and the holy soul of Jesus are now, as it were, one. The heart of the priest and the sacred heart of our Saviour are now one, as it were. The holy heart of Jesus now beats in the heart of the priest. The priest lives no more, but it is Jesus that lives in him. And so it is also with all Christians who receive our Saviour in holy Communion.

Spiritual Communion. When you see the priest and some of the faithful receiving Jesus in holy Communion, you perhaps think: "Oh, could I also receive our Lord! Oh, if He would also come into my heart in holy Communion, how happy would I be"! You have a desire, a longing to receive Jesus. Jesus also longs to be received by you in holy Communion. And if you are not able, or not prepared to receive Him really in holy Communion, you can, nevertheless, receive Him invisibly, spiritually by your ardent desire and by asking Him to come spiritually into your heart. But your heart should be free from sin. How can you then make it free from sin? By praying Jesus to purify your soul, saying: "O my Jesus, purify my heart from every sin. I am sorry for them all; forgive me my sins." Then after saying, "O Lord, I am not worthy," etc., say: "O Jesus, I love Thee above all things, and I desire to receive Thee into my heart; but since I cannot now receive Thee in reality (sacramentally), come at least spiritually into my heart. I unite myself, as if Thou wert already there; permit me not to be separated from Thee." You may make a spiritual Communion not only at the Communion of the priest and the faithful during Mass, but also any other time either in church, or at home, or elsewhere. (Rehearse spiritual Communion.)

The smallest house of God. Our Lord, as you have heard, chooses for His dwelling, the smallest house on earth, that is, the heart of man. Although it is so little, it draws the God of heaven and earth into it. Therefore, children, keep your heart pure and devout, and Jesus will choose it as His dwelling and never more leave it.

CONNECTION — *The Consecration is the most important part of the Mass.* What do the priest and the faithful receive in holy Communion? Under what appearances? When does the bread and wine become the body and blood of Jesus? What were they at the Offertory? Blessed bread and wine. What would they be, if the Communion would immediately follow the Offertory? What would they remain, if there were no Consecration after the Offertory? What would they still remain, at the Communion, if the Communion would immediately follow the Offertory? Which part is, then, the most important in the Mass, which gives the real value to the Mass?

The Consecration is the soul of the Mass. There is a similarity between the Mass and a man. What is the body of a man without the soul? What makes the body a living body? What would the bread and wine in the Mass remain, if there was no consecration? What causes the bread and wine to become in the Mass the living body and blood of Jesus? Therefore, we call the Consecration the soul or heart of the Mass. As the body without a soul is dead, so the Mass would be dead without the Consecration.

SUMMARY. At the Offertory we should offer to God our thoughts, words and actions. Therefore we should resolve to have only good thoughts, good words and good actions. At the Consecration, or elevation we should adore our Saviour, and place our prayer in His heart, so that our heavenly Father may sooner grant it. At the Communion we should receive our Saviour spiritually. It would be well for every child, when they do not sing, to use a prayer-book during Mass, or, at least, to say the beads. (Insist.)

APPLICATION. 1. Ought you not to be glad to go to hear Mass? Would it be too hard for you to get up half an hour earlier in the morning in order to come to Mass? It is hard to believe that there are children who talk in church during Mass. 2. It would be well if you would say sometimes: " O Jesus, come to me, for I long for Thee. Thou art my soul's best friend, I cannot live without Thee. O Jesus, come to me, for I long for Thee."

7. The Worship of the Blessed Sacrament.

DEVELOPMENT.

The whole world is the house of God. Where is God? He is here in the school, in the street, in the fields, in the woods, where the sun rises, and where the sun sets. He is present everywhere all over the world. The whole world is the wonderfully beautiful house of God. Can we see God? No, for God is invisible to our bodily eyes. How, then, is God present everywhere? Invisibly present.

Heaven is the house of God. Where shall we see God? In heaven God is visibly present. Heaven is the wonderfully beautiful palace of God. There He is seated on His golden throne. Around Him are countless angels and saints. They see God face to face; they see His wonderful beauty. They never weary seeing Him. They are continually day and night adoring and praising Him, and loving Him, with all their might, and singing: " Holy, holy, holy Lord God of hosts." Heaven is filled with their beautiful chant.

The church is the house of God. God wishes to be visibly with us, and to dwell visibly among us. What is it that you need to live in? What does God need to live among us? A house. Therefore God allows men on earth to build Him a house of His own. How beautiful is God? How rich? How powerful? How great? What kind of a house should He have? A large and beautiful house. Therefore men build God a house as large and as beautiful as they can. God's house should be the largest and the most beautiful in a place. Inside it is beautifully painted, adorned with fine paintings, statues, altars and stained glass windows. The altars should be especially beautiful. Why? Because there the priest daily says Mass and brings the Son of God down from heaven. At Mass the priest wears beautiful and costly vestments, for he therein serves and worships God. For God's service we should always use what is best and most precious; and even the best and most costly thing in the world is not good enough for the Lord of heaven and earth.

The tabernacle is the throne-room or hall of God in the church. A king, a president has in his house a room that is more beautiful than any other, where he gives receptions to those who go to pay their respects to him. Who can tell which is the heavenly King's throne-room in the church? It is the smallest throne-room in the world. But in this small throne-room in the world is seated the greatest King of the universe, the King of heaven and earth. (Describe the tabernacle in your church — both the outside and the inside.) The ciborium is the golden throne of the Lord of heaven and earth. Its richly embroidered red silk cover is the mantle of this greatest of monarchs. But where is this almighty Lord and King? When the priest opens the ciborium, he bends the knee to the floor, and why? Because in the ciborium is the King Himself. In the stable of Bethlehem there lay a Child so little, so lovely, so beautiful, enveloped in swaddling-clothes in the crib. And yet this Child was the greatest Monarch in the world. But here in the ciborium the same Monarch is still smaller.

The hidden King and God. Suppose you had come with the shepherds, on the night when Jesus was born, to see and adore the Infant Jesus; and Jesus was asleep, and the blessed Virgin had covered Him with her veil; and you could not have seen the Infant Jesus and His pretty face. Would you have said the Infant Jesus was not under the veil, because you could not see Him? Would you for that reason have refused to believe that the Infant Jesus was

the Saviour of the world, the King of heaven and earth?
Would you have refused to adore Him, because the veil
concealed Him from your sight?

But in the ciborium the same divine Infant is really to
be found. But what appearance has He in the Blessed
Sacrament? What color has He under the appearance of
bread? He is there just as if He was covered with a
thick white veil, so that He cannot be seen. Does that
prevent you from believing, that the living Infant Jesus
is really in the ciborium? Did not our Saviour Himself
say that under the white appearance of bread He is wholly
present and alive? To whom did He say this? How did
He say this? Therefore under the white veil of the appearance of bread there is really concealed the same Infant
Jesus, who was enveloped in swaddling-clothes and laid
in the crib. The tabernacle in the church is like the stable
of Bethlehem and the house of Nazareth where Jesus lived;
here we have the same living Saviour, who is seated on a
throne at the right of God the Father. The tabernacle
in God's house is heaven itself on earth.

The most humble adoration. In heaven God can be seen.
During divine service in church on Sunday afternoon or
evening our divine Saviour is exposed outside the tabernacle, so that all may see Him either in the ciborium or in
the monstrance. Around Him many candles are lit. The
priest and altar boys kneel on the lowest step of the altar.
In the body of the church all the faithful, both children
and grown people, are also kneeling, to adore their Saviour
and Redeemer, their Lord and God, their heavenly King.
And from His high throne, the Saviour looks on all present, like a king on his subjects.

How grave and friendly is the house of God! How
dear and lovely! How joyfully and devoutly the people
sing! How they pray from their inmost hearts! And
why? Because God is there! Therefore the faithful
come from far and near into His presence, to adore, thank,

praise and beseech Him. At the end our Saviour gives His blessing to all. Before this the priest bows low to our Lord and incenses Him with the censer; the smoke of incense wafted up to the throne on which Jesus is placed, denotes the prayers, love and adoration of the faithful ascending to Jesus like the sweet-scented incense. The priest then takes in his hands the monstrance in which Jesus is exposed to view under the appearance of bread, and with it makes the sign of the cross over all present in the church. The faithful receive our Saviour's blessing kneeling, bowing low, and striking their breast, adoring their Lord and God.

This reminds us of the wise men before the Infant Jesus at Bethlehem. How did they venerate the Infant Jesus? They prostrated themselves and adored Him. They took off their kingly crowns and bowed down to the ground before the Infant Jesus. Although they were kings, they knew that in presence of the divine Child, they were as a mere nothing. What were the wise men, because they made such little account of themselves before the Infant Jesus? They were humble. And all men, even the bishop, the Pope himself, kings and emperors, the most noble persons on earth, are, in comparison with our Saviour in the Blessed Sacrament, but mere servants. Therefore, how should all men without exception act towards our divine Saviour? In an humble manner. How do we show ourselves humble towards Him? By kneeling and bowing before Him. And, while doing this, what else should we do? Adore Him. Therefore we must adore our Saviour in deep humility. The real presence of our Saviour in the Blessed Sacrament requires that we most humbly adore Him. After benediction (the blessing of Jesus) the Blessed Sacrament is replaced in the tabernacle.

Jesus dwells in the Blessed Sacrament. Here our Saviour dwells among us. Here He has His own house among the houses of the people. He lives in our midst as a friendly neighbor, who came from afar off. And as in the earthly paradise men could converse with God, so now we can come near the tabernacle to converse with our loving Saviour. He remains near us day and night, and will not leave us; so greatly does He love us.

The prayer of Jesus in the Blessed Sacrament. What does our Saviour do in the Blessed Sacrament in the tabernacle? He looks with His all-seeing eye on all who are in the church; He looks at them, when they leave the church; He looks at all who remain at home; He looks also at the graveyard where so many crosses mark the places where lie the dead. And our Saviour extends His hands over all, and prays for them, for the living and the dead, blessing all; He never tires praying and blessing. He watches over all. When all are asleep, our Saviour watches, prays and blesses always. No one can pray so well as our Saviour. He prays best of all, and that so quietly.

The frequent visit to Jesus in the Blessed Sacrament. Have you not some quiet evening entered the church and seen a little red light glittering and trembling? That is the light of the sanctuary lamp always burning before the tabernacle. It is like the bright star that guided the Magi on the way to Bethlehem, and stood still when they reached the stable. What did the Magi learn from this? That the Saviour, newly born, was in there. And when you see that little glittering red light in the church, what do you conclude? Is it not that it is there that our Saviour dwells, watches and prays? Does it not say to you with its fiery little tongue: " Here in the Blessed Sacrament your Lord and God, your best Friend is continually present "?

People love to go often to visit their good friends, and this sometimes every day or even several times a day. And are you not glad to go and see your uncle, your aunt, etc., especially if they always give you something good?

Therefore, what should you do in reference to our Saviour, who is your best friend? Visit Him often. That is what that little lamp tells you, whose light you can see from outside glittering and trembling on the windows of the church. That light tells you: "Oh, come to your Saviour in the Blessed Sacrament, and do not let Him remain always alone." And our Saviour Himself desires your company; for He waits day and night for you to come. He says to each of you: "I am thy God. Oh, come to Me and visit Me." Should you not rejoice to be permitted to visit our Saviour? Nowhere are you more welcome than in church. You should like it as much as your own home. If you are long absent from home, how glad you are to go back to your dear father and mother. In like manner should you not be glad to be able to go to Jesus?

On which day should you always visit our dear Lord in church? Every Sunday. Especially at holy Mass. And at what other time? Which is the best time on week days for doing so? You may visit our Lord during the day, even when there is no divine service in church. Could you not, when passing before a church, step in for a while and pay a short visit to Jesus? Could you not do the same when you have free time for yourself? Our Saviour is always there at home and always has time to listen to you. If you enter the church during the day, you will often find nobody in the church. You are then alone with Jesus. How friendly and lovely does it not seem in church! You can then speak confidently to our Lord, and open your heart to Him.

What then should urge you often to go into the church? The real presence of our Saviour in the Blessed Sacrament, which is in the church. Because Jesus is really there, we should often visit Him.

The adoration full of the most intimate love. On entering the church, be sure to make a genuflexion. The genuflexion is the greeting we owe to our Saviour. In what direction do you look when you genuflect? Towards the tabernacle. Do not make the genuflexion like the old people who can no longer bend down. How far should your knee go down, when you genuflect to our Saviour? Down to the floor (ground). You then go to kneel in your place. It is not becoming to sit down before our Saviour. This may be done only during the sermons and instructions. It is much less becoming to talk, laugh, etc., in presence of the Blessed Sacrament. To do so is very irreverent. The Lord is in His own house; let the whole world be silent before Him.

When you have knelt down in your place, make an act of adoration, saying: " O Jesus, I believe that Thou art really present here in thy church; I adore Thee as my Lord and my God, as my loving Saviour." Then you may continue, saying: " O my dear Saviour, I have come to visit Thee, and to tell Thee how much I love Thee. How happy I am in being now near Thee. How glad I would be, if I could now receive Thee into my heart. How I long to receive Thee; but since I cannot now do so sacramentally, come spiritually into my heart. O dear Infant Jesus, deign to come now into my heart. I embrace Thee, as if Thou wast already there; I unite myself to Thee; permit me not to be separated from Thee." Then pray Jesus to grant you certain graces you desire for yourself, your parents, and all who are dear to you.

What holy boy was so fond of praying in church before the tabernacle? St. Stanislaus. There was his favorite place. How long would Stanislaus remain kneeling before the tabernacle? In what direction was he always looking? He never grew tired of adoring our Saviour in the Blessed Sacrament. What did he then feel in his heart towards our Saviour? How could people perceive exteriorly the love St. Stanislaus bore in his heart towards our Saviour? His face was resplendent with joy. In a word, St. Stanislaus adored our Saviour in the Blessed Sacrament with the deepest love. You should also do the same, when you visit our Saviour in the tabernacle. If you from your inmost heart pray there to our Lord, your heart will beat and your face will brighten, like the face and heart of St. Stanislaus. How then will you adore our divine Saviour? With the deepest love. Why should you do so? Because our Saviour is truly present in the Blessed Sacrament, and His presence therein demands this of us. Prayer is the most beautiful thing in the world. Nowhere can we pray better than before the tabernacle, for therein is the eye of God, the very heart of God. The Saviour looks at you, and you look at the Saviour.

SUMMARY. What does the presence of Jesus Christ in the Blessed Sacrament demand of us? That we should often visit Him and most profoundly, humbly and lovingly adore Him.

APPLICATION — *The feast of Corpus Christi; the feast of the Blessed Sacrament.* How is the feast of Corpus Christi celebrated in Catholic countries? Once a year our divine Saviour comes out of His dwelling in the tabernacle. He allows Himself to be carried in procession through the streets. A beautifully embroidered silk canopy representing heaven is carried above our Lord in the Blessed Sacrament by the best and most prominent men of the place or parish. The others accompany with lighted candles. Girls dressed in white form a kind of wreath around our Saviour. At the head of the procession is the cross; then follow the children, the women, the men, then the altar boys; then little girls dressed in white each with a basket of flowers to scatter them on the way before our Lord; then some altar boys with bells, others with censers to incense the Blessed Sacrament; finally the canopy under which the priest carries the monstrance, exposing our Saviour in the sacred Host to view, having on each side of him the deacon and the subdeacon, all clothed in the most beautiful and costly vestments. The procession passes through the streets and alongside the houses all covered with beautiful arches and decorations. During the procession beautiful hymns are sung by the faithful. Along the route of the procession several altars, or repositories, as they are called, have been erected and grandly decorated. When the Blessed Sacrament arrives at a repository, there is a halt, and the priest places the monstrance containing our Saviour on the repository, and all kneel down wherever they are. The hymn and prayers for benediction are sung, and then the priest gives benediction to all with the Blessed Sacrament. After this the procession is resumed until the next repository is reached, where the same ceremonies are repeated. After leaving the last repository, the procession returns to the church where benediction with the Blessed Sacrament is given with the usual ceremonies. Then the grand hymn of thanksgiving, the *Te Deum* is sung. When this is over, the Blessed Sacrament is replaced by the priest in the tabernacle. Such is the grand Corpus Christi procession, in which Catholics publicly manifest their lively faith in and their deepest love for Jesus in the Blessed Sacrament.

THE SACRAMENT OF PENANCE, AND, AT THE SAME TIME, AN INSTRUCTION FOR THE FIRST CONFESSION.

8. The Institution of the Sacrament of Penance.

PREPARATION — *God alone can forgive sins.* 1. Who commands in your house? What must the children do, when their parents command them something? Who commands or makes laws in a country? What must the people then do? Who commands in heaven and on earth? Almighty God. When God commands, what must men do? How many commandments has God given?

2. When a child does not obey his father, it pains his

father. The child then pains, offends his father. What does a child do to God, when he disobeys God? And what does the child then commit? How does a father feel towards a disobedient child? Displeased, angry. How is God disposed towards the sinner? What does a child deserve for disobeying his father? What does the sinner deserve for disobeying God? What punishment does the sinner deserve for a venial sin? And for a mortal sin?

3. Let us suppose that Charles has offended his father. But Charles is sorry for it, and is anxious that his father should again become pleased with him. What must Charles then say to his father? But Charles goes to his mother and says to her: "Mother, please forgive me for having offended my father." But his mother replies: "You must not come to me for that, but you must go to father." Why does Charles' mother send him to his father to beg pardon for his fault? Because Charles offended his father. His mother cannot forgive him for having offended his father. Only he can forgive who has been offended.

Whom do we offend when we commit sin? From whom then must the sinner obtain forgiveness?

I. OBJECT. I will now show you that God forgives sins.

DEVELOPMENT. Who were the first to commit sin on earth? What did they thereby do to God? How was God disposed towards them on this account? God was angry with them and punished them for it. What did they lose in their soul by their sin? Whose children did they cease to be? Where could they no longer go? Where were they no longer to remain? Where would their soul have gone after their death? But our first parents wished to obtain the forgiveness of their sin. Who could alone forgive their sin? What had they to say to God in order to obtain it? And they really did this. They asked God to forgive them. How must they have silently asked this of God? God then had mercy on them. He promised them a Redeemer, and forgave their sin. The heavenly Father really sent the promised Redeemer. Who is it? Jesus Christ, the Son of God.

II. OBJECT. I will show you to-day that the Redeemer, when on earth, forgave sins.

RELATION. One day Jesus was teaching in a house at Capharnaum. The house was full of people listening to Him. Four men were carrying a paralytic in his bed; they laid him down before Jesus. They believed that Jesus would cure him. When Jesus saw their faith, he said to the paralytic: " Son, be of good heart; thy sins are forgiven thee." Our Saviour wished also to cure him. Therefore He said to him: " Arise, take up thy bed, and go home." The paralytic was cured by these words; he rose, took up his bed and went home.

CONSIDERATION — *The sickness in soul and body.* Where was Jesus teaching on a certain day? A paralytic lived in Capharnaum. . A paralytic is a man who is very sick, and can neither walk nor stand. No doctor could cure that paralytic. This paralytic had got his sickness as a punishment for his sins. His soul, on account of his sins had become more sick than even his body. How then was he sick? When the paralytic heard that Jesus was in the city, he hoped that Jesus would cure him. How did he come to Jesus? Where did those four men place him?

The contrition of the paralytic. When the paralytic was lying down in front of Jesus and gazed on the sacred face of Jesus, he at once thought of his many sins. He reflected on how he had, by his sins, grievously offended God, and this thought pained him in his heart more than his bodily pains. He was very sorry for his sins.

The forgiveness of sins. Our Saviour knew why the paralytic had got so sick. He saw also how sorry he was for his sins, because they offended God. Our Saviour consoled him. What did He say to him? At that moment the soul of the paralytic was purified of all its sins, and was clothed with a bright garment. Which garment do I mean? God and the angels were pleased with him. And whose child did he become? And where would he be allowed to go later on?

The remission of the eternal punishment. What would have become of the paralytic, if he had died in his sins? The devils had already been waiting a long time, to draw his soul down into the abyss of hell, to bury it in the fire. For how long? That would have been the eternal punishment for his sins. The eternal punishment accompanies mortal sin just as the shadow accompanies the child. A child stands in the sunlight. What does he see alongside of him? His shadow. He goes away; what accompanies him? His shadow accompanies him wherever he goes. But if he gets away from the sunlight, what leaves him? His shadow. The same is the case with the eternal punishment of hell. So long as there is a mortal sin in the soul of a child, the eternal punishment of hell stands alongside of him, and it follows him, just like the shadow follows the body. But when mortal sin is removed from the soul, what is it that is also removed? The eternal punishment of hell. What did our Lord forgive or remit to the paralytic besides his sins? The eternal punishment of hell.

The remission of the temporal punishment. But the paralytic's body also was sick. What did our Saviour say to him about it? What did the paralytic do at once? Why had God sent him his sickness? Sickness was, therefore, a punishment for his sins. How long would his sickness have naturally lasted? Until his death. That is, only for a time. A punishment that lasts only for a time, is called a temporal punishment. What kind of punishment was the sickness of the paralytic? What kind of punishment did our Lord remit to him, when He cured him of his sickness? The temporal punishment.

SUMMARY. Tell me what did our Saviour remit to the paralytic? 1, His sins; 2, the eternal punishment due to his sins; 3, the temporal punishment of his sins. And what gift did He bestow on his soul? Whose child did he become? And where had he the right to go?

APPLICATION. How light and glad that man must have felt when on his way home! Everything had been forgiven him. He was cured, and his soul was wonderfully beautiful. There was peace and happiness in his soul. And he was resolved: " I will nevermore in my life commit sin."

TRANSITION. In like manner, our Saviour forgave the sins of many others, when He was still on earth. But He willed that, after His Ascension until the end of the world, men should be able to have their sins forgiven.

III. OBJECT. I will now tell you how this is done.

PREPARATION. I have told you how Charles had to ask his father to forgive him, that his father might again be pleased with him. Why could not his mother forgive him his disobedience? Who has the right to forgive? Now suppose Charles' father says to his mother: " Charles has greatly offended me this day. I have remarked that he is sorry for it. If he comes to you and says that he is sorry for it, you may, in my place, forgive him." What power or commission had Charles' father given his mother? May not his mother in that case forgive him? Yes. Why? Because she received the power to do so from his father. In whose place then does his mother forgive him? His father could have empowered Charles' grandfather or grandmother to forgive him. Who then could also have forgiven him? His father, and every one whom his father would have empowered to do so. Who can alone forgive sins? God.

OBJECT. I will now relate to you how our Saviour gave the apostles the power also to forgive sins.

RELATION. On the evening of the day of the resurrection of Jesus, His apostles were assembled together in a room in Jerusalem. For fear of the Jews they had locked the doors. Suddenly Jesus stood in their midst and said: "Peace be to you. It is I; fear not." The apostles were glad to see our Lord. Jesus again said: "Peace be to you. As the Father hath sent Me, I also send you." When He had said this He breathed on them, and said to them: "Receive ye the Holy Ghost. Whose sins you shall forgive, they are forgiven them; and whose sins you shall retain, they are retained." And then He disappeared.

CONSIDERATION — *Our Saviour imparts to the apostles the power of forgiving sins.* Where were the apostles assembled in the evening? On what day was it? On the day of His resurrection. Who stood suddenly among them? What did our Saviour say to them? The apostles were glad to see our Lord. What did Jesus say the second time to the apostles? And what did He add? "As the Father hath sent Me," etc. For what had our Saviour been sent into the world? To redeem men from sin. He did this. How? By dying on the cross. What did He merit on the cross for us? Grace. Through grace our sins can be forgiven.

Our Saviour willed that men should obtain the forgiveness of their sins through the apostles. Therefore He breathed on them, and what did He say to them? Whom did Jesus breathe into the apostles? What words did Jesus add? "Whose sins (the sins of those men whom) you shall forgive," etc.

What does Charles' father empower his mother to do, if Charles comes to her and tells her he is sorry for having disobeyed father? What power did his father give to his mother? In whose place, then, does his mother forgive him? In this case the mother's forgiveness is just as good as if his father had himself forgiven him. When our Saviour said to the apostles: "Whose sins you shall forgive, they are forgiven them"; He gave them a power, that is, the power to forgive sins in His place. Wherefore, when the apostles said to some one: "Your sins are forgiven you," they were as truly forgiven, as if our Saviour Himself had said it to him.

What did Jesus say to the paralytic, when He forgave him his sins? And what happened, when Jesus had said this? The apostles could do the very same thing, after Jesus had said to them: "Whose sins," etc. By these words He gave the apostles the power to forgive sins. In whose place did the apostles forgive sins? The apostles forgave sins in the place of God.

Our Saviour empowered the apostles to retain sins. Our Saviour did not merely say to the apostles, " whose sins you shall forgive shall be forgiven them," but he also added: " And whose sins you shall retain, they are retained."

Now suppose that Bertha and her brother Francis have each badly burnt one of their hands. The physician wishes to put a poultice on their hands, which at first will cause them pain. Bertha submits and her hand soon gets healed. But Francis, feeling pain, tears off the plaster from his hand. The doctor puts it on again. But Francis at once pulls it off again. Then the doctor says to him: " You can keep your sore hand "; and then the doctor departs. Whose hand has the doctor rid of its soreness? Bertha's. And to whose hand did he leave its soreness?

The same applies to sins. When the apostles said to some one: " Thy sins are retained," what was the effect of these words? Therefore to retain sins means not to take them away, not to forgive them. What power did our Saviour give His apostles, when He said: " Whose sins you shall retain, they are retained "? When the apostles retained the sins of some one, his sins were not forgiven. What the apostles would not forgive, God would not forgive either.

When did Jesus give to His apostles the power of forgiving and retaining men's sins? After His resurrection. How did He give them that power? He breathed on them and said, etc. When our Saviour did and said this, He instituted the sacrament of penance. On what day was that?

Priests also can forgive sins. What power did our Saviour give His apostles at the Last Supper? To whom was this power transmitted? When do bishops and priests exercise this power? In like manner the power of for- giving and retaining men's sins has been transmitted from the apostles to bishops and priests. But they cannot do this in their own name. But in whose place have they this power? In which sacrament do they exercise this power? What, then, is the sacrament of penance? It is a sacrament in which the priest in the place of God forgives sins.

All sins can be forgiven. You have already received a sacrament in which a sin was forgiven you. Which sacra- ment is it? Which sin was forgiven in the sacrament of baptism? What other sins besides does baptism forgive a grown person? But if, after baptism, a person commits a mortal sin, that person cannot have it forgiven by baptism, for baptism can be administered not more than once. And yet a man's mortal sins committed after baptism must be forgiven to enable him to keep out of hell. Wherefore our Saviour instituted another sacrament to forgive the sins committed after baptism. Which sacrament is it? What sins are forgiven by the sacrament of penance? The sins committed after baptism.

Who was it that believed his sins were so great, that God would not forgive him? Cain. Judas also believed that his sin was so great that God would not forgive him. But that is not true. Our Saviour forgave the sins of the par- alytic, of St. Peter, of the robber and murderer on the cross. Cain and Judas could also have obtained the for- giveness of theirs. God is goodness itself, and is willing to forgive. He forgives all sins, even the most grievous. Which sins are forgiven in the sacrament of baptism? Which sins can be forgiven in the sacrament of penance?

In the sacrament of penance the eternal punishment is remitted. What punishment does mortal sin draw upon the sinner? The endless punishment of hell. What punishment does venial sin draw upon the sinner? A temporal punishment either in this world or in purgatory. What did our Saviour remit to the paralytic together with his sins? In like manner, in the sacrament of penance the endless punishment of hell is remitted together with the sins.

In the sacrament of penance at least a part of the temporal punishment is remitted with the sins. What punishment still remained to the paralytic after our Saviour had remitted his sins and their endless punishment? The temporal punishment. What did our Saviour do also with the temporal punishment due to the paralytic? He remitted it also. In like manner, in the sacrament of penance the temporal punishment is remitted, but not always all of it. But a part of the temporal punishment is always remitted in the sacrament of penance.

In the sacrament of penance there is imparted grace and the childship of God. What was imparted to the soul of the paralytic when Jesus forgave his sins? The garment of sanctifying grace. Whose child did he then become? And where could he later on go? The same thing happens to the sinner in the sacrament of penance. In it sanctifying grace is imparted to his soul, he becomes a child of God, and has the right to go to heaven. What is remitted to the sinner in the sacrament of penance? 1, 2, 3. What does he receive in his soul? What does he become? Where has he the right to go after his death?

We must be sorry for our sins. But not all receive these great graces in the sacrament of penance. The priest has not only the power to remit sins, but also the power to retain them. Why did our Saviour remit the sins of the paralytic? Because he was sorry for them. What would our Saviour have done, if the paralytic had not been sorry for his sins? He would not have remitted them, but He would have retained them. The priest acts in like manner in the sacrament of penance. Whose sins does he retain? Whose sins does he forgive? Only the sins of those who are sorry for them.

We must confess our sins. The priest must know our sins before he can forgive them. He cannot see the heart of the sinner. Therefore what must we do, that the priest may know our sins? We must tell them, confess them. To whom must we confess our sins? And where must we confess them? Thus did our Lord command when He instituted the sacrament of penance. What must we do to have our sins forgiven in the sacrament of penance? We must confess our sins. Why must we confess our sins in order to obtain their forgiveness? Because Jesus commanded this, when He instituted the sacrament of penance.

SUMMARY. What must the sinner do to obtain the forgiveness of his sins from the priest? He must be sorry for them and confess them. In which sacrament does the priest forgive sins? In whose place does he do this? What, then, is the sacrament of penance? It is the sacrament in which the priest, holding God's place, forgives sins, if the sinner is truly sorry for them and sincerely confesses them and has the will to make satisfaction for them. (N. B. This will be explained later on.) When did Christ confer the power to forgive sins? After His resurrection when He breathed on His apostles, and said: " Receive ye the Holy Ghost. Whose sins," etc. Can all sins be forgiven? Yes, all sins committed after baptism can be forgiven. Why must we confess our sins to obtain their forgiveness? Because Christ so ordered it when He instituted the sacrament of penance.

APPLICATION. 1. Suppose that you would now make your first confession. You enter the church. There are two confessionals. In one the priest sits, and in the other St. Peter. Now which of them can better forgive sins?

The one can do it as well as the other.   Now suppose there was a third confessional, in which Jesus Christ Himself is seated.   Which of the three can best forgive sins?   Why can Jesus Christ forgive sins?   Because He is God.   Why can the apostles forgive sins?   Why can bishops do so? Why can priests do so?   Because Jesus gave them the power.   When did Christ breathe on them to give them this power?   What is the Holy Ghost?   What is Christ also? Who forgives sins through the apostles, the bishops and priests?   Who then can alone forgive sins?

2. Can your father or mother forgive sins?   Can an angel forgive sins?   Why can they not do so?   From whom has the priest the power to forgive sins?   From whom has the bishop that power?   From whom have all the bishops that power?   From whom have the apostles? Which sacrament do they administer in forgiving sins?

3. How badly off would men be, if Christ had not instituted the sacrament of penance?   Nearly all men fall into sin after their baptism, and how many of them would be cast into hell!   Also all of you have already committed sin.   Perhaps there is one among you who has already committed a mortal sin.   How you should then thank God for instituting the sacrament of penance, by which your sins can be forgiven.   Say with me: " My dear Jesus, I thank Thee from my heart for having instituted the sacrament of penance for us poor sinners."   Rejoice at the thought that you shall soon be admitted to go to confession.

9. The Examination of Conscience.

1. PREPARATION — *Conscience*.   Which   commandment did God give to our first parents?   Did they keep this commandment?   What did they commit by breaking it? After this they were afraid of God.   How do you know this?   And how do you know it also from the words of Adam?   The hearts of the first men beat out of fear.   A

voice in their heart said to them: "Alas! what have you done? You disobeyed God." This voice in their hearts was their conscience.

When Cain had killed his brother, he also heard a voice. What did that voice say to him? You are a murderer. What voice was that? In like manner, every man has a conscience that tells, or reproaches him, when he has done evil. You conscience, like that of Cain, tells you when you have committed any evil. How does it speak to you? This happens every time you do anything bad. If you would go to confession on the same day, you would remember that sin very easily. But some days later your conscience could not so easily tell you your sin immediately. Why? You would have forgotten it. And how would it be, if you had committed many sins, and had to confess only a long time after? Children know their catechism well at home after studying it. But when they have to recite it the next day in school, many do not know it any more. What must you do to remember it? Reflect a little on it.

Object. I will now tell you what you have to do to remember your sins.

2. Development — *Reflect.* What reproaches you every time you commit a sin? The conscience. Whom must you ask when you wish to know again your sins? Conscience. But it may happen that your conscience will not immediately tell you all your sins. Why? Because we have forgotten them. What must you do to remember the catechism lesson which you have forgotten? Try to call it to mind. What must you do to cause your conscience to tell you your sins again? Call them to mind, or reflect. But perhaps your conscience will not be able to tell you your sins again. For it no longer knows them all. Who could tell a child many of the sins he committed at home? Father and mother. Who, then, can help a child to find out his sins? But his parents could not tell them all to him. Why not? Who could tell a child many of the sins he com-

mitted in school? But not all. Why not? *Because he does not know all.*

The Holy Ghost has to help. Who knows all things? Who knows also all the sins, which a child's conscience reproached him with? God. Who can then tell a child all the sins he committed? God has, then, to help you to find out all your sins. Now what must we do, if we wish to have something from God? Pray. Wherefore, if you wish God to help you to find out your sins, you must pray to God. And, indeed, you must pray to the Holy Ghost to enlighten you, that you may find out all your sins. For this repeat this little prayer: " O God the Holy Ghost, deign to give me light, love and sorrow, that I may find out and detest my sins, in order to confess them sincerely. O Blessed Virgin Mary, help me to make a good confession. My dear Guardian Angel, help me to call to mind all my sins." (Rehearse.)

Seeking stains on one's dress. For what do we pray the Holy Ghost to help us? To find out our sins. Now suppose that Bertha wore her fine white dress for the first time in the Corpus Christi procession. In the afternoon she played with other children, and ran against a wagon; her fine dress was torn and covered with black spots. She saw it at once, and began to cry, saying: " Oh, my beautiful white dress! " But soon she forgot all about it, for she was too busy playing, and her dress got a few more black spots. After this she became reckless, and no longer cared if her dress became all covered with black spots. But when she came home, her mother saw the big black spot and the hole in the dress. Her mother said: " Oh, what a big black spot on your dress! How did that happen? " Bertha knew it yet.

Making light. Now her mother wishes to see if there is anything else the matter with the dress. But it was already dark. What does she do? She lights a lamp, and sees more black spots. She asks Bertha: " Where do all those other spots come from?" But Bertha did not know about all of them.

The serious examination. Now Bertha's mother examined the dress all over, carefully and minutely, till she found every spot on the dress. How did Bertha's mother examine the dress?

The stained garment of the soul. We have all received in baptism a much more beautiful dress for our soul than Bertha's fine white dress. Which dress, or garment, do I mean? The white garment of sanctifying grace. Oh, how beautiful was your soul in that splendid garment! The angels gazed at it with love and amazement. And the heavenly Father Himself, full of joy over it, said to the angels: "See, that is My beloved child, in whom I am well pleased."

What happens to the soul's splendid garment through mortal sin? And at once the soul's splendor is gone, and its garment is torn. And every time another mortal sin is committed, a fresh stain is added and a fresh hole is made. And thus is the soul's garment entirely soiled and torn. The soul has lost its splendor and it has become dark and gloomy.

The invocation of the Holy Ghost in order to obtain light for the mind. Now you have to find out your sins in the dark and gloomy soul. What must it first become, that you may see everything clearly? It must become light. What did Bertha's mother do in order to be able to see in the dark room? But we cannot make light in our soul in the usual way. Wherefore we pray to the Holy Ghost to enlighten our soul, saying: "O Holy Ghost, deign to enlighten me that I may find out all my sins."

Enlightening our mind. After praying for light to the Holy Ghost, He will give us light to see into our soul and find out our sins. What then can we see? The spots and holes in the garment of our soul.

Serious reflection. Which spot did Bertha's mother first

notice on her dress? In like manner, we find out the biggest spots more easily in our soul. How had Bertha's mother to examine her dress to find out all the spots in her dress? Seriously and carefully. We must seriously and carefully seek the spots in our soul, and we shall then know all our sins.

The examination of conscience. What told you immediately each time that the garment of your soul was torn or soiled? Conscience. Whom should we then ask which sins have caused all those spots and rents (holes) in the garment of our soul? Our conscience. But our conscience cannot immediately tell us. What must we do to enable our conscience to tell us the sins we have committed? We must reflect over our sins, examine our conscience, and this carefully and seriously. Our conscience will then tell us. This is called the examination of conscience. What is the examination of conscience? To examine our conscience means to reflect earnestly on what sins we have committed. Who has to help us to examine our conscience? In what way is He to help us?

What should we do to obtain the help of the Holy Ghost? Invoke Him, when we are beginning the examination of our conscience. How then should we begin the examination of our conscience? By invoking the Holy Ghost. What is it that we cannot do without the light of His grace? Without the light of His grace we cannot rightly know our sins.

The heart must be moved to be rightly sorry for sin. The paralytic first properly acknowledged his sins, when Jesus cast on him His gracious look. This kind, sorrowful look of Jesus deeply penetrated the soul of the paralytic. He then felt how hateful and ugly sin is, and how greatly it offends God. Thus his heart was entirely moved. It seemed to him as if a sharp instrument had deeply pierced his heart and made a deep wound in it. Oh, how it burnt him and pained him! What did he then feel in his heart? Sorrow, grief and contrition. For what? What did our

Saviour then do, since He saw him so sorry for his sins?

If you wish to obtain the forgiveness of your sins, it is not enough for you to know your sins, but you must also, like the paralytic, reflect how grievously you have offended God, and how ugly your sin has made your soul. What will you then feel in your heart for your sins? Contrition. That you may feel it, you need the help of the Holy Ghost. Therefore say to Him: "O Holy Ghost, deign to move my heart, that I may be duly sorry for my sins."

The heart moved to make a sincere confession. When a child has real contrition for his sins, he is fit to make his confession. But many children are greatly afraid of confession. They need the help of the Holy Ghost that confession may not be too difficult for them. Therefore they should pray: "O Holy Ghost, move my heart that I may sincerely confess my sins."

The heart should be moved to amend. If a child wishes God to forgive his sins, he must do one thing more. He must, like the paralytic, be resolved nevermore to commit sin, and to become better and more devout, and to amend. For this he needs again the help of the Holy Ghost. Therefore he should say: "O Holy Ghost, move my heart, that I really amend my life." For which things do we need help of the Holy Ghost? 1   ., 2   ., 3   4   . What is it that we cannot do without the grace of the Holy Ghost? 1, Know our sins; 2, be duly sorry for them; 3, confess them sincerely; and 4, amend our life, that is, do better in the future. If we would fail in these matters, we could not have our sins forgiven, and our soul would remain sick or spiritually dead. And where is a soul defiled by a mortal sin unable to go? To heaven. Such a soul cannot obtain salvation.

3. Summary. We should begin the examination of our conscience by invoking the Holy Ghost, for without His grace we can neither know our sins, nor be sorry for them,

nor confess them properly as is necessary for our salvation. How should we invoke the Holy Ghost? "Come, O Holy Ghost, enlighten my mind, that I may know my sins well, move my heart, that I may be duly sorry for them, sincerely confess them, and really amend my life." To examine our conscience means to reflect on what sins we have committed.

4. APPLICATION. You should from now daily recite an Our Father to the Holy Ghost, that He may teach you how to make a good confession. Do this after your night prayers. You can say each time: "I will now say one Our Father to the Holy Ghost, that He may help me to make a good confession."

What should you do daily? When is the best time to do it? What should you say each time before the Our Father? Begin this very evening. I will, in a few days, ask you whether you have done it.

10. A practical Examination of Conscience.

PREPARATION. After invoking the Holy Ghost you should begin by reflecting on your sins. Wherefrom have you learned about the sins that we can commit? From the commandments of God. From which other commandments, or precepts? And you have learned also about seven other sins. Which are they? The seven capital sins. In how many ways are sins committed? In thought, word and deed, and omission.

I.

OBJECT. Let us enumerate the sins which we have learned against the commandments of God.

1. Which is the first commandment of God? Of what are we reminded by the first commandment? Of prayer. Which sins can we commit with regard to prayer? He sins, first, who does not say or omits to pray every day, for

it is an omission of what we are bound to do. Secondly, he sins who does not pray devoutly.

2. Which is the second commandment of God? Of what are we reminded by the second commandment? Of the name of God. Which sins in word can be committed with regard to the name of God? He sins against the holy name of God, first, who pronounces it without respect; secondly, he who curses; thirdly, he who swears without necessity.

3. Which is the third commandment of God? Of what are we reminded by the third commandment? Of Sunday. What good action are we obliged to perform on Sunday? What kind of sin can be committed by omitting the good action commanded on Sunday? When we by our own fault omit to hear Mass. What sins can be committed in the church? By irreverence in church.

4. Which is the fourth commandment of God? On what do we think with regard to the fourth commandment? Of parents and superiors. How can sins be committed against parents and superiors? First, he who behaves disrespectfully or insolently towards them. Secondly, he who pains or angers them. Thirdly, he who obeys them badly or disobeys them.

5. Which is the fifth commandment of God? Of what are we reminded by the fifth commandment? Of our neighbor. How can we sin against the body of our neighbor? First, in words by insulting or mocking him. Secondly, in actions by striking him. How can we sin against the soul of our neighbor? By leading him to sin.

6 and 9. Which is the sixth commandment of God? Of what are we reminded by the sixth commandment? Of the vice of impurity. How are sins committed through impurity? He commits such a sin who wilfully thinks on impure things; also he who talks of impure things, and he who wilfully looks on impure things, or listens to impure talk, or who does impure actions.

7 and 10. Which is the seventh commandment of God? Of what are we reminded by the seventh commandment? Of what belongs to our neighbor. How are sins committed in reference to our neighbor's goods? In actions; by pilfering; stealing money at home; stealing things belonging to others; keeping articles found; injuring or destroying the goods of others. Also in thought, by the intention or attempt to steal.

8. Which is the eighth commandment of God? Of what does the eighth commandment remind us? Of lying. In what can sins be committed against the eighth commandment? In words by telling lies, by detraction, by slander. In works by hypocrisy.

Let us now enumerate the sins against the commandments (precepts) of the Church. We have already enumerated the sins against the first commandment of the Church in the third commandment of God. The second commandment of the Church requires us to keep the days of abstinence. Which are they? How can we sin against this commandment of the Church? By wilfully and without necessity eating meat on Fridays and other abstinence days. He who is over seven years of age and does not go to confession at least once a year, sins against the third commandment of the Church. (Attention may be called also to the Easter Communion in as far as the Decree *Quam singulari* of Pope Pius X renders it obligatory on children who have attained the use of reason.)

Which are the capital sins? How can we sin thereby? 1, By being proud; 2, covetous; 3, envious, rejoicing at the misfortunes of our neighbor; 4, excess in eating and drinking; 5, anger; 6, sloth. Nothing more to be said about impurity. Why?

II.

(N. B. All that is here included in brackets may, if necessary, be omitted.— This whole division II is not absolutely necessary. But if it can be given to the children, the time and care devoted to it will surely produce good fruit. Here the children are individually furnished with practical directions how to make a full confession. This will overcome the tendency for making mechanical confessions. It is a difficult matter for children, even of the highest classes to find out the *mean* or average number. In their first confession only highly talented and conscientious children are able to do it correctly. The object of this practical training is to correct this *quasi* abuse.

(The first commandment should be circumstantially treated and also take up some time in the confessional. If the daily prayers are summarily treated, the children have no clear perception of what they should confess. Moreover, the omission of the daily prayers is not always sinful. Nevertheless they are made prominent in all the lists of sins given for the examination of conscience. The reason for this is that the conscience may be impressed with the usefulness and advantages of regular prayer, because everything depends on fervent prayer. This object cannot be obtained by requiring merely a summary examination of conscience on the daily prayers. Although, in reality, the young children who are admitted to make their first confession, do not easily fall into a mortal sin, they must be taught, however, in which cases certain sins are mortal, so that they may confess them as mortal sins in such cases. To judge about the grievousness of the penitent's sin belongs to the confessor.)

Not every child, of course, commits all the sins we have enumerated.

OBJECT. I will now show how each child should act, in order to find out his sins.

DEVELOPMENT. If you wish to know how you look, you have only to look into a mirror. And if you have spots or stains in your face, you will see them. When you wish to see how your soul looks, you have only to examine the list of sins contained in the commandments of God and of the Church, and the seven capital sins, and to examine one after the other.

1. *You must begin with the first commandment of God and ask your conscience:* Did I always say my daily prayers? Which are the daily prayers? When your conscience answers, yes, you know that for this question your soul has no stain; and then you have nothing to say about this in confession. But if your conscience says, no, then you know that you did not always say your daily prayers. Next you must ask: How many times I did not say my morning prayers every week? If you have not said your morning prayers in a week, how many times have you omitted them?

We say the morning prayers in school on every school day, that is, every day in the week except Saturday and Sunday. Therefore, how many times every week have you omitted your morning prayers? How many times in a month? Eight times. But perhaps your conscience tells you: I omitted my morning prayers on two Saturdays. Then you must continue to reflect and ask yourself: Did I omit my morning prayers twice a month all the time since I knew I had to say morning prayers? If you think that there was one month in which you omitted them three times, and again another month, in which you omitted them only once, you should not say in your confession: I omitted the morning prayers twice in one month, three times in another month, and once in another month. That would make your confession too long. But you should prepare yourself to make your confession in this way: I omitted my morning prayers once or twice every month.

There is also the time of vacation, when there is no school. Some children often forget to say their morning prayers during vacation. You should then reflect how many times a week during vacation you did not say your morning prayers. When your conscience tells you: I have omitted my morning prayers in one week twice, in another four or five times, and in the last weeks of vacation, I did not say any. You must then prepare yourself to confess in this way: During vacation I omitted my morning prayers every week from two to five times, and some weeks I did not say any.

What then have you to observe concerning your morning prayers in confession? First, during the time when there was school. During that time I omitted my morning prayers one to three times a month. Secondly, during vacation I omitted my morning prayers every week from three to five times, and some weeks I did not say them at all.

You say your night prayers at home. In many families the mother says night prayers with the children. The children can easily remember if there were any evenings when their mother did not say night prayers with them, and then if, in such cases they said their night prayers alone. If your mother sometimes did not say night prayers with you, and you did not then say your night prayers alone, you should reflect how often did that happen in a month. If you find out that in one month you omitted them twice, and three times in another month, how must you be prepared to confess this? I omitted my night prayers about two or three times a month.

But where the mother very seldom or never says night prayers with the children, it can easily happen that the children forget to say their night prayers almost every evening. When your conscience tells you that you almost never said your night prayers, you must prepare to say in confession: I almost never said my night prayers. But if your conscience tells you that you never said night prayers, you must prepare to say in confession: I never said my night prayers.

Which other prayers, besides morning and night prayers, belong to the daily prayers? The Angelus and the prayers before and after meals. How often is the Angelus said every day? Three times. In the morning it is always said in school. When the Angelus bell rings in the morning, you are asleep and do not hear it. But on Saturdays and Sundays and during vacation you are not in the school. Where then should you recite the Angelus? In many families the children recite the Angelus with their morning prayers. But you omitted your prayers one morning. Which prayer did you also omit? You then omit the Angelus also when you omit your morning prayers. In other families, in which the children do not say the Angelus with their morning prayers, they probably always omit the Angelus, since they are asleep when the Angelus bell rings.

At noon and in the evening you usually hear the Angelus bell ring. Which of you are then obliged to go home to say the Angelus aloud with the other members of the family? Those children always recite the Angelus. Those children who do not go home to recite the Angelus, should examine how many times a week they did not say the Angelus.

And when it is not customary in a family to recite the Angelus, those children know well that they have scarcely ever said the Angelus. What must those children be prepared to confess? I daily twice omitted saying the Angelus. And how often on Saturdays and Sundays and during vacation?

You should also pray before and after your meals. The same happens in this as in the Angelus. In those families in which before and after meals all rise and say together the prayers before and after meals, the children always say those prayers. And in those families that do not pray in common before and after meals, the children always omit them. And what must those children tell about those prayers in confession?

SUMMARY. On what prayers should you examine your conscience for the Sundays in vacation? On the morning prayers and the Angelus in the morning. Which children can know of themselves, if they have almost always said the Angelus at noon and in the evening, and the prayers at meals and the night prayers? Those children belonging to the families that recite these prayers in common. And which children easily know that they have not said the Angelus at noon and in the evening, the prayers at meals and the night prayers? Those children belonging to the families that scarcely ever say these prayers in common. Such children can easily find out the sins they committed by omitting the prayers at meals, the Angelus and the night prayers. What does their conscience tell them about this? I have almost always omitted the Angelus, the prayers at meals and night prayers.

But it is not enough to recite prayers, for we can pray and yet commit a sin at prayer. Who knows how this is done? Children who are fond of prayer, usually pray devoutly. But it may sometimes happen that they think on other things while they are saying their prayers. They should, in this case, prepare to confess this, saying: I have sometimes prayed without attention. The children who are not fond of prayer, usually pray without attention. How should they prepare to confess this? I have often prayed without attention.

APPLICATION. Resolve from this moment nevermore to omit your prayers, and always to pray with attention. You surely all wish to go to heaven. But he who wishes to go to heaven, must pray well, for in heaven prayer is continual. He who does not pray, shall never go to heaven.

2. *The second commandment is:* Thou shalt not take the name of the Lord thy God in vain. In examining your conscience on the second commandment you must ask yourself: Have I used the name of God, or of holy things without reverence? Some children are accustomed to use the word God, Lord, Jesus Christ, etc., without due respect; sometimes they do so ten, or twenty times a day.

Children should ask their conscience: Have I the habit of using with levity, irreverently, the name of God, etc.? If your conscience answers, yes, you must reflect and try to find out about how many times you do this every day. Suppose your conscience tells you, ten times a day. How many fresh stains are there every day on your soul? What, then, must you prepare to say in confession? I have the habit of pronouncing irreverently (with levity) the holy name about ten times every day. Some children have not this bad habit. Nevertheless, they should ask their conscience: How often do I daily pronounce the holy name with levity? If their conscience tells them, once or twice a day, what must they prepare to confess? If your conscience says, Not every day; then ask further: How many times a week? Suppose your conscience replies: Three times a week, what should you prepare to confess?

But cursing is far worse than pronouncing the holy name irreverently. Children, who hear cursing at home, easily acquire the habit of cursing. In examining your conscience ask yourself if there is much cursing done at home. And then ask your conscience: Have I already the habit of cursing? If your conscience says, yes, then ask yourself: How many times do I curse every day? Suppose your conscience answers: About three or four times. How many fresh stains are there every day on your soul? What must you then prepare to confess?

Where there is no cursing or only a little cursing at home, the children do not easily curse. But it might happen that such children cursed a few times. Now what must such a child ask his conscience? Have I cursed? If his conscience says, no, that child's conscience has no stain of cursing on it. But perhaps he remembers having cursed during his life once or twice. How must he prepare to confess it?

On what other sin against the second commandment must

children examine their conscience? Unnecessary swearing. Children do not so easily fall into this sin. Nevertheless, you should ask yourself if you did not swear once or twice, when perhaps a companion would not believe what you said. And if you then swore, you must prepare to confess it.

SUMMARY. On which three sins against the second commandment must you examine your conscience? How can a child know beforehand if he often pronounced the holy name with levity and often cursed?

APPLICATION. Be careful to find out whether you have the habit of pronouncing the holy name with levity or of cursing. Perhaps you have, and do not know it. And if you catch yourself pronouncing again the holy name with levity, or even cursing, say in your heart: "O dear Lord, forgive me. Hallowed be Thy name." And each time resolve: "I will never curse any more."

3. Which is the next commandment? The third. Which sins are committed against the third commandment? Feast days or Holydays of obligation must be kept like the Sundays. What must you now ask your conscience? Have I through my own fault missed Mass on Sundays and Holydays? Have I behaved irreverently in church?

The children who always say their morning and night prayers, and especially who are fond of praying, like also to go to church. The children whose parents always send them to Mass, will not easily miss Mass through their own fault. Nevertheless, they should ask themselves, if perhaps it happened once or twice that they missed Mass. The children, who are not fond of prayer, and whose parents do not send them to Mass, more easily miss Mass. How often does that child miss Mass in a month, who never goes to Mass? Four times.

Therefore ask yourselves: Have I missed Mass every month? If your conscience answers, yes, ask again: How many times every month? And then you must prepare to confess the number of times you missed Mass every month. But if your conscience tells you that you did not miss Mass every month, you must try and find out about how many times in a year. Remember the number of times for your confession.

But even those can commit sin who go to Mass. How? Those children who bring along their prayer-book and read the Mass prayers in it, or who look at and follow the priest at the altar, behave reverently. Yet they ought to ask themselves, if they did not now and then talk or look around during Mass; and if they did, they should remember how many times, that they may confess it. Those children who bring no prayer-book to church, or who do not use it during Mass, are usually irreverent in church. Also the same can be said of those children who try to be always near each other in church, for they do this in order to cut up or misbehave. These children must ask themselves: How often have I (daily) misbehaved in church? Did I disturb others thereby? If your conscience tells you that you did so (daily) five or ten times, or almost all the time, you must remember to confess: I have (daily) misbehaved in church five, ten times, or nearly all the time, and I sometimes also disturbed others.

SUMMARY. Which children easily know that they never or almost never missed Mass? Which children also easily know that they have often missed Mass? Which children know that they seldom misbehaved in church? Which children know that they often or nearly always misbehave in church?

APPLICATION. Resolve from now to behave as piously and devoutly in church as St. Stanislaus.

4. Which is the next commandment? How do children sin against their parents and superiors? What must you now ask your conscience? The conscience of many children tells them, yes, to every question. These children must further ask themselves, how many times every day,

and if not every day, how many times every week, and they should prepare to confess the number of times they have committed each sin.

The conscience of some children does not say, yes, to each of the three questions. There are many children who are not impertinent towards their parents. They have no stains of this sin on their soul, and therefore have no sin of this kind to confess. Most of the sins of children against their parents and superiors are not mortal sins. But if a child has been very impertinent and stubborn towards them, or greatly grieved or angered them, or been very disobedient towards them, his sin is much greater. That is a circumstance which makes the sin, not a venial sin, but a mortal sin. Such a child must, therefore, ask himself how many times he was very impertinent and stubborn, very disobedient, and prepare to confess it: I have been very impertinent, stubborn, disobedient; and say how many times.

APPLICATION. What holy Child was never disobedient to his parents? Try to imitate the Child Jesus, and always obey your parents promptly and cheerfully.

5. Which is the next commandment? By which sins is the fifth commandment transgressed (broken)? What questions should you ask yourselves about this commandment? It often happens that brothers and sisters scold, quarrel with and mock one another. This happens daily among unendurable children. It is also sinful to scold, quarrel with and mock other children. You must, then, ask your conscience: How often have I scolded, insulted, quarreled with and mocked other children? If you did not do it every day, then ask yourself: How often did I do it every week? Then remember the number of times, that you may tell it in confession.

Wicked children also insult and mock their parents, teachers, old people and even the priest. How do we also call the teachers, the priest? Superiors. What must such wicked children examine themselves about? Have I insulted and mocked my parents, my superiors, old people every month, or how many times?

If you have struck or beaten your brothers, your sisters or other children, you should ask yourself: How often have I struck my brothers, my sisters, other children, every day, every week, or every month?

Which is the third sin against the fifth commandment? Into which sins can wicked children lead other children? To missing Mass, disobedience, impurity, stealing and lying. When a child leads another child to disobey, to tell lies, to steal little things, that is a venial sin. But when a child leads another to miss Mass on Sundays, to a sin of impurity, or to steal something valuable, it is a thing that makes the sin greater. How do we call such a thing? A circumstance. In such a case the child that led another into the sin, commits not a venial sin, but a mortal sin. What kind of sin did he commit, who led that child into that sin?

You should now ask yourself: Have I led another child into sin? If your conscience tells you that you have led another child into a mortal sin, you must also remember into what kind of sin you led that child. If you led him only into venial sins, you need only ask yourself how often you did it every week, or every month, and be prepared to confess it.

SUMMARY. On which three sins against the fifth commandment should you examine your conscience? What must you ask yourself besides about those sins? And why should you ask yourself this? Because those sins are no longer venial, but mortal sins. How do we call that which makes a sin greater or worse?

APPLICATION. How beautiful it is, if children are patient and kind with one another, and are like guardian angels to one another!

6 and 9. We now come to the sixth and ninth command-

ments. Which are the sins against the sixth and ninth
commandments? Which word expresses what is a sin
against these commandments? When is it sinful to think,
see, hear, speak and do what is in any way impure? How
should you ask your conscience concerning the sixth commandment? The conscience of some children will always
answer, no. The soul of these children is not stained
by any sin against the sixth commandment, and they have
nothing to confess about this matter.

The conscience of some other children tells them, yes,
concerning thoughts, looks, words and listening. These
children must ask themselves: How often every day, or
every week did I think on impure things, or look at, or
listen to, or speak of impure things? The number of
times your conscience answers, must be told in confession.
You should ask yourself: Did I do anything impure?
If your conscience answers, yes, you must ask yourself:
Did I do it alone, or with some one else, and how many
times did I do it every day, or every week, or in all? You
must be prepared to say in confession: I did something
impure alone, or I did something impure with another; and
tell how many times.

SUMMARY. About which sins against the sixth commandment should you ask yourself? What must you ask
also concerning impure actions?

APPLICATION. Hate and shun impurity. Oh, how beautiful is the virtue of purity in children! They are honored by God and by men.

7 and 10. Which is the next commandment? Let us add
to it the tenth also. Which are the sins against the seventh
and tenth commandments? What must you ask your conscience concerning the seventh commandment? Pilfering
is the sin of children. Some children pilfer every day, or
whenever they get a chance to do so. What must they ask
themselves? How often did I take little things every day?
The number of times should be told in confession. Some

children finding nothing to pilfer at home, steal money at home, in order to buy sweetmeats and trifles; some even pilfer, or steal money from other people. If what they stole at home or from others is valuable, their sin is greater. Such children must ask their conscience: Did I steal money at home? Have I stolen anything from other people? If their conscience says, yes, they should ask themselves: How often did I steal money at home, and how much was it? How often did I steal from other people, and what did I steal? The number of times must be told in confession.

You must not keep stolen things. What should be done with them? You must also make restitution, that is, restore what you have stolen. When must we also make restitution? When we have found something that was lost. You should ask yourself, whether you have still what you stole or found. If your conscience says, yes, you must tell it in confession.

Which are the other sins against the seventh commandment? Hence you should ask yourself: Did I not cause any damage to others? If your conscience says, yes, you should ask yourself: What damage did I cause, and how often did I cause it? If the damage is but trifling, you need only tell in confession: I caused a little damage to others; and tell how often you did so. But if you caused a great damage to others, you must tell in confession what the damage was, and how often you did it. What else must you do concerning the damage you caused? If you have not repaired the damage, or paid the worth of what you damaged, you must tell it in confession.

There is one sin more to be confessed. Which sin is it? I desired, or intended or attempted to steal. You must ask your conscience about that sin, and if it says, yes, you must confess it.

SUMMARY. About which sins against the seventh and tenth commandments must you ask your conscience? You must find out also the number of each sin. As to stealing, finding, causing damage you should find out two things more. What, how often, and whether I made restitution. Moreover, ask: Did I wish, intend or attempt to steal?

APPLICATION. Dear children do not accustom yourselves to pilfer, for those who never do so at home, will not do so either from their neighbor. Consider your neighbor's goods as sacred, after the example of St. Paschal.

8. Which is the next commandment? Which are the sins forbidden by the eighth commandment? What should you ask yourself about this commandment? Some children have accustomed themselves to tell lies. They can hardly speak without telling a lie. And when their parents or their teachers ask them: Why did you not go to church; why did you not learn your lesson; why did you not do that work? They say: "I had pains in the stomach; I had headache; I had toothache; I had no time; my mother was sick," etc. And all these excuses are lies. You should then ask your conscience: Have I the habit of telling lies? How many lies do I tell every day or every week, or every month? You must tell in confession what your conscience answers you.

Which are the other sins against the eighth commandment? Hypocrisy, detraction or backbiting, and slander. You should then ask your conscience: How many times a week, or a month, have I played the hypocrite? How often have I been guilty of backbiting my neighbor? How often have I slandered my neighbor? You must tell in confession the number of times you committed each of these sins.

SUMMARY. About which sins against the eighth commandment must you examine your conscience? What else should you ask your conscience about lying?

APPLICATION. Never tell a lie! You are children of God. Liars are children of the devil!

THE COMMANDMENTS OF THE CHURCH. Which are the commandments of the Church? We need not now take the first commandment of the Church, for we have done so together with the third commandment of God. Which is the second commandment of the Church? To keep the days of abstinence. Which day is especially a day on which flesh-meat is forbidden? Friday. How many Fridays in a week? in a month? How often in a month can this commandment be broken? You should ask your conscience: Did I eat meat on Fridays and other forbidden days? If your conscience says, no, your conscience is not stained with that sin, and you have nothing to confess about it. But if your conscience says, yes, you must ask further: How many times did I eat meat on forbidden days? And then you have to tell in confession: I ate meat on forbidden days (number of) times. (N. B. He who eats meat twice or three times on a forbidden day, commits a sin each time.)

APPLICATION. Why is meat forbidden on Fridays? To remind us of the suffering and death of our Saviour Jesus Christ. For His sake we should deny ourselves some satisfaction.

THE SEVEN CAPITAL SINS. Which are the capital sins? What should you ask your conscience about these sins? If your conscience tells you that you were guilty of pride or covetousness, you should ask yourself: How many times a week have I been proud, have I been covetous or miserly? You must then tell it in your confession.

Envy is a sin easily committed by children. They are usually jealous of the fine dresses, of the fine playthings, etc., of other children. Brothers and sisters are usually jealous of one another for getting more sweetmeats, or for being better liked, or more smart. If your conscience tells you that you were envious or jealous of others, you should ask: How often every day, or every week, was I jealous or envious of others? You should tell it then in confession. Jealous children are apt to be glad when others have to suffer some loss, or undergo some punishment. This also is a matter for examination and confession.

Intemperance in eating and drinking is not very common among children. You should, however, ask: Have I sometimes eaten too much? If so, how often? Did it make me sick?

Anger is a sin very common among children. You must ask yourself: How often did I get angry every day, or every week, or every month? How often did I make others angry? You must tell all in confession.

Some children are slothful, or lazy in studying, others are so at work; and others do not wish to study or to work. Ask yourself: How often was I lazy every day, or every week, and tell it in confession.

If any of you committed some sin, which we have not enumerated, you should tell it in your confession.

SUMMARY. Which commandments should you examine by turns to find out the sins you committed? The commandments of God and of the Church. And which sins should you also examine? The seven capital sins.

III.

The table of sins. Where do you look to find out the spots in your face? How does the soul become stained? Where are the sins enumerated, which children commit in thoughts, words and actions? We have placed them together in a long list. You must examine this list in order to find out your sins. And whom must you ask what sins you have committed in thought, word, action and omission? In which way can you examine your conscience? We can examine our conscience by going through the commandments of God and of His Church and the seven capital sins, and asking ourselves how we have done wrong in thought, word, action and omission. And then look at yourself through the list of sins, as you would look at yourself in a looking-glass (mirror), to find out whether you have committed any of those sins, whether your soul is stained by any of them. The list of sins is like a mirror which shows us the stains of sins in our soul. And why should you look for your sins in that mirror? Therefore, it is called a list, or table, or mirror of sins.

What do you look for in the list of sins? For our sins. What must you also seek concerning each kind of your sins? Their number. The number is not put down on that list. How do you find their number? By examining ourselves. It is well, and I like it, if every child tries to find out the number of his sins. Concerning venial sins the number is not so important. But with regard to mortal sins, each of you must carefully try to find out their number.

Circumstance. With regard to some sins, such as stealing and sins against your parents, it is not always enough to know their number. There are sometimes some things about these sins that make them much worse. What is it that makes a sin more grievous? The circumstance. There is sometimes such a circumstance about these sins. On what must you, then, examine yourself concerning those sins? On their circumstances. Why? Because such circumstances make them mortal sins. What must you first examine concerning your sins? Their number. Of which sins is it well to know their number? And what should you next examine concerning your sins? Their circumstances.

SUMMARY. Should you examine into the number and circumstances of your sins? Yes, at least of the mortal sins. In what way can you examine your conscience? By going through the list of sins forbidden by the commandments of God and the Church, and through the capital sins, and asking ourselves how we have sinned in thought, word, action and omission.

APPLICATION. You surely desire to have a heart free from sin and your soul clothed with the white garment of grace. Therefore, take great care to make your examination of conscience well. Some children are too light-minded in everything they do. All they care for is to get through with it. If such a child is not very earnest in making his examination of conscience, he can easily forget or pass over a mortal sin through his own fault. And then God would not forgive his sins. Therefore all the children, especially the light-minded, should resolve to be very earnest in examining their conscience. Therefore at your night prayers, when you come to the Our Father in honor of the Holy Ghost for a good confession, reflect: I will now say this Our Father to the Holy Ghost, that He may help me to examine my conscience carefully.

11. Idea of Contrition.

1. PREPARATION — *Sorrow.* You have all experienced sorrow. What things have given you pain, made you sorry? How do we know that children are in pain, or feel very sorry? When they weep. Children weep when scolded, when their parents punish them. What do they then feel? Sorrow, pain, grief. They then feel no headache, no pain in their arms, in their feet. Who knows where they feel pain or sorrow? In their heart, in their soul. At the death of their parents, children feel pain or grief in their soul, and this especially when they see them laid out in their coffin.

Horror. Surely none of you would like to remain alone all night in a room, where a corpse is laid out. And why? You are afraid; it disgusts you; it makes you shudder. Three days after a person's death his corpse begins to corrupt and to emit a disagreeable odor. Would you dare to lie in bed alongside such a corpse? That would disgust you, horrify you, and make you shudder still more. Yes, as soon as a corpse begins to corrupt, no one cares any more to look at it. Hence it disgusts us even to look at it.

Have you already heard people saying of some man:

"That man is really disgusting"? Of what kind of men is this said? Of one who is extremely harsh with his parents, who is a drunkard, and quarrelsome. People are disgusted with those who do very wicked things.

OBJECT. I will now relate to you what filled the apostle Peter with sorrow and disgust.

RELATION. On the night when Jesus was arrested all His apostles abandoned Him and fled. Only Peter and John followed Jesus into the court-yard of the highpriest. In the middle of the yard there was a fire where the high-priest's men and maid-servants warmed themselves, for it was chilly. Peter sat down among them to see what would be done to Jesus. A maid-servant asked him: "You were with Jesus of Nazareth?" Peter got frightened and said: "No; I do not know Him." The cock now crowed for the first time. A few moments later another maid-serv-ant said to him: "You also were one of the disciples of Jesus." Peter swore and said: "No, I am not; I do not know that man." About an hour later one of the men-servants said to Peter: "Yes, you are one of the disciples of Jesus." Peter again swore and cursed himself, saying he did not know the man. Whilst he was yet protesting, the cock crowed the second time. At that very moment, Jesus was led out of the court and passed in front of Peter. Jesus turned towards Peter and cast on him a very sad and sorrowful look. This look of Jesus was like a sword that pierced Peter through the heart and filled it with great sor-row. And Peter went out and wept bitterly. And the longer he reflected on his sin, the more ungrateful and wicked he appeared to himself. And he was filled with hatred and horror of himself.

CONSIDERATION — *Peter's sin.* How did the apostles be-have when Jesus was arrested? Which apostles followed Him? Jesus was dragged all the way by the soldiers and servants into the house of the highpriest. Where did the servants and soldiers remain? The night was chilly.

What had they done on account of this? Relate what happened in the court-yard, whilst Jesus was in the high-priest's house? How often did Peter deny Jesus? What did he reply to the first maid-servant? What sin did he commit thereby? Told a lie. What did he say to the second maid-servant? How many sins did he commit thereby? Mention them. He lied and swore falsely. What did he say to the man-servant? How many sins did he commit by his third denial? Mention them. He lied, swore falsely and cursed himself. How many sins in all did he commit in the court-yard? Which of these sins are the most grievous? False swearing and cursing one's self.

The grievousness of Peter's sins. What did Peter do to our Saviour by his sins? Our Saviour loved Peter very much, and bestowed many favors upon him. He had made Peter one of His apostles, and kept him with Him for three years. At the Last Supper He had given Himself as food to Peter. How it must have pained our Saviour deeply, when Peter said: "I do not know the man." Our Saviour showed this when He was led out in front of Peter. How did our Saviour show how deeply He was pained? He turned to Peter and looked at him. Oh, how painful and sad was that look! By this painful look Jesus meant to say: "O Peter, what hast thou done to Me? Did I deserve this of thee?"

Peter's sorrow. This look of our Saviour was a look of grace for Peter. Peter saw at once how ungrateful he had been towards the Saviour, and how fearfully he had offended Him by his denial. How did Peter feel our Saviour's look penetrating into his heart? Like the thrust of a sword, for it went through his heart, to its inmost depth. What does a man feel when he is cut with a knife? What kind of pain does that cause? And when the dagger goes as far as the heart? An exceedingly great pain, so much so, as to make one feel as if he were dying.

What did Peter feel when our Saviour's look went through his heart like a dagger, a sword? Pain. And how great was the pain that went through his heart to its inmost depth? An exceedingly great pain, a deathly pain. He felt as if some one had plunged a dagger into his heart and made a great wound in it. Oh, how the wound in his soul made him sorry! He felt as if he could die of pain and grief. Now he could no longer remain in the court-yard. What did he do, as he was going out? He wept. Behold the grown-up man, Peter, weeping and crying with sorrow and grief, outside the court-yard like a child. He weeps the whole night, and can find no consolation. Tears roll continuously down his cheeks. Oh, how bitter were his tears! Therefore we say: "Peter wept bitterly." And this thought was always in his mind: "Oh, what have I done? I have offended my Saviour. He loved me so much; He was always so kind to me. I should have loved Him with my whole heart; and I said: "I do not know Him. Oh, how it pains me for having done so, and how sorry I am for it. I could weep my eyes out for having done it. Oh, had I rather died than deny Him. Oh, how wicked have I been! O God, how could I do such a wicked thing! How ungrateful have I been! I should be unmercifully beaten for being so wicked. I do not deserve that the Saviour should look at me. I deserve to fall dead on the spot and to be cast into the very bottom of hell!"

Peter's disgust. How had our Saviour always treated Peter? How did Peter treat our Saviour? Ungratefully and wickedly. What do you feel in the presence of a wicked man? Disgust. Peter considers himself a very wicked man. And what did he consider that he did not deserve our Saviour should do to him? What did Peter think that men should do to him on account of his denial? He even thinks he deserves even worse than that. What should have been done to him on the spot, as he thinks? What were Peter's feelings about himself, because he had so wickedly and ungratefully offended our Saviour? Disgust. What did Peter feel, if we judge by his weeping? Sorrow. Where did Peter feel disgust and sorrow? In his heart, in his soul. Why did he feel in his soul disgust and sorrow? Because he had denied the Saviour, offended Him; because he had sinned; he was sorry for his sins. He who has sorrow and disgust for his sins, has contrition. What had Peter conceived for his sins? Contrition.

Contrition, the most necessary part of the sacrament of penance. Because Peter was sorry for his sins, our Saviour forgave him his sins. Who else had his sins forgiven by our Saviour? Why did Jesus forgive the sins of the paralytic? To whom did God first forgive their sin? What did Adam and Eve feel on account of their sin? God requires the same of all men. He who wishes God to forgive his sins, must be sorry for them. A confession without sorrow (contrition) is like an empty nutshell. What is an empty nutshell worth? Nothing. In like manner, a confession without contrition is worth nothing. God does not forgive the sins of him who has no contrition for them. Contrition is the most necessary part of the sacrament of penance.

For a true contrition we need God's grace. Peter at once was sorry for his sins. When did he begin to be sorry for his sins? When our Saviour looked at him. What kind of look did Jesus cast on him? This look of grace excited contrition in Peter's heart. On whom did Jesus cast also a similar look of grace? On the paralytic. What did it excite in the heart of the paralytic? Contrition. The same has to happen to every one who has sinned. No one can excite true contrition in himself. Indeed, it is not so very easy to have true contrition. No matter how hard you may try, you could never succeed by yourself in having true contrition. It is necessary that God should cast a look of grace into your heart, to enable you to have true contrition for your sins. True contrition is found only there where God has cast a look of grace. And where there is no true contrition, there is no forgiveness of sins.

What must we do to obtain the grace of God? To whom should we especially pray for this? To the Holy Ghost. How should you pray to Him to obtain true contrition for your sins? And the Holy Ghost will help you to awaken in your heart true contrition. The Holy Ghost helps us to awaken true contrition.

Summary. What does he feel in his heart, who has true contrition? Sorrow and disgust. For what? For the sins he has committed. Therefore contrition is a sorrow in the soul and a disgust for past sins. Contrition is the second part of the sacrament of penance. It is the most necessary part of the sacrament of penance. God does not forgive those who have no contrition for their sins. To awaken a true contrition we need the grace of God.

Application. 1. What must you have in your heart, if you wish God to forgive your sins? You have often told lies like Peter. Have you bitterly bewailed your lies as he bewailed his? Some of you have also cursed as Peter did in the court-yard. Has your soul ever felt contrition for it? Some have sworn without necessity or falsely. Had they any disgust for their sin? There is no forgiveness without contrition. Could God forgive you without it?

2. Our Saviour looked at Peter. Peter went out and wept bitterly. Our Saviour's look of grace excited contrition in his heart. You must make earnest efforts to have true contrition. For this pray to God: "Excite, O Lord, contrition in my heart by a look of Thy grace." I told you to recite every night an Our Father. For what? From now recite the Our Father, in order that the Holy Ghost may help you to have a true contrition for your sins.

12. The Qualities of Contrition.

Object. You shall hear which is the greatest evil on earth.

PREPARATION. What did the apostles do after they had received the Holy Ghost on Pentecost? They preached about Jesus. What did the chief priests do concerning the preaching of the apostles? They said to the apostles: "You must not preach any more about Jesus, otherwise you shall be put into prison." To be put into prison would have been an evil for the apostles. But what would the apostles have committed, if they had not preached? Why? To commit a sin would have also been an evil for them. The apostles were obliged to choose between two evils. What did the apostles do? Which evil did they consider to be the greater? What happened then to the apostles? They were cast into prison. When the apostles were set free from the prison, what did the highpriests say to them? "If you again preach about Jesus, you shall be scourged." Scourging would have been a greater evil for the apostles than imprisonment. What would the apostles have committed, if they had stopped preaching? The apostles had now again to choose between two evils. Which evil did they now consider to be the greater? Sin. After being scourged the apostles were threatened with death, if they would again preach about Jesus. What did they allow to be done to them rather than cease preaching and committing sin? What did they fear more than martyrdom? Sin. Because sin is a greater evil than martyrdom. What do we do to God, when we sin? We offend Him. How does God feel towards the sinner? By mortal sin we make God our enemy. Oh, what a great evil it is to have God for our enemy! What does our soul lose by mortal sin? Our soul becomes poor, poorer than the poorest beggar. What punishment does mortal sin deserve? How long do the torments of hell last? Which is the greatest evil, to be imprisoned, scourged, put to death in great torments, or to have God as our enemy, to be poorer in our soul than the poorest beggar, and to burn forever in hell? And how do we draw upon us these three dreadful evils? By mortal sin.

Because by mortal sin we offend God, lose divine grace, and deserve hell, sin is the greatest of evils.

What a frightful misfortune it is for us, if we commit a mortal sin! Can such a sin be forgiven? Oh, yes. What then is the most necessary for us to obtain the forgiveness of our sins? Contrition.

I.

OBJECT. I will show you, from the example of St. Peter, what contrition ought to be.

DEVELOPMENT. Peter had committed several sins. Were all these equally grievous? Which were the most grievous? What did Peter feel about all his sins? He had contrition for all of them. How deep in his soul was his contrition? To the inmost depth of his soul. Why was St. Peter so sorry for his sins? Peter was so sorry for his sins, because he had offended our Saviour. What had the soul of Peter lost by his sins? Peter's soul had lost sanctifying grace by his sins.

How could God have immediately punished Peter for his sins? What punishment in the next life did Peter deserve for his sins? To lose grace, to die and to deserve hell are also a great misfortune. Peter could also have been sorry for his sins, because by them he had lost grace, deserved death and hell. But Peter had not thought of these, for his contrition was so great. What would Peter in his contrition have preferred to his having sinned? Death. What kind of evil did he consider sin to be? What did he feel concerning sin? Horror. How much horror had Peter for sin? He hated sin as the greatest of evils. And what did Peter wish concerning his sins? He wished: "Oh, if I only had not done this!"

The hope of forgiveness. Peter had often witnessed how our Saviour had willingly forgiven others their grievous sins. Give an example. The paralytic. How did Peter for this reason pray in his heart to our Saviour? And what did he expect Jesus would do? Peter expected that Jesus would forgive him. Hence we can say: Peter hoped that our Saviour would forgive him his sins. Our Saviour did, indeed, forgive him. (Repeat.)

Tell me which apostle had committed a more grievous sin than Peter. But Judas was also sorry for his terrible sin. Yes, he was frightfully sorry for it. It burnt like a red hot iron in his breast. Our Saviour would also have forgiven him. Jesus is so good; He came upon earth to redeem men from sin. He forgives all who repent of their sins. What should Judas have expected from our Saviour? He should have hoped for pardon from Jesus. Yes, Judas should have gone to kneel down under the cross and besought Jesus to forgive him, and Jesus would have forgiven him. But Judas was afraid and thought his sin was too great for our Saviour to forgive him. What was wanting to the sorrow of Judas? The hope of forgiveness. Therefore our Saviour did not forgive him. Both apostles, Peter and Judas, were sorry for their sins. What did Peter include in his sorrow? The hope of being forgiven. And what did Jesus do to him on that account? What was wanting to the sorrow of Judas? And what did Jesus not do on that account? When does God forgive sin? When does he not forgive the sins of those who are sorry for them?

SUMMARY. What must be united with sorrow (contrition)? The hope of pardon must necessarily be united with contrition.

II.

OBJECT. I will now tell you how Bertha repented of her sins.

1. DEVELOPMENT — *Exteriorly, interiorly.* Bertha, by her disobedience greatly offended her mother. Her mother is very angry with Bertha for it. But Bertha is indifferent. But because it is Christmas eve, Bertha is afraid that she

will not get a Christmas gift. Therefore she says to her mother: " Oh, dear mother, had I only not disobeyed you; I am so sorry for having done so! Please forgive me." But her mother did not forgive her.

CONSIDERATION — *Exteriorly.* Bertha says she is sorry for having offended her mother. What does he feel in his heart about his sins, who is really sorry for them? Sorrow and hatred (horror). But Bertha feels no sorrow and no hatred. How do you know that? She is very indifferent. Her sorrow, therefore, does not penetrate to her heart. Where is her sorrow for her disobedience? Only in her tongue. Her sorrow is only in her mouth. Her mother sees that. Her mother sees that Bertha talks in that way, for fear of not getting a Christmas gift. Will her mother forgive her? Why not?

CONNECTION — *Contrition must be interior.* Where are our sins? Where the sins are, there also must be the contrition. Therefore Peter was sorry for his sins not merely with his tongue. How was he sorry for his sins? He was sorry for his sins not only in words, but especially in his heart. His contrition penetrated to the inmost depth of his heart. How much did he detest his sins? Peter detested his sins in his heart as the greatest of evils.

Sincere. What did Peter wish concerning his sins? " Oh, had I only not done that!" What does Bertha say, when asking her mother's forgiveness? " Oh, dear mother, had I only not disobeyed you; I am so sorry for having done so." What cares Bertha for having offended her mother? She merely says she is sorry, but does not mean it. Does she really feel sorry in her heart? He who says something with his lips, but does not mean it in his heart, is not sincere. Peter wished he had not offended our Saviour; he said this with his lips, but meant it much more in his heart. Therefore Peter sincerely wished that he had not offended our Saviour. Which three things have you now learnt about Peter's contrition?

Our contrition is interior, if we are sorry in our heart for our sins, if we detest them in our heart as the greatest evil, and if we sincerely wish we had not committed them. What should we say about Peter's contrition? His contrition was good; therefore our Saviour forgave Peter his sins. How is Bertha sorry for her sin? With her lips. What kind of sorrow is it? Her sorrow is not good. Therefore her mother did not forgive her. If Bertha's contrition in confession is of the same kind, God will not forgive her. What kind of sorrow must she have to obtain God's forgiveness?

SUMMARY. When is contrition interior? Our contrition is interior if we are sorry for our sins not merely with our lips, but also from our heart, and detest them as the greatest of evils, and sincerely wish we had not committed them.

2. OBJECT. I will now tell you all about Frank's contrition.

RELATION — *Not universal; universal.* Frank had not studied his lesson well in school, and Fred got ahead of him in class. Being angry with Fred for this, Frank tore out many leaves from Fred's book, cut up his book and expressed the wish: "I wish that Fred would get very sick." When he went to confession, he was sorry for both his mortal and venial sins, except that he was still angry with Fred, and was not sorry for having caused him so much damage.

CONSIDERATION — *Mortal sin. The room for laying out corpses.* In what did Frank offend Fred? That was surely a mortal sin. Why is such a sin called mortal? Because such a sin is like a death-thrust into the soul of the sinner, which kills the soul spiritually, takes its life for heaven away. Every time a man commits a mortal sin, his soul receives a death-thrust. How many death-thrusts in the soul of him who has committed three mortal sins? Of him who committed two? Of him who committed one?

The room in which corpses are laid out is called a mortuary room. What does the heart of a man become, who has committed mortal sin? A mortuary room.

Venial sin, not a mortuary room. The soul does not receive mortal wounds from venial sins, but only slight wounds. What happens to the soul of him who commits only venial sins? Hence the heart of such a one is not a mortuary room. The Holy Ghost does not leave his soul. But what happens when a mortal sin is committed?

We must be sorry for every mortal sin. If a sinner wishes the Holy Ghost to return to his soul, all his death-thrusts of mortal sin must be healed, and this all together. If the soul has received three death-thrusts, the soul cannot regain life, if all three are not healed at once; the soul would remain dead if only one, or only two were healed. What is required for the Holy Ghost to enter again the soul that has received many death-thrusts, and for the soul to get alive again for heaven? All the soul's death-thrusts must be healed. The death-thrusts are healed by contrition. But Frank had no contrition for one of his mortal sins. What was not healed in his soul? But if one death-thrust is not healed, none of them are healed, and the soul remains dead; and the Holy Ghost does not enter it, and all the sins, even those for which the sinner was sorry, all remain in the soul.

There is no obligation to have contrition for venial sins —unless no mortal sins are confessed. Suppose a person has committed both mortal and venial sins. Which kind must he be sorry for, that his soul may recover life? All his mortal sins. What kind of wounds do venial sins inflict on the soul? Slight wounds. Who does not leave the soul on account of venial sins? He can dwell in a soul that is stained only by venial sins. Venial sins only would not prevent the Holy Ghost from entering a soul. It is not necessary to be sorry for every venial sin that the soul may recover the life of grace.

It is well to be sorry for venial sins also. What do venial sins cause in the soul? Therefore it is well to be sorry for all of them. This will make the soul much more healthy and pure, and more pleasing to God. (Necessity of being sorry for at least one kind of venial sins confessed, if no mortal sins are confessed or included.)

CONNECTION — *Universal.* Mention the sins Peter committed. How many mortal sins was Peter sorry for? But what about Frank's sorrow? He had no contrition for one of his mortal sins. How many sins were forgiven to Peter? How many to Frank? None. Why? When are all mortal sins forgiven?

What do you know about Peter's contrition for his venial sins? Peter was sorry for all his venial sins also. What happened to him concerning his venial sins? Frank was also sorry for his venial sins. Were they forgiven him? Why not? Were any of his mortal sins forgiven? Were any of his venial sins? Did he obtain forgiveness for any of his sins? When is no sin forgiven? When contrition for a mortal sin is wanting. When are all mortal sins forgiven? When we have contrition for every one of them.

In which case are all sins committed, both mortal and venial, forgiven? When we are sorry for all of them, our contrition is universal. True contrition should be universal. Which kind of sins must we be sorry for? All of our mortal sins.

SUMMARY. When is our contrition universal? Our contrition is universal, when we are sorry for all our sins, or, at least, for all our mortal sins.

3. OBJECT. I will now tell you how Rudolf was sorry for his sins.

RELATION — *Natural, supernatural.* Rudolf had climbed a neighbor's cherry tree to steal cherries. But seeing the gardener coming, he quickly jumped down and broke his leg. Rudolf had to remain long in bed and suffered very much. He wept a good deal. When he got well, the other children made fun of him and called him a thief. He would get mad and weep every time. He would keep away from other children as much as possible.

CONSIDERATION — *Temporal injury.* What did Rudolf commit in stealing, or trying to steal cherries? A sin. What happened to him, when he jumped down from the tree? He broke his leg. His playmates could go out to play, but he could not. What injury did his broken leg cause him? He had to stay in bed and suffer much. What must he have thought during that time about his stealing? " Oh, would that I had not done it." How did he feel about it? He felt sorry. Why was he sorry? Because he had to stay in bed and suffer much; because it had injured him. How long did that injury last? Until his leg was healed. Therefore Rudolf's stealing caused him temporal injury. Why was Rudolf sorry for his theft, for stealing? He was sorry because it caused him temporal injury.

Disgrace. What did the other children call Rudolf for stealing? Thief. Every time he was called thief, he got very angry. And why? Because he was ashamed. What was it for Rudolf to be called a thief? A disgrace. This disgrace pained him deeply. How did he show that this disgrace pained him? What thought would then come into his mind? " Oh, would that I had not done it." How did he feel about his theft? Sorry. He repented of his theft, because it disgraced him. And for what else did he repent of his theft? Because it had caused him temporal injury.

Natural contrition. It was quite natural for Rudolf to be sorry for his theft because it caused him temporal injury and disgrace. Therefore we call his contrition a natural contrition.

CONNECTION — *Supernatural contrition.* Why was St. Peter sorry for his sins? For which other reasons could he have been sorry? Because he had lost sanctifying grace and deserved hell. He who is sorry for his sins because he offended God, lost grace and deserved hell has supernatural contrition. When is our contrition supernatural? Our contrition is supernatural, when we are sorry for (repent of) our sins, because we have offended God, lost grace and deserved hell.

Contrition must be supernatural. Whom do we offend by our sins? Who is to forgive our sins? Of whom should we think in our contrition? How is the contrition called which makes us think of God? True contrition makes us think of God, and is therefore supernatural.

Natural sorrow or contrition is of no use. What kind of contrition did Rudolf have? What did it make him think of? Of whom should he have thought? If he had thought of God, what kind of contrition would he have had? A supernatural contrition. And what would God have done about his sins? But because Rudolf had only a natural sorrow for his sin, God did not forgive him. What profit did he get from his natural sorrow? His natural sorrow did not at all profit him. What is it that makes our sorrow supernatural and deserving of God's forgiveness? To think of God in our contrition. Would it, then, not be sufficient for us to repent of our sins on account of the temporal injury or disgrace they caused us? To repent of our sins, because they caused us temporal injury or disgrace, is only natural sorrow, which does not profit us.

SUMMARY OF THE WHOLE. What is contrition? Contrition is a sorrow of the soul and a horror of our past sins. Which are the qualities of contrition? It must be, first, interior; second, universal; third, supernatural. When is our contrition interior? Our contrition is interior, when we repent of our sins not only with our lips, but from our heart and detest them as the greatest evil, and sincerely wish we had not committed them. When is our contrition universal? Our contrition is universal, when we repent of all our sins, or at least of all our mortal sins. When is our contrition supernatural? Our contrition is supernatural, when we repent of our sins, because we have

offended God, lost His grace and deserved hell. Would it
not be sufficient, if we repented of our sins on account of the
temporal injury they caused us? He who repents of his
sins merely on account of the temporal injury and disgrace
they caused him, has only a natural sorrow, which does
not profit him. With what must contrition be accompanied? Hope of forgiveness must accompany our contrition.

APPLICATION — 1. *Peter.* Peter's contrition for his sins
lasted all his life. Every night when he heard a cock crow,
he would begin again to weep. His many tears made fur-
rows in his face.

2. *Magdalen.* Mary Magdalen bitterly repented of her
sins, as we read in Bible History (Gospel). She had been
a wicked sinner. She once heard that our Saviour had
been invited to dine with a pharisee. She entered the
pharisee's house, cast herself at our Saviour's feet, and began to weep bitterly over her sins. Her tears ran over
the feet of Jesus. She wiped His feet with her hair and
repeatedly kissed them. Jesus said to her: " Thy sins
are forgiven thee."

3. *You have all sinned.* What must you feel concerning
your sins, that God may forgive you? Have you already
been sorry for your sins? It is well, if a child is so sorry
for his sins, that he weeps over them, like Peter and
Magdalen. But it is not necessary for you to weep over
your sins. Where must you feel sorry for your sins? In
our heart. The chief thing is to be sorry in your heart
for your sins. Have you not already said: " O my God,
I am sorry for having cursed, told lies, been disobedient,"
without being at all sorry in your heart? What did such a
sorrow profit you?

13. The Purpose of Amendment, or the Resolution to sin no more.

CONNECTION. It is not enough to be sorry for our sins, we must also resolve never to sin any more.

I. THE WORTHLESS RESOLUTION.

OBJECT. I will now tell you how John resolved not to sin any more.

RELATION. John was a bad boy. He was disobedient and impudent towards his parents, and was addicted to cursing and lying. He often stole money out of the drawer, until his father caught him at it. His father then reproached him with all the evil things he knew about him; and then he brought him before the crucifix, saying: "Look at our divine Saviour who suffered so much for the sins of men. And now you have again so grievously offended Him. You have even stolen and become a thief. Do you not see that you deserve to be punished?" Then his father punished him severely with a rod. John began to cry aloud, and said: "Oh, I am so sorry for being so wicked. I will never do it again. I will surely never steal any more." Then his father stopped punishing him, and locked the money drawer, and took the key out. John, who was still crying, watched his father to see where he would hide the key. For what did he watch his father?

CONSIDERATION — *The earnest or firm will.* What sins had John committed? What was John doing when his father found him out? Where did his father bring him? What did he say to him? What did John get for the evil he had done? What did John cry out, when he was getting punished? John said that he was sorry from his heart. What else did he say? He also said: "I will never do it again; I will never steal any more." Therefore we say: John was resolved never to do anything bad, and especially never to steal any more. (Repeat.) That was a resolution, a purpose of amendment, of doing better. At what was John looking when he was still crying? What did he do that for? What did he really intend to do again? Therefore when he said: I will never do it again, he really intended to do it again; we say; he did not mean what he said. What do you say about John saying: "I will not steal any more"? John did not mean it.

Summary. What does John say that he resolved? What do you say about this? John did not mean what he said.

II.

Object. If you wish that God should forgive your sins, you must be sincerely resolved not to sin again; you must mean it. This I will show by the example of St. Peter.

Development. Where did Jesus go on the night before His death? What did He do there? What did our Saviour urge Peter, James and John to do? What did they do instead? If Peter, instead of falling asleep, had prayed, he would not have committed such grievous sins that night. What sins did he commit? What did Peter feel in his heart afterwards concerning his sins? And what did he wish? "Oh, would that I had not done it." He thought how well it would have been for him, if he had obeyed our Saviour, and watched and prayed. And he said to himself: "From now I will pray more fervently. Not for the whole world will I again deny our Saviour. Before all men I will profess that I am His disciple, even if I had to be arrested and put to death for it." What was Peter resolved to do?

Peter was resolved to amend his life. How will Peter repair his neglect of prayer? He is resolved to pray fervently. How does he intend to atone for (repair) his denial of our Saviour? He will profess before everybody that he is our Saviour's disciple. Peter, therefore, is resolved henceforth to do better. How then will his life be with regard to the past? Better. What kind of a life is Peter resolved henceforth to lead? A better life. We may also say: Peter is resolved to amend his life; or Peter intends to lead henceforth a better life. This is his resolution, his firm purpose of amendment.

Peter resolved never to sin any more. Peter also said what he intended not to do any more. What? To deny our Saviour, to tell lies, to curse and swear. What had Peter committed by doing those things? Sins. What is he resolved never more to do? He is resolved nevermore to sin. Or we may say: Peter has the firm purpose of never committing any more sins. That is a resolution.

The resolution. Therefore Peter is resolved to do a certain thing, and also nevermore to do certain things. Tell what. Peter is resolved to amend his life, and never to sin again. And what is this called? A resolution.

CONNECTION — *Firm, earnest, sincere.* What was John's resolution? Did he mean it? No, he did not mean it; he was not sincere. How do you know that? What is Peter resolved to undergo rather than sin again? How was Peter disposed when he made that resolution? He meant it.

The good resolution. Therefore we say: Peter's resolution was good. But who did not mean what he said he resolved to do? Was John's resolution good? No. What did Peter resolve to do? What did John resolve to do? Both resolutions sounded alike, and yet they were really very unlike. Why was John's resolution bad? Because he did not mean it. Why was Peter's resolution good? Because he really meant to amend his life and nevermore to sin. A good resolution is an earnest, or sincere, will, or a firm purpose to amend our life and nevermore to sin.

Peter's resolution was united to contrition. What did John say he felt about his sins? And what did he say he was resolved to do? And what did he intend to do again? If a man says he detests something and yet means to do it again, we can easily see that he really does not detest it. On the contrary, he finds pleasure in it. And, therefore, he is not truly sorry for it. What did Peter feel about his sins? And what did he say he was resolved to do? What would he rather undergo than sin again? Peter really detested sin. How do you know that Peter really detested sin? Peter joined the firm purpose of amendment with his contrition.

The firm purpose of amendment, or the resolution never to sin any more, must be joined to contrition. Wherefore Peter's contrition was good, and our Saviour forgave him his sins. But what did John mean to do again? What, then, was not joined to his sorrow? A good resolution. Therefore John's sorrow was worthless. How can you know if your contrition is good? If I have a good resolution along with it.

SUMMARY. What must necessarily accompany (or be joined to) contrition? A good resolution must always accompany contrition. What is a good resolution? The sincere will, or firm purpose, to amend one's life and to sin no more.

APPLICATION. Dear children, remember that a good resolution, that is, a firm purpose of amendment, must accompany our contrition. He who has cursed must resolve: " I will not curse again." He who missed Mass on Sundays through his own fault, must resolve: " I will never stay away from Mass any more." He who disobeyed his parents, must say to himself: " I will henceforth be obedient, even if I find it hard." He who was impure in speech, or even in action, must be resolved: " I will never do so again for the whole world; no, not even to save my life." And if some one would promise you plenty of money, or would threaten to beat or even kill you, as was done to St. Paschal, in order to make you sin, you should tell the seducer, as St. Paschal did: "You can beat and even kill me, but I will not commit sin."

III.

OBJECT. I will now tell you what qualities the good resolution must have.

DEVELOPMENT — *When is the good resolution interior?* Who had a good resolution? Why was Peter's resolution good? Because he meant it. He not only *said:* "I will not deny our Saviour again," but he really willed in his heart never to do it again. How did he show this afterwards? Why was John's resolution bad? Because he did not mean it. John said, indeed: "I will never do it again"; but what was wanting to him? How did we call the contrition which comes from the lips only? How should we call John's resolution, which came from his lips only? Peter also said with his lips: "I will never again deny our Saviour." But where did his resolution come from? How do we call contrition when it comes from the heart? How shall we call the resolution that comes from the heart? Interior. When is our resolution interior?

The resolution must be interior. I have told you about contrition that God does not consider what we say with our lips so much as what we mean in our heart. What value before God has the contrition that comes from the lips? None at all. In like manner, the resolution that comes only from the lips has no value before God. Where must our contrition be, if we wish that God should forgive our sins? In the heart. In other words? Interior. The resolution also must be interior in order to be good. Where then should we have our resolution? In our heart, in our interior. Hence the resolution must be interior like the contrition.

Peter's resolution was supernatural. Why did Peter resolve never to sin again? How did we call Peter's contrition because he was sorry for having offended our divine Saviour? Supernatural. How can we also call his resolution, because he intended to avoid sin and never again offend our Savior? Supernatural. In like manner, if we resolve not to sin any more in order not to lose the grace of God, in order not to be cast into hell, our resolution is also supernatural. When is our resolution supernatural?

The resolution must be supernatural. Whom do we offend when we sin? Why, then, should we be resolved to avoid sin? What kind of resolution is that? What must our contrition be? What must our resolution be? Supernatural.

When is the resolution universal? How many sins should we be sorry for? For all sins, both for the mortal and the venial. For which sins especially should we be sorry? Of what kind, then, is our sorrow? Universal. Our resolution should likewise be universal. Which sins must we at least be resolved to avoid? Of what kind, then, is our sorrow? Universal.

The resolution must be universal. What would happen if we were not sorry for one of our mortal sins? Suppose a child would not be resolved to avoid a certain one of his mortal sins. What would he, then, do to God? Therefore God would not forgive him; and why not? What kind of resolution should we have? Our resolution must be universal, like our contrition. What is the kind of resolution we should have?

The proximate occasion. We must be resolved to avoid something more than our sins. You can learn this from Joseph, when he lived in Putiphar's house. Who was trying to seduce him (to lead him into sin)? What did Joseph say to her? But that bad woman went again after him. What did she even do on a certain day? In Putiphar's house Joseph was well treated, and his master liked him very much. But Joseph preferred being cast into prison, than to live in that place where he was in danger to commit sin. What did he do when that bad woman took hold of his cloak to lead him into sin? He let go his cloak and ran away.

In like manner, you must not go into or stay in a house where sin is committed. Because there you would see and hear wicked things, and you would soon do the same. Nor should you go with bad companions. Place a nice sound apple alongside a rotten apple, and what will happen? The sound apple will soon get rotten. How does this happen? The sound apple gets infected by the rotten one. He who goes with bad companions, soon becomes bad himself, and soon tells lies, curses, steals and talks bad, and does bad things just as they do. And why? Because he has constant occasion to see, hear and do evil things. For him the occasion of committing sin is always very near or proximate. Therefore such places and such companions are called a near or proximate occasion of sin. What was Putiphar's house with regard to Joseph? Give me an example of another proximate occasion of sin. What resolution must you make, if you have been in wicked places or with wicked companions? "I will never again go into that house; I will never again go with those bad companions"; in other words: "I will avoid that house and those evil companions." Otherwise what could easily happen to you? What are such houses, such bad companions to you? Proximate occasions of sin. What must you then resolve to avoid?

SUMMARY. Which are the qualities of a good resolution? Like contrition, our resolution should be 1, interior, 2, universal, and 3, supernatural. When is our resolution interior? When is it universal? When is it supernatural? Our resolution must accompany our contrition. What must we be resolved to avoid? The good resolution is the third part of the sacrament of penance.

APPLICATION. Reflect a little, that you may know if any of your companions have already led you to curse, to say or do bad things, to steal, or if you often go to a house or place where you hear and see evil things. If such is the case, you must resolve to avoid that house, that place, those companions. It will, perhaps, be difficult for you to keep away from such companions, whom you liked to be with, or to stay from that house or place, where you enjoyed yourself. But God and your soul should be dearer to you than such companions or such places. Promise this to God, saying with me: "O my God, I detest all my sins, and I am resolved never more to offend Thee, my most beloved Lord, and carefully to avoid all occasions of sin."

14. The awaking of Contrition and the good Resolution.

CONNECTION. Whose help do you need to awake in you a true contrition? What should you do to obtain the help of the Holy Ghost? What should you say to Him for this?

OBJECT. I will show you how to awake a true contrition.

I. MOTIVES OF LOVE.

I. THINK ON GOD THE FATHER. That you may, with the grace of the Holy Ghost, awake true contrition in your heart, think on God the Father, and listen to what He says to each of you. He says: "First, I created you, otherwise you would not exist (be in this world). I gave you a healthy body. If you have been sick, I made you well again. I give you every day food and drink (to eat and drink), clothing and a home, and all the good things you have. If it were not for Me, you would have died long ago. Secondly, and how well I cared for your soul! In holy baptism I clothed you with sanctifying grace and made you My child. I gave an angel to guard and protect you in body and soul. And lastly, I gave you what is dearest to Me, My only-begotten Son. Thirdly, what did I demand of you for all this? All I demanded of you was to love Me very much. Therefore I said to you: My child, give Me your heart. Fourthly, but what have you done? You committed sin. How often did you offend Me, your good Father! You prayed so carelessly, pronounced My name so irreverently, and behaved so badly in church. You disobeyed your parents. You have been so immodest, so impure. O how ungrateful you have been towards Me, your greatest Benefactor! Fifthly, come back to Me, you poor, stray sheep and say to Me with a sorrowful heart: O dear Father, I am so sorry for having offended Thee. Deign to forgive me! And I will forgive you again, and take away your sins and bury them in the bottom of the sea; I will wash them away, and never more think on them. I will again make you My dear child, embrace you and press you to My heart. O allow yourself to be moved!"

Beg pardon of God the Father, saying with me: "O dear Father, how good art Thou to me, Thy poor, sinful child! I should have loved Thee with all my heart; but I have so grievously offended Thee by my anger, my sloth, my disobedience and my other sins. O how ungrateful have I been! How could I so shamefully commit sin? Would that I had rather died than offend Thee! Deign to forgive me. O dear Father, never will I again offend Thee. I will never miss Mass through my fault. Never again will I quarrel with others or strike them. Never will I again tell lies or steal. Never will I again disobey my parents. Never more will I speak or act immodestly. Henceforth I will willingly say my prayers, obey my parents, behave well in church. I will not, for the whole world, offend Thee again. I am resolved rather to die than to commit sin. I am sorry for all my sins from my inmost heart, because I have offended Thee, my most loving Father. Forgive me. I hate and detest all my sins, and I am resolved never more to offend Thee, the best of fathers."

2. THINK ON GOD THE SON. Now look up to our dear Saviour hanging on the cross. He looks at you with so much love and sorrow, as He once did on St. Peter; and He says to each of you:

" My child, I have redeemed you. For you I came down from heaven and became man. For you I was born in a stable at Bethlehem, and laid on straw in a manger. For you I underwent for thirty-three years heat and cold, hunger and thirst; and at last for you I was nailed to the cross. Look at Me well. Look at My head. It is cruelly wounded and pierced by sharp thorns. O how fearfully it pains Me, and all this on account of your angry and envious thoughts. But I suffer all for your sake, that you may not be lost. Look at My eyes. They wept bloody tears on account of their great pains. O how fearfully they suffer! And this on account of your immodest and envious looks. But I bear all this willingly for your sake, that you may not be lost. Look at My mouth. My lips are blue, My tongue is all afire, it cleaves to My palate, and for pain it can no longer talk. And all this on account of your lies, your cursing, your unchaste talk. But I suffer it all for your sake, that you may not be lost. Look at My hands, with which I did so much good for men, cured so many sick and blessed so many children. See how they are pierced with thick nails and attached to the cross! O how frightfully they pain Me, because you use your hands to do immodest things, to steal, to strike others. But I willingly bear all this for your sake, that you may not be lost. Look at My feet, pierced and torn by the nails, and bruised and almost broken. O how frightfully do they pain Me, because you go to forbidden places with evil companions. But I willingly bear all this for your sake, that you may not be lost. Look at My whole body. It is all covered with wounds from head to foot, and with

My back all sore and bruised leaning against the hard cross, hanging on the cross by four nails. O what horrible pains must I bear in My whole body, because your body has been the instrument of your many sins. But I willingly bear all this for your sake, that you may not be lost.

And how have you repaid My excessive love? Instead of loving Me in return, you continued to sin and to shamefully offend Me, your Redeemer, your best Friend. Child, have you a single spark of love for Me in your heart? If you had, by chance, mortally wounded your mother, you would fall on your knees and cry out weeping aloud: O mother, dear mother, forgive your unfortunate child! And you could not stop weeping, and mingling your tears with her blood. And after piercing My heart with your sins, the heart of your divine Redeemer, of your best Friend, should not your heart melt with sorrow, pain and love? Should you not weep out both your eyes? Or would you say: I am not the cause of Thy death, for it was the Jews that caused it. But have you never committed any sin? Did I not have to suffer for your sins? Oh, come now to Me, beg My forgiveness, and tell Me that you are heartily sorry for your sins, and that you will love Me, your best Friend, from your heart. See, My arms are opened to receive you and press you to My heart, and to forgive all your sins."

Beseech God the Son to forgive you; and say with me:

O my Jesus, Thou didst endure too much for me, a poor sinful child. It pains even my sinful heart so much. Thou didst suffer all to save me. Oh, deign to help me now to be sorry from my inmost heart for having so ungratefully repaid Thy excessive love. By my pride I helped to press those sharp thorns into Thy sacred head. By my thefts I caused Thy burning thirst, and by my immodesty I helped to scourge Thee so frightfully. By my sloth, I made Thy cross so heavy. O Lord, I embrace

Thy sacred body on the cross, I kiss Thy wounds a thousand times and bedew Thy feet with my hot tears. O Jesus, how sorry I am for having so greatly offended Thee. O dearest Saviour, do not let Thy blood be wasted on me. O crucified Jesus, have mercy on me, and forgive me my sins. O Jesus, be merciful unto me. O Jesus, pardon me my sins. O Jesus, show me mercy. Oh, how could I be so ungrateful! Would that I had died rather than ever have offended my beloved Saviour!

O my Saviour, I beg Thee a thousand times pardon. Henceforth, I will never again offend Thee. I will not, for the whole world offend Thee by committing sin. Rather to die than sin again. O my God, I am sorry for all the sins of my whole life from my inmost heart, because I offended Thee, my most amiable Redeemer. I hate and detest them all, because they displease Thee. (Repeat in part.)

3. THINK ON GOD THE HOLY GHOST. Now think on the Holy Ghost, and listen to what He says to you. "I have sanctified you. In holy baptism I entered your heart and made your body My holy temple, and have dwelt therein from that time. I brought to your soul the white garment of sanctifying grace. In this precious heavenly garment your soul was My wonderfully beautiful image. The heavenly Father looked upon you with pleasure, and said to the angels: See, that is My beloved child, in whom I am well pleased. In order to make My image in your soul still more beautiful, I bestowed daily new graces upon you. Like a painter, I have worked and painted on My image in your soul for years since your baptism. And how glad I felt when I saw it becoming more and more beautiful. And what did I demand from you for all this? Only that you should not defile My image, and that you should keep the garment of sanctifying grace. Therefore I daily spoke to your heart, urging you to do good, and warning you against evil. But how have you repaid My

love? You committed venial sins and defiled the white garment of your soul with many, many little stains. Oh, how you would feel ashamed before the angels and saints, if you could see the stains on your soul's white garment!

Or you have even committed mortal sins! Oh, unfortunate child, what have you done? You have torn your soul's white garment, lost sanctifying grace, cast Me out of your heart, and destroyed My image in your soul. So long had I worked on it, and now it is all useless. Oh, how it pains Me! Heaven weeps over you; the angels weep over you; the divine Saviour even shed blood over you; and yet you alone will not weep."

Beseech the Holy Ghost to forgive you. Therefore say with me:

"O my dear Lord, how good art Thou towards me, a poor sinful child! I should have loved Thee with my whole heart, and now I have so grievously offended Thee. Deign to forgive me. O dear Lord, never again shall it happen that I again offend Thee. I will not even for the whole world commit another sin. I would rather die. O my God, I am sorry for all the sins of my whole life, etc.

4. THINK ON THE INFINITE GOOD. O what beautiful and good things the Father, the Son and the Holy Ghost have given you, have done for you! But God is still more beautiful and good than all that. Oh, could I but tell you how beautiful and good, how rich and powerful God is! He is more beautiful than the sun, more gentle than the moon, more bright than the stars, more splendid than the angels and saints. He is above all monarchs and rulers, more mighty than all the angels and saints. He is far more loving than your brothers and sisters, than your parents. He is the highest, the best, the most lovely Good. And you have offended the highest, the best, the most lovely Good. Oh, what have you done?

How bad you feel when you have offended your father or your mother! But how much should it pain you for having offended God, the highest, the best, the most lovely Good! Should it not break your heart? Beg pardon of God, the highest and greatest Good, and say with me:

"O my God, I am heartily sorry for all the sins of my whole life, because I have offended Thee, the highest and most lovely Good. Oh, had I rather died than offended Thee. My dear Lord, forgive me; be merciful unto me. I hate and detest all my sins; I am firmly resolved never again to offend Thee, my most amiable Good, and to avoid carefully the occasions of sin. I will rather die than offend Thee again."

II. MOTIVES OF FEAR.

1. THINK ON HEAVEN. He who offends God, the highest (chief) Good, by a mortal sin, cannot go to enjoy Him in heaven, because he lost heaven by his sin. Oh, if you only knew how beautiful heaven is! St. Paul once had a little glimpse of heaven. Being asked what he had seen there, he replied: "No man can think or guess, nor can any one say how beautiful heaven is; no man has ever seen anything so beautiful." The angels and saints are around the throne of God, seeing His unspeakable beauty and filled with His love. They never get tired or weary seeing and loving Him. All their desires are fulfilled. And in their love and gratitude they pray and sing full of joy and happiness. "Holy, holy, holy Lord God of hosts." And near God's throne on a brilliant seat is Mary, the Mother of God, the Queen of heaven, wearing a crown of twelve bright stars. And among the saints parents see their children, children see their parents, their relatives, their companions, all as bright as the sun, and in perfect joy and happiness. In heaven there is no sorrow, no complaint, no weeping, no pain, no sickness, no death, no quarrels, no bitter feelings, no separation, but peace, love, life everlasting and endless bliss. And by committing mortal sin you have lost that beautiful heaven! Oh, how miserable

you have made yourself! Should you grieve and weep over such a misfortune?

2. THINK ON PURGATORY. On account of your sins you have already deserved that God should punish you already in this life. The punishments your parents inflict on you are nothing in comparison with the punishments of God. God sends all sickness; He permits those who sin to be wounded, crippled, or to meet with sudden or violent deaths. And if you had died in your venial sins, where would you have gone? You would be in the flames of purgatory. Your soul would be undergoing pains and torments to expiate those sins.

No one can tell how fearfully the souls must suffer in purgatory. Sometimes we see a picture of purgatory. In it we see the poor souls burning in those flames and raising their hands to God, begging for mercy, praying to be freed from their punishment and taken up to heaven. But they must remain in purgatory until they have been perfectly purified from every stain of sin, and fit to enter heaven. The pains of purgatory are much greater than all the pains that are endured on earth! Now if you were to die in your venial sins, and without any mortal sin, you would have to suffer in purgatory for days and months, till you are fit to enter heaven.

You see now how you have injured your soul even by your venial sins. Therefore beg pardon of God, and say with me:

"O my God, how many sins have I already committed during my life? Although I am still so young and so small, I have already deserved great punishments. Often I prayed carelessly, got angry with my companions, disobeyed my parents, told lies, etc. O my God, deign to forgive all the sins I have committed during my whole life, and remit the punishments I have deserved thereby. Be merciful unto me, a sinner. Henceforth I will keep Thy commandments more faithfully, punctually obey my parents and superiors, be kind towards my brothers and sisters and my companions; no more will I again steal, tell lies, or do or say anything immodest. I would rather die than sin again. O my God, I am sorry," etc.

2. THINK ON HELL. When a soul defiled by mortal sin leaves her body, she beholds before her Jesus, our most amiable Saviour, our greatest Benefactor, our best Friend, our chief and most lovely God. Jesus is there to judge her. The soul knows her sinful state and her mortal sins. And yet she cannot believe that Jesus will cast her away. Hence she hastens towards Jesus. But Jesus repels her, says: Depart from Me. During your life on earth, you did not wish for Me, and now I will not have you. "Depart from Me." Almost dead from fear the soul looks terrified at our Saviour. She then advances towards Him, falls on her knees, joins her hands in supplication and says: "O kind, good Shepherd, pardon Thy stray sheep and receive me again. O my most loving Redeemer, Thou hast so greatly suffered for me, do not let Thy blood be shed for me in vain. Forgive Thy disobedient, unhappy child, and receive me again." But Jesus again repels her, saying: "Away from Me; I am no longer your Redeemer; you are no longer My child. Depart from Me!" But the poor soul knows not what to do now. She sees the Blessed Virgin, and hastens to her, and says, weeping: "O dear Mother Mary, thou art my Mother. Beseech thy divine Son to forgive thy unhappy child and to receive me again." The wretched soul strives again to approach our Saviour; but He says: "Away from Me and from My Mother. My Mother is no longer your Mother; My angel is no longer your angel; My saints are no longer your saints. You no longer have any part with Me. Depart from Me."

"Depart, accursed, from Me. You served the devil, and not Me. Be now accursed in body and soul! Accursed be your eyes for yielding to sinful looks. Accursed be your ears, for listening to detraction and backbiting! Accursed be your lips for uttering lies, etc. Accursed be your hands for stealing. Accursed be your feet for going with evil companions. Accursed be your heart for entertaining envious and impure thoughts and desires.

"Depart from Me, you accursed, into fire; into that fiery dungeon, where the floor is of fire, the walls are of fire, where the ceiling and roof are of fire, where the air is of fire, the breath is of fire; where the food and drink are of fire, and the tears are of fire. All the members of your body shall be of fire; you shall be like a red hot coal in the furnace of hell!" How horrible are the torments! And for how long? For an hour, a day, a week, a month?

"No," our Saviour says: "Depart from Me, you accursed, into everlasting fire. You shall dwell forever in those frightful flames, forever weeping, forever burning, if you die with a mortal sin on your conscience." But is there no one in hell, to console the damned? Our divine Saviour says:

"Depart from Me, you accursed, into the everlasting fire, prepared for the devil and his angels. You served the devil during life; you shall be his companion in the fire of hell for all eternity. He shall be your tormenter forever. You shall have there numberless companions who will add to your sufferings at every moment." In hell, as our Saviour says, there is weeping and gnashing of teeth, and the worm dieth not. That the worm of conscience shall always torment the damned. It will constantly reproach them with their sins, and tell them how easily they could have been saved, if they had only tried seriously, if they had kept from bad company, if they had obeyed their parents, if they had followed the admonitions of the priest, if they had made a good confession, if they had prayed to Jesus and Mary when they were tempted to commit sin. Their conscience will constantly tell them how easily they could have been saved and enjoy forever the delights of heaven, if they had imitated the good example of some of their companions now in heavenly bliss, sharing the very happiness of God, their Father.   But now it is too late for the damned; the time for penance, for forgiveness is over, for out of hell there is no redemption!

But for you children, it is not yet too late; you can still obtain forgiveness by making a good confession and keeping henceforth your good resolutions.   Ask God's forgiveness, and say with me:

"O Jesus, I have deserved hell; be merciful unto me. O Jesus, let not Thy blood be lost for me.   O Jesus, forgive me my sins.   I hate and detest all my sins.   Rather let me die than ever sin again.   I will never miss Mass by my own fault; I will pray with attention; I will never again curse, never again disobey my parents and superiors, never think or speak of, or do immodest or impure things; I will never again tell lies, steal or get angry; I will always behave well in church, and be obedient.   O my God, I am heartily sorry for all my sins, because I have offended Thee the highest and most lovely God, and because I have justly deserved Thy punishments both in this life and in the next. I detest my sins; I am resolved never more to offend Thee, my most amiable God, and carefully to avoid the occasions of sin."

15. Confession.

OBJECT.   I will now tell you how our sins are forgiven.

PREPARATION.   You have already heard that Jesus forgave sins.   To whom did Jesus give the power also to forgive sins?   When did Jesus give this power to the apostles?   To whom did the apostles transmit this power? The priest must know the sins, in order to forgive them. They must be made known to him.   What must we do to make our sins known to the priest?   We must tell or confess them to him.   In confession we tell our sins to the priest, that he may know and forgive them.   Where do we make our confession? In the confessional. 'And what does the priest then do? He forgives our sins, or absolves us from our sins by giving us absolution.

OBJECT. I will now show you how to make a good confession from the example of two boys.

RELATION. Antony and Albert were two bad boys. They had committed many sins together. Antony had five times caused Albert to go into the woods on Sundays instead of going to Mass. Another time there was a circus. Antony said to Albert: "I have ten cents; now try to get some more at home, so that we may go together to the circus and have a fine time." Albert managed to steal at home two dollars. They both went to the circus instead of going to school. After going to the circus, they felt hungry and entered a restaurant and, although they knew it was Friday they ordered and ate meat. Antony also had a bad picture, and often showed it to Albert, and they talked and laughed about it. And Antony once committed an act of impurity when he was alone. Both committed also many venial sins. Now both of them went to confession.

Albert was the first to enter the confessional. He confessed his sins in the order of the ten commandments. When he came to the third he said: "I missed Mass five Sundays through my own fault; and I ate meat on a Friday knowingly." When he came to the sixth commandment he said: "I looked with another boy at an indecent picture from three to five times a week." At the seventh commandment he said: "I took once two dollars from my parents." He was very near crying aloud when he told these sins. The priest then asked him: "How did you come to steal so much money from your parents?" Albert replied: "Another boy led me to do it." Then the confessor asked him further: "What did you do with that money?" Albert replied: "We spent it in the circus and for a lunch and other things."

The confessor then asked him: "Did that other boy lead you into other sins?" Albert answered: "He led me into staying away from Mass, and into looking at an indecent picture and speaking of indecent things." Then the confessor said to him: "Consider how you have grievously offended God by these sins. If God had punished you for them by a sudden death, where would you now be? O how unhappy you have made yourself by your sins!" Albert began to cry. But the confessor encouraged him: "Do not be discouraged; God will willingly forgive you all these sins, and all will be right again with you, if you are firmly resolved never again to offend God grievously. Moreover, you must no more associate with the boy that led you into these sins. Do you promise me that?" Albert replied: "Yes, I promise you. I will never again go with him." The confessor then said to him: "For your penance you shall say three Our Fathers and three Hail Mary every day for three days." The confession then gave him absolution.

Antony next entered the confessional. He was greatly afraid. The devil whispered in his ear: "What will the confessor think of you? If you tell all, you must be fearfully ashamed of yourself." Antony began to tell his sins according to the commandments. At the third he said: "I missed Mass five times on Sundays through my fault." When he came to the fifth, and was to confess that he had led another boy into sin, his heart began to beat through fear. But he said: "I have led another boy into grievous sin five to seven times a week." But he said the word *grievous* so low that the confessor might not understand it. When he came to the sixth commandment, he said: "I looked with another boy at an indecent picture from three to five times a week." But when he was about to say: I have done an indecent thing alone, he got ashamed, and did not confess it. About the seventh commandment he confessed: "I stole money at home." With regard to the commandments of the Church he said: "I ate meat on a Friday, but I did not know it was Friday."

When Antony got through, he was in great fear. A voice in his heart said to him all the time: "You have made a bad confession." Therefore he could hardly pay attention to what the confessor was saying to him. He almost failed to understand the penance the confessor gave him. On the way home all the boys who had gone to confession, felt so glad and so happy, for their heart was light. Albert said: "When I get home I will weigh myself to see how much lighter I have become." Antony alone was not cheerful. He went home gloomy and peevish.

On the following day the priest said at school: "Dear children, you are now happy; your souls are entirely pure, and you are again holy children of God." At these words Antony first blushed deeply, and then turned deathly pale, for a voice constantly said to him: "But you are not a child of God. You made a bad confession." And from that time Antony could not feel really happy again. When the other children were at play, he was standing in some corner with a gloomy face. And when he sometimes played with them, he never found much pleasure in it. Sometimes he suddenly stopped playing in the middle of a game, for his conscience had whispered to him: "You have made a bad confession." At last he said to himself: "I can no longer stand feeling so uneasy and so unhappy. In my next confession I will tell all." And he meant to do it. But when he was in the confessional, the devil again inspired him with a great fear, and he again concealed his sin. And he did the same in the following confessions. He now felt really miserable. He found no pleasure in praying; he could hardly learn anything more; he had no more rest. He was almost always alone, and seldom went with his schoolmates. They could not explain why he was so different from what he had been before. This lasted for many years. When he was twenty-one years old, the news spread all over: Antony is dead. How do you think he died? He had hung himself in a barn.

CONSIDERATION. The sins of Antony and Albert. Which was the worse boy? Why?

1. Into what sins was Albert led by Antony? To missing Mass for five Sundays; to looking at an indecent picture, and to indecent conversation; to steal money at home. How had Albert to confess those sins? How had Antony to confess them? As to the seventh commandment there was a difference: what was it?

2. What grievous sin had Antony committed alone? An act of impurity. How should he have confessed the sin of eating meat on Friday? How was Antony to confess the sins he led Albert into?

The good Confession — Entire. Which of the two boys entered the confessional first? Albert made his confession in the same order as you have learned in the examination of conscience. With what sins did he begin his confession? With the sins against the first commandment. Albert had only venial sins to confess against the first and second commandments. I did not mention them to you. Which sins did he commit against the third commandment? How did he confess them? Did he join to the third commandment the sin he committed against the second commandment of the Church? Which sin was that? How did he confess it? His confession concerning the third commandment was therefore good. What kind of sins did he commit against the fifth commandment? How did he confess the sins he had committed against the sixth commandment? Which sin had he committed against the seventh commandment? What kind of sin was that? Why? Because his parents were very poor. If he had taken only twenty cents from them, what kind of sin would it have been? A venial sin. What makes a theft a mortal sin? The value of the thing stolen, and also the poverty of the person from whom it is stolen. What do you call the thing which changes a venial into a mortal sin? A circumstance. How did Albert confess his sin against the seventh commandment? Was his confession of that sin good? Albert confessed also the sins he had committed against the other commandments.

It is well to confess venial sins also. What happens to our soul when we commit a venial sin? Venial sin does not kill the soul, nor does it cause the Holy Ghost to leave the soul. Therefore we are not bound to confess our venial sins, and also there are other means of obtaining the pardon of them. But what effect do venial sins produce in our soul? Therefore it is well to confess them. But what happens to our soul, if we commit a mortal sin? Mortal sin kills our soul and causes the Holy Ghost to depart from it. Therefore we must confess at least all our mortal sins. Albert confessed all his mortal and all his venial sins.

What did Albert add to each sin he confessed? The number of times he had committed it. What did he add to the sin he confessed concerning the seventh commandment? The circumstance. How did Albert confess? He first told each sin he had committed; then he told the number of times he had committed each one; and lastly the necessary circumstance. He who confesses in this manner confesses well; and his confession is entire, that is, complete. (Questions on this point.) When is our confession entire or complete?

In confessing his sins against the sixth commandment Albert did not give a fixed (or determinate) number. But how did he express the number? Why did he say from three to five times a week? Because he did not know the exact number of times. What must we do, when we do not know the exact number of our sins? We must tell about the number we commit every day, or every week, or every month. But, children, be careful not to tell the number that may chance to present itself to your mind, but you must first think over it and try to find out the number as near as you can, and then confess that number which you really believe to be as near right as possible.

Sincere. When the confessor thinks that the penitent was not able to tell a sin correctly enough, he asks questions about it. What questions did the confessor ask Albert? What did Albert answer to each question?

Mention no one by name. How could Albert have said instead of: "Another boy led me into sin?" If he had said: "Antony N. led me into sin"; he would have told the boy's name; but that would have been very wrong, for in our confession we are not allowed to give the name of the person with whom we sin, or who led us into sin. We would be guilty of detraction, if we did so. Therefore, we must never mention any one by name in our confession.

What other questions did the confessor ask Albert about the boy who had led him into sin? Did Albert answer truly? Albert told all he knew, with discretion and humility. How did we call Peter's contrition, because he said with his lips just what he felt in his heart? What should we call Albert's answers? What must we do, when the confessor asks us questions? When the confessor asks us questions (questions us) we must answer sincerely and humbly.

Contrite. How did Albert feel when he confessed his grievous sins? He felt like weeping. Why? Because he was contrite, that is, he felt sorry for his sins. Where did he feel this sorrow? In his heart; in his soul. Because Albert felt sorry for his sins when he confessed them, we say that his confession was contrite. (Repeat.) Our confession must be contrite.

Confession defined. How must we confess our sins? What kind of acknowledgment or telling of sins is confession? Confession is a contrite acknowledgment of one's sins. To whom is this acknowledgment of sins made? To the priest. For what purpose? That he may absolve us from our sins; or to obtain the absolution of sins from him. Therefore we say: Confession is a contrite acknowledgment or telling of past sins to the priest, in order to obtain the absolution of them.

The Admonition. Before absolving a penitent, the priest usually gives him some admonition, or some advice, encouragement, or some direction. What admonition did the priest give Albert? What did Albert do? How did the priest console or encourage him? What effect did this produce on Albert? It encouraged him.

The Penance. What did Albert promise? You can easily imagine how attentively Albert listened to the confessor's admonition. What did the confessor tell Albert to say? These prayers are called the penance. (Repeat.)

The Absolution. Albert's sins were not yet forgiven. The principal thing was yet wanting. What was it? The absolution. Now the priest gave him absolution. By it all Albert's sins were forgiven. And he left the confessional.

3. THE BAD CONFESSION — *Fear.* How did Antony feel before his confession? Why was he so much afraid? What did the devil whisper to him? In the beginning Antony told all his sins right. What sins against the third commandment did he confess? How did he confess them? He also told his sins right against the fourth commandment. What sins had he committed against the fifth commandment? They were grievous sins. When he was about to confess them, he felt still more afraid; and the devil again whispered to him: "You cannot tell that."

Not clearly. What did Antony say? "I led another boy into grievous sins." But he pronounced the word grievous so low, in order that the confessor should not understand him. In the confessional we must not talk aloud, lest those who are outside should understand. Now if, when you are outside the confessional waiting for your turn to make your confession, and you would chance to hear what another said in confession, or what the priest said to him, you must never mention to any one what you overheard. It would be sinful for you to do so. That no one outside the confessional should hear what the penitent or the priest says in confession, it is necessary to speak there in a whisper or very low tone of voice (softly). But the penitent must not speak too low or too softly, otherwise the priest will not understand what he says. Therefore when you make your confession, you must speak so that those who are outside cannot understand you, and so that the priest may hear and understand everything you confess; then your confession is clear. When is the confession clear? How did Antony confess the word grievous? Why? How did this make Antony's confession bad? Because it was not clear. When a person wilfully, purposely tells his sins indistinctly (that is, not clearly), so that the confessor cannot understand him, his confession is bad, is worthless. Therefore, no sins can be forgiven in such a confession. Moreover, such a person adds another very grievous sin to his other sins, that is a bad or sacrilegious confession. If such a one has ten mortal sins on his conscience when he enters the confessional, how many mortal sins has he on his conscience when he leaves the confessional?

Concealing. What sins had Antony committed against the sixth commandment? How should he have confessed them? But how did he confess them? Which sins did he confess correctly? Which did he conceal? (Repeat.) Which sins had he committed against the seventh commandment? Which sin had Antony committed against the second commandment of the Church? How did he confess it? What kind of a sin had he committed? What did he say to excuse it? Was that true? He therefore told a lie! Therefore he concealed his sin, for he knew it was Friday, and yet he said he had not eaten it wilfully; and gave as his reason that He did not know then it was a Friday. His confession was not sincere; therefore it was a bad, a sacrilegious confession. His excuse was no real excuse, for it was a lie. His confession was not sincere. Our confession is sincere, when we tell our sins just as we know they are before God, without concealing or excusing what is really a grievous sin.

APPLICATION. Suppose you are making your confession, saying: "I took little things every day." And the priest asks you: "Did you take any money from your parents?" You should say right away: "No, I did not." But you must reflect a little, and then sincerely and humbly tell the priest what you remember about it. Children who are in the habit of telling lies, must be very careful at confession. The devil is glad when he sees such children going to confession. He thinks: "These are my children. I will go into the confessional with them and prevent them from making a sincere confession." Such children should, before going to confession, pray devoutly to the Holy Ghost to help them to make a sincere confession.

4. BENEFITS OF A GOOD CONFESSION. In the first place, a good confession gives joy to God. To whom do we confess our sins? In whose place does the confessor hear confessions? To whom, then, do you really make your confession? But God already knows our sins, because He knows all things. God knew the sin of Adam and Eve. And yet what did He ask them? God knew also the grievous sin of Cain. And yet what did He ask him? Why did God ask Adam and Cain what they had done? Because He wished that they should confess their sin. So you see God wishes the confession of sins. When you confess your sins, you do what God wishes you to do. And what does your confession give to God? Pleasure. Secondly, the angels also are pleased when a child makes a sincere confession. They rejoice in heaven every time a sinner makes a sincere confession of his sins. Thirdly, the guardian angel is full of joy when the child he guards sincerely confesses his mortal sins. He then thinks: "How

glad I am now to see the child I care for, become again a child of God." But more than all our divine Saviour rejoices, when a child sincerely confesses his mortal sins. He then says: " Oh, I am so glad of it; for I died for that child. I redeemed that child with My sufferings, and shed all My blood to save him. He belonged to Me, but his grievous sins tore him away from Me and gave him to the devil. How happy I am because he is again Mine."

The other boys had also gone to confession with Albert. How did they feel on their way home? Joy! They were greatly pleased. Albert also felt light-hearted. What did he say? And he found it easier to pray, to obey and become fond of study.

5. THE BAD EFFECTS OF A BAD CONFESSION — *An uneasy life*. But it was quite different with Antony. What did he feel in his heart? Fear and anxiety. This began already in the confessional immediately after he had told his sins. What did a voice in his heart say to him? Whose voice was it? How do you see his fear (dread) while the confessor was admonishing him? How did he show it also when the priest was giving him his penance? How did he behave on his way home? Why could he not be cheerful? On the following day, when the priest came into the school, Antony showed again his fear and anxiety. What did the priest say to the children? What happened then to Antony? Antony could no longer feel easy, for his conscience always kept on reproaching him.

Cain. What is the name of the man mentioned in Bible History, whose conscience always kept reproaching him with his crime? What did his conscience say to him? Cain wandered about the country from place to place to escape hearing the reproaches of his conscience. But wherever he went, he heard that voice saying: " You are a murderer." What is it that he could find nowhere?

Antony also heard everywhere the voice of his conscience. Therefore he could never again be cheerful.

What did he do when the other boys were playing? Why did he sometimes suddenly stop playing in the middle of a game? What did that voice say to him when he rose in the morning, and when he retired to rest at night? What is it that he could not find anywhere? What kind of life did he live in his sins? A restless life. What did this cause him? To feel as if he no longer could stand it. What did he then resolve to do? To make a good, sincere confession. Did he try to fulfil this resolution? What then happened to him at confession? And then what did he do? He again concealed his sins, and made another bad confession. He did the same thing every time he went to confession afterwards.

A miserable death. What was said about him, when he became twenty-one years old? How did he die? What kind of sin did he commit by hanging himself?

Where do they go who die without sin on their conscience? To heaven. Such a death is a happy death. But where does he go, who has one or more mortal sins on his conscience when he dies? To hell. That is the greatest misfortune. Therefore we call Antony's death an unhappy or a bad death. What was the cause of Antony's unhappy death? His want of sincerity in confession.

The shame on the last day. The sins which Antony concealed in his confessions will one day be published to all mankind. On the day of the general judgment all the sins of the damned will be visible as horrible spots on the faces of the damned so that all men and all angels may see and know them. Then everybody will say: "Look at so and so, how ugly and hideous he looks. Look at so and so; see how awful he looks for concealing his sins in confession!" What a shame will it then be for the sinner, for him who concealed his sins in confession, when God, the angels and the saints will know and read his sins marked on his face!

How did Antony live after his bad confession? How

did he die? What shall happen to him on the last day? He shall be put to shame before the whole world! How will he then feel? He would wish the earth to open and swallow him up, that all men might not see his sins!

Heaven grieves over him. What should he have done to prevent all this misery and shame? When Antony entered the confessional, the heavenly Father had His arms already extended to press him to His fatherly heart. His guardian angel was standing alongside of Antony, thinking: "If he only confesses all his sins well!" Even the Blessed Virgin and his holy patron were ready to celebrate a joyful feast on his account. But, alas! Antony's confession was not sincere. Hence the heavenly Father had to repel him with horror. His guardian angel weeping left his side, and the Blessed Virgin and his holy patron grieved over him.

Hell exults over him. But there was one who greatly rejoiced over him. Who could that be? Yes; not only one devil, all in hell rejoiced at the insincere confession of Antony. Therefore the devil had whispered to him in the confessional: "You cannot tell that, otherwise," etc. The devil frequently does that. When a child fears committing a sin, the devil whispers to him: "You need not be ashamed; do it. That is not so very bad. That is nothing." But when the child goes to confession, the devil comes again; but he speaks quite differently. "What! you cannot tell that. You would have to be terribly ashamed before the priest, if you would tell it." But that is not true; the devil lies.

The confessor is kind. The priest in the confessional is like a good mother, a very kind father. Suppose a child has done something very bad. He goes to his mother or to his kind father, full of sorrow, and sincerely acknowledges the wicked thing he has done. Will his father treat him harshly? Will he be very severe towards him? Oh, no; God has given the father a kind heart to forgive a child that sincerely tells his fault and is heartily sorry for it.

God has also given the priest in the confessional a good, kind heart for the penitent. When a child tells all his sins sincerely, the priest rejoices over it, for he sees then that the child is in earnest and wishes to do right. He treats the penitent in a friendly and kind manner, as a good father does his child. Therefore we address the priest in the confessional by the name of " Father." The confessor will not scold a sincere child; on the contrary, he will feel only too happy to absolve him and to love and honor him as a good child of God.

The confessor is discreet. A child needs never be afraid that the confessor will tell others anything of the child's confession. The confessor will never say a word about it. He quickly forgets what is told him in confession. And even if he should remember, he dare not say a word about it. God has strictly commanded him to keep silent on what is confessed to him. A man who does not repeat what he hears, is called discreet? Why is the confessor discreet?

The seal of confession. When a person writes an important letter, he not only closes it, but he carefully seals it, that no one may be able to read it, except him to whom it is addressed. In like manner, the priest is most strictly obliged to keep his mouth sealed about all that he hears in confession. He to whom the sealed letter is addressed, is the only one who has the right to break the seal to open the letter. But no priest is ever allowed to break the seal of confession. A confessor must rather undergo any suffering, any hardship, and even death itself, than ever to reveal what he heard in confession.

Why should no one be ashamed to tell his sins sincerely, in confession to the priest? The confessor is so kind; the confessor is discreet. Antony should have thought of that. What would have been the result, when he was making his confession? In his after life? He would not have lived in sin and worry. At his death? He would not have died an unhappy death. What would he then avoid on the last day?

Which is better, to conceal your sins in confession out of shame, or to tell your sins sincerely to a kind and discreet priest? What misfortune follows during life an insincere confession? At death? On the last day? What then should a child consider, when he feels ashamed to tell some sin or other in confession? He should consider that it is far better to confess his sins to a discreet priest, than to live worrying in his sins, to die a bad death, and to be disgraced on the last day before the whole world.

Dear children, if you have had the misfortune to commit some grievous sin, for instance, against the sixth or the seventh commandment, and you are very much afraid or ashamed to tell it to the priest in confession, you should pray fervently before going to confession to the Holy Ghost, to the Blessed Virgin and to your guardian angel for grace and courage to tell it sincerely in confession. Pray to the Holy Ghost: "O Holy Ghost, give me the grace and courage to tell all my sins in confession sincerely, especially this sin (mention it); do not permit that I should conceal it." Then say three times the Glory be to the Father, etc., in honor of the Holy Ghost. After this say: "O Mary, Mother of Jesus and my Mother also, refuge of sinners; I am a sinful child and have not the courage to confess this sin (mention it). O dear Mother, help me to confess it sincerely, so that I may not offend Jesus still more and lose my soul. O Mary, help me." Then say the Hail Mary three times. Then say: "O my good guardian angel, my protector, do not forsake me now. The devil is doing all he can to keep me from telling all my sins in confession, in order to drag me into hell. God has appointed thee to help me. Now I am in great need of thy help. Help me to make a good confession and to

tell this sin (mention it) to the priest." Then say one
Our Father, one Hail Mary, one Glory be to the Father,
etc., in honor of your guardian angel. And if when you
are in the confessional you lose courage, say to the priest:
"Father, I committed a sin (or some sins) which I have
not the courage to confess sincerely; please help me to do
so." Then the priest will kindly ask you some questions
to find out what sin you have not the courage to confess,
in order to help you to tell it. Remember that the priest
is only too glad to help you to make a good confession.
But be sure to give a true answer to every question. If
you do so, how happy you will feel! It will be like a big
load taken off your heart, for your sins shall be forgiven.
(Ask questions and rehearse the prayers. All this is very
important.)

SUMMARY. What is confession? Confession is the contrite acknowledgment of past sins to a priest, to obtain
the absolution of our sins from him. Which are the qualities of confession? Confession must be complete (entire),
sincere and distinct (clear). When is the confession complete? When we confess at least all our mortal sins, together with their number and their necessary circumstances.
If we do not know their exact number, what must we do?
We must tell it as near as we can. If a sin is habitual,
we may confess it by saying about how often we committed
it every day, or every week, or every month. Are we
obliged to confess our venial sins? Although we are not
obliged to confess our venial sins, it is well and profitable
to do so. When is our confession sincere? When we
confess our sins just as we know them before God, without
concealing or excusing them. What should we consider,
when we feel ashamed or afraid to confess some grievous
sin? We should consider: "It is a thousand times better
to confess them to a discreet priest, than to lead a restless
and worried life, to die an unhappy death, and to be disgraced on the last day before the whole world." When

is our confession distinct? Our confession is distinct when we tell our sins, so that the priest can understand all we say to him.

APPLICATION. There was over five hundred years ago a very cruel king in Bohemia. He wished to find out what sins the queen told the priest in confession. He sent for her confessor, who was a real saint. His name was John Nepomucene. The king said to him: "I want you to tell me what the queen said to you in confession." But John answered not a word. The king then cried out: "If you do not tell me, you will find out what I will do to you." But the holy priest paid no attention to what the king said. Then the king ordered his body to be burned with torches. But the priest remained steadfast and would not tell even a word of the queen's confession. Then the bad king condemned the holy priest to death. He was cast into the river with a big stone tied to him, and he was drowned. He had preferred to suffer death rather than reveal what he had heard in confession. A number of other priests have died, others have suffered imprisonment rather than break the seal of confession. And every priest is bound to suffer every kind of torment, and even death, rather than reveal a penitent's confession. Therefore, you can safely tell all your sins to the priest in confession.

Here is a beautiful picture. Look at it. What do you see? A lamb. What is around the lamb? Thorns. The lamb got entangled in these thorns and can no longer get loose from them. What would happen to it? It would die. Who is kneeling beside the lamb? A man. What has He in His hand? A staff. A shepherd's staff. The man is a shepherd. What is He doing? He is loosening the lamb from the thorns. Here is another picture. Where has the Shepherd put the lamb? On His shoulders. After freeing the lamb from the thorns, the Shepherd, full of joy, placed the lamb on His shoulders to bring it home.

Who is this Good Shepherd? It is Jesus. Who is that

stray lamb? It is a child that got entangled into his sins. That child cannot free himself from his sins. And what would then happen to him? He would die in his sins and be condemned to hell. But Jesus, the Good Shepherd, comes to his help. In confession He frees the sinner from the thorns of his sins; and then He takes him again as His child, and brings him back to the heavenly Father.

Dear children, you are going to confession. Are you going to confess like Antony, or like Albert? Are you going to give joy in your confession to the devil or to your guardian angel? From this day say a prayer daily to the Holy Ghost, to the Blessed Virgin, to your guardian angel till the day of your confession, that you may make a good confession.

16. Satisfaction.

OBJECT. Have we done all that was necessary, when our confession is over? Need we do anything more? Let us see.

I. DEVELOPMENT.

1. ATONING FOR THE TEMPORAL PUNISHMENT DUE TO SIN — *Expiating or paying up.* Charles stole ten dollars from his neighbor. When his father found that out, he said: "Wait, boy, you shall pay me for that. I will soon cure you of stealing." What would you say, if Charles' father would give him only one blow of the rod? That will not do; that is not enough. One stroke of the rod is not sufficient for so great a sin. What did Charles deserve for it? A severe punishment; a rigorous penance. But he received severe punishment from his father. It was only when Charles had enough, that his father ceased punishing him. And why? Because the punishment had its effect, and therefore, it was enough. Charles had sufficiently atoned for his theft. Why was Charles punished? To expiate (atone for) his sin.

All men have deserved punishment. Who committed the first grievous sin on earth? How did God punish Adam and Eve for it? They were driven out of paradise, condemned to work hard, to sweat, to suffer cold; Eve would have much to suffer from her children; and both were to die. How long did those punishments last? Until their death. These punishments were not everlasting, but only for a time, only temporal.

Temporal punishments. Where are these punishments expiated? Where should Adam and Eve have gone after their death to be punished? Because all men are children of Adam and Eve, all men should have gone there also after their death. By what sin does a man deserve the punishment of hell every time he commits it? How long will the pains of hell last? Forever. What are they, therefore, called? Eternal punishment.

Our divine Saviour atoned for the eternal punishment we deserved. God created men not for hell, but for heaven. Therefore the Son of God said to His heavenly Father: "Do not cast men into hell; I will atone (suffer punishment) for them." How did the Son of God atone for us? In His passion and death our Saviour underwent such great sufferings, as if He had been burnt in hell for us. In this manner He atoned for the eternal punishment we deserved. And what did He deserve for us at the same time? Grace. Where is grace contained? In which sacraments are our sins forgiven? What must we do to obtain the forgiveness of our sins in the sacrament of penance? Be sorry for them and confess them. What is forgiven us together with our mortal sins? The eternal punishment is remitted to us together with our mortal sins. This is the case in every good confession.

We must also do penance ourselves for a time. It would not be right, if we had nothing to suffer for our sins, since our innocent Saviour suffered so much for us. Therefore God wills that we also should do some penance for our sins. For this reason He sends to men sickness, poverty, misfortune, storms, death, and sends them for a long time to purgatory. How do we call the punishments that we have to undergo on earth and in purgatory? Temporal punishments.

Some have to atone more, others less. Who will receive more temporal punishment, he who has committed few sins, or he who has committed many sins? He who has committed mortal sins, or he who has committed only venial sins?

The paralytic atoned for all his temporal punishment on account of his great contrition. He had committed many grievous sins. What punishment had he to suffer? He was sick for thirty-eight years. But he was very sorry for his sins. Therefore our Saviour not only remitted his sins and their everlasting punishment in hell, but also completely cured him. Which punishment did he thereby remit? The temporal punishment.

God remits to us also at least a part of the temporal punishment. If we are as sorry for our sins as we can possibly be, God remits to us in the sacrament of penance all the temporal punishment due to us. But to those who are not so sorry as that, God remits in the sacrament of penance only a part of the temporal punishment. This is usually the case at confession. Which punishment does God not always remit with our sins? Which punishment does He always remit with our sins? God always remits the eternal punishment together with our sins, but not always all the temporal punishment. The rest of the temporal punishment we must atone for ourselves.

For this purpose the confessor imposes a penance. How did Charles' father make him expiate his theft? He punished him. At confession the confessor punishes us in God's place for our sins, by giving us a penance. For instance, he says to us: " For your penance say five times the Our Father and five times the Hail Mary "; or, " say the Litany of the Blessed Virgin "; or, " say the rosary or beads."

Which punishment for sin do we atone for by fulfilling the penance the confessor gives us?   The temporal punishment.   By this penance we satisfy for our sins.   How did Charles' father punish him?   Until he had enough; until he had atoned (satisfied) for his theft.   We also atone for our sins, till we have done enough.   That is why the confessor imposes a penance upon us.   If by our penance we atone for as much punishment as we deserve, we have done enough, and satisfied God.   By doing the penance the priest gives us in confession, we satisfy God.

II. THE AMENDMENT OF LIFE.

We shall see what the punishment was for besides, which Charles received for his theft.   If his father had not punished him, Charles would most probably have stolen again, and would get accustomed to steal and become a regular thief.   But what did he think every time he felt tempted to steal?   And what would such a thought do to him?   It would keep him from yielding to the temptation and stealing again.   What help did those blows afford him?   Helped to keep him from stealing; helped him to become a better boy; helped him to amend his life.   What did his father say to him when punishing him?   Why did his father punish him?   To amend his life.

God wills that, after our confession, we should be more on our guard against committing sin, for instance, against stealing, disobeying, telling lies, cursing, etc.   Therefore the confessor, in God's place, imposes a penance on the penitent; and the confessor gives such a penance as will help him to become better.   For instance, to a child who curses, the confessor may say: " For your penance you shall say every time you curse again: Our Father, who art in heaven; hallowed be Thy name."   Now suppose such a child curses again soon after his confession.   What must he then do? His conscience tells him right away: " You have cursed again, you must do your penance, and say with devotion: Our Father, who art in heaven; hallowed be Thy name." The child does this, and afterwards takes more care to keep from cursing. Perhaps he curses again the next day. What does his conscience tell him? What does he do? After this he takes still better care to keep from cursing. His penance is always before him, when he feels tempted to curse. And then in a short time he is able to get rid of his bad habit of cursing, and he amends his life. So you see that that child, by means of his penance atones for the temporal punishment due for his sins, and succeeds in amending his life.

The salutary penance. You have a sore finger, and you put on it a poultice. Why do you do that? A bad habit, such as cursing or telling lies is like a disease or a sore on the soul. And the medicine or the poultice that is to heal it, is the penance imposed by the confessor. What is the use of that penance for the soul's sickness or sore? It is intended to cure it. Therefore we call it salutary penance, that is, a penance that cures. In confession we ask the confessor for such a penance.

Definition of Satisfaction. What do you give to God, when you perform the penance the confessor has given you? Satisfaction. Therefore we say: Satisfaction is the performance of the penance imposed by the confessor. (Repeat.) Satisfaction is the fifth part of the sacrament of penance.

III. THE PERFORMANCE OF THE PENANCE.

Not to perform the penance. You should willingly recite the penance given you by the confessor. As soon as he tells it to you, you should think: " God sends me this penance; I will willingly perform as a punishment for my sins." But if you would immediately think in the confessional: " That penance is too big; I will not say it ";

you would commit a mortal sin and cause your confession to be bad. What are the effects of a bad confession?

Punctually to perform the penance. 1. You must perform the penance exactly as the confessor told you. If he told you: " Say five Our Fathers kneeling," you must say them kneeling, and not standing or sitting down. If he says: " Say five Our Fathers before the cross," you say them there and nowhere else. 2. Suppose the confessor says: " Say three Our Fathers and three Hail Marys "; how many times must you say those prayers? Only once. When the priest does not tell you the number of times, it means that you should say them only once. 3. If the confessor tells you: " Say three Our Fathers and three Hail Marys for three days." What does he mean? He means that I should say three Our Fathers and three Hail Marys on the day of my confession; the same on the next also, and the same also on the second day after my confession. But a child may say: " I always say all my penance at once after my confession, because, if I did not, I might forget it." But this is not what the confessor wishes you to do. He wishes you in this case to say some of it every day for a number of days, partly in order not to give you too long a penance to say at once, and partly in order to make you think longer of your confession and of the good resolutions you made. Nevertheless, it would not be a mortal sin, if you said the penance all at once after your confession.

The forgotten Penance. Suppose a child receives the penance of saying three Our Fathers and three Hail Marys for three days. He thinks: " That is not much; I will willingly say those prayers." Therefore after leaving the confessional he says three Our Fathers and three Hail Marys for the first day. But he is light-minded and forgets to say his penance the two following days. Is his confession bad? No, he confessed sincerely, and intended to do the penance; but on account of his levity he may have committed a venial sin; and he surely lost many graces by his forgetfulness. If he later on remembers the penance, he should say it, and in his next confession he should tell the priest: "I forgot twice to say my penance."

Rigorous penances of ancient times. Now-a-days the confessor does not usually impose big penances, but only light ones. In olden times the penances imposed in confession were very much heavier. Those who swore through levity, had to fast for seven days, eating only dry bread, and drinking only water. Therefore we call it a seven-days' fast on bread and water. For talking in church the penance was a ten-days' fast on bread and water. For disrespect of parents, it was a forty-days' fast on bread and water. For a sin of impurity, a fast on bread and water for forty to one hundred days.

Now think how long some of you would have to fast, if the confessor would now impose similar penances for grievous sins! How long would you have to fast merely for talking in church! Make it out when you go home. If this were now practised, some children would have to fast all their life on bread and water!

Formerly the penance given by the confessor sufficed to atone for all the temporal punishment due for sin. In those times those who conscientiously performed those rigorous penances, surely atoned for all the temporal punishment due for their sins. Such persons satisfied God entirely by these penances. Where did such persons go immediately after their death?

God still demands now from us as much penance as formerly. And now compare with such penances the light penances the confessor imposes on you. Do you believe that by such light penances you can satisfy for all the temporal punishments you owe for your sins? Or do you believe that now-a-days God is not so strict as formerly? God demands now as much temporal punishment as formerly for light-minded swearing, for disrespect to parents, etc., because these sins are now just as great as formerly. Hence you shall have to undergo the temporal punishments your sins deserve. You can satisfy for them by performing some penance of your own accord.

The temporal punishments due for sins must be atoned for either on earth on in purgatory. Suppose you were to die, before satisfying for all of them. Where would you be obliged to satisfy for them? In the fire of purgatory until they would all be atoned for. We must satisfy for the temporal punishment due to our sins either during life on earth, or in purgatory after our death.

SUMMARY. What is meant by due satisfaction in the sacrament of penance? The performance of the penance imposed by the confessor. Why does the confessor impose a penance? The confessor imposes a penance, first, to satisfy for the temporal punishment due for sin, and secondly, to amend our life. Does God remit all punishment when He remits sins? He always remits the eternal punishment with the sins, but not always the temporal. Which is the temporal punishment of sin? It is the punishment which we must undergo either on earth or in purgatory for our sins.

APPLICATION. Dear children, none of you would like to atone for your sins in purgatory. We can escape purgatory, if we do some little penances of our own for our sins. I will tell you how you can do it. For instance, a boy has cursed; "for cursing," he says, "I will say: Hallowed be Thy name"; or, "Glory be to the Father," etc. A girl came a little late to Mass on Sunday. She performs for this the penance of going once or twice extra to Mass on a week day. A boy was playing; his mother called him home; but he disobeyed her. A good penance for him would be not to go out into the street for one day; or only for an hour. A child has taken little things at home; a good penance would be for each time to do without sugar in his coffee, or without butter on his bread.

Another ate a piece of meat on a Friday; let him do without fruit, without cake, or eat what he does not like. Another told lies; let him say an Our Father, or a Hail Mary for each lie. Another talked in church; let him say an Our Father kneeling. A child has a sore, has toothache, etc., let him say: " I will bear it all as a penance for my sins, especially for.   ." Dear children, punish yourselves, that God may not need to punish you. Who will impose penances in himself for his sins? I will ask you another time, who did so.

17. A practical Confession.

PREPARATION. We shall soon get through the instructions on the sacrament of penance. I have but one point more to explain. The day is near when you will all be glad; that day you have longed for. Which day is that? The day on which you will be admitted to make your first confession. The day of your first confession is for you a day of great joy.

After baptism your soul was wonderfully beautiful. You were perfectly free from sin and adorned with the white garment of sanctifying grace. You were children of God, and were allowed to call Him Father. Many, perhaps all of you have always remained until now children of God. Perhaps not one of you has committed a mortal sin, and your soul is still adorned with the garment of sanctifying grace, which you received in baptism. May God be a thousand times thanked for this. How happy you are now for this.

But all of you have committed venial sins. Some of you have perhaps committed a great many of them, such as, praying without attention, pronouncing with levity the holy name of God, being irreverent in church, disobedient to your parents, telling lies, etc. Each of your venial sins made a little stain on your soul's white garment of sanctifying grace, and it is no longer quite as beautiful as when you received it in baptism.   On account of these stains you must feel ashamed before God and His angels and saints. And so long as even only one stain remains, you are not fit to enter heaven.

Perhaps some one among you has even committed a mortal sin, perhaps through immodesty.   O poor child, how unhappy you have made yourself by that sin.   You have fearfully stained and torn the garment of your soul. You are no longer a child of God.   If you were to die thus, God would have to cast you into hell.

But, O joy, O happiness, all that can still be repaired. He who is no longer a child of God, can again become one, and then his heart will again be pure from sin, and he will receive a brand new garment of sanctifying grace.   And those who have only little stains in their soul, can remove them all, and their garment of grace will again be as white as fresh fallen snow, and as bright as the sun.   Who can tell how this will happen?   By making a good confession. So you see how everything depends on how you make your confession.

I.

OBJECT.   I will now tell you how a good boy made his confession.   From this you will learn how to make yours.

1. RELATION.   The boy's name was Charles.   He wished to make a very good confession, and yet he was somewhat afraid lest he should not do everything properly.   Therefore he resolved: " I will pray fervently to God to help me."   On the evening previous to his confession he took his prayer book (or catechism) and went into the church. The altar lamp before the tabernacle was shining in so friendly a way, like the evening star.   Have you ever noticed how its little flame trembles and flares?   It is like a little tongue silently, quietly saying to us: " Come here, my child; come here, for here dwells our loving, sweet

Jesus, who is so fond of children." Charles knelt down right in front of the altar. He began to pray: "O my dearest Jesus, to-morrow I am to make my first confession. Oh, deign to help me to do it right. O Mary, ever Virgin, Mother of Jesus and my Mother also, pray for me. My holy guardian angel, assist me." Then he invoked the Holy Ghost: "Come, Holy Ghost," etc. Charles now opened his prayer book (catechism), and said the prayer before the examination of conscience.

After this he began to examine his conscience carefully. He reflected on all his life as far back as he could remember, and asked himself: "What sins have I committed against the first commandment?" After finding out all he could remember, he examined what sins he had committed against the second commandment. Thus he went through the commandments of God, the commandments of the Church, and the seven capital sins. He found out sins almost against every commandment, and also the number of times he had committed them. He thought over them and their number so carefully that he should remember them well. He was not in a hurry, but took his time. And why?

After this Charles excited contrition in his heart for his sins. He thought of God the Father, God the Son and God the Holy Ghost, or God the Chief Good, whom he had offended by his sins, and asked forgiveness of God the Father, God the Son and God the Holy Ghost. He thought also of purgatory, of the pains of hell which he, perhaps, had deserved on account of his sins. And again besought God for forgiveness. He was sorry from his heart for his sins, and resolved never to sin again. He resolved especially to combat his favorite fault, anger. He also resolved never again to associate with the bad companions, who had already led him into sin a few times. Then he slowly recited from his heart the act of contrition: "O my God, I am heartily sorry," etc.

The next day was the day appointed for his confession. In the morning Charles went to Mass and prayed very devoutly. When the time for the children's confession came, he was already in church repeating his preparation of the previous evening. (A few questions on this.) He continued doing so, and making acts of contrition kneeling around the confessional, silently waiting for his turn to make his confession, and reading from his prayer book the prayer before confession.

2. When his turn came, Charles entered the confessional and knelt down. The confessor gave him his blessing, and Charles made the sign of the cross, saying: " Bless me, Father, for I have sinned." Then he recited the *Confiteor* until " through my fault." After this he sincerely confessed his sins and the number of each as far as he could remember, in the same order as he had made the examination of his conscience; then he said: I am heartily sorry for all these sins and for all that I do not remember; I ask pardon of God for them, and penance of you, Father, and absolution if you judge me worthy. Then he finished the *Confiteor*. After this the confessor asked Charles a few questions, and Charles sincerely answered them. The priest then spoke a few words of admonition to Charles and gave him a penance. Charles listened very attentively to what the priest said to him, and humbly received his penance. Then whilst the priest was giving him absolution, Charles renewed the act of contrition, and made the sign of the cross, whilst the priest was saying: " I absolve thee from thy sins, in the name of the Father," etc. Charles then left the confessional.

3. After Charles had returned to his place, he knelt down and began to pray thus within himself: " O how happy I feel now! I am again a child of God. O my good God, I thank Thee a thousand times for this." Then he opened his prayer book and slowly read the prayer after confession. Then he said the prayers the confessor had imposed

on him for his penance, and, of his own accord, recited the Litany of the Blessed Virgin and other prayers. Moreover, he made this resolution: "Henceforth I will fight against my favorite sin, anger, and be on my guard against it." He then went home.

II. CONSIDERATION. WHAT WE SHOULD DO ON THE EVE OF CONFESSION.

We must first pray. What is the name of the boy I have spoken about? Charles wished to go to confession. What did he feel a little before making it? He wished to do it well. How did he begin? He began by praying. What must we know before confession? But we have usually forgotten most of our sins. What must we do to remember them? Examine our conscience. Who is to help us in doing so? What should we do to obtain the assistance of the Holy Ghost? What was Charles going to do to obtain it?

We should go into the church. Therefore Charles went into the Church the evening before. What did he take along? The altar lamp was shining in so friendly a manner before the tabernacle. What did that lamp's trembling flame invite him to do? Where did Charles kneel?

To whom should we pray. How did Charles begin his prayer? To whom, then, did he pray first? To Jesus. To whom did he pray next? To Mary and his guardian angel. Whom did he finally invoke in a special manner? The Holy Ghost. How did he pray to Him? You may also use your prayer book (or catechism) for this. (If the catechism in use contains instructions and prayers for confession, tell the children to open their catechism and go through said prayers with them, the examination of conscience, etc. Children should have and use prayer-books in church from the time they can read a little. Where this is not done, children will hardly use a prayer-book later on, and that is why so many grown up boys and girls are seen at Mass, holy Communion without prayer books, staring distractedly all over the church, and making very careless confessions.)

4. *Examination of conscience.* What did Charles do after praying? He began to examine his conscience. How should we examine our conscience? With what commandment did Charles begin to examine his conscience? What did he ask himself concerning the first commandment? "Have I omitted my morning prayers?" etc. After each question which he answered by yes, he asked himself: "How many times did I do that?" And he tried earnestly to find out the number of times as near as he could; if he could not find out the exact number, he tried to find out about how many times it was. Then concerning some of his sins, such as sins against the sixth and seventh commandments, he examined whether there had not been some circumstance which would change a venial sin into a mortal sin. Charles examined his conscience not for the past week or two, but as it was his first confession, he examined it concerning the sins of his whole life as far as he could remember. And as this will be your first confession, you must do the same. You must examine your whole life as far as you can remember, and try to find out all the sins you have ever committed, their number, and those that special circumstances caused sins venial in themselves to become mortal sins.

5. *Contrition.* It must be sincere. Contrition is the most necessary part of the sacrament of penance. What had Charles to feel in his heart, in order that God should forgive him? Of whom did he think in order to excite himself to contrition? Of God the Father, God the Son, God the Holy Ghost; of God, the highest and Chief Good. And what did he pray for? For forgiveness. Of what else did he think? Of purgatory and hell. What did he again do? And what did he resolve to do? What prayer did he then say? The act of contrition, as given in the

catechism. But that was not enough. What other prayer did he say? The act of contrition in his prayer book after the examination of conscience. Where did Charles then go? (Repeat.)

6. *You may examine your conscience also at home.* If you have a room at home in which you can be alone for some time, you may examine your conscience at home also.

7. What you should do before confession on the day of your confession. A good confession is a great grace for which we should earnestly pray God. Where did Charles go in the morning for that purpose? He put on his best clothes to go to confession, and took his prayer book along. He did not tarry in the street on his way. He was already in church half an hour before the time. To whom did he pray first? And then what did he do? He repeated to himself the sins, their number and circumstances which he was to confess, that he might not omit anything in confession. What did he do next? He made a sincere act of contrition and the good resolution. This should never be forgotten before going to confession. Then he read slowly in his prayer book the prayers before confession. You must all do the same. If after this you have to wait some time before your turn comes to enter the confessional, you must not remain idle, looking around, talking and laughing; you should then review in your mind what you have to confess, and say some prayers, that you may make a good confession.

2. WHAT TAKES PLACE IN THE CONFESSIONAL — *The priest's blessing.* What did Charles do when his turn came to make his confession? He entered the confessional, and knelt down. His guardian angel accompanied him with joy. Then he said to the priest: Bless me, Father, for I have sinned. When the priest was blessing him, Charles made the sign of the cross very devoutly. Then he recited the *Confiteor* until, "through my fault." To whom did Charles confess his sins? Whose place does the con-

fessor take in the confessional? To whom do we really tell our sins in confession? God sees our heart, and knows well whether we are going to tell our sins sincerely. Charles thought of this when he was saying the *Confiteor.*

The Confession. After saying the first part of the *Confiteor,* Charles told the priest that this was his first confession. He then began by confessing the sins he had committed against the first commandment, and the number of each. He continued to tell his sins and their number in the order of the commandments, etc.

In what direction should you tell your sins? In the direction of the little grate, where the priest has his ear that he may easily hear what you are confessing. (As to those children who are very small, and the grate is too high for them, they should make their confession standing, otherwise they cannot hear what the priest may ask or tell them, and the priest cannot either understand them.) In telling your sins speak slowly, distinctly and softly so that the priest may understand you, and that those who are outside may not hear what you are confessing. Those outside who happen to overhear what the priest or the penitent says in the confessional, must never speak about it to any one. If you happen to forget some sin in the course of your confession, go on and tell the rest without worrying over it; if you remember it when you are through with the other sins, tell it at the end. What did Charles say at the end of his confession? You must say the same, but with attention and slowly.

How often did Charles make an act of contrition for his confession? Three times. When? Twice before it and once at the end of his confession. If you happened to forget making an act of contrition before your confession, you must at least make it before the priest gives you absolution. Contrition is more important than anything else in confessing your sins. To omit making an act of contrition before absolution, renders the confession null and void (worthless). How do you say that little act of contrition at the end of confession before the priest questions you and gives you a penance and absolution? " I am heartily sorry for all these sins," etc. (see I. 2). By these words you express your contrition for all your sins, not only for those you have actually confessed, but also for all those which you have forgotten.

The Confessor's Questions and the Penitent's Answers. After Charles had finished the prayer at the end of his confession, the confessor asked him some questions. The confessor will perhaps ask you also some questions. If you do not understand what the priest asks you, say to the priest: " Please, Father, I do not understand what you ask me." The confessor will ask you again. How did Charles answer the confessor's questions? Sincerely. Do not, before answering, try to find out some excuse for your sins. God knows them; you cannot deceive Him. You must tell the truth in your answers; that is, you must be sincere, and tell your sins just as they are. Therefore answer the priest sincerely and humbly.

The Admonition. The confessor also admonished Charles. What did Charles do, when the confessor was admonishing him? He listened to him very attentively. The confessor will also give you a short admonition. He may perhaps tell you not to go any more with certain companions, or to certain places; or he will tell you to do certain things. You must after your confession do exactly what he has said to you in his admonition. Like Charles, you must listen very attentively to all that he says, so that you may well remember it, and do it faithfully.

The penance. The confessor also told Charles a certain thing he should remember and do after his confession. What was that? The penance. The confessor will also give you a penance. You must, therefore, pay great attention, that you may understand it, and remember and do it after your confession. What must you pay attention to in confession?   To what the confessor asks, and to what he tells us.   How must you answer his questions?

You must understand the penance given you.   When you have understood the penance, answer: " Yes, Father "; or say: " Thank you, Father."   But if you did not understand the penance, do not say: " Yes, Father "; but say: " Please, Father, I did not understand the penance."   Be sure not to go out of the confessional till you understand the penance.   Sometimes the confessor may ask you before he gives you the penance: " Have you anything else (or any more sins) to confess? "   If you do not remember anything else, say: " No, Father."   But if you remember some other sin or sins, tell it (them) right away.

The Absolution.   It is not yet all over.   There remains the principal thing to be done.   The penitent is not yet rid of his sins.   How are our sins taken away or forgiven? How did the priest give absolution to Charles?   What did Charles do when receiving it?   You must do the same.

The Effects of the Absolution.   Have you ever reflected on what happens at that solemn moment when the priest gives absolution to a penitent?   The Holy Ghost comes into the penitent's soul, washes away all his sins, and his soul becomes what it would have been, had he committed no sin.   His soul puts on again the garment of sanctifying grace, and becomes pleasing to God.   He becomes again a child of God, and God loves him again, as before; and if he dies in that state, God will admit him into heaven. Such is the great benefit of the priest's absolution.   No angel can do what the priest does by giving absolution to a penitent sinner.

Leaving the Confessional.   Now the confession is all over, and the penitent leaves the confessional.   (Repeat in order what takes place in the confessional.)

3. *A hearty thanksgiving.*   Where did Charles kneel, when he came out of the confessional?   What did he then do?   He first prayed in silence in his own words.   What

did he say in his heart? What does a beggar say when he receives alms? What do you say when your father gives you something good? In confession God bestows on you an immense benefit; He forgives your sins, and again makes your soul pure and beautiful. What should you say to God after your confession? Why did Charles then say: "O my good God, I thank Thee a thousand times for this"? This thanksgiving of Charles was rather short. Therefore he opened his prayer book and read therein slowly and attentively the prayers after confession. You should do the same.

Performing the Penance. What prayer did Charles say after his thanksgiving? He performed his penance exactly as the confessor had imposed it on him. You should do the same. You should, whenever it is possible, perform your penance immediately after thanking God. In what case you need not perform the penance immediately after thanking God for forgiving you your sins? But suppose when you come to your place after leaving the confessional, you remark that you do not know any more what penance the priest gave you. What must you then do? Return to the confessional and tell the priest you forgot what penance he gave you. But if the priest has already left the confessional, you must say in your next confession: "I did not say my penance the last time, because I forgot what it was."

Voluntary penance. When Charles had performed the penance the confessor had given him, he thought it was too little. What other penance did he perform of his own accord for his sins? What special resolution did he also make? You should likewise impose on yourself some little penance of your own choice for your sins? What voluntary penance could you do? Why should you do that?

Going home. What did Charles do, when he had finished his voluntary penance? You also should go directly home after finishing your penance. Do not wait for the other children, but go home in silence. People should be aware that you have been to confession, and you should reflect that God now looks upon you with complacency.

Do not speak about your confession. It would be wrong to tell one another what the confessor said to you in confession.

The amendment of life. The day after your confession you should all go to Mass, in order to thank God for the great grace He bestowed upon you. Remember that not everything is over, when you have made your confession. On the contrary, you must now earnestly begin a new life. You should start on the very day of your confession. You should so behave at home that your brothers should never hear you say a wrong word again. You should always think: "Now I will try to be a better child." You should especially try to overcome your favorite (predominant) fault. What would you say of a child that promised in confession to do better, and yet commits again all his former faults immediately after confession? What kind of resolution did such a child make? He did not mean it! He made it with his lips, but not from his heart. How can you know when a child meant what he promised? Which is the surest sign of a good confession? If we amend our life after confession. "Go and sin no more." Repeat now in proper order what you have to do after confession.

SUMMARY. What is the most necessary thing to obtain forgiveness of our sins? Contrition. When should we excite in us contrition for our sins when we go to confession? We should do so before confession, or at least before receiving absolution. How should you begin your confession? How should you conclude it? What should you then do? Listen to and sincerely answer the questions of the confessor. What should you do next? Pay great attention to the confessor's admonition and to the penance he gives. When should you perform the penance? Immediately after our thanksgiving, if it is possible.

Which is the surest sign of a good confession? If we really amend our life after confession.

APPLICATION. The catechist should make a confession, so that the children may learn practically how to tell their sins, with their number and necessary circumstances. Appoint one of the most talented to repeat the confession you have made; but be careful to direct him not to tell his own sins.

18. Extreme Unction.

PREPARATION. When our divine Saviour lived on earth, He did good to all men. Whom did he love in a special manner? Children, the poor and the sick. How did He show His love for the sick? What did people say of Him on this account? "He has done all things well; He gives sight to the blind," etc. The blind, the deaf, etc., were sick in their body. How can we get sick in our soul? By committing sin. How can sin be removed from the soul? Then the soul recovers health. Our Saviour cured also the souls of men. Can you name some whose souls He cured? How did He do so? How well they were afterwards, and how joyful and happy they felt! Our Saviour when on earth cured many others that were sick in soul and in body. Jesus cares even now for the sick. He instituted a special sacrament for those who are very sick, to benefit them in both body and soul. It is the sacrament of extreme unction.

OBJECT. I will now tell you how the sacrament of extreme unction benefits in both body and soul those who are very sick.

RELATION. There was once a boy thirteen years old who was very sick. The physician was sent for; but all his medicines did him no good. He grew worse. The sick boy suffered great pains. He sometimes cried out: "I suffer so much; I believe I am going to die." But when saying this, he began to think of his sins. This thought made him very much afraid, for after death comes judgment; and he thought: "What will then happen to me?" The devil also tormented him. He tried to lead the sick boy into sin, that he might prevent him from going to heaven. He tried to make him murmur and complain against God, for letting him get sick. He inspired him with wicked thoughts; he said to him: "You shall come to hell with me, because God will not forgive you."

The sick boy continued to complain, and cried out: "Oh, how afraid I am and worried in soul! O dear Lord, do not abandon me; forgive me." His mother said to him: "We are going to send for the priest, and he will prepare you for death." The boy consented. The priest soon came with the Blessed Sacrament, preceded by altar boys carrying lighted candles. The sick boy then made his confession, and was absolved from his sins. Then he received our Lord in holy Communion. Then the priest took a small silver vase containing blessed oil in his left hand, and dipped the thumb of his right hand into the oil and made the sign of the cross with it first on the boy's closed eyes, then on his ears, his nostrils, his lips, his hands and feet, praying, at the same time, God to forgive him the sins he had committed in his life with his eyes, his ears, his smell, his taste, his tongue, his hands and his feet. Soon after the priest left the house. And now, how wonderful! the sick boy became quiet and patient; he no longer complained. But he said: "Oh, how glad I feel now! I feel so light and so well in my heart. I am not afraid now to die. If it is God's will, I am content to suffer longer, or to die." But this was not all. His bodily pains began to diminish. Each day the sick boy's health improved, and in a short time he was perfectly well again. He lived many years since then; and when he reached the age of seventy-two years, he got sick again, and shortly after again receiving extreme unction, he died calmly. Such was God's holy will.

CONSIDERATION — *Sickness.* The boy of whom I have been speaking, was very sick. Who is called to help or cure the sick? The doctor was sent for. What did he prescribe? Did the medicines help? He grew worse.

Bodily pains. What pains did the sick boy suffer in his body? He could not sleep, breathed with difficulty, had a high fever, etc. What complaints did he make? The sick usually make the same complaints. What does sickness cause the body? Pains.

Worry of the soul. The sick boy thought he would die. What thoughts did the fear of death bring to his mind? What does the thought of death make the sick feel? Worry. What happens when a person dies? Where would his soul go, if he is in the state of sin? He thinks of that. And what does his thought bring to his mind? Dear children, how painful is death to those who have committed mortal sin! They are very much afraid. They dread the judgment of God. They do not know what will happen to them. They fear they will be condemned to the endless torments of hell.

The temptations of the devil. What else torments the sick boy's soul? The devil will not let sick people suffer in patience, or think on God or love God. He tries to bring them to hell with him. He wishes to keep them out of heaven, because he himself cannot enter it. When a person is very sick and seems likely to die, the devil thinks: "Now is my chance. If that person dies with a mortal sin on his conscience, he belongs to me, and I will take him to hell with me." To what does the devil wish to tempt the sick? He tempts them to impatience, so that they may murmur against God, saying: "Why did God let me get sick?" The devil also tries to make the sick angry, so as to scold and curse others. The devil tries also to make them commit other sins, to bring bad thoughts to their mind. He tells the sick person: "God will not forgive you your sins; you shall surely go to hell." In this way the devil acted towards that sick boy. He tried to make him commit sin; to make him murmur against God; to make him believe: " God will not forgive me my sins." What did the sick boy then feel in his soul? A great fear and worry. How did he complain? " O how I feel worried in my mind! O dear Lord, help me, and do not abandon me."

The last sacraments. What did his mother ask him? He was glad to have the priest called. What did the priest bring with him? How could people know that the priest was bringing our Lord! What was the first thing the sick boy had to do? Confess his sins. What effect did this have on his soul? What did the Holy Ghost bring to his soul in the sacrament of penance? What did the sick boy receive next? Our divine Saviour in holy Communion. He who has Jesus in his soul, possesses all graces. From whom do all graces come?

Extreme unction. What did the priest take in his left hand? The oil had been blessed by the bishop. It is then a holy oil. What did the priest then do with the thumb of his right hand? What did he anoint with the oil? How did he anoint the sick boy's eyes, etc.? And what prayer did the priest say at each anointing? He besought God to remit to the sick boy all the sins he had committed by the sense he was anointing. (Repeat all.)

What sins are committed with the eyes? With the ears? With the mouth? etc. The priest anointed the sick boy's five senses; sight, hearing, smell, taste (and speech), feeling (*tactus*). With what did he anoint each sense? And when the priest was anointing his eyes, what happened in his soul? The Holy Ghost came into his soul with His grace, and remitted the sins he had committed by his sight. (Same question and answer for each of the other senses.) Whence does grace flow into our soul? From the cross in seven streamlets, which are the seven sacraments. The sick boy received one of the seven sacraments; it is called extreme unction, or the last anointing. The first anointing with holy oil takes place in baptism; the second in confirmation. (Then in the sacrament of Order.) And the last in the sacrament instituted for those who are very sick and in danger of dying.

The grace of God for the benefit of the soul. After receiving extreme unction, the sick boy becomes quiet at once. His soul is now better. What does he say? " Oh, how I feel better! I have nothing more to fear, nothing more to worry about." What did he receive from the sacrament of extreme unction? The grace he received in extreme unction has cured his soul. The sacrament of extreme unction benefited the sick boy's soul. The same happens to all the sick who receive extreme unction with due dispositions. They receive in it the grace of God for the benefit of their soul.

The grace of God for the benefit of the body. Besides benefiting the sick person's soul, extreme unction often benefits the body also. That sick boy after receiving it, did not feel so much the pains of his body. How did he get along every day? And what did he at last get? Well. When did he begin to grow better? Hence extreme unction benefited his body also. What do the sick receive for their body in the sacrament of extreme unction? The grace of God for the benefit of their body. Which was the first benefit of extreme unction for the sick boy? Which was the second? What then do the sick receive in the sacrament of extreme unction? The sick receive in the sacrament of extreme unction the grace of God for the benefit of their soul and of their body.

The second administration. This boy lived to be an old man till what age? Then he got sick again. And then which sacrament did he again receive? He became again easy and quiet in his soul. He did not either complain about his bodily pains. But what happened to him this time? He did not get well, for so God willed it, for He wills that old people should die. Often it is better for the young, who get sick, to die than to get well. They go more easily to heaven. Extreme unction does not benefit the bodies of these.

CONNECTION. How many times did that sick boy receive extreme unction? How many times did it benefit his soul? Why did it fail the second time to benefit his body? What effect extreme unction does not always produce? When does it benefit the body? What did extreme unction benefit each time?

Which sacraments did that sick boy receive before receiving extreme unction? Which did he receive first? What effect did the sacrament of penance produce in him? What was it that the Blessed Sacrament brought to his soul? Our divine Saviour and many graces. What effect did extreme unction produce in his soul? Many more graces. How many times did the sick receive graces for his soul? What effect did it produce the first time in his body?

SUMMARY. What do the sick receive in the sacrament of extreme unction? How is extreme unction administered?

APPLICATION. 1. You see now, children, how good our Saviour is towards those who are very sick, and how He cares for them. For them He instituted a special sacrament. How often doctors and other persons have said: "There is no hope for that sick person; he cannot get well." But after receiving extreme unction so many very sick persons have got well again. 2. Mostly all who are very sick, are afraid to die. But extreme unction enables them to think quietly on death, to think much on God, to whom they are soon to go. 3. Suppose you now see a priest going to prepare a sick person for death. What should you do? Adore inwardly Jesus, whom the priest carries, and pray for the sick person, that he may worthily receive the last sacraments and be prepared to die well.

19. Holy Order.

PREPARATION. Last time I spoke about a very sick boy who received extreme unction. Who administered extreme unction to him? Why did they not call some other man to do this? Because only a priest can do it. The priest receives power of administering the sacraments when he is ordained priest by the bishop.

OBJECT. I will tell you to-day what powers the priest receives when he is ordained priest.

RELATION. He who wishes to become a priest, must first study for many years. After this the bishop ordains him during Mass. The bishop lays both his hands on the head of him who is being ordained and prays that the Holy Ghost may come down upon him. Then the bishop anoints his hands with holy oil, to consecrate them to God. After this the bishop makes him touch the chalice and the little gilt plate with a host on it. Next the new priest says Mass aloud with the bishop. At the consecration he pronounces with the bishop these words of Christ over the bread: "This is My body"; and over the wine: "This is My blood." After holy Communion the bishop again holds both hands over the new priest's head, saying: "Receive the Holy Ghost; whose sins you shall forgive, they are forgiven them; whose sins you shall retain, they are retained." Thus is a priest ordained, and receives all the powers of a priest and all the graces contained in the sacrament of Holy Order, and soon says his first Mass.

CONSIDERATION — *How our divine Saviour during Mass ordained the apostles priests [and bishops].* He who wishes to become a priest, has to prepare himself for many years. In what manner? Then he is ordained priest. By whom? The highest and holiest priest on earth was Jesus Christ. The priest has to offer sacrifice. Which was the sacrifice Jesus Christ offered? Where is this sacrifice offered in our times? Under what appearances does

Jesus sacrifice Himself during Mass? Through whose hands? When did Jesus sacrifice Himself for the first time to His heavenly Father under the appearances of bread and wine? That was the first Sacrifice of the Mass on earth. But Jesus willed that the apostles also should offer the holy Sacrifice of the Mass. What did He say to the apostles for this purpose? " Do ye this for a remembrance of Me." By these words He ordained them priests. What power did He give them, when He said this? He said this during the first Mass. When did Jesus ordain the apostles priests? Jesus ordained the apostles priests during the first holy Sacrifice of the Mass.

Our Saviour did not need many words to ordain priests. He has only to say it, and they are real priests. Just as He did in creating the world. He said only: " Let it be," and the earth and the heavens were there. When Jesus said to the apostles: " Do this for a remembrance of Me," they became priests.

The apostles also ordained priests. Our Saviour willed that the Sacrifice of the Mass should be offered until the end of the world. But the apostles could not do this so long, for they did not live so long. Therefore Jesus gave them the power of ordaining other priests and bishops. Therefore the apostles prayed over other men and imposed hands upon them, in order to ordain them bishops and priests. To some they gave all their power, and these became bishops, to others they gave only a part of their power, but the most beautiful (that of sacrifice). These became priests. These bishops ordained others as bishops and priests. The same happens also now.

How the bishop ordains priests. When did our Saviour ordain the apostles priests and bishops? What sacrifice did our Saviour offer at the Last Supper? Where does the same thing now take place? Therefore bishops ordain priests during Mass. The bishop begins the Mass. After some time, he stops, and those who are to be ordained

priests, kneel down. The bishop then begins the ceremonies of the ordination. What does he do first? The
bishop lays both hands on the head of each one that is to
be ordained, and prays over him, and beseeches the Holy
Ghost to come down upon him. And whilst the bishop lays
his hands over the one who is to be ordained, the bishop's
power is communicated to him and the Holy Ghost interiorly descends upon him with His grace; and in this
manner he is made a priest of God. Which sacrament does
he thus receive?

The power of offering sacrifice. The most beautiful of
the priest's powers is that of offering the holy Sacrifice
of the Mass. The newly ordained priest has that power.
The sacrament of Holy Order is conferred on him for this
purpose. To offer the Sacrifice of the Mass, the priest
needs a consecrated gilt chalice and paten (small gilt plate)
with a host and wine. After anointing and consecrating
the hands of the new priest with holy oil, the bishop makes
him touch the chalice, paten and host with his hands, to
impart to him the power of offering the holy Sacrifice of
the Mass. After this the bishop continues the Mass. And
what does the new priest do together with the bishop? He
says Mass aloud together with the bishop. Which is the
most essential part of the Mass? What takes place at
the consecration? Which are the words of the consecration? The new priest pronounces these words aloud with
the bishop over the bread and the wine that are on the altar.
He now, together with the bishop, for the first time
changes bread and wine into the true body and blood of
our divine Saviour. After this he continues to say Mass
together with the bishop until the third principal part of
the Mass. Which is the third principal part of the Mass?
What does the bishop then do? The new priest also receives our Saviour in holy Communion from the hand of
the bishop.

The power of administering the sacraments. After the

Communion the bishop again lays his hands on the head of the new priest. What does he say whilst he is doing this? "Receive the Holy Ghost;" etc. Who first spoke these words? To whom? What power did these words impart to the apostles? The power to forgive sins. This power is imparted by the sacrament of Holy Order to the newly ordained priest. The sacrament of Holy Order imparts the power to forgive sins. In which sacrament does the priest forgive sins? Which sacrament can the newly ordained priest administer? In which other sacrament does the priest forgive sins? In the sacrament of baptism. There is another sacrament in which the priest can forgive sins; which is it? The sacrament of extreme unction. The newly ordained priest can administer all these sacraments. What other power, already mentioned, does the priest receive in the sacrament of Holy Order? The power of offering the holy Sacrifice of the Mass.

Which are the two great powers conferred on the priest by the sacrament of Holy Order? These two powers are called the priestly power. The priestly power is the grace conferred by the sacrament of Holy Order. Moreover, when the bishop anoints and consecrates the hands of the new priests, he confers on him the power of blessing persons and things, for he says: "Whatever these hands will bless, shall be blessed." Not long after his ordination the new priest celebrates his first Mass. Who has assisted at a priest's first Mass?

The special grace. The priesthood is a holy and difficult office. What must the priest do in church? In the school? In the houses of his parishioners? He has to go into the houses of the rich and of the poor. He must love them all alike. He must pray for all. He says Mass for all on Sundays and feast days. He is like a good father, a good shepherd. To enable him to perform his duty well, the Holy Ghost entered his heart at his ordination. And what did the Holy Ghost bring to him? He brought to him the special grace to discharge well the duties of the priesthood.

SUMMARY. In the sacrament of Holy Order the priestly power is conferred together with the special grace to discharge properly the duties of the priesthood.

APPLICATION. A certain saint said: If I would meet a priest and an angel at the same time, I would greet the priest first, for the dignity and the power of the priest are greater than those of the angel. What powers has the priest, which the angel has not? Whom does the priest represent in administering the sacraments and in saying Mass? He is the representative of God, and therefore greater than an angel. Therefore also you ought to greet the priest before any one else. Priests like to greet children. You should revere the priest, love him and pray for him.

20. Marriage.

OBJECT. I will relate to you the marriage of Adam and Eve. Who was the first man on earth? Adam had no one to speak to. What did God say on this account? "It is not good for man to be alone," etc. What did God, therefore, send to Adam? What did He do whilst Adam was sleeping? What did God do when Adam awoke? Therefore Adam rejoiced very much; he said: "This is bone of my bone, and flesh of my flesh." What name did he give her? Woman. Now Adam and Eve knelt down before God, and God married them. Adam was the bridegroom and Eve the bride. Adam and Eve joined hands, and God blessed them. They were now husband and wife. Thus Adam and Eve had their wedding. Our divine Saviour made marriage a sacrament.

OBJECT. We shall learn to-day what graces husband and wife receive in this sacrament.

RELATION. When a man and a woman wish to get married, they go together into the church. They are usually accompanied by their parents, relatives and friends. They have all put on their best clothes. They come before the altar. When the priest comes, he stands before them, and the man and woman kneel down. The priest first asks the man: " N. wilt thou take N. here present for thy lawful wife according to the rite of our holy Mother the Church?" The man answers: " I will." The priest then asks the woman: " N. wilt thou take N. here present for thy lawful husband according to the rite of our holy Mother the Church?" She answers: "I will." They join their right hands and the priest says: " I join you in marriage in the name of the Father, and of the Son and of the Holy Ghost. Amen." He makes the sign of the cross over them, and sprinkles them with holy water. Now they are married; they are husband and wife and belong to each other. After this the priest says Mass for them. During Mass they go twice to the altar to receive special blessings from the priest, and at the Communion they receive holy Communion together. After Mass they have a little wedding feast. From that time they live together, and God gives them children. The father has to work and care for the mother; the mother cares for the father at home and does all he requires. And both the father and the mother care for the children. Father and mother remain together until death separates them. And from the day of the marriage, if they are good, God is with them and helps them with His grace in all things.

CONSIDERATION — *The marriage.* You have all seen a marriage. Who are invited to it? How are all dressed? Who are the best dressed? What does the bride wear? What does the bridegroom wear? Where is the marriage ceremony performed? Where does the bridal party place themselves? Where does the priest stand? Who kneels down during the ceremony? What does the priest ask of the bridegroom? What does he answer? What does the priest ask of the bride? What does she answer? What is done next? What does the priest do while the bride-groom and the bride have joined their right hands? (Blessing of the ring, etc.). Then the priest says Mass for the newly married. What do they do twice during the Mass? For what? When do they receive holy Communion? Why do they go to Communion? That our divine Saviour may be always with them and help them with His grace. Where does the marriage feast take place? Henceforth they live together and God gives them children. Thus were your father and mother married, and God has given them you and your brothers and sisters.

Duties of the husband. Who supports the wife after the marriage? The husband has to do it. How does he support her and the children? By his work or business. He must earn the money necessary for this, and also use his earnings for this. He received in the sacrament of marriage special grace from the Holy Ghost to do this properly.

Duties of the wife. The wife must care for her husband's wants at home; and she must also follow his directions, and obey him, for he is the head of the family. God said that already in Paradise. The Holy Ghost gave her special grace for all this in the sacrament of marriage.

Duties of the married. The father must support and care for the mother, and the mother must care for and attend to the wants of the father. And the father and the mother must care together for their children. How do they care for the bodies of their children? How do they care for the souls of their children? They must have them baptized; when they begin to speak, they must teach them to pray, to be good, to be obedient. And if the children are disobedient, are bad? The parents must correct and punish their faults. In a word, they must train, bring up, educate their children. Which are the duties of father and mother towards their children? To care for their wants, to educate them. The sacrament of marriage, which they received, imparted to them the special grace to do this properly. They must do all they can, and grace will enable them to succeed in this duty.

The family circle. Father and mother can give great pleasure to the children. For instance, in the long winter evenings after supper, after the mother has put the baby to sleep, and all the other children are assembled with their father and mother around a bright fire; sometimes the children are playing together, or studying the next day's lessons; or the father or the mother relates stories; or one of the children reads something interesting out of a good book, and the others listen; or all join in singing together some pious hymn. Then at the appointed time all kneel together before a little altar, on which is a statue or picture of the Blessed Virgin and a crucifix between two lighted candles, and night prayers are said in common by the father and mother and the children. After this the children bid their father and mother good night, and then retire to rest each in his own little bed. The blessing of God is with such a family.

Until death. The duties of the married are difficult. The mother has much to endure from the children. What punishment did God pronounce over Eve after her sin? Your mother has much trouble with you. Her children are sometimes disobedient or quarreling; some are crying; sometimes they are sick, and cannot sleep. The mother can have no rest, cannot get a chance to sleep; she often cannot help weeping over her troubles, saying: " Oh, what a heap of trouble and worry the children cause me!" It is much worse, if the father gets sick. Can the mother then say: " I am going away, I cannot stand this any longer "? No; she must stay, and now, more than ever, must she care for the children and for their sick father.

The father has also many cares on account of the children. His hours of work are often long and hard. When he comes home, he is very tired, and, nevertheless, he often has to do some work at home also. If the mother is sick, he must care for her and do a good part of her work. Sometimes he cannot get work, and then he knows not where he can get means to support the family. He can never say: " I am going away, and I will leave the mother and the children to care for themselves." No, he cannot; for now more than ever he must stay with the mother and the children and care for them and work to support them. The father and the mother must remain together until death separates them. That is a sacred duty of the state of marriage.

Which are the duties of the father towards the mother? Which are the duties of the mother towards the father? Which are the duties of the father and the mother towards the children? How long must married persons remain (live) together? How long then must married persons fulfil the duties of the marriage state? Until death. What did they receive for this in the sacrament of marriage? A special grace from the Holy Ghost to enable them to perform those duties until death separates them.

SUMMARY. Married people receive in the sacrament of marriage a special grace to perform properly the duties of the state of marriage until death.

APPLICATION. Father and mother have duties towards each other and towards the children. Which are the duties of the children towards their parents?

How beautiful it is to see love and harmony reign in a family, between father, mother and children! To see how they help and care for one another. This was seen in the Holy Family at Nazareth. Have you seen a picture of the Holy Family at Nazareth? How many persons are represented in it?

ST. JOSEPH IS THE FATHER. What is he doing? He is working to care for and support the family. So does your father for you. The Blessed Virgin Mary is the mother. What is she doing? Doing the house-work. Your mother also does the same. What is the Child Jesus doing? He is helping St. Joseph. He also helped Mary, His Mother. He always obeyed immediately and cheerfully. What did His obedience cause to Mary and Joseph? Much pleasure. How can you also give pleasure to your parents? Are you very willing to help them? Strive always to imitate the Child Jesus.

THE END